T0351840

Human Capital in History

A National Bureau of
Economic Research
Conference Report

Human Capital in History
The American Record

Edited by **Leah Platt Boustan, Carola Frydman, and Robert A. Margo**

The University of Chicago Press

Chicago and London

LEAH PLATT BOUSTAN is associate professor of economics at the University of California, Los Angeles, and a research associate of the National Bureau of Economic Research. CAROLA FRYDMAN is assistant professor of economics at Boston University and a faculty research fellow of the National Bureau of Economic Research. ROBERT A. MARGO is professor of economics at Boston University and a research associate of the National Bureau of Economic Research.

The University of Chicago Press, Chicago 60637
The University of Chicago Press, Ltd., London
© 2014 by National Bureau of Economic Research
All rights reserved. Published 2014.
Printed in the United States of America ·

23 22 21 20 19 18 17 16 15 14   1 2 3 4 5
ISBN-13: 978-0-226-16389-5 (cloth)
ISBN-13: 978-0-226-16392-5 (e-book)
DOI: 10.7208/chicago/9780226163925.001.0001

Library of Congress Cataloging-in-Publication Data
Human capital in history : the American record / edited by
    Leah Platt Boustan, Carola Frydman, and Robert A. Margo.
        pages ; cm. — (A National Bureau of Economic Research conference report)
        ISBN 978-0-226-16389-5 (cloth : alk. paper) — ISBN 978-0-226-16392-5 (e-book) 1. Human capital—United States. 2. Labor supply—United States—History. I. Boustan, Leah Platt. II. Frydman, Carola. III. Margo, Robert A. (Robert Andrew), 1954– IV. Series: National Bureau of Economic Research conference report.
        HD4904.7.H858425 2014
        302.0973—dc23
                                                                                        2014008636

♾ This paper meets the requirements of ANSI/NISO Z39.48-1992 (Permanence of Paper).

Relation of the Directors to the
Work and Publications of the
National Bureau of Economic Research

1. The object of the NBER is to ascertain and present to the economics profession, and to the public more generally, important economic facts and their interpretation in a scientific manner without policy recommendations. The Board of Directors is charged with the responsibility of ensuring that the work of the NBER is carried on in strict conformity with this object.

2. The President shall establish an internal review process to ensure that book manuscripts proposed for publication DO NOT contain policy recommendations. This shall apply both to the proceedings of conferences and to manuscripts by a single author or by one or more co-authors but shall not apply to authors of comments at NBER conferences who are not NBER affiliates.

3. No book manuscript reporting research shall be published by the NBER until the President has sent to each member of the Board a notice that a manuscript is recommended for publication and that in the President's opinion it is suitable for publication in accordance with the above principles of the NBER. Such notification will include a table of contents and an abstract or summary of the manuscript's content, a list of contributors if applicable, and a response form for use by Directors who desire a copy of the manuscript for review. Each manuscript shall contain a summary drawing attention to the nature and treatment of the problem studied and the main conclusions reached.

4. No volume shall be published until forty-five days have elapsed from the above notification of intention to publish it. During this period a copy shall be sent to any Director requesting it, and if any Director objects to publication on the grounds that the manuscript contains policy recommendations, the objection will be presented to the author(s) or editor(s). In case of dispute, all members of the Board shall be notified, and the President shall appoint an ad hoc committee of the Board to decide the matter; thirty days additional shall be granted for this purpose.

5. The President shall present annually to the Board a report describing the internal manuscript review process, any objections made by Directors before publication or by anyone after publication, any disputes about such matters, and how they were handled.

6. Publications of the NBER issued for informational purposes concerning the work of the Bureau, or issued to inform the public of the activities at the Bureau, including but not limited to the NBER Digest and Reporter, shall be consistent with the object stated in paragraph 1. They shall contain a specific disclaimer noting that they have not passed through the review procedures required in this resolution. The Executive Committee of the Board is charged with the review of all such publications from time to time.

7. NBER working papers and manuscripts distributed on the Bureau's web site are not deemed to be publications for the purpose of this resolution, but they shall be consistent with the object stated in paragraph 1. Working papers shall contain a specific disclaimer noting that they have not passed through the review procedures required in this resolution. The NBER's web site shall contain a similar disclaimer. The President shall establish an internal review process to ensure that the working papers and the web site do not contain policy recommendations, and shall report annually to the Board on this process and any concerns raised in connection with it.

8. Unless otherwise determined by the Board or exempted by the terms of paragraphs 6 and 7, a copy of this resolution shall be printed in each NBER publication as described in paragraph 2 above.

In memory of and with deep gratitude to
Gary Becker and Robert Fogel, teachers and
mentors of many, beacons to Claudia Goldin

Contents

Acknowledgments

We would like to express our appreciation to the National Bureau of Economic Research and to the Spencer Foundation for their financial support of the "Human Capital in History" conference and the conference volume, and to the NBER Conference Department for its assistance with conference management.

We also thank the following scholars who served as formal discussants or gave prepared remarks at the "Human Capital in History" conference:

David Autor, MIT and NBER (Katz and Margo)
Sarah J. Reber, UCLA and NBER (Gordon)
Robert Whaples, Wake Forest University (Kuziemko and Ferrie)
Richard H. Steckel, Ohio State and NBER (Bleakley, Costa, and Lleras-Muney)
Francine D. Blau, Cornell University and NBER (Olivetti)
Richard B. Freeman, Harvard University and NBER (Boustan and Collins)
Richard Easterlin, University of Southern California (Bailey, Guldi, and Hershbein)
Cecilia E. Rouse, Princeton University and NBER (Goldin)
Matthew E. Kahn, UCLA and NBER (Glaeser and Ma)
Stanley L. Engerman, University of Rochester and NBER (prepared remarks)
Gary Becker, University of Chicago (prepared remarks)

Introduction

Leah Platt Boustan, Carola Frydman, and
Robert A. Margo

Human Capital and American Economic Growth: Introductory Remarks

The United States has one of the highest standards of living in the world, the result of a remarkably steady increase in per capita real income over the past two centuries. By definition, the growth rate of per capita real income is the sum of the growth rates of output per worker and of the labor force participation rate. The chapters in this volume illuminate the role of human capital in increasing both labor productivity and the labor force participation rate, particularly among women, over the course of American history.

Labor productivity increases if technology improves or if capital per worker rises. However, this standard decomposition obscures the complementary role of human capital in the growth process. Given that physical and human capital have been relative complements throughout the twentieth century, the accumulation of physical capital contributes more readily to growth when augmented by an educated workforce. As advanced technologies diffuse through the economy, the allocation of workers of different skills and education to the tasks of production is also altered.

Shifts in the demand and supply of educated, highly skilled workers have transformed the level and composition of human capital embodied in the average worker in the United States, with corresponding effects on growth.

Leah Platt Boustan is associate professor of economics at the University of California, Los Angeles, and a research associate of the National Bureau of Economic Research. Carola Frydman is assistant professor of economics at Boston University and a faculty research fellow of the National Bureau of Economic Research. Robert A. Margo is professor of economics at Boston University and a research associate of the National Bureau of Economic Research.

We are grateful to Stanley Engerman, Claudia Goldin, and two referees for comments on an earlier draft. For acknowledgments, sources of research support, and disclosure of the authors' material financial relationships, if any, please see http://www.nber.org/chapters/c12887.ack.

There is strong evidence, for example, that the demand for highly educated workers relative to less educated workers has increased steadily throughout the twentieth century, except for a brief slowdown during the 1940s (Goldin and Katz 2008). On the supply side, changes in the distribution of educational attainment in the labor force derive from two sources—workers who obtain an education in the United States, and workers of varying levels of schooling who immigrate to the United States. When growth in demand for educated workers outstrips growth in supply, the earnings gap between workers with different levels of education, such as those with a college degree versus those with a high school degree, or between workers in occupations that demand high skills versus workers in occupations requiring less formal schooling, will increase. In the United States the earnings of skilled workers relative to less skilled workers followed a U-shaped pattern over the twentieth century, declining during the first half of the century and increasing in the second half (Goldin and Katz 2008).

In addition to enjoying a higher material standard of living, individuals today live longer and healthier lives. Improvements in health and longevity arguably are complementary to increasing educational attainment because individuals have a longer period of time over which to reap the benefits of investments in schooling and related skills. In turn, increases in educational attainment, particularly those in the twentieth century, have played an important causal role in reducing morbidity and increasing life expectancy.

Growth in per capita real income can also be attributed in part to a rising labor force participation rate, particularly among women.[1] The increasing participation of women in the workforce is perhaps the most significant transformation experienced by American labor markets in the last century. Over the longer run, the level of female labor force participation has followed a U-shaped pattern, with participation falling in the nineteenth century and then rising sharply in the twentieth century among married women, albeit with important differences by race. The factors that caused the rise in female labor participation have also encouraged women to upgrade their educational attainment. These include both structural changes in the economy that altered the returns to skill for women employed outside of the household and shifts in a social and political climate that once made gender and racial discrimination ubiquitous but what is now largely (and thankfully) a thing of the past.

Rising female labor force participation and the associated expansion in

---

1. Goldin (1986) examines the impact of changes in the participation of women in the workforce on per capita income in the United States from 1890 to 1980. Over this period the female labor force participation rate (age 15–64) rose by 40 percentage points (from approximately 20 percent to 60 percent) and the female-to-male earnings ratio rose from 0.46 to 0.60. According to Goldin, the rise in female participation coupled with growth in their relative earnings led to a rise in per capita income that was between 16 to 28 percent higher than the rise in male earnings over the same period.

women's human capital have contributed to changes in household formation and fertility. Throughout the twentieth century in the United States, the increase in the workforce participation of women has been negatively correlated with fertility. This negative relationship reflects the combined impact of changes in the timing of household formation within the life cycle, the type of household formed (married versus cohabitation), fertility decisions within household type, and rates of household dissolution (e.g., divorce). Household formation and fertility, in turn, influence levels of human capital because successive generations of parents have substituted child quality—greater investment in human capital per child—for child quantity. Historically and at present there are pronounced differences in these processes by race, ethnicity, and social class, which ultimately affect the rate of growth of human capital in the aggregate economy.

Volume Summary

This book presents ten chapters addressing topics on the role of human capital in American economic development and the increased participation of women in the workforce, as outlined above. The chapters are revised versions of papers presented at a conference held in Cambridge, MA, in December 2012. The conference was sponsored by the National Bureau of Economic Research and the Spencer Foundation.

Chapter 1 by Lawrence F. Katz and Robert A. Margo focuses on the evolution of the demand for skilled labor over two centuries of American economic history. Katz and Margo begin with the well-known observation that technical change is often embodied in physical capital (for example, modern computers). Throughout the twentieth century, physical capital and skilled or educated labor are relative complements, so that increases in physical capital per worker are associated with shifts in relative demand for skilled workers. Goldin and Katz (2008) show that the relative demand for skilled labor has increased in every decade of the twentieth century, with the exception of the 1940s.

Conventional wisdom about the relationship between physical capital and skilled labor in the nineteenth century, however, is quite different. Previously, economic historians have argued that capital deepening in nineteenth-century manufacturing reduced the relative demand for skilled labor, a process referred to as "de-skilling." The artisan shop, overseen by a master craftsman, was displaced by the factory, in which production tasks were divided up such that each could be performed by a relatively unskilled worker. According to this argument, the shift to modern capital-skill complementarity arises with the diffusion of electricity, which dramatically reduced the need for unskilled workers on the shop floor (Goldin and Katz 1998).

Katz and Margo instead argue that the complementarity between physical capital and skilled labor has been a central feature of the US economy from the dawn of industrialization to the present. Their chapter makes three points. First, while the share of artisans in the manufacturing sector declined over time throughout the nineteenth century, the shares of both unskilled labor and white-collar workers increased. This change in the occupation distribution is better described as "hollowing-out" rather than de-skilling. Second, in the economy as a whole, rather than simply in the manufacturing sector, the aggregate shares of low skilled jobs decreased, middle skill jobs were roughly constant, and high skill jobs expanded during the second half of the nineteenth century. Lastly, Katz and Margo show that, over the course of the nineteenth century, the relative wage of white-collar workers—the best available proxy for educated labor—increased, also suggesting that the origins of the long-term trend in the relative demand for educated labor began quite early in American economic development.

Katz and Margo use a wide variety of historical evidence to document their points, including establishment-level data from the 1850 to 1880 manuscript censuses of manufacturing and occupation and industry information from various Integrated Public Use Microdata Series (IPUMS) samples. In addition, Katz and Margo use archival evidence to construct new wage series for artisans, common labor, and white-collar workers over the 1860s and 1870s. Taken together with previous series constructed by Margo (2000), the new series document relative wages by occupation for most of the nineteenth century.

Katz and Margo appeal to recent task-based models put forth by Autor, Acemoglu, and others to develop a consistent explanation for the impact of technical change on the relative demand for skilled labor. In this framework, the labor market assigns workers with preexisting skills, such as education, to perform various tasks (for example, accounting). New technology alters the worker-task assignment matrix, which then affects the demand for educated workers. The task-based approach illustrates that technical change is not always uniformly skill biased one way or the other, but instead can complement skills in certain tasks while substituting for skills in other tasks.

Goldin and Katz (2008) document that the rate of return to schooling declined sharply during the first half of the twentieth century, and then rose just as sharply after 1970. If the supply of educated workers adjusted quickly to changes in demand, we would expect the rate of return to a year of schooling to remain roughly constant over time. The V-shaped pattern in the return to schooling implies that, to the contrary, the supply of skilled workers grew more quickly than demand during the high school movement from 1910 to 1940, but it did not keep pace with growing demand in the last several decades.

In recent decades, this imbalance between supply and demand has manifested itself quite starkly in a stagnant rate of high school graduation. This observation is the starting point of chapter 2 by Nora Gordon on the role of educational institutions in producing the supply of educated workers.

Drawing on Goldin and Katz's estimates, Gordon documents that, in 1900, less than 10 percent of youths graduated from high school, whereas, by 1970, the high school graduation rate increased to nearly 80 percent. Over the next thirty years (1970–2000), however, the high school graduation rate remained constant despite the sharply rising relative demand for college graduates and the fact that a high school degree is a prerequisite for college attendance.

As Gordon observes, the stagnant high school graduation rate between 1970 and 2000 is a puzzle that only deepens when we consider that real per-pupil spending at the elementary and secondary levels has increased dramatically since 1950, and that much of that has been mandated by state and federal programs intended to help groups of students at the highest risk of dropping out. In theory (if not always in practice) spending on education should be complementary to time spent in school, so, given the increase in funding, we would expect that high school graduation rates should have increased, rather than remaining constant. Gordon finds that in the absence of state school finance equalization reforms, the (counterfactual) high school graduation rates may have declined more than they actually did. For economic historians and others who are unfamiliar with the recent education literature, Gordon's chapter also provides an excellent overview of the relevant legislation.

The second key point of Gordon's chapter concerns the effect of income inequality on high school graduation rates, with inequality's impact on spending acting as a potential intermediate mechanism. On the one hand, the rising income inequality since the 1980s increased the return to a college degree, and increases in inequality at the top of the distribution lowered the tax price of spending for the median voter; yet, on the other hand, a widening income distribution—or any increase in fractionalization—can weaken the electorate's willingness to spend on public education as it involves subsidizing the children of other groups. In their analysis of state-level differences in high school graduation rates in the early twentieth century, Goldin and Katz (2008) note that high levels of inequality were associated with lower rates of graduation. If this pattern were still present today, it might account for some of the stagnation in high school graduation rates. Using state-level panel data, Gordon investigates the relationship between income inequality and graduation rates. She finds little support for the hypothesis that graduation rates are lower in states with high levels of inequality. Instead, and consistent with recent work on the latter part of the twentieth century (Corcoran and Evans 2010; Boustan et al. 2013), increases in inequality are associated with increases in graduation rates and with higher levels of school spending. In short, the rise in income inequality after 1970 does not appear to be a major cause of the stagnation in high school graduation rates.

The relative supply of skilled labor in the United States is determined not only by the production of educated workers in local schools but also by "importing" workers of various skills from abroad. Throughout American history, immigration has accounted for a quantitatively significant portion of the growth in population and the labor force. Consequently, the skill composition of the US labor force is fundamentally shaped by the initial selection of who chooses to immigrate to the United States and by the extent to which immigrants assimilate into the labor market once they arrive.

Convergence between immigrants and the native born can occur over a single lifetime, as an immigrant develops his labor market network, or it can take place across generations, as children surpass their immigrant parents and move up the occupational ladder. Traditionally, economists have assumed that parents can influence the assimilation rates of their children through human capital investments and neighborhood choice. Chapter 3 by Ilyana Kuziemko and Joseph Ferrie proposes the novel hypothesis that children, in turn, can exert a profound influence on the assimilation of their parents. Children may enhance the human capital of the adults if, for example, they teach the local language to their parents. When parents learn from their children, immigrants with young children in the household will assimilate faster. Alternatively, parents may rely on their children to navigate economic life in the destination, and substitute for their own human capital with that of their children. In this case, parents will lean on their children to conduct transactions and will delay their own language acquisition, thereby assimilating more slowly.

Kuziemko and Ferrie analyze the role of children in helping or hindering the language assimilation of immigrants for two waves of immigrant arrivals to the United States, one arriving during the Great Migration of the late nineteenth and early twentieth centuries and the other arriving after 1970. These two arrival cohorts differ in fundamental ways. In the past, immigrants were less likely to arrive with children, whereas today immigrants are more likely to arrive in family groups. Furthermore, when measured by the earnings score relative to the native born or the ability to speak English, immigrants who arrived during the Great Migration assimilated more rapidly than immigrants from recent cohorts. This pattern holds even after controlling for declining cohort quality within each migration wave. Finally, Kuziemko and Ferrie show that, in the past, immigrants with children at home assimilated more quickly than did immigrants in childless households (regardless of the gender of the head of household and of the children), whereas today the opposite is true. Thus, immigrants of the Great Migration "learned" from their children, but more recent immigrants "lean" on them.

Despite potentially high returns to human capital, poor health levels in the population may have curtailed investments in formal schooling or job training at points in American history. Over the past three decades, economic historians have made major advances in understanding the evolution of early health and nutritional status, using data on birth weight and adult height as proxies. Scholars have shown that adult height fluctuated over the nineteenth century; periods of improvement were followed by periods during which average height declined, signaling a worsening of nutritional status and possibly of health more generally (Costa and Steckel 1997). Improvements in early childhood health may have been a precondition for the expansion of schooling. In particular, children who were in poor health would likely attend school less frequently, especially prior to the early twentieth century when compulsory attendance laws were weakly enforced or nonexistent. Although there is some evidence that historical shocks to health did affect investment in schooling (see, for example, Bleakley 2007), systematic analysis has been limited thus far.

Chapter 4 by Hoyt Bleakley, Dora Costa, and Adriana Lleras-Muney seeks to fill this lacuna. The chapter summarizes existing evidence and presents new data on long-term trends in early health, including birth weights and mothers' health. The authors then use microdata from the nineteenth and twentieth century to investigate changes in the relationships between health, human capital, and productivity over time. Although adult height increases educational attainment and income throughout the twentieth century—suggesting that early child health, which is a determinant of adult height, matters for socioeconomic outcomes—good childhood health was not strongly correlated with time spent in school in the nineteenth century. Bleakley, Costa, and Lleras-Muney speculate that shifts in economic structure—in particular, an increase over time in the relative return to cognitive skills—may be responsible for this pattern. Given that health is an input into both physical strength and cognitive skill, and that the relative return to physical strength was higher in the past than it is today, some healthier individuals chose to specialize in manual labor in the nineteenth century. Therefore, poor health alone is not a sufficient explanation for low levels of educational attainment in the nineteenth century; rather, this supply-side explanation must be combined with low labor demand for skilled work, and hence low returns to education.

The remaining chapters in the book study changes in the female labor force over time, and associated shifts in household formation and fertility. Underlying the analysis in all of these chapters is an awareness of the U-shaped relationship between female labor force participation and economic development in the United States, first documented in Goldin (1990, 1995). Goldin argues that, in the early to mid-nineteenth century, women worked on family farms, often combining childcare and home production with market-oriented work. As the manufacturing sector grew in the late nineteenth and early twentieth centuries, employment increasingly took place in dirty, unpleasant factories, leading married women to retreat from paid employment. The return of women to the labor force in the mid to late twentieth century coincided with, and was in part caused by, a second economic transition from manufacturing into services and the attendant expansion of education in the workforce.

Chapter 5 by Claudia Olivetti builds on this logic by looking for the presence of the U-shaped relationship between economic development and female employment in a long panel of sixteen developed countries (1890–2005) and a shorter panel of nearly 200 countries (1950–2005). She finds evidence of a U-shaped relationship in both samples, even after focusing on variation in economic development within a country over time. However, after excluding the early Organisation for Economic Co-operation and Development (OECD) countries, the U-shape relationship is considerably attenuated. Olivetti interprets the attenuation as evidence that the timing of a country's transformation from agriculture to manufacturing determines whether female labor force participation experiences the downward portion of the U-shaped relationship. Manufacturing industries of the late nineteenth century required heavy manual labor and took place in dark, dirty settings considered unfit for women. The cleaner, more precision-based manufacturing of today may be less likely to trigger norms against women's work. Olivetti concludes that the U-shaped association between economic development and female labor force participation does not hold in all historical periods and regions of the world but is, instead, a feature of certain economies—including, but not limited to, the American economy—that went through a transition from agriculture to manufacturing in the nineteenth century.

Chapter 6 by Leah Platt Boustan and William J. Collins turns to the evolution of racial differences in women's work within the United States over time. In the decades after slavery's end, black women were more likely than white women to work outside of the home, even after controlling for the (limited) set of socioeconomic characteristics available in the census. The racial gap in market work narrowed significantly between 1920 and 1950 as white women began graduating from high school in large numbers and entering the growing number of "clean" office jobs. Black women, in contrast, remained heavily concentrated in agriculture and domestic service until the last third of the twentieth century. Only by 1990 did the racial gap in female labor force participation disappear entirely.

Boustan and Collins emphasize that, in the antebellum United States, white and black women participated in very different types of agriculture; white women often lived on small family farms and engaged in limited work outside of the home, while black women were mostly enslaved, living on farms that operated with little gender differentiation in work activity. Following Goldin (1977), Boustan and Collins argue that these initial differences by race in work behavior, a legacy of slavery, had persistent effects on female labor force participation over time through the intergenerational transmission of attitudes, skills, and labor market networks from mother to daughter.

The chapter presents two estimates of the intergenerational correlation between mothers' and daughters' work behavior. The first approach focuses on daughters born immediately after Emancipation. Boustan and Collins find that black daughters whose mothers were born into slavery in the South were themselves 5 to 9 percentage points more likely to be in the labor force in the 1900 census, even after controlling for region of residence. Their second approach analyzes a cohort of young women born in the mid-twentieth century who were followed over time by the National Longitudinal Survey (NLS). Daughters whose mothers worked outside of the home were 3 to 4 percentage points more likely to be in the labor force around age thirty, even after controlling for extensive family background controls. According to these estimates, the intergenerational transmission of labor force behavior can explain a sizable but declining share of the racial gap in female participation, as the work behavior of black and white mothers converged over time.

Labor supply is only one of the many economic choices that women make that differ by race and socioeconomic status. Chapter 7 by Shelly Lundberg and Robert A. Pollak documents differences in the probability of cohabitation, nonmarital fertility and divorce by race and educational attainment, and the widening of these gaps over time. By 2010, over two-thirds of black births occurred to nonmarried mothers, compared to less than one-third of white births. Within each race, the probability of having a nonmarital birth falls with education level, although the gradient is steeper for whites.

Since 1970, the economic value of marriage has declined for couples across the socioeconomic spectrum, as the value of women's time in market work rose (due, in part, to the transition from manufacturing to services emphasized by Olivetti in chapter 5). Yet marriage rates have remained relatively high for whites, particularly for white college graduates, a pattern that Lundberg and Pollak attribute to the interest of this group in raising "middle class" children, an outcome that is more readily achieved in a two-parent household.

Until recently, women had to choose between marrying or remaining single. Today, the option of cohabiting outside of marriage is also available. Lundberg and Pollak point out that the existing economic theories of marriage emphasize the returns to joint household production through specialization and division of labor, benefits that are also available to couples who cohabit without entering into a formal marriage contract. Couples may choose to marry rather than cohabit because marriage bolsters the intertemporal commitments that facilitate successful child rearing.

The recent changes in fertility and marriage markets documented by Lundberg and Pollak are part of a longer-run transformation in demographic outcomes that began with a decline in childbearing in the United States in the late nineteenth century. However, this fertility decline was interrupted when birth rates increased by roughly 60 percent during the baby boom from 1940 to 1960 but declined sharply thereafter. Are the changes in childbearing in the post-1960 period merely a return to this long-run trend, or are they instead the response to forces fundamentally different from those driving the declines in fertility a century ago? Chapter 8 by Martha J. Bailey,

Melanie Guldi, and Brad J. Hershbein tackles this question by contrasting the sharp decline in childbearing after 1960 with the earlier fertility transition.

From 1900 to 1930, fertility rates and average completed childbearing declined as rapidly as they did during the post-1960 period, even after controlling for compositional changes in the population. Yet the authors find that many other characteristics of marriage and childbearing decisions differ across these two transitions. The variance in childbearing was much lower in the recent transition, with more women having exactly two children and a smaller fraction remaining childless. Cohorts reaching childbearing age in the post-1960 period formed households roughly at the same age as did the early twentieth century cohorts, but more recent cohorts were more likely to do so through nonmarital cohabitation. Thus, women in the later cohorts exhibited a higher age at first marriage, delayed motherhood and, conditional on getting married before having children, waited longer from first marriage to giving birth. These delays occurred even as women became sexually active at a younger age. The second fertility transition was also accompanied by an increase in premarital sex and in the fraction of nonmarital births, particularly for the youngest cohorts. Thus, the post-1960 fertility decline has been characterized by a decoupling of sex, marriage, and childbearing that was not present in the first fertility transition.

Bailey, Guldi, and Hershbein also find that the association between fertility outcomes and a mother's education has changed over time. For each birth cohort, they compare the outcomes for women with high educational attainment relative to those for women in the lower quantiles of the education distribution. During the early fertility transition trends in children ever born, childlessness, marriage rates, nonmarital childbearing, and age at first birth evolved similarly for all educational groups. In contrast, the dispersion in the age at first birth and nonmarital childbearing increased steadily across the educational distribution since the 1960s.

The varying features of the two fertility transitions may help to shed light on the applicability of various models of fertility decline, and suggest that different factors may have influenced fertility decisions in each period. For example, the decline in the variance in the number of births, and the decoupling of sex, marriage, and childbearing are indicative of the large role that the availability of modern contraceptive technology has played in reducing the cost of exerting control over one's fertility in the later twentieth century fertility transition.

Unlike the chapters by Olivetti, and by Boustan and Collins, which place the rise of female labor force participation into the broader context of industrial or technological change, the final two chapters focus on shifting forms of discrimination against women. Sex segregation and gender differences in earnings were pronounced in the early twentieth century. Chapter 9 by

Claudia Goldin proposes that some of these differences are due to gender-based discrimination that can be explained by men's desire to protect the status or prestige of traditionally male occupational groups.

Goldin presents a theoretical framework in which society confers prestige on a given occupation based on the minimum perceived level of a productivity-related characteristic required to perform the job. When a woman attempts to break into an occupation that is traditionally male, the prestige of the occupation is reassessed and assumed to be equal to the female average, because the skills of specific female entrants are unknown by society. Given the lack of information on the characteristics of new entrants, society may infer that a technological shock has downgraded the required level of productivity when women are hired in male occupations. In this way, even the entry of highly qualified women may "pollute" the occupation, leading men to be hostile toward female coworkers, or to try to bar women from entering the occupation. Which occupations are integrated by gender depends on the characteristic distributions for men and women, and on the minimum required level of productivity. Sex segregation will be greater for occupations requiring a level of the characteristic above the female median. Occupations will also be more segregated at the tails of the female characteristic distribution. New occupations, in contrast, are more likely to be integrated.

The long-run evolution of sex segregation is consistent with the pollution model proposed by Goldin. In the early 1900s, manufacturing work required considerable strength, a trait much more prevalent among men than among women. The limited overlap in the strength distribution may explain why segregated occupations in manufacturing were found at the upper tail of the female earnings distribution. With the rise of clerical jobs, and the increasing importance of brains relative to brawn, the characteristic distributions began to have greater overlap starting in the 1930s.

Using an extensive data set on the characteristics of clerical and office workers and on firms' personnel policies in 1940, Goldin finds that hiring restrictions were particularly prevalent in the higher-paying occupations. Accounting jobs, for example, were generally restricted to men. Typist positions were often restricted to women. But many middling occupations, including clerks and correspondents, were not restricted by gender. As the model predicts, occupations with annual earnings above the female median were among the most restricted, whereas hiring was not restricted for those occupations below or around the female median.

Occupations at the upper end of the education scale remained restricted to women until the 1970s, even though the fraction of college-educated women had increased rapidly for several decades. The pollution theory suggests that increased public information on the qualifications of women would remove entry barriers. Thus, the increased credentials associated with occupations that emerged in the 1970s and 1980s may have contributed to the decline in sex segregation and in wage discrimination for the most educated women in the late twentieth century.

Beliefs about women's ability to work outside the home may also explain why female labor force participation rates were low in the early twentieth century, especially for married women, and why they have increased steadily since then. Goldin's model suggests that women may be kept out of certain occupations, and perhaps out of the workforce altogether, if society perceives their average ability to perform on the job to be too low. As men (and women) change their beliefs about women's ability to perform tasks outside of the home, women will start entering the labor market. But why would beliefs about women's ability to work change over time? And how would these discriminatory beliefs form in the first place? These questions are the basis of chapter 10 by Edward L. Glaeser and Yueran Ma.

While Goldin's framework emphasizes that beliefs about average ability reflect reality, Glaeser and Ma allow for the possibility that beliefs are formed by perception and are systematically different from women's innate ability. The formation of gender-related stereotypes will likely differ from models of discriminatory racial, religious, or ethnic-based beliefs based on hatred of an "out group" because men will not consider women to be innately evil. The authors quickly discard various sources of the formation and dissemination of gender stereotypes, such as politicians, producers of consumer goods, and coworkers. Instead, Glaeser and Ma focus on parental formation of beliefs for female children. In their framework, grandparents often have a stronger desire for their children to reproduce than their own children do, and will therefore try to persuade their daughters to forgo work in the formal labor force. Parents shape their daughters' beliefs about their own ability through their investment in education; in equilibrium parents underprovide education to their daughters, who therefore receive a negative signal about their ability. These beliefs and the lower investment in formal education reduce the returns from participating in the workforce relative to childbearing, and lead to higher fertility.

The mechanism proposed by Glaeser and Ma will be disrupted, however, when young women begin to work outside the home before childbearing, and are therefore able to obtain an independent assessment of their talents. Medical technologies, such as the Pill, that allow women to control the timing of fertility, and the elimination of institutional barriers that kept women away from top occupations likely diminished the ability of false beliefs to persist, and reduced the incentives for parents to underinvest in their daughters' education. These mechanisms may explain why gender stereotypes began to erode with the cohorts born in the 1940s, and may contribute to the transformative changes in female labor force participation and in household formation experienced by the American economy over the twentieth century.

Concluding Remarks

In bringing together the various chapters into a single volume, our primary goal is for the research presented in this book to advance understanding of the role of human capital in American economic development, and to encourage further related work on the United States as well as on other countries. But the volume is more than the proceedings of a conference; it also honors the scholarly work of Claudia Goldin, whose research has done much to shape knowledge about the issues considered in this volume and many other key topics in American economic history The motivations for the various chapters arose organically from every phase of Goldin's research, from her earliest published work on black and white women in southern labor markets to her widely cited and very influential work on the changing role of women in economic development, and finally, to her recent interest in how technological change and educational attainment together determine the growth and distribution of income. The volume concludes with a brief, personal essay by Stanley L. Engerman that recounts and assesses Goldin's profound and ongoing impact on the fields of labor economics and economic history.

References

Bleakley, Hoyt. 2007. "Disease and Development: Evidence from Hookworm Eradication in the American South." *Quarterly Journal of Economics* 122:73–117.

Boustan, Leah P., Fernando Ferreira, Hernan Winkler, and Eric Zolt. 2013. "The Effect of Rising Income Inequality on Taxation and Public Expenditures: Evidence from US Municipalities and School Districts, 1970–2000." *Review of Economics and Statistics* 95 (4): 1291–1302.

Corcoran, Sean, and William N. Evans. 2010. "Income Inequality, the Median Voter, and Support for Public Education." NBER Working Paper no. 16097, Cambridge, MA.

Costa, Dora L., and Richard H. Steckel. 1997. "Long-Term Trends in Health, Education, and Economic Growth in the United States." In *Health and Welfare During Industrialization*, edited by R. H. Steckel and R. Floud, 47–89. Chicago: University of Chicago Press.

Goldin, Claudia. 1977. "Female Labor Force Participation: The Origin of Black and White Differences." *Journal of Economic History* 37:87–108.

———. 1986. "The Female Labor Force and American Economic Growth: 1890–1980." In *Long Term Factors in American Economic Growth*, Studies in Income and Wealth, vol. 51, edited by S. Engerman and R. Gallman, 557–94. Chicago: University of Chicago Press.

———. 1990. *Understanding the Gender Gap: An Economic History of American Women.* New York: Oxford University Press.

———. 1995. "The U-Shaped Female Labor Force Function in Economic Development and Economic History." In *Investment in Women's Human Capital and Economic Development*, edited by T. P. Schultz, 61–90. Chicago: University of Chicago Press.

Goldin, Claudia, and Lawrence F. Katz. 1998. "The Origins of Technology-Skill Complementarity." *Quarterly Journal of Economics* 113:693–792.

———. 2008. *The Race between Education and Technology.* Cambridge, MA: Harvard University Press.

Margo, Robert. 2000. *Wages and Labor Markets in the United States, 1820–1860.* Chicago: University of Chicago Press.

Technical Change and the Relative Demand for Skilled Labor
The United States in Historical Perspective

Lawrence F. Katz and Robert A. Margo

1.1 Introduction

Skill-biased technical change has been a pervasive feature of the twentieth-century American economy (Goldin and Katz 2008). At the ground level, technical change is frequently embodied in new capital goods, whose price relative to output or labor becomes cheaper over time. As the relative price of capital declines, more capital per worker is used, and capital "deepening" occurs. In the twentieth century, physical capital and skill have been shown to be relative complements so that capital deepening has increased the demand for skilled relative to unskilled labor (Griliches 1969). Technology-skill complementarity has also been widespread over the past century with new technologies from those associated with the electricity revolution in the early twentieth century to the computer revolution in the late twentieth century being relative complements with human capital (Goldin and Katz 1998; Autor, Katz, and Krueger 1998). Goldin and Katz (2008, 297, table 8.1), using educational attainment as a proxy for skill, show the growth in the

Lawrence F. Katz is the Elisabeth Allison Professor of Economics at Harvard University and a research associate of the National Bureau of Economic Research. Robert A. Margo is professor of economics at Boston University and a research associate of the National Bureau of Economic Research.

This is a revision of a paper presented at the "Human Capital in History: The American Record" conference held in Cambridge, Massachusetts, in December 2012. The conference was supported by the NBER and the Spencer Foundation. Comments from David Autor, Jeremy Atack, Leah Boustan, Stan Engerman, Carola Frydman, Caitlin Rosenthal, two referees, and seminar participants at the "Human Capital in History" conference, at the 2013 World Cliometrics meetings in Hawaii, at Harvard University, at the University of Tennessee, at the University of Montreal, and at the 2014 ASSA meetings in Philadelphia are gratefully acknowledged. For acknowledgments, sources of research support, and disclosure of the authors' material financial relationships, if any, please see http://www.nber.org/chapters/c12888.ack.

demand for skilled labor greatly outpaced that for unskilled labor in every decade of the twentieth century, with the possible exception of the 1940s.[1]

The apparent pervasiveness of complementarities between capital and skilled labor in the twentieth century has naturally led economists and economic historians to ask whether such complementarity has been an inherent feature of technical change since the onset of modern economic growth in the United States, or whether it is a more recent phenomenon. Drawing almost entirely on evidence from manufacturing, the conventional wisdom is that technical change was predominantly "de-skilling" in the nineteenth century—capital and unskilled labor substituted for skilled labor with mechanization (Brown and Phillips 1986; Atack, Bateman, and Margo 2004).[2] In manufacturing, de-skilling occurred as the factory system began to displace the artisanal shop as the United States began to industrialize in the 1820s, and it picked up pace as production increasingly mechanized with the adoption of steam power after 1850 (Goldin and Sokoloff 1982; Atack, Bateman, and Margo 2008). However, beginning in the late nineteenth century and continuing into the early twentieth century the familiar modern pattern of capital-skill complementarity emerged. This emergence, according to Goldin and Katz (1998), can be traced to the diffusion of electricity as a source of inanimate power and with the technological shift from traditional factories to continuous-process and batch production methods in many manufacturing industries. The conventional wisdom, in other words, suggests a discontinuity between the nineteenth and twentieth century in the impact of capital deepening on the relative demand for skilled labor.

In this chapter we revisit the issue of the historical evolution of capital-skill complementarity and with it, shifts over time in the relative demand for skilled labor. Our chapter makes three points. First, although de-skilling in the conventional sense did occur overall in nineteenth-century manufacturing, a more nuanced picture is that the occupation distribution "hollowed out." By hollowing out we mean the share of middle-skill jobs—artisans—declined while the shares of high-skill—white-collar, so-called nonproduc-

---

1. The 1940s was the decade of the "Great Compression," during which wage differentials by education and skill declined sharply. A portion of this decline can be attributed to a shift in relative demand in favor of less skilled labor that reflected the impact of World War II on labor demand in agriculture and manufacturing, sectors that were more intensive in the use of less skilled labor (see Goldin and Margo 1992).

2. In their computable general equilibrium analysis of long-term trends in inequality, Williamson and Lindert (1980) made the prior assumption that capital and skilled labor were relative complements in nineteenth-century manufacturing, citing evidence from the twentieth century. Williamson and Lindert purported to find a rise in skilled-unskilled wage premium between 1820 and 1860, which they attributed in part to capital deepening, in line with the complementarity assumption. However, Williamson and Lindert's claim of an antebellum "surge" in wage inequality has been challenged (see Margo 2000) as has their assumption of capital-skill complementarity in manufacturing. It is fair to say that the conventional wisdom among economic historians, as noted in the text, is that capital deepening in nineteenth-century manufacturing was de-skilling.

tion workers and low-skill operatives and laborers—increased. Second, unlike the pattern observed in manufacturing, de-skilling did *not* occur in the aggregate economy; rather, the aggregate shares of low-skill jobs decreased, middle-skill jobs remained steady, and high-skill jobs expanded from 1850 to the early twentieth century. It is incorrect, in other words, to infer the pattern of occupational change in the economy at large from that occurring in manufacturing. The pattern of monotonic skill upgrading in the aggregate economy continued through much of the twentieth century until the recent period of hollowing out and "polarization" of labor demand since the late 1980s (Autor, Katz, and Kearney 2008; Autor 2010). Third, new archival evidence on wages suggests that the demand for high skill (white-collar) workers grew more rapidly than the supply starting well before the Civil War to the end of the nineteenth century.

Our argument begins with the observation that much technical change in manufacturing in the nineteenth century was embodied in "special purpose, sequentially implemented" machinery (US Bureau of Labor 1899; Hounshell 1984). The machines were "special purpose" because they were designed to accomplish specific production tasks that had previously been performed with hand tools by skilled artisans. These machines were "sequentially implemented" in that a partially finished good would be operated on by one machine, followed by another, until the production process was completed or nearly so. Over time, such machines became much cheaper relative to output or skilled labor, and manufacturing became much more capital intensive as a result.

Although special purpose, sequentially implemented machinery displaced artisans from certain tasks in production, the machines could not run on their own—they required "operatives." Operatives were less skilled than the artisans they displaced in the sense that an artisan could fashion a product from start to finish, while the operative could perform a smaller set of tasks aided by machinery.[3] But operatives were not without skills—rather, it is more accurate to say that the skills they acquired were those necessary to operate productively the machinery to which they were assigned (Bessen 2012). Further, skilled workers (engineers and mechanics) were still needed to install and maintain the equipment, as well as design it (and assist in its manufacture) in the first place (Goldin and Katz 1998).

As Adam Smith famously described, the substitution of machines for skilled artisans in manufacturing production raised labor productivity through pure division of labor alone. However, the effects on productivity through division of labor appear to have been relatively modest and exhausted at fairly low levels of output (Sokoloff 1984, 1986). Much larger

---

3. In referring to operatives as less "skilled" we are following tradition in economic history although, as pointed out in the text, operatives had skills needed to operate machinery. While such skills might be acquired quickly compared with the standard apprenticeship in an artisanal shop, they were by no means insubstantial in an absolute sense.

effects on productivity could be had, however, if the machinery could be powered inanimately, particularly if steam was the energy source. Furthermore, the productivity gains were increasing in firm size, thereby enhancing the division of labor (Atack, Bateman, and Margo 2008).[4]

If the displacement of artisans from production tasks was the dominant effect of capital deepening in manufacturing, the shift toward mechanized factory production would be associated with a reduction in the share of artisans in the manufacturing labor force.[5] However, as the establishments became larger in size and served geographically expanded markets, managerial tasks increased in number and complexity (Chandler 1977). As noted earlier, a more refined portrait of change is that the manufacturing labor force in the nineteenth century hollowed out, a decline of middle-skill artisan jobs in favor of highly skilled white-collar nonproduction jobs and less skilled operatives and unskilled workers.

The conventional view draws its evidence on de-skilling from manufacturing. However, while manufacturing was a growing share of the gross national product (GNP) in the nineteenth century, it was (very) far from the whole economy. The United States experienced a substantial shift of labor out of agriculture during the nineteenth century. Even if the share of operatives was increasing due to organizational change within manufacturing and overall manufacturing growth, it does not follow that the share of unskilled labor was rising in the aggregate economy, because some of the growth in the share of operatives may have come at the expense of a decrease in the share of workers employed as low-skilled farm laborers in agriculture. But farm *operators*—arguably, a middle-skill job like artisan—were also in relative decline due to the growth of the nonfarm economy, and the overall share of white-collar jobs was boosted by the growth of the service sector. The net effect of these shifts on the aggregate relative demand for skill is unclear a priori and cannot be intuited from shifts occurring in manufacturing alone.

We use a variety of historical microdata sets to document the narrative just sketched. Using establishment-level data from the 1850 to 1880 censuses of manufacturing (Atack and Bateman 1999), we examine the relationship between de-skilling and establishment size, building on previous work by Sokoloff (1982, 1984), Goldin and Sokoloff (1982), and Atack, Bateman, and Margo (2004). We find that capital deepening was greater in larger firms than in smaller firms. Much of this difference is attributable to the diffu-

---

4. A variety of factors contributed to the growth in establishment size in manufacturing, including the transportation revolution (Atack, Haines, and Margo 2011), growth in the supply of less skilled labor through immigration (Rosenbloom 2002), development of financial markets (Rousseau and Sylla 2005), and legal changes in business organization (Lamoreaux 2006; Hilt 2008).

5. We should note that in making this statement we are abstracting from the diversity of skills that may have evolved in the artisan labor force as factory production spread (see Scranton 1999).

sion of steam power, which was positively correlated with establishment size (Atack, Bateman, and Margo 2008).

Next, we use the manufacturing samples to study the relationships between establishment size, inanimate power, capital intensity, and the various proxies for the relative use of unskilled labor. When we do not control for establishment size, we observe positive relationships between steam power, capital intensity, and the relative use of unskilled labor. The positive correlations largely disappear, however, when we control for establishment size, which is positively related to the percent unskilled, similar to Goldin and Sokoloff's findings for the first half of the nineteenth century (Goldin and Sokoloff 1982). We make use of information on occupation and on imputed industry of employment in the 1850–1900 Integrated Public Use Microdata Series (IPUMS) samples to further examine employment changes by skill in manufacturing.[6] We construct broad occupation distributions for manufacturing at the national level. These distributions go beyond the labor force definition used by the IPUMS (only covering those age sixteen and older) to include child labor (age ten to fifteen), which was an important component of the nineteenth-century manufacturing labor force (Goldin and Sokoloff 1982). The manufacturing distributions exhibit hollowing out between 1850 and 1910—a declining share of skilled artisans and rising shares of operatives and white-collar workers. Next, we use the IPUMS as a base to construct more detailed occupation distributions for the overall economy between 1850 and 1910. The distributions for the aggregate economy show a decrease in the share of unskilled labor, a rise in the share with high skills (professional, technical, and managerial workers), and—unlike manufacturing—comparative stability in the share of skilled artisans and the overall share of middle-skill workers (skilled artisans plus clerical and sales workers plus farm operators).

The occupation distributions provide evidence on the quantity side of labor demand versus supply, but to fully interpret the trends they need to be compared with time series of wages by occupation. Building on previous work by Margo (2000) we provide new archival-based, annual estimates of wages for common labor, skilled artisans, and white-collar workers for the 1820–1880 period. We find a modest secular rise in the premium for white-collar workers from 1820 to 1880. The new wage series suggests that the relative demand for white-collar workers outpaced the relative supply over the nineteenth century. This pattern contrasts with that observed during the "high school movement" of the early twentieth century, but is similar to the pattern observed in the late twentieth century (Goldin and Katz 2008).

6. The pre-1910 population censuses recorded occupation but not industry directly. However, the census manuscripts contain sufficient information for the IPUMS staff to impute industry. While arguably less reliable than the actual information reported in 1910 and subsequently, we believe that the imputed data are sufficiently reliable to distinguish manufacturing broadly from other sectors (see appendix B).

In the final section of the chapter we examine changes in the occupational distribution of employment from 1920 to 2010 to compare recent changes with those occurring in the nineteenth century. The employment share of highly skilled occupations (professional, technical, and managerial) has increased steadily from 1850 to the present. Monotonic skill upgrading is apparent over most of the twentieth century. The occupational distributions in the aggregate economy and manufacturing since 1990 exhibit a hollowing out with a decline in the number of workers with middle-skill jobs relative to workers with lower-skill jobs. The recent decline in the employment and earnings in middle-skill occupations (Autor, Katz, and Kearney 2006; Autor 2010) has a counterpart in the nineteenth-century de-skilling of manufacturing. But the modern distributions also suggest, in conjunction with our overall results for the nineteenth century, that relative demand shifts in favor of more-educated labor can be traced back to at least 1850, and quite possibly even earlier.

There are substantial similarities between our arguments concerning technical change and labor demand shifts by skill in nineteenth-century manufacturing with those embedded in the application of recent "task-based" models of computerization and skill-biased technical change to post-1970 changes in the distribution of wages and occupations starting with Autor, Levy, and Murnane (2003). In a task-based framework, individuals come to the labor market with a set of premarket skills, most notably their education. In equilibrium the labor market assigns workers to tasks at a point in time. Over time, technical change alters the assignment of workers to tasks, thereby feeding back on the demand for the underlying skills. In recent years, for example, there has been dramatic erosion in demand for workers in middle-skill white-collar work, as these tasks can now be more cheaply undertaken by computer-based technologies, which also facilitate international outsourcing. However, while the demand for middle-skill jobs has eroded, the demand for those with higher levels of skills—for example, those who can design and market new software applications or invent more powerful algorithms or design faster computer chips—has increased. Task-based models demonstrate that technical change need not be uniformly skill-biased but rather can be complementary with skills in some tasks while substituting for skills in other tasks (for example, Autor, Katz, and Kearney 2006; Acemoglu and Autor 2010, 2012; Autor and Dorn 2013; Autor 2013).

A task-based framework illuminates an essential continuity to the effects of technical change across the two centuries. In both centuries, the diffusion of new capital goods altered the assignment of workers to tasks. Some of these reallocations displaced skilled labor, while others did the opposite. On net in both centuries, technical change has tended to increase the relative demand for educated labor. The demand side of the "race" between technology and education as described by Goldin and Katz (2008) for the twentieth century has its roots much earlier in American history, perhaps as far back as early industrialization itself.

1.2   Interpreting Historical Complementarities: A Simple Framework

It is useful to have a simple economic framework to interpret historical relationships between technology and skills. The framework we present here is a modest elaboration of Goldin and Katz (1998) in which we consider how the various steps, or tasks, performed in manufacturing production by skilled or unskilled workers were affected by technical and organizational change.[7] As in the original Goldin-Katz (1998) framework, we assume that there are three technological regimes in manufacturing: the "artisanal shop," the "factory," and "continuous processing." We focus on the transition from the first to second regime, with some discussion of the transition to the third regime at the end of this section.

We begin by restating the original Goldin-Katz framework. There are two production tasks to be performed. In the first task, skilled labor is combined with "raw" capital to construct an intermediate input called "operating" capital. In the artisanal shop, most operating capital consists of partially completed goods—the artisan will be directly involved in making the good, even if he does not put on the finishing touches. However, in the factory, operating capital will primarily be machinery, and artisans devote their energies and talents to installing and maintaining such equipment. We follow Goldin and Katz and assume that the ratio of skilled labor to raw capital is higher in the artisanal shop than in the factory.[8]

In the second production task, operating capital is combined with unskilled labor to produce a finished good. In the artisanal shop unskilled labor puts on the finishing touches, whereas in the factory unskilled labor operates the machinery that is used in fashioning the finished product. Following Goldin and Katz (1998) we assume that inputs are chosen efficiently in task number two. Thus, in particular, the desired ratio of unskilled labor to operating capital will be a positive function of the ratio of the rental price of operating capital to the unskilled wage and the level of output.[9] Exactly how the ratio of unskilled labor to operating capital changes with respect to output depends on the nature of the production process. For example,

---

7. Our exposition of the framework is verbal; readers desiring a simple mathematical treatment should consult the NBER working paper version of this chapter (Katz and Margo 2013) or the original Goldin and Katz (1998) paper (see also Atack, Bateman, and Margo 2004).

8. The basis for this assumption is the belief that the production of a good by an artisan, even if in partially completed form, was more time intensive than machine installation and maintenance. Empirical evidence from the late nineteenth century suggests there were economies of scale in the installation and maintenance of specialized machinery. For example, in a sewing machine factory whose operations were examined by the US Bureau of Labor (1899) there were just three machinists in a workforce of fifty-seven whose functions were listed as "making dies and keeping machinery in order." They were among the higher paid workers in the plant, earning $2.50 per day, compared with just $3.00 for the engineer and $3.50 per day for the foreman who oversaw the establishment.

9. There is good historical evidence of capital-labor substitution for the nineteenth-century United States. Manufacturing in the South after the Civil War became much less capital intensive as interest rates (a component of the rental price of capital) rose relative to the wages of unskilled labor (Hutchinson and Margo 2006).

if division of labor becomes finer at higher levels of output, the amount of labor used per unit of operating capital may actually increase at higher levels of output.

Another critical difference is that factories used higher ratios of unskilled labor to operating capital in the second production task. A higher ratio of unskilled labor per unit of operating capital is the very essence of de-skilling. Factory owners subdivided the specific steps of production so these could be performed by a relatively unskilled worker using a specialized machine. For example, in the machine manufacture of curved sewing machine needles, the workers operated automatic cutting machines, cold-swaging machines, pointing machines, a marking machine, grooving machines, clipping machines, burring machines, bending machines, eye-scouring machines, and point-finishing machines as well as more general purpose machines such as punch presses and polishers and hand tools such as pliers, gauges, and tongs (US Bureau of Labor 1899, 1342–43). These highly specialized machines had essentially no uses outside of the specific task for which they were developed (although they could be used in other establishments in the industry operating in the same manner).

In our empirical work we examine the relationship between inanimately powered machinery and skill using establishment-level data from 1850 to 1880. For this period, the key issue is the diffusion of steam power. Measured by horsepower, use of steam in manufacturing increased by nearly sixtyfold from the late 1830s to the late 1870s (Fenichel 1966; Atack, Bateman, and Weiss 1980). The use of steam power had offsetting effects on the demand for blue-collar skills. On the one hand, steam engines were fickle beasts requiring specialized expertise to install and maintain—in terms of the framework, this increases the ratio of skilled labor to raw capital in the first production task. However, there is good evidence that steam power enhanced the division of labor in production; in addition, steam required coal, and hauling coal on the shop floor and feeding the steam engines were performed by unskilled labor. Thus in steam-powered plants, we would expect a higher ratio of unskilled labor to operating capital in task number two (Atack, Bateman, and Margo 2008). If this second effect dominates, we would predict that the use of steam-powered machinery would be associated with a higher unskilled labor share, but the correlation would turn negative once we control for establishment size—and this is what we find in our empirical analysis.

Although the original Goldin-Katz framework is well suited to illuminate the general phenomenon of artisanal de-skilling, it is not well suited to examine hollowing out. To examine hollowing out it is necessary to distinguish a third production task not directly considered in the original Goldin-Katz framework. This task consists of overall management, record keeping, the formation of business strategy, the design of new products, and pricing and marketing decisions—in short, activities performed by what are traditionally (and rather inaccurately) called "nonproduction" workers. Nonproduction activities, like those in task number one, require skilled labor, although the skills involved are white-collar and therefore quite different from artisanal skills. We assume that the amount of skilled labor used in this third task is in proportional to the amount of unskilled labor used in task number two, and that the factor of proportionality is higher in the factory than in the artisanal shop. In the artisanal shop the apprentice would work alongside the master, without a need for further supervisory personnel. Artisanal shops served limited, local markets, unlike factories that needed sales and (possibly) advertising personnel. Record keeping in the artisanal shop could be quite casual, but the factory needed to keep close track of personnel, raw materials received and used, along with revenues.[10]

In the modified Goldin-Katz framework it is now possible, theoretically, that the share of unskilled labor might decline during the transition from the artisanal shop to the factory. This will occur if the reduction in the share of artisanal labor is more than offset by an increase in the share of nonproduction workers. However, a better way to think about the modified framework is that the shift from the artisanal shop to the factory lowered the proportion of skilled artisans, while raising the shares of operatives *and* nonproduction workers. Following the recent literature on task-based models, we refer to this more nuanced view as hollowing out. Instead of limiting attention to the overall share of skilled labor, thereby lumping nonproduction workers and artisans together, the more nuanced view suggests that it is fruitful to distinguish between the two.

We can think of artisans as a type of middle-skill worker, whereas operatives are unskilled (or low skill) and nonproduction workers are high skill.[11] The delineation of skill groups in this manner fits the nineteenth-century wage hierarchy reasonably well in which artisans were (much) better paid than common labor but not as well paid generally as white-collar workers who performed nonproduction tasks (Margo 2000).[12]

---

10. The discussion in the text, however, does not do full justice to nonproduction activities in that it neglects a key difference between the artisanal shop and the factory; namely, the role of product design. In the artisanal shop most products were custom designed by the artisan to fit the needs of the customer. However, the whole point of the so-called "American system" was to create an idealized product—a model—which then could be replicated by operatives using specialized, sequentially implemented machinery in a factory setting. The design process in the factory was clearly subject to increasing returns, unlike the design process in the artisanal shop. The net effect of this shift on skills is not clear; however, fewer custom goods entail less demand for artisans, but model design, not to mention the design and construction of the associated machinery, was a very highly skilled activity.

11. An even more refined framework would allow for different types of skills among nonproduction workers and the possibility of capital deepening altering the relative demand for such workers. In particular, Rosenthal (2012, ch. 4) documents how the development and diffusion of "ready reckoners" and other mathematical devices permitted less educated workers to perform clerical and accounting tasks that otherwise would have required a highly trained clerk.

12. Later in the paper we expand the definition of middle and low skill for the nineteenth and early twentieth centuries to include farm operatives, clerical and sales workers (middle), and farm laborers (low). The acquisition of human capital in farming involved the moving up of the "agricultural ladder" from farm laborer to farm operator. This process was not unlike

We have stressed the transition from the artisanal shop to factory regime in this section because the empirical work that follows focuses on this transition. The third regime of continuous processing deserves some brief comment. This third regime differed from the factory in that a higher ratio of capital to unskilled labor was the norm, and electricity was the power source (Devine 1983; Goldin and Katz 1998). The availability of electric power dramatically altered the architecture of manufacturing plants by eliminating a whole category of unskilled jobs involving the movement of bulky raw materials and product from one place to another in the plant. Use of electricity was associated with a substantial increase in the demand for skills acquired in formal schooling, even for blue-collar workers, and much higher levels of output, generating new management challenges. The effects of the shift from steam to electricity altered the relationship between size and skill. In the nineteenth century, larger establishments used relatively less skilled labor overall (including nonproduction workers), but in the twentieth century skill and establishment size are positively correlated (Brissenden 1929; Davis and Haltiwanger 1991; Goldin and Katz 1998; Atack, Bateman, and Margo 2004).

1.2.1 De-Skilling and Division of Labor in Nineteenth-Century Manufacturing: Evidence from the 1850 to 1880 Censuses of Manufacturing

Because of limitations of coverage and comparability across the various censuses of manufacturing, the full extent of capital deepening in nineteenth-century manufacturing is difficult to quantify. However from 1850 to 1880, for which representative samples of manufacturing firms from the censuses exist, one recent estimate is that capital per worker in manufacturing increased by between 75 to 94 percent, adjusting for changes in the price of capital goods and various biases and omissions in the census data (Atack, Bateman, and Margo 2005, 586). The increased intensity in capital usage in manufacturing occurred in tandem with a shift away from artisanal to factory production. Early in the nineteenth century workers in the typical artisanal shop used relatively limited and nonspecific capital goods—general purpose hand tools in a workshop that could be used for many different purposes. In the factory, tasks were subdivided and performed by less skilled workers using specialized, sequentially implemented machines (Hounshell 1984). To maximize effectiveness and, sometimes, simply to be

---

that involved in becoming the owner of an artisanal shop—both were, at the core, small businesses. Although clerks were better paid on average than artisans and the clerk-artisan wage ratio was growing over time (see Margo 2000) the wage gap between the two was not very large, absolutely, and clerical and sales jobs can certainly be viewed as middle skill compared with, say, managerial positions. Margo (2000) provides evidence for the antebellum period that, within local labor markets (e.g., counties) wages of farm laborers and common nonfarm laborers were essentially equalized.

used at all, such machines often required more power than could be delivered by human muscle and instead were driven by inanimate sources of energy. Water power had long been used for such purpose, and the eastern United States, where manufacturing first took hold, was blessed by a dense endowment of water power sites (Hunter 1979). Increasingly after 1850, steam became the power source of choice over water, displacing and then greatly surpassing water power use. Steam was preferred to water chiefly on grounds of cost and because steam-powered establishments could be footloose–they need not be located next to a water power site (Fenichel 1966; Temin 1966; Atack, Bateman, and Weiss 1980; Hunter 1985).[13]

The shift toward factory production was a proximate cause of capital deepening in manufacturing. Table 1.1 shows nominal capital-labor ratios computed from the 1850 and 1880 Atack-Bateman manufacturing samples by establishment size.[14] Adjustments are made to the original data to take account of the possible underreporting of the entrepreneurial labor input and working capital (Sokoloff 1984; Atack, Bateman, and Margo 2005). The key finding in table 1.1 is that, when we control for industry and location, capital deepening was much greater in larger-size establishments than in smaller establishments, particularly those with more than 100 workers (see also Atack, Bateman, and Margo 2005, 591).[15] The table also demonstrates that, over time, the manufacturing labor force shifted away from small establishments to large establishments—that is, the artisanal shop was displaced by the factory. Not only were more workers employed in factories in 1880 than in 1850, capital deepening was disproportionately concentrated in factories rather than in artisanal shops.

The primary reason why capital deepening was more extensive in larger than in smaller firms after 1850 was that the diffusion of steam power was not neutral with respect to establishment size. Traditional accounts of the diffusion of steam in American economic history emphasize decreases in the user costs of steam compared with water power and also the geographic spread of markets for coal, which was facilitated by the transportation revolution (Taylor 1951; Atack 1979; Atack, Bateman, and Weiss 1980). While

13. For further discussion and general background on the growth of manufacturing in nineteenth-century America, see Field (1980), Sokoloff (1982, 1984, 1986), Wright (1990), and Engerman and Sokoloff (2000).

14. For a detailed discussion of capital data in the nineteenth-century manufacturing censuses, see Atack, Bateman, and Margo (2005); the consensus of opinion is that the data refer to market values. Because capital goods prices declined between 1850 and 1880, changes in nominal capital intensity understate capital deepening in the aggregate. We do not deflate by capital goods prices in table 1.1 because the currently available price deflator (see Atack, Bateman, and Margo 2005) does not distinguish by size class of establishment. The 1880 figures in table 1.1 are reweighted to take account of the underreporting of so-called "special agent" industries; see note 18 and Atack, Bateman, and Margo (2005).

15. Table 2 of Atack, Bateman, and Margo (2005, 591) shows that factories (those with sixteen or more workers) were more capital intensive in 1880 than nonfactories, but does not present the contrast with 1850, as does table 1.1 in the present chapter.

Table 1.1 Nominal capital-labor ratios in manufacturing, 1850 and 1880 (number of workers)

Number of workers	1–5 workers	6–15	16–100	100+	1–5 workers	6–15	16–100	100+
Adjustment for entrepreneurial labor input?	No	No	No	No	Yes	Yes	Yes	Yes
Adjustment for working capital?	No	No	No	No	Yes	Yes	Yes	Yes
1850 sample mean, Ln (K/L)	5.77	5.70	5.75	5.74	5.88	6.08	6.18	6.08
1880 sample mean, Ln (K/L)	6.17	6.05	6.26	6.03	6.20	6.41	6.65	6.47
Δ (1880–1850), Ln (K/L)	0.40	0.35	0.51	0.28	0.32	0.33	0.47	0.39
Δ (1880–1850), Ln (K/L) in size class, relative to 1–5 workers		−0.05	0.11	−0.12		0.01	0.15**	0.07
(standard error in parentheses)		(0.08)	(0.07)	(0.07)		(0.06)	(0.05)	(0.05)
Regression adjusted, Δ (1880–1850), Ln (K/L) in size class, relative to 1–5 workers (standard errors in parentheses)		−0.09	0.21**	0.28**		−0.10	0.16**	0.37**
		(0.06)	(0.05)	(0.07)		(0.04)	(0.04)	(0.05)
1850, share of total employment:	0.214	0.164	0.343	0.279	0.241	0.177	0.309	0.273
1880, share of total employment:	0.141	0.139	0.335	0.385	0.158	0.152	0.321	0.369
Δ (1880–1850) share of total employment	−0.073	−0.025	−0.008	0.106	−0.083	−0.025	0.012	0.096

Sources: For 1850 and 1880 Atack-Bateman national manufacturing samples, see Atack and Bateman (1999). For adjustment for entrepreneurial labor input and working capital, see text and Atack, Bateman, and Margo (2005, 587n7). Establishments are included in the sample if they reported positive employment (males + females > 0 in 1850, and children + adult females + adult males > 0 in 1880), capital invested, outputs produced, raw materials, and value added (value of output – value of raw materials). We also deleted observations whose estimated rate of return on capital invested in either census year fell outside the 1st through 99th percentiles of the distribution of such returns (see Atack, Bateman, and Margo 2005) as well as observations in miscellaneous manufacturing (SIC = 999) and gas works and distribution (SIC = 492). These assumptions assure compatibility with the samples analyzed in Atack, Bateman, and Margo (2005). We also exclude establishments reporting more than 1,000 workers (only a handful of establishments fall into this group). For regression-adjusted changes from 1850 to 1880, the reported coefficient in each column is the coefficient on the interaction between size class of establishment (e.g., 6–15 workers, 16–100, 100+) and dummy variable for year = 1880; the regression also includes a dummy variable for year = 1880, integer values of the total number of workers hired, dummy variables for urban status (establishment located in a city or town of population 2,500 or larger), state, and three-digit SIC industry code; 1850 and 1880 samples are pooled to estimate the regressions. There are 4,905 establishments in the 1850 sample and 7,175 establishments in the 1880 sample. Standard errors are shown in parentheses.

**Significant at the 5 percent level or better.

these features of the diffusion of steam power are certainly important, the traditional account misses the critical role played by establishment size—larger establishments were more likely to use steam than smaller establishments. The size-steam pattern is evident as early as 1850 and, moreover, becomes steeper over time because changes in steam use were disproportionately concentrated in larger establishments (Atack, Bateman, and Margo 2008). A primary reason why diffusion of steam was concentrated in larger establishments is that the labor productivity gains from steam were increasing in establishment size, relative to water power or pure division of labor alone (Atack, Bateman, and Margo 2008).[16]

We would like to be able to explore how the shift to capital-intensive, steam-power production affected the allocation of tasks in nineteenth-century manufacturing. The prevailing hypothesis, as discussed earlier, is that mechanization-*cum*-capital deepening promoted the substitution of operatives for skilled artisans. In steam-powered establishments, artisans were less involved in the production process from start to finish—rather, they were needed primarily to install and maintain the machinery. But the establishments were also larger in size, which entailed new and more complex managerial responsibilities. In small establishments the shop owner—the master artisan—would undertake managerial tasks, but in larger establishments these, too, were subject to division of labor. As long as the extent of division of labor of managerial tasks was less than that in installation and maintenance of equipment, however, we should observe that the percent operative should be higher in steam-powered, capital-intensive establishments, when other factors are held constant.

For the twentieth century there are a variety of data that can be used to shed light on complementarities between skilled labor and capital in manufacturing, as well as the trends in the relative demand for skilled labor in the broader economy (Goldin and Katz 2008). For the nineteenth century, the available data are sparser and any analysis is suggestive rather than definitive. We present two types of (more or less) direct evidence on skill intensity in this section.[17] The first, following Goldin and Sokoloff (1982), examines the relative use of female and child labor across different types of manufacturing establishments. The idea is that, on average, female and, especially,

---

16. Productivity gains are not the only reason why steam power diffused more rapidly among larger establishments. For example, because steam engines were relatively costly, larger establishments may have been more able to finance their purchase out of retained earnings (see Atack, Bateman, and Margo 2008).

17. An alternative approach pioneered by Atack, Bateman, and Margo (2004) makes use of indirect evidence on skill intensity as reflected by the average wage at the establishment (the "establishment wage" to use Atack, Bateman, and Margo's terminology). The idea is that, if the percent operative effect dominates, and all other factors affecting skill intensity or wage rates are controlled for, the establishment wage should decrease as establishment size increases. Atack, Bateman, and Margo show that this was the case in both 1850 and 1880; further, the distribution of establishment wages shifted to the left, as the density of employment at larger establishments with lower average wages increased between 1850 and 1880.

child labor was less skilled than adult males, and thus the percent female/ child is a proxy for the percent operative. Our second analysis makes use of information that was collected as part of the 1880 census of manufactures, most of which was never compiled in the published census volumes. In particular, the census asked two questions pertaining to the average daily wages of "common labor" and "mechanics." We explore how the incidence of reporting to these questions varies across establishment characteristics. We also use these data, in conjunction with an estimate of the overall average daily wage, to construct a proxy for the overall percent unskilled.

Economic and social historians have long been aware of the role played by female and child labor in early industrialization, but scholarly understanding was advanced significantly in a celebrated article by Claudia Goldin and Kenneth Sokoloff (1982; see also Goldin and Sokoloff 1984). In contrast to previous work, which was anecdotal or focused on particular firms or industries, Goldin and Sokoloff systematically examined census and related microdata for the first half of the nineteenth century, drawing on the 1820 and 1850 manuscript of federal censuses of manufacturing, and the 1832 McLane Report prepared by the US Treasury Department.

Goldin and Sokoloff's principal focus was the relationship between the relative use of female and child labor, as measured by the share of workers who were children or women, and the size of the establishment, as measured by the total number of workers. The key finding was that the percent female or child was positively correlated with establishment size. Importantly, the positive correlation remained even after controlling for the level of urbanization in the country where the firm was located, a New England regional dummy, and industry. These controls are important because they demonstrate that the establishment size pattern was quite general, not driven by particular, well-known examples such as cotton textiles, or local geographic or labor market factors.

Our empirical analyses draw upon the Atack-Bateman manufacturing samples for 1850–1880 (Atack and Bateman 1999) covering the period of much of the diffusion of steam power in US manufacturing (Fenichel 1966; Atack, Bateman, and Weiss 1980). The power data were only tabulated in the published census starting in 1870 (Atack, Bateman, and Weiss 1980).

The information reported on the labor force varies before and after the Civil War. For 1850 and 1860 the schedules report the number of male and female workers separately, whereas for 1870 and 1880 the data are more detailed—children, females, and males, the latter two for age sixteen and older. Unfortunately, there is no easy way to make these data fully comparable over time. For 1850 and 1860, we specify the dependent variable to be the percent female; for 1870 and 1880, it is percent of workers who were children or female.

The regressions of child and female employment are shown in table 1.2. To be included in the regression samples, establishments had to report positive

Table 1.2   **Regressions of percent female (1850–1860) or percent female and child (1870–1880): US manufacturing**

A. 1850–1860

Dependent variable	Percent female		Percent female, county fixed effects		Percent female		
Sample	Pooled	Pooled	1850	1860	Pooled, steam powered	Pooled, water powered	Pooled, nonpowered
Steam power = 1	0.012**	−0.030**	−0.041**	−0.018**			
	(0.005)	(0.005)	(0.009)	(0.007)			
	{0.014**}	{−0.028**}					
Water power = 1	0.003	−0.005	−0.003	−0.005			
	(0.005)	(0.004)	(0.008)	(0.007)			
	{0.007}	{−0.005}					
Ln (capital/value added) x 10⁻¹	0.014	0.018	0.040	−0.017	−0.011	0.027	0.021
	(0.010)	(0.013)	(0.022)	(0.020)	(0.033)	(0.018)	(0.019)
	{0.010}	{0.011}			{−0.009}	{0.028}	{0.019}
Ln (# of workers)	0.043**	0.043**	0.051**	0.034**	0.023**	0.040**	0.049**
	(0.001)	(0.001)	(0.002)	(0.002)	(0.003)	(0.002)	(0.002)
	{0.042**}	{0.042**}			{0.022**}	{0.041**}	{0.047**}
Mean value of dependent variable	0.052	0.052	0.055	0.048	0.034	0.036	0.062
	[0.231]	[0.231]	[0.219]	[0.243]	[0.102]	[0.390]	[0.206]
Mean value, # of workers	9.41	9.41	9.04	9.78	18.59	9.13	7.87
Adjusted R-square	0.492	0.546	0.513	0.510	0.539	0.660	0.529
# of establishments	10,122	10,122	5,039		1,144	2,646	6,332

(continued)

Table 1.2   (continued)

B. 1870–1880

Dependent variable	Percent female and child		Percent female and child, county fixed effects		Percent female and child		
Sample	Pooled	Pooled	1870	1880	Pooled, steam powered	Pooled, water powered	Pooled, nonpowered
Steam power = 1	0.021**	-0.029**	-0.023**	-0.029**			
	(0.005)	(0.005)	(0.010)	(0.008)			
	{0.024**}	{-0.026**}					
Water power = 1	-0.008	-0.025**	-0.017	-0.034**			
	(0.007)	(0.0070)	(0.013)	(0.010)			
	{-0.010}	{-0.027**}					
Ln (capital/value added) x 10^{-1}	-0.017	-0.029	-0.044	-0.041**	-0.006	0.015	-0.048**
	(0.016)	(0.016)	(0.030)	(0.023)	(0.030)	(0.024)	(0.022)
	{-0.028}	{-0.043**}			{-0.031}	{0.026}	{-0.052**}
Ln (# of workers)		0.041**	0.045**	0.038**	0.028**	0.026**	0.046**
		(0.017)	(0.003)	(0.002)	(0.003)	(0.030)	(0.002)
					{0.028**}	{0.023**}	{0.046**}
Mean of dependent variable	0.077	0.077	0.077	0.077	0.081	0.033	0.085
	[0.270]	[0.270]	[0.239]	[0.286]	[0.236]	[0.200]	[0.330]
Mean of # of workers	12.36	12.36	12.89	12.08	27.51	10.07	7.47
Adjusted R-square	0.347	0.383	0.360	0.323	0.361	0.548	0.375
Number of establishments	11,084	11,084	3,885	7,199	2,323	1,464	7,208

Sources: For panel A, 1850 and 1860 samples of manufacturing establishments, Atack and Bateman (1999). Pooled regressions include dummies for urban status, three-digit (SIC) industry code, year (1860), state, and state x year. Coefficients in { } are for regressions with county fixed effects rather than state fixed effects. Nonpowered establishments include observations for which the power source is not reported. For panel B, 1870 and 1880 samples of manufacturing establishments, Atack and Bateman (1999). Regressions include dummies for urban status, three-digit (SIC) industry code, year (1880), state, and state x year. Coefficients in {{s}} are for regressions with county fixed effects rather than state fixed effects. The 1880 observations are reweighted to correct for underreporting of special agent establishments (see Atack, Bateman, and Margo 2004). Nonpowered establishments include observations with unreported power source. Numbers in [ ] are the mean of the dependent variable when establishments are weighted by reported employment.

**Significant at the 5 percent level or better.

values of total employment, capital invested, gross value of outputs and inputs, and value added (= value of outputs—value of raw materials). In addition, we excluded establishments whose estimated rate of return on capital was either so high or so low to raise questions about the accuracy of the data. The various data screens are the same as used in previous work (see, for example, Atack, Bateman, and Margo 2008). The 1880 sample is reweighted to take account of the underreporting of so-called special agent establishments.[18]

Panel A shows results for 1850–1860 and panel B for 1870–1880. The structure of the panels is identical. In column (1), we control for inanimate power use—dummy variables for steam and water power and the log of the capital-labor ratio. We expect the power and capital intensity coefficients to be positive in sign, although because power use and capital intensity are positively (and strongly) correlated, they may not be precisely estimated (that is, statistically significant). In column (2), we add the number of workers to the specification. We expect that this variable will have a positive and significant coefficient, and controlling for it should explain the positive effects of capital intensity and power use in column (1), possibly even reversing their signs. The remaining columns either add county fixed effects (columns [3] and [4]) or estimate the regressions separately by power source, and are meant as robustness checks.

There are two key results, which are remarkably consistent across the samples despite the difference before and after the Civil War in the definition of the dependent variable. First, the percent female or female and child is positively and significantly related to the use of steam power. We also generally observe a positive effect of capital intensity, controlling for power, although these are not statistically significant given the multicollinear relationship between power use and capital intensity.

Second, if we add establishment size to the regression (the number of workers) its coefficient is uniformly positive and significant. The positive effect of size is consistent with Goldin and Sokoloff (1982). Note that, when we control for size, the coefficient on steam power becomes negative. In

18. Although the samples analyzed here are nationally representative of the surviving manuscript schedules, they are not necessarily nationally representative of all manufacturing establishments because some establishments were missed and some schedules have not survived. We can presume that these omissions are random except in 1880. In 1880, however, certain industries (including textiles and iron and steel) were assigned to special enumerators chosen for their specialized knowledge about the industry. Their enumerations were not deposited with the other census data and the records have never been found (Delle Donne 1973). Fortunately, not all enumerators followed the instructions and, in fact, there are firms from the special agent industries contained in the regular schedules (and thus included in the Atack-Bateman samples). We use these establishments to construct a set of weights to correct for the underrepresentation. Although this reweighting is a clear improvement over no adjustment at all, it is unlikely to fully correct for the problem; as a result the 1880 sample, even when reweighted, has too few large establishments in it. Thus, our substantive findings with respect to size are likely to be understated even when the 1880 data are reweighted.

terms of the Goldin and Katz (1998) framework, steam-powered machinery required installation and maintenance and these were tasks for skilled labor, even if semiskilled operatives or unskilled workers could operate the machinery.

Although compelling, the evidence on size and relative use of female and child labor does not reflect the full extent of division of labor in nineteenth-century manufacturing, because many establishments did not hire women or children, and yet were relatively large. Thus, additional direct evidence is desirable. Specifically, the 1880 census of manufacturing collected data on the average daily wages of "mechanics" and "ordinary" laborers. Although neither term was defined explicitly in the instructions to enumerators, it is clear from the context that "mechanics" referred to skilled artisans like machinists, blacksmiths, and engineers while ordinary labor meant "common laborer." Except for a few industries these data were not compiled in the 1880 census volume on manufacturing, but they are available in the manuscripts and also in the Atack-Bateman 1880 sample (Atack and Bateman 1999).

The instructions to enumerators on collecting the wage data are extremely sparse, but one particular instruction is still very useful to us. Referring to the column where the data on the average wage of ordinary laborer was to be recorded, the census noted that "[i]n many establishments (as carpenter shops, blacksmith shops, etc.) it will be found that no ordinary laborers are employed. In this case column 11 will not be filled" (Wright 1900, 316). We infer from this instruction that the wage data were supposed to refer to individuals employed at the establishment, and if no such labor was employed, the column would be left blank.

With this instruction in mind, we created a variable, ART, which equals one if the establishment reported a wage for mechanics but not for ordinary labor. We also created a second variable, BOTH, taking the value one if the establishment reported both types of wages. As can be seen from table 1.3, the majority of establishments in 1880 (67 percent) reported both types of wages but a substantial minority, 25 percent, reported just the mechanic's wage. The likelihood of reporting just the mechanic's wage was significantly decreasing in the number of employees, whereas the likelihood of reporting both was increasing in the number of workers. Note, as well, that use of steam power reduced the likelihood that just the skilled wage was reported. These patterns are consistent with the hypothesis that division of labor increased with establishment size and was enhanced by mechanization.

Last, we use the information on the reporting of skilled and unskilled wages, total wages paid, the number of workers hired, and operating times to construct a proxy for the overall share of workers in an establishment who were unskilled. The details of constructing this proxy are given in appendix A. We concede that our proxy is clearly biased, but we believe that the biases

Table 1.3   Regressions of reporting of skilled daily wages and of estimated percent unskilled: Manufacturing establishments in 1880

A. Report of skilled daily wage: 1880 manufacturing establishments

	Artisan wage reported only	Artisan wage reported only	Both artisan and unskilled wage reported	Both artisan and unskilled wage reported
Ln (# of workers)	-0.075** (0.010)	-0.052** (0.010)	0.089** (0.011)	0.061** (0.011)
Ln (capital/workers)		0.013** (0.005)		-0.002 (0.006)
Steam power = 1		-0.165** (0.016)		0.201** (0.017)
Water power = 1		-0.083** (0.021)		0.045** (0.023)
Sample mean of dependent variable	0.245	0.245	0.667	0.667
Adjusted R-square	0.113	0.126	0.095	0.113

B. Percent unskilled

Dependent variable	Percent unskilled	Percent unskilled	Percent unskilled	Percent unskilled, steam-powered establishments	Percent unskilled, water-powered establishments	Percent unskilled, nonpowered establishments
Steam power = 1	0.130** (0.019) {0.145***}	0.005 (0.021) {0.016}	0.005 (0.021) {0.016}			
Water power = 1	0.076** (0.027) {0.070***}	0.032 (0.027) {0.030}	0.033 (0.027) {0.030}			

(*continued*)

Table 1.3 (continued)

Dependent variable	Percent unskilled	Percent unskilled	Percent unskilled	Percent unskilled, steam-powered establishments	Percent unskilled, water-powered establishments	Percent unskilled, nonpowered establishments
Ln (capital/value added)	0.015**	0.014**	0.014**	0.006	0.006	0.017**
	(0.006)	(0.006)	(0.006)	(0.014)	(0.019)	(0.007)
	{0.016**}	{0.013**}	{0.013}	{0.012}	{0.043}	{0.015}
Ln (# of workers)		0.090**	0.090**	0.077**	0.035	0.096**
		(0.006)	(0.006)	(0.012)	(0.029)	(0.008)
		{0.091**}	{0.091}	{0.085**}	{−0.01}	{0.096**}
Controls for operating times?	No	No	Yes	Yes	Yes	Yes
Adjusted *R*-square	0.147	0.188	0.188	0.168	0.038	0.123
					{−0.026}	
Sample mean, dependent variable	0.428	0.428	0.428	0.609	0.606	0.349
	[0.685]	[0.685]	[0.685]	[0.745]	[0.640]	{0.391}
Mean value, no. of workers	11.30	11.30	11.30	30.3	3.90	6.41
Number of establishments	4,428	4,428	4,428	796	506	3,084

Sources: For panel A, 1880, Atack-Bateman manufacturing sample. Number of establishments is 7,119. Establishments are reweighted to correct for undersampling of special agent establishments; see text and Atack, Bateman, and Margo (2004). For panel B, 1880, Atack-Bateman sample of manufacturing establishments (Atack and Bateman 1999). See appendix A for construction of dependent variable. Establishments are reweighted to correct for underreporting of special agent industries (see Atack, Bateman, and Margo 2004). All regressions include dummy variables for urban status, three–digit industry (SIC) code, and state; coefficients in { } are from regressions with county fixed effects instead of state fixed effects. Mean values shown in brackets reweight establishments by reported employment (adjusted for underreporting of special agent industries).

**Significant at the 5 percent level or better.

go against our finding that the percent operative increased with establishment size (see appendix A). Panel B of table 1.3 reports regressions of this proxy on establishment characteristics. We find that, not controlling for establishment size, the proportion unskilled was increasing in the use of steam power and also in capital intensity but, as we found in the analysis of female and child labor, the effect of steam power disappears once we control for establishment size, which is positively associated with the percent unskilled.

In summary, we have used the 1850–1880 Atack-Bateman manufacturing samples to shed light on the relationship between steam power, capital intensity, and the percent unskilled. We find, not controlling for size, that steam power and the percent unskilled were positively correlated, as were capital intensity and percent unskilled. Echoing Goldin and Sokoloff (1982) and Atack, Bateman, and Margo (2004), we find that larger establishments were more likely than smaller establishments to substitute unskilled labor and capital for skilled labor.

1.2.2 Occupations in Nineteenth-Century America: Did Technical Change "Hollow Out" the Distribution?

Our analysis of the manufacturing samples is consistent with the view that technical change in nineteenth-century manufacturing displaced artisans from production tasks, replacing them with operatives and machines. We are also interested in whether the occupation distribution in manufacturing hollowed out. However, we cannot investigate hollowing out using the 1850–1880 manufacturing samples because the census of manufacturing did not separately identify nonproduction workers until 1890.

At first glance, it might also seem that hollowing out cannot be investigated using information collected in the census of population, either. From 1910 onward the census collected information separately on each worker's occupation and industry, but prior to 1910 industry of employment was not separately recorded. However, sufficient information was reported in the manuscripts to permit the development of protocols by the IPUMS to impute industry of employment prior to 1910.[19] This is because in answering the occupation question, individuals also gave information sufficient to identify the industry of employment. And, even if this did not happen explicitly, industry can in many cases be inferred directly from the occupation. Importantly, when imputing industry, the protocols used by the IPUMS staff do *not* have our question of interest in mind—that is, they did *not* impute industry with the conscious desire to show hollowing out in the manufacturing distribution.

We have scrutinized the IPUMS protocols for assigning industry and believe them to be reasonable. Although there is no question that the imputed

19. See IPUMS-USA (n.d.) for a detailed discussion of the protocols.

industry codes are less accurate than their twentieth-century counterparts, we believe they are adequate for the type of broad analysis undertaken here—distinguishing manufacturing overall from other sectors.[20]

Appendix B describes our procedures for computing the occupation distributions. Our goal is to make the coverage of the distributions as comprehensive as possible—that is, the entire labor force, as opposed to a specific subgroup.[21] In brief, we begin with the IPUMS samples, which pertain to persons in the labor force, age sixteen and older. To these we add estimates for child workers age ten to fifteen, and we also make a series of technical adjustments that we believe produce more accurate occupational classifications. Because we rely on the IPUMS for the basic estimates, we cannot provide distributions for 1890 (there is no IPUMS sample for 1890).

Panel A of table 1.4 shows our estimates of occupations in manufacturing, distinguishing between white-collar (profession/technical/manager and clerical/sales), skilled blue-collar (that is, artisan), and operative/unskilled. Even as early as 1850, almost 60 percent of manufacturing workers are classified as operative or unskilled. This is perhaps less surprising as it might seem, however—the shift away from the artisanal shop was well underway even before steam power diffused (Goldin and Sokoloff 1982; Sokoloff 1984; Atack, Bateman, and Margo 2008). We cannot, however, document the pre-1850 transition precisely, however, because the pre-1850 censuses did not report occupations in sufficient detail.

That said, consistent with the results of the previous section, there is clear evidence of de-skilling in the traditional labor history sense in panel A: the proportion artisan in manufacturing declines from 39 percent in 1850 to 23 percent in 1910. The decline is continuous, although it did not occur at the same rate across decades—the downward shifts in percent blue-collar were more dramatic during the 1860s and between 1900 and 1910. The flip side of de-skilling, of course, is the rise in the percent operative/unskilled, from 58 percent in 1850 to 65 percent in 1910. But de-skilling is not the full

---

20. We are less sanguine that the imputed industry data are sufficiently accurate to analyze differences in hollowing out across manufacturing industries. That said, there are any number of interesting hypotheses to could be tested—for example, we might expect more hollowing out to have occurred in manufacturing industries with broader, more geographically integrated markets because these may have required larger clerical/sales labor forces.

21. We want the distributions to be comprehensive because historically the labor force included groups—child labor and slaves, in particular—whose occupations were not recorded at all in the population census (for example, slaves) or who were incompletely enumerated (children). For example, if we failed to include slaves in the antebellum distributions, emancipation would be associated with a shift in the occupation distribution (a sudden increase in the share of unskilled labor) that reflects the fact that the occupations of former slaves were enumerated in 1870, but not in 1860. On the other hand, comprehensiveness is not without cost because the adjustments that we make for slave and child occupations are necessarily crude, and also because at present the wage series that we present later in the chapter is not as comprehensive in its coverage (see the discussion in the next section).

Table 1.4   Occupation distributions: US labor force, age ten and older: 1850–1910

	1850 (%)	1860 (%)	1870 (%)	1880 (%)	1900 (%)	1910 (%)
A. Manufacturing industries						
White collar	3.1	3.2	4.8	4.7	6.8	**11.9**
Prof-tech-manager	3.0	3.1	4.2	4.0	5.2	5.6
Clerical-sales	0.1	0.1	0.6	0.7	1.6	6.3
Skilled blue collar	**39.4**	**38.5**	**31.8**	**29.2**	**28.7**	**22.8**
Middle skill 2 (skilled blue collar + clerical/sales)	**39.5**	**38.6**	**32.4**	**29.9**	**30.3**	**29.1**
Operative/unskilled	**57.5**	**58.3**	**63.4**	**67.8**	**64.5**	**65.4**
B. Aggregate economy						
White collar	**6.9**	**8.3**	**10.6**	**11.6**	**17.1**	**19.7**
Professional-technical	2.3	2.6	2.9	3.4	4.3	4.6
Manager	3.1	3.6	4.4	4.3	5.7	5.6
Clerical/sales	1.5	2.1	3.3	3.9	7.2	9.5
Skilled blue collar	**11.6**	**11.2**	**10.7**	**9.1**	**11.0**	**11.9**
Operative/unskilled/service	**28.7**	**30.1**	**32.4**	**37.7**	**36.4**	**37.9**
Agriculture	**52.7**	**50.5**	**46.4**	**41.6**	**35.3**	**30.5**
Operator/supervisory	23.9	23.2	24.8	24.8	20.0	16.6
Farm laborer	28.8	27.3	21.6	16.8	15.5	13.9
C. Skill groups, aggregate economy						
High skill 1 (white collar)	6.9	8.3	10.6	11.6	17.1	19.7
High skill 2 (prof/tech/man)	5.4	6.2	7.3	7.7	10.0	10.2
Middle skill 1 (blue collar + agricultural operator/supervisory)	35.6	34.3	35.5	33.9	31.1	28.5
Middle skill 2 (no. 1 + clerical/sales)	37.1	36.2	38.8	37.8	38.3	38.0
% Low skill (oper/ unsk/serv/farm lab)	57.5	57.4	54.0	54.5	51.9	51.8

Sources: For panel A, 1850 to 1910, census IPUMS; see appendix B. Manager includes proprietors and officials. For panel B, 1850 to 1910, census IPUMS; see appendix B. For panel C, computed from panel B.

story—we also observe an upward trend in the percent white-collar from 3 percent in 1850 to almost 12 percent in 1910. Prior to 1880 most of this growth was concentrated among managers rather than clerical or sales workers, whose proportion began to grow rapidly in the late nineteenth century.

Our evidence suggests, therefore, that the occupation distribution in manufacturing hollowed out between 1850 and 1910. The hollowing out is clearly evident if we consider high-skill jobs in manufacturing to be all white-collar jobs, or even if we follow the definition of middle skill used later in the chapter in our analysis of twentieth-century trends, treating clerical-sales positions as middle skill, along with skilled blue collar.

Did the hollowing out extend beyond manufacturing? We address this question in panels B and C by presenting occupation distributions for the aggregate economy. As for manufacturing, we construct the overall distributions by starting with samples drawn from the IPUMS. To these initial distributions we add child labor, slaves (1850 and 1860), and also make a series of technical adjustments (see appendix B).

In panel C, we rearrange the occupation shares into skill groups: high skill 1 (white-collar workers), middle skill 1 (the sum of skilled blue-collar and farm operators), and low skill (the sum of operative-service-unskilled in nonfarm jobs and farm laborers). Following the classification in panel A (as also used later in the chapter) we also present results in which the high-skill group is limited to professional/technical/managerial and the middle-skill group is expanded to include clerical/sales. These skills groups correspond (roughly) to their average position in the wage distribution for the nineteenth century and, we believe, in the distribution of schooling at the time, although we lack detailed data to verify this.

The hollowing out evident in manufacturing does *not* extend to the position of artisans in the overall economy, at least after 1850. As shown in panel A, there is a modest decline in the percent skilled blue collar from 12 percent in 1850 to 9 percent in 1880, which is subsequently reversed such that the artisan share in 1910 is slightly higher than in 1850. Although the artisan share declines in manufacturing, the employment of artisans was relatively high in manufacturing compared with other sectors, and the percent manufacturing grew after 1850. The economy also became more urban over time, which fueled the growth of the construction industry, which was also relatively intensive in the use of artisan labor.

Our second finding is that, in the aggregate economy, the share of high-skill workers, whether defined narrowly (professional/technical/manager) or more broadly (all white collar) rose monotonically from 1850 to 1910, while the share of low-skill jobs fell. The share of low-skill jobs fell entirely because the share of farm laborers declined to more than offset the rise in the share of operatives, unskilled labor, and service workers in the nonfarm economy.

Note that when we define the middle-skill group to be artisans plus farm operators, this share also falls over time, absolutely and relative to the low-skill group.[22] In other words, between 1850 and 1910 there was relatively more growth in high-skill jobs and relatively less decline in low-skill jobs, compared with middle-skill jobs—a type of hollowing out, although nowhere near as dramatic as occurred in manufacturing proper. But if one moves clerical and sales workers into the middle-skill group, then there is substantial stability in the middle-skill share from 1850 to 1910. Perhaps

---

22. The ratio of the middle- to lower-skill group was 0.55 in 1910, compared with 0.62 in 1850. The decline in the relative share took place after 1870.

the most important point, however, is that absolute and relative growth occurred in white-collar occupations between 1850 and 1910.[23] Because the nineteenth-century censuses did not record educational attainment, we cannot directly measure the schooling levels by occupation in the nineteenth century. However, from abundant descriptions of such jobs and workers, white-collar workers were better educated than the average, and they routinely used literacy, numeracy, and related skills acquired in formal schooling to a greater extent than was true of artisans, operatives, or common laborers.[24]

1.2.3   Occupational Wage Differentials in the Nineteenth Century: Supply or Demand?

We have shown that the share of white-collar workers in manufacturing increased from 1850 to 1910, while the share of skilled artisans decreased and that of operatives increased. In the aggregate economy the share of artisans was stable while the share of unskilled labor fell, but the white-collar share followed the same upward trend as it did in manufacturing.

Our story about capital deepening and firm size is a labor demand-side explanation of the occupation trends in manufacturing. We have not tried to claim that the story in its particulars is relevant outside of manufacturing, but it would be easy to point to technological change outside of manufacturing that could have increased the relative demand for white-collar workers. For example, the transportation revolution fueled growth in the service sector as well as urbanization, and as a byproduct increased the demand for white-collar workers (Haines and Margo 2008; Atack, Haines, and Margo 2011).

The occupation distributions in the previous section refer to quantities, and we cannot conclude from these alone that shifts in labor demand were responsible for the relative growth in white-collar workers. In particular, school enrollment rates and educational attainment were increasing over time. To distinguish between demand and supply explanations, we need information on wages.

Previous work by Margo (2000) and by Goldin and Katz (2008) gives some insight into this issue. Margo (2000) provides annual wage series for common labor, artisans, and white-collar workers from 1821 to 1860, while Goldin and Katz (2008) provide benchmark estimates of wage ratios—for example, white collar to operatives—for the late nineteenth and early twen-

---

23. See Rosenthal (2012, figure 4.4, 170) for additional evidence on the growth of white-collar workers from 1850 to 1900. In particular, Rosenthal uses the original occupational "strings" (that is, the text) to compute the number of clerical and accounting workers per 100,000 people. Her series increases from approximately 550 such workers per 100,000 in 1850 to approximately 1,200 per 100,000 people in 1900.

24. Goldin and Katz (2000, 2008) directly document using the Iowa state census of 1915 that white-collar workers had much higher levels of formal schooling than other workers in the early twentieth century.

tieth century. According to Margo's time series, the wage ratio of white-collar to common labor increased from 1820 to 1860, and Goldin and Katz's benchmark estimate of this wage ratio for the late nineteenth century is higher than Margo's estimate for the late antebellum period. By contrast, Margo finds a slight decline in the wage ratio of artisan to common labor from 1820 to 1860, and Goldin and Katz's benchmark for this wage ratio in the late nineteenth century is similar to Margo's estimate circa 1860. These results suggest that the relative demand for artisans (net of relative supply growth) was quite stable over the nineteenth century, while the relative demand for white-collar labor increased rapidly given increasing educational attainment levels. But the precise time path of relative wages in these occupations between 1860 and Goldin and Katz's benchmarks is not known.

In this section, we provide some additional evidence on occupational wage differentials for the nineteenth century. This evidence draws on the same source used by Margo for his antebellum series, namely the so-called *Reports of Persons and Articles Hired* for army forts in the nineteenth century.[25] The data specifically analyzed here pertains to the period 1866 to 1880, and is used to generate national aggregate series of daily wages for common labor and artisans, and monthly wages for white-collar workers, analogous to the series previously published by Margo for the antebellum period.[26] The data set contains approximately 17,000 wage observations (the unit of observation is a person-month).

Following Margo (2000), hedonic wage regressions are estimated for unskilled labor, artisans, and white-collar workers. Separate regressions by census region (Northeast, Midwest, South Atlantic, and South Central) are estimated for artisans and unskilled labor, but the sample sizes are such that only a national regression can be estimated for white-collar workers. The dependent variable is the log of the daily (or monthly) wage. The independent variables include dummy variables for separate occupations (for example, mason), the month of the year, the pay period (for example, monthly versus daily), fort (or state), and year.

The series for common labor are extensively benchmarked at the regional

25. Margo (2000, ch. 2) provides extensive evidence to show that that wages at the forts were very similar to those in the purely civilian economy in the local labor market. This evidence pertains to the antebellum period, but there is no reason to suppose that the patterns would be different for later in the century. That said, we recognize that the forts differed substantially as economic organizations from manufacturing and other types of firms in the civilian economy, and for all sorts of reasons the workers at the forts could differ from those in the civilian economy and consequently cause the trends in wages at the forts to deviate. We think that any such bias is likely to be minimal for the common labor wage series because of the extensive benchmarking, but we cannot make the same claim for the artisan or white-collar series.

26. Thus far no data have been collected for the Civil War years (1861–1865). Although such data are available for some forts, a separate study is necessary to determine their usefulness for capturing trends in the civilian economy.

level.[27] The series for artisans and white-collar workers, unfortunately, cannot be so extensively benchmarked. Instead, a national average wage for artisans and white-collar workers is computed using census data for 1880.[28] As far as possible, the benchmarking is done so as to produce a consistent series with those previously published by Margo (2000). Once the benchmarks are available, it is straightforward to use the coefficients of the time dummies to generate nominal wage series. Further details of the construction of the wage series can be found in appendix C.

Although the new wage series are, in our opinion, superior to any previously available, they have important limitations that should be kept in mind. First and foremost, the series at present pertain to narrow slices of the labor force—(free) white males whose skill levels are judged to be typical (or modal) for their occupation. Thus, for example, the series for artisans pertains to those of average skill—not, say, master carpenters or apprentice masons. This limitation is important because the occupation distributions presented in the previous section are more comprehensive in coverage than the wage series. Whether this affects our substantive conclusions is difficult to say, although our operative belief is that any bias is small.[29] Second, while the skills demanded at the forts were in widespread use in the general economy, the economic organization of the forts was not the same as, say, the typical manufacturing establishment. On the other hand, there is good evidence that wages at the forts were sensitive to local economic conditions and, in general, were very similar to what the workers would have commanded in the purely civilian economy (Margo 2000).

Panel A of table 1.5 shows five-year and decadal averages of the full (1820 to 1880) series along with estimates of the coefficients of linear time trends. Panel B shows wage ratios based on the decadal averages in panel A. Looking first at the wages of skilled artisans relative to common labor, we observe a shallow U-shaped pattern—a decrease in the relative wage of skilled artisans before the Civil War followed by a modest rise in the 1870s. Overall,

---

27. The regional series were published in summary form (e.g., five-year averages) in Margo (2004) and the annual series are available in Margo (2002).

28. The 1880 wage data come from the so-called Weeks Report. The white-collar data from Weeks are chosen to reflect the tasks performed by white-collar workers at the forts—standard clerical and bookkeeping skills that were also in widespread use in the purely civilian economy.

29. The principal issue is the inclusion of child and female labor, and slaves before the Civil War, in the wage series. Margo's (2000) antebellum regressions do control for slave status for forts located in the South, but the number of observations on slaves is insufficient to estimate separate wage series. Female and child workers were paid much less than adult white males, and including these workers in the series would reduce the level of the common labor wage series, thereby increasing the level of the skill premium for artisanal and white-collar workers. Goldin and Sokoloff (1982) present evidence that the wages of child and female workers in manufacturing increased relative to adult men between 1820 and 1850; this suggests, for example, that a more comprehensive series might show a smaller increase in the ratio of wages of white-collar to common labor before the Civil War and perhaps a larger decline in the ratio of wages of skilled artisans to common labor.

Table 1.5   Wages of common labor, skilled artisans, and white-collar workers: Aggregate time series, 1820–1880, by five-year periods and by decades

A. Nominal wage series

Pay period	Common labor Day ($)	Skilled artisan Day ($)	White collar Month ($)
1821–1825	0.71	1.31	33.62
1826–1830	0.70	1.38	35.12
1831–1835	0.73	1.45	35.23
1836–1840	0.82	1.56	43.75
1841–1845	0.79	1.40	42.43
1846–1850	0.81	1.41	44.70
1851–1855	0.90	1.57	51.00
1856–1860	1.01	1.83	52.29
1866–1870	1.47	2.47	71.52
1871–1875	1.40	2.64	74.38
1876–1880	1.11	2.29	72.69
1821–1830	0.70	1.36	34.45
1831–1840	0.78	1.51	39.49
1841–1850	0.80	1.40	43.56
1851–1860	0.95	1.70	51.65
1861–1870	1.47	2.47	71.52
1871–1880	1.26	2.46	73.53
Coefficient of linear time trend, log wage regression	0.0135 (0.0011)	0.0127 (0.0010)	0.0159 (0.0006)

B. Wage ratios

	Artisan/ common labor	Clerk/ common labor	Clerk/artisan
1821–1830	1.94	1.89	0.97
1831–1840	1.94	1.95	1.01
1841–1850	1.75	2.09	1.19
1851–1860	1.79	2.09	1.17
1861–1870	1.68	1.87	1.11
1871–1880	1.95	2.24	1.15

Sources: For panel A, see appendix C. Standard error of coefficient reported in parentheses. Panel B computed from panel A. Wages ratios for clerks assume twenty-six days per month (daily wage = monthly wage / 26); see Margo (2000).

however, there is no secular trend in the wages of skilled artisans relative to common labor. The occupation distribution for the overall economy in table 1.4 also follows a shallow U-pattern, but is probably better summarized by saying there was little overall trend in the relative shares of skilled artisans versus unskilled labor (see panel C of table 1.4).

For white-collar labor there is an upward trend in relative wages over the 1820 to 1880 period, which coincides with the upward trend in the percent white-collar in the overall economy. It follows that the relative demand for white-collar workers increased compared with relative supply over this time period. The extent to which relative demand grew faster than relative supply seems to have been modest, however, since the relative wages of clerical workers compared with common labor were approximately 10 percent higher circa 1880 than in 1850, whereas the share of white-collar workers in the economy more than doubled.[30] To the extent that the gap in the educational skills embodied in the typical white-collar worker relative to other workers remained reasonably stable over the course of the nineteenth century, the rise in the white-collar wage premium also suggests that the relative demand for educated labor increased faster the relative supply of educated labor. Goldin and Katz (2008) provide extensive documentation that the relative demand for educated labor increased throughout the twentieth century. Our results suggest that these increases began rather earlier in American history, at least as far back as the middle of the nineteenth century. Although the census does not allow us to trace occupation distributions prior to 1850, it is almost certainly the case that the share of white-collar workers in 1820 was lower than the share in 1850. Since the increase in relative wages of white-collar workers appears to begin in the 1820s, the increase in relative demand for educated workers probably began with the onset of industrialization in the United States.

1.3   Technical Change and Occupations in the Twentieth Century

Skill-biased technical change from electrification in the early twentieth century to computerization in recent decades has driven a rapid secular growth in the relative demand for more-educated workers. But the supply of skills at least kept pace with the demand for skills over most of the twentieth century (Goldin and Katz 2008). Growth in the supply of skills was largely due to the increased educational attainment of successive cohorts fueled by increased access to public high schools in the early twentieth century and later to colleges and universities. The upshot of these factors was that educational wage differentials narrowed from 1915 to 1980.

But US educational wage differentials and overall wage inequality have increased sharply since 1980. Goldin and Katz (2008) show that a slowdown in the growth of the supply of skills of the US working population combined with continued growth in the relative demand for skills can substantially explain the recent increase in educational wage differentials.

The rate of growth of the relative demand for more-skilled workers does not seem to have accelerated since 1980, but there is much evidence that changes in skill demand have shifted since the 1980s from being monotonically rising in skill to a polarization of labor demand that is U-shaped in skill

---

30. See Rosenthal (2012, chapter 4) for evidence that a wide variety of educational institutions emerged after 1850 to meet the growing demand for clerical, accounting, and related skills.

favoring high-wage jobs and lower-wage, in-person service jobs relative to middle-skill jobs. This pattern of skill demand shifts is consistent with a shift from the monotonic widening of the US wage structure in the 1980s to the divergence of upper-half and lower-half wage inequality since the late 1980s with upper-half wage inequality continuing to increase and lower-half wage inequality growth (if anything) slightly reversing in the 1990s (Goldin and Katz 2007; Autor, Katz, and Kearney 2008; Autor 2010).

Changes in the organization of work associated with computerization raise the demand for the cognitive and interpersonal skills used by highly educated professionals and managers and reduce the demand for the routine analytical (nonmanual) and mechanical (manual) skills that characterize many middle-educated, ordinary white-collar positions and manufacturing production jobs. Computerization has less direct impact on the demand for nonroutine manual skills in many low-wage, in-person service jobs and in the building trades (Autor, Levy, and Murnane 2003; Autor, Katz, and Kearney 2006; Acemoglu and Autor 2010; Goos, Manning, and Salomons 2011).

We next examine changes in the occupational distribution of employment from 1920 to 2010 in table 1.6 to gain insights into the post-1980 pattern of skill demand changes relative to those over much of the twentieth century and those in the second-half of the nineteenth century (shown earlier in table 1.4). We focus on the occupations of individuals employed in the civilian work force age sixteen or older using the IPUMS microdata for the 1920 to 2000 decadal censuses of population and the 2010 American Community Survey (ACS). Occupations are classified into occupational groupings using 1950 census occupation codes and the consistent coding of each census and ACS year's occupation codes into the 1950 codes by the IPUMS.

Panel A of table 1.6 displays changes in the occupation distribution for the aggregate civilian economy from 1920 to 2010. We focus on a categorization of occupations based on recent rankings by education and wages into high skill (professional, technical, and managerial occupations that increasingly require at least a bachelors' degree), middle skill (clerical, sales, skilled blue collar, and farm operators), and low skill (operatives, laborers, farm laborers, and service occupations). The employment share of high-skill workers (as well as of the overall white-collar workforce) secularly increased from 1920 to 2010, continuing a trend going back at least to 1850 with the high skill share more than tripling from 12 percent in 1920 to over 39 percent in 2010. Monotonic skill upgrading is seen in the occupational distribution throughout most of the twentieth century (through 1980) with the share in high-skill occupations rising, middle-skill occupations holding steady, and low-skill occupations declining. The stability of the middle-skill group from 1920 to 1980 hides a rise the clerical/sales share, stability for skilled blue collar, and a steep decline for farm operators. The declining share of low-skill employment is driven by farm laborers in the first half of the twentieth century and by operatives and laborers (largely in manufacturing) in

Table 1.6 Occupation distributions (in percent): US civilian employment, age sixteen and older, 1920 to 2010

Detailed occupations	A. Aggregate economy									
	1920	1930	1940	1950	1960	1970	1980	1990	2000	2010
White collar	25.5	30.8	31.9	37.5	43.3	48.5	53.8	58.8	61.8	62.5
Professional-technical	5.6	6.9	7.7	8.9	11.9	15.5	17.5	20.4	23.4	25.1
Manager	6.7	7.8	8.0	9.0	8.9	7.9	10.4	12.8	14.2	14.3
Clerical/sales	13.1	16.1	16.2	19.6	22.6	25.1	25.9	25.5	24.2	23.1
Skilled blue collar (craft)	14.1	12.7	11.6	14	14.3	13.6	12	10.5	9.8	8.1
Operative/laborer/service	35.5	34.2	39.1	36.8	36	34.8	31.9	29.2	27.1	28.3
Operative/laborer	27.3	24.3	27.4	26.5	24.4	22.1	19.2	15.9	14.1	12.6
Service occupations	8.2	9.9	11.6	10.3	11.6	12.6	12.9	13.2	13.0	15.7
Agricultural occupations	24.9	22.4	17.4	11.7	6.3	3.1	2.2	1.6	1.2	1.1
Farmer/supervisory	16.3	13.7	11	7.7	4.1	1.9	1.3	0.9	0.6	0.4
Farm laborer	8.6	8.6	6.4	4.1	2.2	1.3	0.9	0.7	0.6	0.7
Skill groups										
High skill (prof/tech/manager)	12.4	14.7	15.7	17.9	20.7	23.4	27.8	33.3	37.6	39.4
Middle skill (Clerical/sales/farmer/craft)	43.6	42.5	38.9	41.3	41.0	40.5	39.3	36.9	34.6	31.6
Low skill (Operative/laborer/farm laborer/service)	44.1	42.8	45.4	40.8	38.3	36.0	32.9	29.9	27.7	29.0

(continued)

Table 1.6 (continued)

B. Manufacturing industries

Occupational groups	1920	1930	1940	1950	1960	1970	1980	1990	2000	2010
White collar	14.8	19.4	21.5	23.5	28.4	30.5	33.5	39.3	41.5	45.6
High skill (prof/tech/manager)	6.1	8.2	7.9	9.7	13.0	15.3	18.1	23.9	27.6	31.7
Clerical/sales	8.7	11.2	13.6	13.9	15.4	15.2	15.5	15.4	13.9	13.9
Skilled blue collar (craft)	24.8	23.0	18.9	19.6	20.1	19.3	19.3	19.0	18.0	15.8
Middle skill (clerical/sales/craft)	33.5	34.2	32.5	33.4	35.5	34.5	34.8	34.4	31.9	29.7
Low skill (operatives/laborers/service)	60.4	57.6	59.5	56.9	51.4	50.2	47.2	41.7	40.5	38.6

Sources: 1920 to 2000, census of population IPUMS and 2010 American Community Survey IPUMS.

Notes: Occupation shares are reported in percent. Occupations are classified into occupational groups based on 1950 occupation codes using the consistent coding of occupations in all years into 1950 codes (the OCC1950 variable) in the IPUMS. For 1930 to 2010, the samples include all individuals age sixteen or older who were employed in the civilian workforce during the reference week for the census or American Community Survey (EMPSTAT = 1, excluding those in the armed forces) and who reported a valid occupation (OCC1950 from 0 to 970). Employed individuals (those with EMPSTAT = 1) are excluded from the sample as being members of the armed forces if they are categorized in the armed forces by the detail EMPSTAT codes (EMPSTAT = 13 in 1930 to 1950, and EMPSTAT = 14 or 15 in 1960 to 2010) or they list a military occupation (OCC1950 = 595). For 1920, the sample includes all individuals age sixteen or older in the civilian labor force (LABFORCE = 2) excluding those listing military occupations (OCC50 = 595). The 1940 census occupation codes do not allow one to separate accountants (a professional occupation) from bookkeepers and cashiers (a clerical occupation) with all three groups being in occupation code 210. We allocate individuals in 1940 occupation code 210 in the 1940 census IPUMS into professionals (27.7 percent) and clerical occupations (72.3 percent) using the share of accountants among accountants, bookkeepers, and cashiers in the 1950 census IPUMS sample.

the second half of the twentieth century. In contrast, the share of employment of service workers—the other low-skill and currently the lowest wage occupational group—increased (almost doubling) from 1920 to 2010 with the most rapid growth in the last decade. Panel B of table 1.6 shows a similar pattern of monotonic occupational skill upgrading in manufacturing industries from 1920 to 1980.

A hollowing out of the occupational skill distribution with a declining share of jobs in middle-skill occupations is apparent both in the aggregate economy and in manufacturing since 1980 and especially from 2000 to 2010. The high skill employment share has continued to increase rapidly since 1980. And the decline of the low skill employment share has slowed since 1990 with an actual increase in the aggregate low skill share from 2000 to 2010, driven by the rapid relative growth of in-person service jobs. More detailed analysis of the full set of three-digit occupations by average education levels and wages in 1980 show a shift from monotonic occupational skill upgrading through the 1980s to a polarization pattern of the upper and lower ends gaining against the middle since 1990 (Autor, Katz, and Kearney 2008; Autor 2010).

The employment share of high-skill occupations that increasingly require at least a college degree has more than tripled since 1920. And the college wage premium, after declining in the first half of the twentieth century, has risen substantially since 1980 back to at least the level prevailing in 1915 in the face of a growing relative supply of college-educated workers (Goldin and Katz 2008). This pattern indicates strong secular relative demand shifts favoring more-educated labor over the last century. And the evidence on occupation employment shares and relative earnings in the nineteenth century in tables 1.4 and 1.5 indicate that rapid increases in the relative demand for more-educated workers dates back at least to 1850. Furthermore, the recent period of the hollowing out of middle-skill jobs associated with the reorganization of work from computerization in the aggregate economy and manufacturing has parallels to the decline in middle-skill artisans in US manufacturing in the nineteenth century with the shift from the artisanal shop to the factory.

1.4   Conclusion

Technology has been an engine of economic growth in the United States since the onset of industrialization. In the twentieth and twenty-first centuries technology has been skill-biased overall, favoring more-educated labor. But the conventional wisdom among economic historians is that technical change in the nineteenth century may have had the opposite effect—de-skilling. The switch to capital-skill complementarity allegedly occurred in the early twentieth century with the diffusion of electricity as an inanimate power source.

In this chapter we have revisited the question of the historical evolution of capital-skill and technology-skill complementarity in the United States. In contrast to the conventional wisdom, we have instead stressed the continuity of the effects of technical change on the relative demand for skill. It is true, as we document extensively in this chapter, that in nineteenth-century manufacturing, technical change reduced the relative demand for artisans in favor of machines operated by less skilled workers and, in that sense, certainly was de-skilling. But a more nuanced picture shows that the manufacturing workforce hollowed out: in addition to operatives, nonproduction workers, who on average were more educated, not less, increased their employment shares relative to artisans. And in the aggregate economy of the nineteenth century we find no evidence of de-skilling overall but rather the opposite, as demonstrated by a persistent, long-term increase in the share of white-collar workers. In the twentieth century technical change has largely had a monotonic effect on the relative demand for skill, until quite recently. But the occupation distribution has again hollowed out since the 1980s. Drawing on the recent literature on task-based models (Acemoglu and Autor 2010), we argue that there is a common theme to the effects of technical change across the two centuries, displacing skilled labor from some tasks, but increasing its use in other tasks.

We have stressed the effects of technical change on the relative demand for skill in this chapter, but our results also have important implications for the historical evolution of social mobility in the United States. Throughout much of the nineteenth century the pathway to middle class status was through ascending the agricultural ladder to farm operator status or via an apprenticeship to artisan status. By the end of the century, however, both pathways had narrowed, replaced by white-collar occupations that, unlike farming or artisanal skills, required more formal schooling. Indeed, our new wage series imply that the demand for white-collar skills increased relative to supply, which suggests that the returns to schooling trended upward during much of the nineteenth century. Careful study of how the shifts in relative demand and wages influenced the decisions of individuals in the mid- to late nineteenth century to invest in schooling rather than agricultural or artisan skills could shed considerable light on the historical evolution of the race between technology and education in the American case.

Appendix A

Construction of Percent Unskilled: 1880 Manufacturing Sample

The 1880 census reports sufficient data with which to compute an estimate of the average daily wage of workers at the establishment level (see Atack,

Bateman, and Margo 2004). The census also inquired about the average daily of unskilled labor and the average daily wage of "mechanics." We use these data to construct a proxy for the percent skilled.

First, for firms that reported both types of wages, we use the following equation to estimate, u, the percent skilled

$$w = w_u u + w_s(1 - u).$$

Here, w is the average daily wage at the establishment level, u is the share unskilled, and s is the share of skilled blue collar. We compute the estimate of u with this equation, retaining only those observations such that u is nonnegative. For firms that report the skilled wage but not the unskilled wage, we set $s = 1$. For firms that report the unskilled wage but not the skilled, we set $s = 0$.

Our estimate of u is clearly biased because our procedure assumes, in effect, that all employees were production workers, which is obviously incorrect. It is straightforward to show that our estimate of u will be biased downward. Let m be the share of nonproduction workers, and w_m the average daily wage of nonproduction workers. Then the correct estimate of u is given by the equation

$$u = \frac{w - (w_m - w_s)m - w_s}{w_u - w_s},$$

whereas our estimate is

$$u^* = \frac{w - w_s}{w_u - w_s}.$$

Both the numerator and denominator of the right-hand side of the expression for u or u^* are negative, but the numerator of the right-hand side of u^* will be biased toward zero, hence our estimate of u^* will be smaller than the correct estimate, u. However, this bias is likely to be very small, because m was still relatively small for most establishments in 1880. The bias will be increasing in absolute value as establishment size increases, so the coefficients on size in the regressions in panel B of table 1.3 are biased downward. The downward bias reinforces the substance of our argument, namely that the percent of operatives/unskilled was increasing in establishment size.

Appendix B
Construction of Occupation Distributions

In table 1.4 we present estimates of the occupation distribution in manufacturing and in the overall economy from 1850 to 1910. Our estimates pertain to individuals age ten and older. The estimates are based on detailed adjustments to occupation distributions that are derived from the various IPUMS samples over the same period. IPUMS samples exist for every census year between 1850 and 1910, except 1890. The IPUMS occupation and industry data pertain to free persons age sixteen and older in the labor force; persons are considered to be in the labor force if they reported a gainful occupation.

Estimation of Occupation Distribution in Manufacturing

The 1910 census was the first to ask individuals about their industry of employment as well as occupation. While there have been several attempts by scholars to produce estimates of the share of the labor force in manufacturing for the pre-1910 census years, to the best of our knowledge there have been no attempts to provide estimates of the occupation distribution within manufacturing.

Our estimates make use of the imputed IPUMS variable IND1950. The IPUMS staff created this variable after observing that in the census manuscripts individuals very frequently provided information recorded in the occupation column that readily identify the industry of employment. Nineteenth-century census officials were long aware of this characteristic of the data collection; indeed, this was a primary reason why the census created the separate question in 1910. The IPUMS staff has devised a set of protocols to determine industry of employment based on the information contained in the census manuscripts (IPUMS-USA n.d.). Importantly, these protocols were designed to provide a series that could link up to 1910, not to answer the question addressed in this chapter. While we do not believe that the imputed industry classifications are accurate enough to produce reliable estimates of the occupation distribution at, say, the three-digit SIC code, we do believe the classification is accurate enough to broadly distinguish the manufacturing and nonmanufacturing labor force.

A small caveat to our estimates is that we make no adjustment for slave labor in manufacturing for 1850 or 1860 because we believe the available data to make such an adjustment are too sparse. Slaves were certainly employed in antebellum manufacturing; the best known example is the tobacco industry in Richmond, Virginia (Goldin 1976). Excluding slaves biases downward the share operative/unskilled in 1850 and 1860; however, the numbers are too small in the aggregate to noticeably alter the levels of the estimates, much less the trends that we observe.

As in our estimates for the overall occupation distribution (see below) we begin with samples of individuals drawn from the IPUMS with LABFORCE = 2. We then retain all observations for which IND1950 indicates a manufacturing industry. Using the variable OCC1950, we classify the manufacturing labor force into white-collar, skilled blue-collar, and operative/unskilled. This constitutes our preliminary distribution.

We make a series of adjustments to the preliminary distribution. In summary form, the adjustments are:

Reallocation of shoemakers and operatives in boots and shoe industry. See the discussion below.

Adjustment for female labor, 1850. The 1850 census reported occupations for males only. We assume that the ratio of males to the total manufacturing labor force, age sixteen and older by occupation group (white collar, skilled blue collar, operative/unskilled) was the same in 1850 as in 1860. Applying these ratios to the IPUMS totals by occupation group in 1850, we produce estimates of the occupation distribution in manufacturing for both genders, age sixteen and older.

Adjustment for free child labor, age ten to fifteen. For 1870–1910, we use the published census of manufacturing to compute the ratio of child workers (age ten to fifteen) to the sum of adult females and males. We multiply this ratio by the number of individuals in our preliminary occupation distribution; this generates an estimate of the number of child workers to be added to the total. We assume that all child workers are employed as operatives. For 1850 and 1860, we assume that the ratio of child workers to the sum of adult males and females was the same as in 1870.

Estimation of Overall Occupation Distribution

Our estimates of the overall occupation distribution do not rely on the imputed IPUMS variable IND1950, but do make use of the IPUMS variable OCC1950, which classifies occupations. We use this variable to divide up the labor force into seven occupation groups. The first five are nonfarm occupations and the remaining two are farm: professional/technical, managerial/official/proprietor, clerical/sales, skilled blue collar, operative/unskilled/service, farm operator/supervisor, and farm laborer. The first three occupations are the traditional subdivisions of the white-collar labor force. In panel C of table 1.4, we present calculations that define the unskilled share of the labor force to be the sum of the shares in operative/unskilled/service and farm laborer.

For each IPUMS census year we begin by extracting a sample of individuals, selecting those for whom the variable LABFORCE = 2 (in the labor force). All such individuals in the IPUMS are age sixteen or older, and all report a gainful occupation. Using the variable OCC1950, we create a preliminary occupation distribution for the seven occupation groups listed above. We then make a series of modifications to the preliminary distribution. In summary form, these adjustments are:

Adjustment for free female labor force, age sixteen and older, in 1850. The 1850 census only reported occupations for free males. We make an initial imputation of the free female labor force by occupation group by assuming the ratio "total free labor force, age sixteen and older/male free labor force, age sixteen and older" was the same in 1850 and in 1860. We then adjust the occupation group totals for females so that the overall gender composition matches Weiss's (2006, tables Ba1-10, Ba40-49) estimates for 1850.

Adjustment for laborers not elsewhere classified, living on farms, age sixteen and older. In the preliminary distribution, persons for whom OCC1950 = 970 (laborers, not elsewhere classified) are allocated to the operative/unskilled/service group, regardless of their residential location. However, it is widely believed by economic historians that such individuals who lived on farms were almost certainly farm laborers rather than nonfarm. Therefore, the number of individuals who report OCC1950 = 970 and also FARM = 2 is subtracted from the operative/unskilled group and added to the farm laborer group.

Adjustment for child labor, free labor force. Using Weiss (2006), we compute ratios by gender of the labor force age ten to fifteen to age sixteen and older. We apply these ratios to the IPUMS sample totals, thereby generating estimates of children workers whose occupations were not reported in the labor force. Next, for each IPUMS census year, we extract a sample of individuals, age ten to fifteen, computing the proportion, by gender, who were living on farms (FARM = 2). We multiply our estimated number of child workers by the share living on farms (by gender), and call the result the number of child workers employed in agriculture. We assume all such workers were farm laborers. The remainder is assigned to the operative/unskilled/service group.

Adjustment for shoemakers and operatives in shoe factories, 1850–1870. According to the 1850 and 1860 occupational classifications in the IPUMS, virtually all persons who were employed in the boot and shoe industry were classified as skilled artisans (shoemakers, or OCC1950 = 488) rather than operatives in shoe factories. However, according to the Atack-Bateman-Weiss samples from the manufacturing census, fully two-thirds of all labor employed in boots and shoes worked in establishments of sixteen or more workers—the commonly used definition of the "factory"—as early as 1850. In the 1870 IPUMS sample, the proportion of operatives in boot and shoes is much closer to two-thirds than in 1850 or 1860. Consistent with the general trend toward factories, the proportion employed in boot and shoe establishments of sixteen or more workers increased between 1850 and 1880, but the trend is a gentle one, not abrupt. We believe that in 1850 and 1860 the census had difficulty in distinguishing shoemakers in artisanal shops from those working as operatives in establishments; the 1870 and 1880 censuses, however, contain instructions to enumerators to pay close attention to such distinctions in manufacturing. For 1850 to 1870, therefore, we assume that 65 percent of workers age sixteen and older in the boot and shoe industry were operatives, and 35 percent were skilled artisans. We adjust the preliminary occupation distribution in these years to reflect this assumption. For 1880, we assume that the occupation classification for persons in boots and shoes are correct, as indicated by OCC1950.

Adjustment for slave occupations, 1850 and 1860. We use Weiss (2006) estimates to calculate, by gender, the ratio, "slave labor force/free labor force."

We apply these ratios to the adjustment number of free workers, by gender (i.e., the adjustments described above). This generates an estimate number of slave workers, to be included in our occupation distributions. We use Olson (1992, 139, table 8.1) to allocate our estimated number of slave workers to the occupation groups. For men this results in allocations to the skilled artisan, operative/unskilled/service, farm operator/supervisor, and farm laborer groups; for women, the allocations are to operative/unskilled/service and farm laborer. It is likely that this procedure underestimates the number of skilled artisans among male slaves because the Olson table is based on probate and plantation records and, as such, probably underweights slaves in urban areas; however, any bias is likely to be very small, because the share of slaves in urban areas was less than 5 percent in the decade before the Civil War (Goldin 1976).

Appendix C
Construction of Wage Series, 1866–1880

We provide annual estimates of nominal wages for three occupations: common labor, artisans, and white-collar workers (clerks). The data source is the *Reports of Persons and Articles Hired* (Record Group 92, National Archives) used extensively by Margo (2000) in his construction of analogous wage series for the antebellum period. The data pertain to civilians hired at US army installations, and cover the period 1866–1880. The data were extracted (by hand) from monthly payrolls at the forts, which have survived and have been deposited at the National Archives. There are approximately 17,000 wage observations available in the data set (a wage observation refers to a person month; for example, a carpenter hired at St. Louis for one or more days during the month of October in 1879). Like those for the antebellum period, the data appear to reflect labor market conditions in the labor market surrounding the fort.

Wage series are produced from hedonic regressions. In these regressions, the dependent variable is the logarithm of the daily wage (if a worker is hired on a monthly basis, the daily wage is computed by dividing by an assumed twenty-six days of labor per month). Control variables include occupation dummies, month of the year, place of hire (or state in which the fort is located), other characteristics of the worker, if known (e.g., race), and year.[31] For common labor and artisans the regressions are estimated separately by region. For white-collar workers the number of observations is insufficient

---

31. In some cases, the year dummies refer to groups of years rather than single years. In such cases we linearly interpolate to produce the annual series.

to estimate regional series and instead a national regression is estimated with extensive controls for location.

From the year dummies we produce annual indices of nominal wages. These annual indices are then benchmarked to wage estimates from other sources (see Margo [2002] and [2004], and the text of the current chapter). For common labor the benchmarking is extensive (multiple years between 1866 and 1880), and the year-by-year values of the indices are adjusted to reflect the benchmarking.

The data for common labor has previously been analyzed, and annual wage series for census regions (Northeast, Midwest, South Atlantic, and South Central) produced in Margo (2002, 2004). Except for California during the Gold Rush period (see Margo 2000), no series have been produced for the western United States.

For this chapter we estimated annual series of daily wages for artisans by region and an annual series for white-collar workers (see above regarding the white-collar regression). For common labor and artisans we aggregated the regional series using region-specific weights. To compute these weights we drew extracts from the 1870 and 1880 IPUMS samples and estimated regional shares of occupations for 1870 and 1880. We linearly interpolated the shares between 1870 and 1880. For 1866–1869 we used the 1870 weights.

References

Acemoglu, Daron, and David H. Autor. 2010. "Skills, Tasks, and Technologies: Implications for Employment and Earnings." In *Handbook of Labor Economics*, vol. 4, part B, edited by O. Ashenfelter and D. Card. New York: Elsevier.

———. 2012. "What Does Human Capital Do? A Review of Goldin and Katz's *The Race between Education and Technology.*" *Journal of Economic Literature* 50:426–63.

Atack, Jeremy. 1979. "Fact or Fiction? The Relative Costs of Steam and Water Power: A Simulation Approach." *Explorations in Economic History* 16:409–37.

Atack, Jeremy, and Fred Bateman. 1999. "US Historical Statistics: Nineteenth Century US Industrial Development through the Eyes of the Census of Manufactures." *Historical Methods* 32:177–88.

Atack, Jeremy, Fred Bateman, and Robert A. Margo. 2004. "Skill Intensity and Rising Wage Dispersion in Nineteenth Century American Manufacturing." *Journal of Economic History* 64:172–92.

———. 2005. "Capital Deepening and the Rise of the Factory: The American Experience in the Nineteenth Century," *Economic History Review* 58:586–95.

———. 2008. "Steam Power, Establishment Size, and Labor Productivity Growth in Nineteenth Century American Manufacturing." *Explorations in Economic History* 45:185–98.

Atack, Jeremy, Fred Bateman, and Thomas Weiss. 1980. "The Regional Diffusion and Adoption of the Steam Engine in American Manufacturing," *Journal of Economic History* 40:281–308.

Atack, Jeremy, Michael Haines, and Robert A. Margo. 2011. "Railroads and the Rise of the Factory: Evidence for the United States, 1850–1870." In *Economic Evolution and Revolution in Historical Time*, edited by J. Rosenbloom and D. Weiman, 162–79. Palo Alto, CA: Stanford University Press.

Autor, David H. 2010. "The Polarization of Job Opportunities in the US Labor Market." Working Paper, Center for American Progress and The Hamilton Project, April.

———. 2013. "The 'Task Approach' to Labor Markets: An Overview." NBER Working Paper no. 18711. Cambridge, MA.

Autor, David H., and David Dorn. 2013. "The Growth of Low-Skill Service Jobs and the Polarization of the US Labor Market." *American Economic Review* 103:1553–97.

Autor, David H., Lawrence F. Katz, and Melissa S. Kearney. 2006. "The Polarization of the US Labor Market." *American Economic Review* 96:189–94.

———. 2008. "Trends in US Wage Inequality: Revising the Revisionists." *Review of Economics and Statistics* 90:300–23.

Autor, David H., Lawrence F. Katz, and Alan B. Krueger. 1998. "Computing Inequality: Have Computers Changed the Labor Market?" *Quarterly Journal of Economics* 113:1169–213.

Autor, David H., Frank Levy, and Richard J. Murnane. 2003. "The Skill Content of Recent Technological Change: An Empirical Exploration." *Quarterly Journal of Economics* 116:1279–333.

Bessen, Jim. 2012. "More Machines, Better Machines . . . or Better Workers?" *Journal of Economic History* 72:44–74.

Brissenden, Paul F. 1929. *Earnings of Factory Workers, 1899–1927: An Analysis of Payroll Statistics*. Washington, DC: Government Printing Office.

Brown, Martin, and Peter Phillips. 1986. "Craft Labor and Mechanization in Nineteenth Century Canning." *Journal of Economic History* 46:743–56.

Chandler, Alfred. 1977. *The Visible Hand: The Managerial Revolution in American Business*. Cambridge, MA: Harvard University Press.

Davis, Steven J., and John Haltiwanger. 1991. "Wage Dispersion between and within US Manufacturing Plants, 1963–1986." In *Brookings Papers on Economic Activity: Microeconomics* 1991:115–80. Washington, DC: The Brookings Institution.

Delle Donne, C. R. 1973. *Federal Census Schedules, 1850–1880: Primary Sources for Historical Research*. National Archives and Records Service Reference Information Paper no. 67, General Services Administration, Washington, DC.

Devine, Warren D. 1983. "From Shafts to Wires: Historical Perspective on Electrification." *Journal of Economic History* 43:347–72.

Engerman, Stanley, and Kenneth Sokoloff. 2000. "Technology and Industrialization, 1790–1914." In *The Cambridge Economic History of the United States, Volume Two: The Long Nineteenth Century*, edited by S. L. Engerman and R. Gallman. New York: Cambridge University Press.

Fenichel, A. H. 1966. "The Growth and Diffusion of Power in Manufacturing, 1839–1919." In *Output, Employment and Productivity in the United States After 1800*, Conference on Research on Income and Wealth. New York: National Bureau of Economic Research.

Field, Alexander. 1980. "Industrialization and Skill Intensity: The Case of Massachusetts." *Journal of Human Resources* 15:149–75.

Goldin, Claudia. 1976. *Urban Slavery in the American South, 1820–1860: A Quantitative History*. Chicago: University of Chicago Press.

Goldin, Claudia, and Lawrence F. Katz. 1998. "The Origins of Technology-Skill Complementarity." *Quarterly Journal of Economics* 113:693–732.

———. 2000. "Education and Income in the Early Twentieth Century: Evidence from the Prairies." *Journal of Economic History* 60:782–818.

———. 2007. "Long-Run Changes in the Wage Structure: Narrowing, Widening, Polarizing." *Brookings Papers on Economic Activity* 2:135–67.

———. 2008. *The Race between Education and Technology.* Cambridge, MA: The Belknap Press of Harvard University Press.

Goldin, Claudia, and Robert A. Margo. 1992. "The Great Compression: The Wage Structure in the United States at Mid-Century." *Quarterly Journal of Economics* 107:1–34.

Goldin, Claudia, and Kenneth Sokoloff. 1982. "Women, Children, and Industrialization in the Early Republic: Evidence from the Manufacturing Censuses." *Journal of Economic History* 42:741–74.

———. 1984. "The Relative Productivity Hypothesis of Industrialization." *Quarterly Journal of Economics* 99:461–88.

Goos, Maarten, Alan Manning, and Anna Salomons. 2011. "Explaining Job Polarization: The Roles of Technology, Globalization, and Institutions." Working Paper, University of Leuven, November.

Griliches, Zvi. 1969. "Capital-Skill Complementarity." *Review of Economics and Statistics* 51:465–8.

Haines, Michael, and Robert A. Margo. 2008. "Railroads and Local Economic Development: The United States in the 1850s." In *Quantitative Economic History: The Good of Counting*, edited by J. Rosenbloom. London: Routledge.

Hilt, Eric. 2008. "When Did Ownership Separate from Control? Corporate Governance in the Early Nineteenth Century." *Journal of Economic History* 68:645–85.

Hounshell, David. 1984. *From the American System to Mass Production.* Baltimore, MD: Johns Hopkins Press.

Hunter, Louis C. 1979. *A History of Industrial Power in the United States: 1780 to 1930. Volume One: Waterpower in the Century of the Steam Engine.* Greenville, DE: Eleutherian Mills-Hagley Foundation.

———. 1985. *A History of Industrial Power in the United States: 1780 to 1930. Volume Two: Steam Power.* Greenville, DE: Eleutherian Mills-Hagley Foundation.

Hutchinson, William, and Robert A. Margo. 2006. "The Impact of the Civil War on Capital Intensity and Labor Productivity in Southern Manufacturing." *Explorations in Economic History* 43:689–704.

Integrated Public Use Microdata Series (IPUMS)-USA. n.d. "Integrated Occupation and Industry Codes and Occupation Standing Variables in the IPUMS." http://usa.ipums.org/usa/chapter4/chapter4.shtml.

Katz, Lawrence F., and Robert A. Margo. 2013. "Technical Change and the Relative Demand for Skilled Labor: The United States in Historical Perspective." NBER Working Paper no. 18752, Cambridge, MA.

Lamoreaux, Naomi. 2006. "Business Organization." In *Historical Statistics of the United States: Earliest Times to the Present*, millennial ed., vol. 3, part C: Economic Structure and Performance, edited by S. Carter et al. New York: Cambridge University Press.

Margo, Robert A. 2000. *Wages and Labor Markets in the United States, 1820–1860.* Chicago: University of Chicago Press.

———. 2002. "The North-South Wage Gap, before and after the Civil War." NBER Working Paper no. 8778, Cambridge, MA.

———. 2004. "The North-South Wage Gap, before and after the Civil War." In *Slavery in the Development of the Americas*, edited by D. Eltis, F. Lewis, and K. Sokoloff. New York: Cambridge University Press.

Olson, John F. 1992. "The Occupational Structure of Southern Plantations during the Late Antebellum Era." In *Without Consent or Contract, Markets and Production*, Technical Papers, vol. 1, edited by R. W. Fogel and S. L. Engerman. New York: W.W. Norton.

Rosenbloom, Joshua. 2002. *Looking for Work: Searching for Workers: Labor Markets during American Industrialization*. New York: Cambridge University Press.

Rosenthal, Caitlin C. 2012. "From Memory to Mastery: Accounting for Control in America, 1750–1880." PhD diss., Department of History, Harvard University.

Rousseau, Peter, and Richard Sylla. 2005. "Emerging Financial Markets and Early US Growth." *Explorations in Economic History* 42:1–26.

Scranton, Phillip. 1999. *Endless Novelty: Specialty Production and American Industrialization, 1865–1925*. Princeton, NJ: Princeton University Press.

Sokoloff, Kenneth. 1982. "Industrialization and the Growth of the Manufacturing Sector in the Northeast, 1820–1850." Unpublished PhD diss., Department of Economics, Harvard University.

———. 1984. "Was the Transition from the Artisanal Shop to the Non-Mechanized Factory Associated with Gains in Efficiency? Evidence from the Manufacturing Censuses of 1820 and 1850." *Explorations in Economic History* 21:351–84.

———. 1986. "Productivity Gains in Manufacturing during Early Industrialization: Evidence from the American Northeast, 1820–1850." In *Long Term Factors in American Economic Growth*, Studies in Income and Wealth, vol. 51, edited by S. L. Engerman and R. Gallman. Chicago: University of Chicago Press.

Taylor, George R. 1951. *The Transportation Revolution, 1815–1860*. New York: Holt-Rinehart and Winston.

Temin, Peter. 1966. "Steam and Waterpower in the Early Nineteenth Century." *Journal of Economic History* 26:187–205.

US Bureau of Labor. 1899. *Thirteenth Annual Report of the Commissioner of Labor, 1898*. Two Volumes. Washington, DC: Government Printing Office.

Weiss, Thomas. 2006. "Workforce." In *Historical Statistics of the United States, Earliest Times to the Present*, millennial ed., vol. 2, part B, Work and Welfare, edited by Susan B. Carter, Scott Sigmund Gartner, Michael R. Haines, Alan L. Olmstead, Richard Sutch, and Gavin Wright. New York: Cambridge University Press.

Williamson, Jeffrey, and Peter Lindert. 1980. *American Inequality: A Macroeconomic History*. New York: Academic Press.

Wright, Carroll D. 1900. *The History and Growth of the United States Census*. Washington, DC: US Government Printing Office.

Wright, Gavin. 1990. "The Origins of American Industrial Success, 1879–1940." *American Economic Review* 80:651–68.

Explaining Trends in High School Graduation
The Changing Elementary and Secondary Education Policy Landscape and Income Inequality over the Last Half Century

Nora Gordon

2.1 Introduction

In *The Race between Education and Technology*, Goldin and Katz (2008) comprehensively examine the forces behind changes in returns to skill in the United States over the twentieth century. Their title summarizes key forces influencing the supply of and demand for skilled labor. They write, "Our central conclusion is that when it comes to changes in the wage structure and returns to skill, supply changes have been critical, and changes in the educational attainment of the native-born have driven the supply side" (323). This chapter examines one dimension of the puzzle remaining at their conclusion: Why did high school graduation rates plateau in the latter portion of the twentieth century? Labor economists study this pattern in the context of increasing returns to skill; though returns to a high school diploma itself have diminished, it continues to serve as a gateway to college and its associated increasing labor market rewards. In this chapter, I focus on the role income inequality may have played in affecting graduation rates, and whether it did so in part through educational institutions.

In contrast to Goldin and Katz (2008), who find that income inequality slowed the local establishment of public high schools from 1910 to 1938, recent evidence (Boustan et al. 2013; Corcoran and Evans 2010) shows that increases in income inequality at the local level from 1970 to 2000 increased elementary and secondary school spending. In this chapter, I review major changes in education over the past half century, including a massive aggre-

Nora Gordon is associate professor of public policy at Georgetown University and a research associate of the National Bureau of Economic Research.

For acknowledgments, sources of research support, and disclosure of the author's material financial relationships, if any, please see http://www.nber.org/chapters/c12898.ack.

gate increase in school spending, the decline in the inequality of resources across local school districts, and the civil rights focus on various groups of students historically less likely to graduate. I then describe the relationships between within-state income inequality and mean state spending on state-level graduation rates and, separately, school spending, to see if the data suggest any part of the increases in spending induced by inequality went toward productive investments in students on the margin of dropping out. Following the plateau in graduation rates, what appears to be an uptick since 2000 sparks further speculation about the relationship between education policy and graduation outcomes.

Becker's model of human capital provides a useful starting point for considering potential determinants of high school graduation and educational attainment more generally. Individuals optimize their investments in human capital by considering the expected costs of acquiring it and the stream of returns they anticipate earning from it. School quality, as determined by inputs and technologies, can affect both costs and benefits. Much of the education literature implicitly assumes that improvements in school quality reduce psychic costs of human capital acquisition by making the school experience more enjoyable or effective, and thus considers graduation to be an indicator of school quality, holding the demand for skilled labor constant.[1] If the skill level of the entire workforce is increasing—whether due to the increasing returns to skill we see over this period (Freeman 1976) or improvements in school quality—excess supply of skilled labor could depress returns to the point that individuals anticipating this response would lower their investments in human capital. I confine my discussion to the potential impact of changes in the supply of education, rather than labor market-induced changes in its demand, though of course both forces shape individual decisions about attainment.[2]

High school graduation rates are a relevant outcome for several reasons. As a measure of human capital, they have implications for productivity and economic growth. Studies of high school dropout point to the importance of achievement levels at younger ages, so studies of high school graduation can indirectly allow us to study the elusive education production function at the elementary and early childhood levels as well as the secondary level. The extent to which educational inputs are associated with student outcomes has long been a popular question among researchers, the media, policymakers and the public, most prominently emerging with the Coleman

---

1. Intended improvements in schools could well make schooling more costly, however. Changes in educational production could improve achievement *conditional on constant enrollment* but discourage enrollment and ultimately attainment, potentially to the point that the net effect is negative: consider high school exit exams, longer school days and years, or longer commutes to nonneighborhood schools due to desegregation or choice policies.
2. For the evolving return to high school graduation and postsecondary education over this period, see Autor, Katz, and Kearney (2008).

Report in 1966 and defining an entire subfield of the literature studying what are known as education production functions. The central difficulty in this literature—which I will not surmount in this chapter—is identifying exogenous sources of variation in educational inputs. Depending on the choice and measurement of inputs (e.g., school spending, class size, teacher salary) and outcomes (levels or gaps, achievement or attainment, exceeding minimum proficiency levels or more finely detailed distributional measures), researchers debate the extent to which outcomes have improved, stagnated, or declined with increased inputs. Many conclude that money does not matter in the production of education (e.g., Hanushek 1997), though this assessment of the literature is far from universal (e.g., Krueger 1998).

One natural extension to this line of questioning is how what one *does* with the money (in the language of Goldin and Katz, productivity versus resources alone) matters. Here researchers have had more success in constructing methodologies to credibly identify causal impacts, though often in highly specific contexts not readily amenable to generalization. They also have more frequently estimated statistically significant positive relationships between specific inputs and student outcomes, perhaps most notably with Project STAR's experimental design randomly assigning Tennessee students to smaller and larger classes. A major recent emphasis in this literature is a focus on the impact of individual teachers characterized by their "quality" based on past value added to student achievement (e.g., Rockoff 2004). At least in part as a response to some of this research, major education policy initiatives at the state and federal levels currently focus much more on encouraging the use of particular "scientifically based" inputs or practices rather than on increasing—or maintaining, in the current budgetary climate—levels of overall resources.

This chapter focuses on one outcome, the high school graduation rate, so I emphasize at the outset that there are multiple ways an individual could change investments in human capital without changing one's status as a high school graduate or dropout: for example, dropouts or graduates can exert variable levels of effort and correspondingly acquire different skills and levels of proficiency, and graduates could attain more or less postsecondary schooling. High school graduation does in most cases serve as a gatekeeper to postsecondary education, however, so high school graduation trends can influence trends in postsecondary attainment as well (see Heckman and LaFontaine 2010).

Figure 2.1 replicates Goldin and Katz's figure 9.2, which shows high school graduation rates from 1890 to 2000. These rates grow throughout the period until peaking at 77 percent in 1969.[3] The period from 1910, when only 8 percent of students graduated from high school, through 1940, the

---

3. Goldin and Katz calculate these rates by dividing annual counts of graduates from education agencies by the age-appropriate (17-year-old) population at the state level.

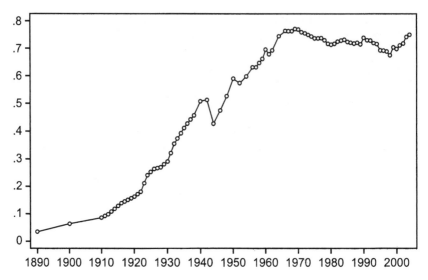

Fig. 2.1   US high school graduation rates, 1890–2004
Source: Goldin and Katz (2008, fig. 9.2).

first year in which the median student continued through graduation, is known as the "high school movement" during which public high schools were established in local school districts throughout the nation. In *The Race between Education and Technology*, Goldin and Katz analyze differences in geographic trends in these rates, establishing important roles both for factors that affected family demand for education (manufacturing job prospects related to the opportunity cost of education, and average income) and the likelihood that local school districts would reach consensus to provide a public high school education (income inequality, and the stability of a community, proxied for by the share of the population over age sixty-four). Graduation rates continued to increase through 1969 followed by what Goldin and Katz describe as subsequent "backsliding" and then plateau.

Figure 2.2 shows national and regional graduation rates from 1963 to 2007. I define these rates using data from educational agencies with counts of high school graduates as the numerator and counts of students enrolled in eighth grade five years earlier as the denominator. I exclude General Education Development (GED) recipients from the defined group of high school graduates.[4] On average, 76.5 percent of US eighth graders persisted to graduate from high school in 1963. This increased to 81.7 percent by 1969, but dipped below the 1963 level, to 76.1, by 1979. By 2007 the national rate

---

4. As Heckman and LaFontaine note, this may be impossible for some observations in which states include GED recipients in the administrative counts of high school graduates reported to NCES annually; they give New Jersey as one such example.

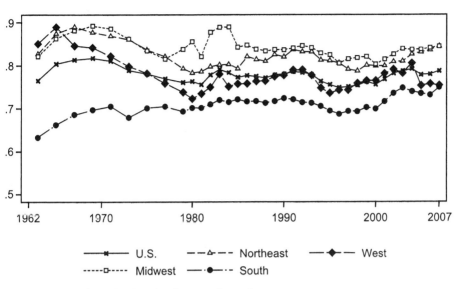

Fig. 2.2   High school graduation rates by region

Notes: Graduation rates are calculated as the count of graduates (excluding GEDs where possible) divided by eighth grade enrollment five years previously. Graduate and enrollment by grade data are from state educational agencies (as reported in *Statistics of State School Systems* and *Digest of Education*, various years).

was 78.7 percent, similar to the 1991 level and only 2.8 percent higher than in 1963.

The relevant question for studying how the supply of elementary and secondary education relates to graduation rates in the latter part of the twentieth century changes from that asked by Goldin and Katz of the high school movement—Why did some places establish high schools sooner than others?—to whether variation in intensive measures of the supply margin, such as school spending, days of schooling per year, and teacher characteristics helps explain variation in graduation rates. Might the same forces underlying the initial establishment of public high schools, most notably income inequality, continue to promote school quality decades later and thus correlate with higher graduation rates? While I am primarily interested in elementary and secondary school quality as a mechanism for these relationships, the descriptive nature of this investigation precludes any causal conclusions. Most importantly, I cannot determine the extent to which income inequality affects graduation via school quality (or other factors affecting human capital acquisition prior to or concurrent with formal schooling) or due to labor market expectations based on changing returns to skill shaping demand for schooling.

In section 2.2, this chapter summarizes what we know about trends in high school graduation and the forces behind them, from analyses of both aggregate and microlevel data. I then describe major changes in American elementary and secondary education over the past half century and how they might be expected to affect high school dropout in section 2.3. Section 2.4 presents a descriptive analysis of the relationships among education policies, demographics, and high school graduation rates at the state-year level. Section 2.5 concludes by discussing other potential explanations for observed graduation patterns and future policy directions for improving educational attainment.

2.2 Trends in High School Dropout and What (Little) We Know about Its Causes

2.2.1 Literature on Aggregate Trends in High School Graduation

Heckman and LaFontaine (2010) present a comprehensive review of the literature describing high school dropout. They note that much of the literature focuses on levels and gaps at a point in time, rather than on demonstrating historical trends, and emphasize the widely disparate levels reported across studies for ostensibly the same groups at the same points in time due to different approaches to measuring the graduation rate. These differences matter for first-order questions about the nature of trends in aggregate levels and gaps across groups, as well as in calculating estimates of returns to education and trends in inequality over time. One central difference across measures used by researchers is whether they are derived from measures of educational attainment in the adult population, backing out graduation cohorts from respondents' ages, or are based on counts of high school graduates produced by education agencies, relative to estimates of a cohort's size (measures used for reporting to state and federal governments fall into the latter category). Within each of these approaches, there are a number of variations based on data sources.[5] Depending on the time period of interest and desired level of geographic and demographic aggregation, researchers often do not have a choice among measures.

Heckman and LaFontaine show that these discrepancies across data sources—including census and Current Population Survey (CPS) data used to measure attainment in the adult population, administrative data on graduates and completers (the latter group includes recipients of the General Educational Development [GED] high school equivalency certificate) from educational agencies, and longitudinal research samples—can be resolved by ensuring that both the numerator and denominator of the high school

---

5. In particular, there is much discussion in the literature normalizing a school system's graduate counts by a cohort's enrollment in that system in previous years about *which grade* to use as a proxy for cohort size. Increased likelihood of retention in grade nine makes the choice of grade nine versus eight or ten, or an average, matter in some cases. This method is standard in the current literature. See Swanson (2004) for more.

graduation rate meet uniform criteria.[6] They report trends quite similar to those reported by Goldin and Katz and shown in figure 2.1 of this chapter, with graduation rates peaking around 1970.

To get a sense of just how much measurement choices can yield differences in first-order characterizations of these patterns, consider that Mishel and Roy's (2006) analysis of CPS data from 1962 to 2004 describes "remarkable progress in raising . . . high school completion rates." This qualitatively different assessment hinges on the use of completion (defined to include GED recipiency) as an outcome rather than high school graduation. Their estimated trends differ qualitatively from those in figure 2.1 throughout the time period and do not exhibit a peak around 1970. Murnane (2011) follows the general strategy of Heckman and LaFontaine while incorporating more recently released data from the American Community Surveys of 2002–2010; this exercise reveals an increase in graduation (not completion) rates from later, 2000 to 2010, while confirming the general aggregate trend identified by Heckman and LaFontaine (and, again, generally consistent with figure 2.1) prior to 2000. Overall, the analyses of *graduation* rates by Goldin and Katz, Heckman and LaFontaine, and Murnane identify very similar trends as each other and as I do later in this chapter.

Within the aggregate graduation trend, figure 2.2 reveals significant regional variation. The most immediately visible regional deviation from the national average is in the South, which started out behind in the 1960s with a 63 percent graduation rate compared to rates exceeding 80 percent in the three other census regions. This is unsurprising given the inferior educational opportunities available to blacks in the South, but, as Goldin and Katz and others note, also was due to poor outcomes for southern whites. Though the South did experience brief periods of decline subsequently, the general trend over the decades was much more positive than in the other regions, with the graduation rate reaching 75 percent by 2007. Trends for the Northeast and Midwest were relatively similar to one another, starting out high (at 83 and 82 percent, respectively, in 1963) and peaking soon after before prolonged decline. By 2007, graduation rates had not yet returned to their peaks, with rates of 85 percent in the Northeast and 84 percent in the Midwest. The West, which started out with the highest graduation rates of any region at 85 percent in 1963, experienced the greatest decline over the period, and is the sole region ending the period far below its initial level, with only 75 percent of students graduating in 2007. Differential demographic trends are one obvious potential explanation for such regional differences; consider, for example, increased immigration and enrollment of language

---

6. They focus on a sample that includes all students attending school in the United States and only those students—including those later incarcerated, and excluding immigrants who arrive in the United States after completing their schooling, for example—and use administrative data on GED test takers to exclude GED recipients from high school graduate counts derived from census data.

minority students in the West. How demographics affect graduation rates also could be changing over time differentially across regions; for example, the remarkable improvement in attainment in the South is likely related to the impact of desegregation. Regional differences could also be attributable to different trends in the level and distribution of school resources. The data analysis in section 2.4 begins to examine these questions.

2.2.2   Literature on Factors Influencing Graduation Rates

Little of the literature attempting to disentangle the determinants of high school graduation (often framed as understanding dropout, rather than graduation) tries to do so by understanding long-term historical trends. Goldin and Katz's analysis of the high school movement points to the importance of both supply and demand factors for early adoption of public secondary schooling and graduation rates (see their table 6.1). The mechanism for generating variance in high school graduation rates in these early decades is a first-order one: one is more likely to graduate from high school if one has access to a free public secondary school.

One related contemporary literature asks what forces shape gaps in graduation rates across demographic groups (but still at aggregate levels) over time. Although recent work points to the growing importance of socioeconomic gaps in educational outcomes (see Reardon 2011), racial gaps have received more attention in the accumulated literature to date. These attempts have generally concluded that trends in black graduation rates drive the observed trends in the gap, and that much of the timing of this stagnation and reversal is unexplained (see Neal 2006; Ferguson 2008), though some of it can be attributed to policy changes (see Vigdor and Ludwig [2008], on the role of school segregation levels). Recent work by Evans, Garthwaite, and Moore (2012) proposes the crack cocaine epidemic as an explanation for this timing. In this chapter, I focus on aggregate trends rather than trends within or gaps across groups to study a longer historical period, including earlier years in which administrative graduation data disaggregated by demographic groups are not available.

Another literature investigates determinants of graduation outcomes at the individual level. Such research is necessarily limited to years in which sufficiently rich microlevel data are available, and cannot provide annual estimates like the literature on gaps or aggregates. This cost comes alongside the considerable benefit of richer data. Recent work by Altonji and Mansfield (2011) analyzes two such databases, the National Education Longitudinal Study (NELS 1988), which tracks the spring 1988 eighth-grade cohort slated for "on-time" high school graduation in 1992, and the Education Longitudinal Survey (ELS 2002), which tracks the spring 2002 tenth-grade cohort who would graduate on time in 2004. They assess the correlations between students' home, school, and community characteristics and their likelihood of graduating from high school. They emphasize that they cannot estimate the causal impact of these factors, but rather are illuminating the extent to which school and community characteristics have explanatory power beyond aggregating individual characteristics. This distinction is crucial, particularly in the context of highly publicized research describing so-called "dropout factories"—the public high schools with disproportionately high concentrations of poverty, concentrated in northeastern cities and in the South—that Balfanz and Legters (2004) show disproportionately "produce" the nation's high school dropouts. If the school-level socioeconomic characteristics of these high schools exert a significant and negative independent force on graduation rates *after* controlling for the independent role of those same variables at the student level, policies to reduce the concentration of poverty in schools—for example, school desegregation by poverty, income, or other sufficiently highly correlated student characteristics—could improve graduation rates absent any reduction in child poverty rates. Alternately, if school-level demographics appear to operate primarily through the aggregation of individual-level characteristics, one would look primarily to public policies aimed at poverty itself to improve educational attainment.

Altonji and Mansfield find a statistically and economically significant relationship between school and community characteristics[7] and the likelihood that any given student will graduate from high school.[8] They also examine the across-school variance in the composite quality measure for both these cohorts and the high school senior class of 1972, revealing significant increases in between-school variance from 1972 to 1993, and a slight increase from 1993 to 2005. This is consistent with the documented trend of increased residential segregation by income over that time period (Watson 2009), given the dominance of residentially determined school attendance and the authors' use of peer socioeconomic characteristics as an input into their composite school quality measure. Altonji and Mansfield emphasize, however, that for both the NELS and ELS cohorts the relationship between *school and community* characteristics and individual dropout behavior is much weaker than the relationship between *individual* students' characteristics and dropout outcomes. Among individual students' characteristics affecting within-school probabilities of graduation, the typical observable characteristics—family structure and various components of socioeconomic status—matter, and unobservable characteristics explain even

7. These characteristics include both student characteristics aggregated up to the school level, and school characteristics such as teacher turnover and student-teacher ratios. They combine these characteristics into a single dimension of school quality, as determined by what predicts student outcomes, by which they rank schools.

8. Specifically, they estimate that moving a given student from a high school at the 10th percentile of the school quality composite index to the 90th percentile is associated with being 7 percentage points more likely to graduate from high school in the NELS: 88 cohort, for whom the average dropout rate was 9 percent, and 9 percentage points more likely in the ELS: 2002 cohort, for whom the average dropout rate was 10 percent.

more of the variance. Their results therefore suggest that increased income inequality over time would be negatively correlated with graduation rates, but is not the primary mechanism behind the individual outcomes for those students at the bottom of the income distribution.

2.3   A Brief History of Recent Changes in US Education Policy and Teacher Labor Markets

Systems of public elementary and secondary education finance and governance in the United States today differ markedly from those in place in the decades when graduation rates were climbing. Some of the most prominent policy changes—for example, court-ordered desegregation, state-level school finance equalization reforms, and the federal requirement of a free and appropriate education for students with special needs—were designed with the intent of improving educational outcomes for specific groups; these students were also those historically less likely to graduate from high school. To affect graduation rates, these policies would need to reach those targeted students and to engender effective changes in educational practice, neither of which are straightforward goals. Whatever funds "stick" to district budgets must be allocated across schools within districts (this is relevant even for districts with one high school, given the correlation between academic achievement prior to high school and persistence to graduation), and within schools, allocated to particular instructional settings and therefore not benefiting all students in the school uniformly. We know relatively little about both these processes and how they may have changed over this time period.

Alongside federal, state, and local changes in elementary and secondary education policy over these years came significant changes in the teacher labor market and in the demographic composition of students. As attractive labor market options beyond teaching have expanded for college-educated women, they have disproportionately drawn women from the upper part of the distributions of various measures of cognitive skill from the pool of potential teachers. Changes in family structure have led to increasing numbers of students coming from single-parent homes, which is positively correlated with high school dropout (McLanahan and Sandefur 1994). The time-series data alone, showing stagnating graduation rates alongside major education policy initiatives, thus do not necessarily imply that we are not better off with particular reforms than we would have been without them.

In the following subsections, I detail key changes in federal, state, and local revenues and programs. Many of these changes are captured by figure 2.3, which shows the evolution of revenue and spending per pupil. For most of the United States' history, and in most states, the vast majority of school spending was funded through locally generated revenue streams.[9] This reli-

---

9. Local revenue refers to that generated at the school district level. In the minority of states in which school districts are "dependent" on parent governments such as counties, cities, or

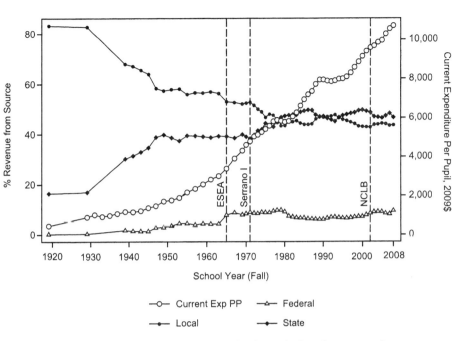

Fig. 2.3   Trends in spending per pupil and the share of education revenue from local, state, and federal sources, 1919–2008

Notes: Spending and revenue data from NCES *Digest of Education*, various years.

ance on local revenue was accompanied by a great deal of local control. Though states assume constitutional responsibility for education and have no obligation to allow local control, they historically have devolved much of education governance to local districts, while retaining control over decisions such as ages of mandatory attendance, minimum required days per school year, and requirements for teacher credentialing at the state level (Briffault 2005). Over the same time period that graduation rates declined and stagnated, centralization increased in school finance, with increased roles for the federal and state governments.

Figure 2.3 and table 2.1 also reveal the marked increase in school spending over the past half century. The national average for current spending (excluding capital investments), discussed throughout in per pupil terms in 2009 dollars, rose from under $500 to over $11,000 from 1963 to 2007. This has not gone unnoticed: education policy discussions nearly always frame trends in achievement and attainment in the context of this dramatic increase. The rest of this section discusses major changes in federal, state, and local policy, as well as changes in teacher labor markets.

---

other local governments, the taxes are levied and revenue collected by the parent government rather than by the school district itself; for both independent and dependent districts, "local" revenue is raised from the geographic area contiguous with the school district.

Table 2.1   Descriptive statistics

	1963		2007	
	mean	s.d.	mean	s.d.
A. Weighted by school-aged population				
High school graduation rate	0.767	0.115	0.789	0.070
Current spending per pupil (thousands of 2011$)	3.416	0.855	12.009	3.044
90/50 family income ratio	1.979	0.168	2.551	0.234
50/10 family income ratio	2.989	0.83	4.074	0.454
Median family income	45,881	8,314	59,957	9,063
Percent school-aged children nonwhite	13.69	11.32	30.08	10.52
Percent school-aged children in poverty	22.81	11.72	16.88	3.57
B. Unweighted				
High school graduation rate	0.740	0.107	0.789	0.082
Current spending per pupil (thousands of 2011$)	3.208	0.704	11.938	2.800
90/50 family income ratio	1.989	0.184	2.476	0.481
50/10 family income ratio	3.067	0.879	4.000	0.791
Median family income	44,586	8,454	59,988	10,603
Percent school-aged children nonwhite	14.57	16.8	27.26	15.66
Percent school-aged children in poverty	24.47	11.76	16.11	4.55

Sources: Income, poverty, and race data are from decennial censuses (Ruggles et al. 2010), linearly interpolated between years. School finance equalizations (SFEs) are from Corcoran and Evans (2008). Graduation rates are calculated as the count of graduates (excluding GEDs where possible) divided by eighth-grade enrollment five years previously. Spending, graduate, and enrollment by grade data are from state educational agencies (as reported in *Statistics of State School Systems* and *Digest of Education*, various years).

2.3.1   Changes in Federal Education Policy

The federal role in elementary and secondary school finance initially emerged in a significant way with the Elementary and Secondary Education Act (ESEA) of 1965. The ESEA and its largest program, Title I, changed the nature of federal education policy in three key ways. First, it was a sizeable amount of revenue for some districts. The federal government provided funds to districts (always via their state education agencies) earlier through a few categorical programs, with Aid to Federally Impacted Areas and the National Defense Education Act as the largest funding streams, but these other sources together totaled only about 3 percent of what the average district spent. Southern districts, with their high poverty rates, benefited disproportionately from Title I, with program revenues equal to about 15 percent of preexisting spending levels in southern districts. While Title I significantly increased federal spending, however, it is important to remember that all federal revenue still constitutes just under 10 percent of total school district revenues in the United States today.

Second, the Title I program aims to provide compensatory education and is explicitly designed to be redistributive, with funding based primarily on child poverty counts in a district. Title I as a share of spending has therefore always varied by district. In figure 2.3, we see the average change, with federal revenue overall accounting for 7.9 percent of spending in 1965 compared to 4.4 percent just the year before. The extent to which Title I redistributed resources to less advantaged *students* remains an open question. It would first need to resist crowd-out of state and local revenues to supplement spending at the district level. Cascio, Gordon, and Reber (2013) show that nearly half of Title I revenues did ultimately supplement local spending on average in the late 1960s, and significantly more so in districts experiencing larger shocks from Title I grants relative to their existing budgets. Gordon (2004) shows that this was unlikely by the mid-1990s. Conditional on "sticking" to school spending at the district level, Title I funds might not make their way to the most disadvantaged students within districts—who are disproportionately those on the margin of choosing to drop out of high school. Cascio, Gordon, and Reber examine the South of the 1960s and find that Title I–induced net increases in district-level spending were associated with improvements in high school graduation rates for whites but not blacks. Extensive qualitative data publicized by advocates from the NAACP Legal Defense Fund also suggests that local officials often found ways to use federal funds in unintended ways (Martin and McClure 1969).

The regulatory framework meant to ensure that funds make their way to the most disadvantaged students has grown more logistically complex and legally binding over time, but recent work (Roza 2010; Heuer and Stullich 2011) suggests that the (generally opaque to the researcher) ways in which districts allocate resources across their schools have tended to offset the redistributive intent of the Title I program. This clearly violates the spirit of the law and its regulations. Further, the accounting systems of state and local education agencies make it difficult to capture resources in dollar units (as opposed to full-time equivalent staff, or FTEs) at the school level. Federal regulators thus allow districts to comply with Title I by smoothing FTEs rather than dollars across schools before layering on Title I funds, in what is known as the "comparability loophole."

Third, and perhaps most significantly, offering such sizeable grants allowed the federal government to require that school districts meet conditions of their choosing in order to receive the funds, providing a mechanism for the federal government to intervene in a policy sector in which it otherwise has no constitutional right to do so. This conditionality of funding was most relevant at the inception of Title I not in the context of ensuring that funds benefited disadvantaged students within a district (to which the federal government devoted little effort at the time), but rather in enforcing the desegregation requirements legislated in the Civil Rights Act of 1964, which withheld federal funds to discriminatory public agencies across policy functions (see Cascio et al. 2010). Most recently, the 2001 reauthorization of ESEA as the No Child Left Behind Act withholds Title I funds from states that fail to establish accountability systems meeting its requirements. This prompted resistance from states and districts that have come to rely on Title I funds, litigation, and ultimately a ruling from the US Court of Appeals for the Sixth Circuit that NCLB provides conditional aid rather than an unfunded mandate and is therefore legal (*Pontiac v. Secretary of Education* 2009).[10] Research suggests that the net impact of NCLB on achievement is neutral to positive, depending on the outcomes measured (Dee and Jacob 2011). Overall, the use of conditions with federal funds has magnified their influence beyond that implied solely by the relatively small share of total revenue they constitute.

While some of the increase in federal funding over time has come through increases in allocations to the Title I budget, new federal programs have also contributed to the rise. Perhaps more notable than the funds provided by these programs is their categorical nature and the extent to which they have attempted to force local districts to channel resources to groups of (variably defined) disadvantaged students. The introduction of federal categoricals was followed by increasing numbers of states adopting more categorical funding streams. If this relationship is casual, the impact of federal funds extends far beyond dollars appearing as federal revenue in district financial reporting. These categorical programs are notable for the various groups they aim to serve and to whom they provide legal recourse; the amount of funding provided through them, however, is generally small compared to all federal education revenue, which is in turn small compared to total education revenue.

The introduction of new programs, with the exception of ESEA, thus generally does not register as remarkable in the time series of federal revenue or current spending displayed in figure 2.3. For ease of reference, the figure does not note all programs; close examination reveals noticeably *absent* upticks for new programs for the Individuals with Disabilities Education Act of 1970, in 1972 for Title IX promoting gender equity, and in 1968 for the Bilingual Education Act (see Gordon [2008] for more detailed discussion of these and other federal education programs). Some of the most significant federal interventions in elementary and secondary schooling in these decades comes through the federal judicial actions to desegregate schools (see Cascio et al. [2008] for further discussion); these mandates do not appear as revenue either, though desegregation has been associated with increased likelihood of graduation for blacks (Guryan 2004; Reber 2010).

Also not shown in the historical time series of figure 2.3 is the most recent increase in federal education funds, much of which was due to the American Recovery and Reinvestment Act (ARRA). Rather than solely expanding funding for existing programs, such as the traditional form of ESEA Title I,

10. *School Dist., Pontiac v. Secretary, US Dept. Educ.*, 584F. 3d 253 (6th Cir. 2009).

the ARRA funds were targeted to several new initiatives that differ qualitatively in their approach to the federal role in education. Two of the ones that are most significant, in both the magnitude of funds allocated and in their departure from the traditional structure of federal aid, are the School Improvement Grants and Race to the Top programs.

School Improvement Grants (SIGs) are similar to the federal Comprehensive School Reform (CSR) grants program of the 1990s, but on a much larger scale. Both SIGs and CSR often channel funds through school districts to private contractors for tasks—related to school management, curriculum, and instruction—typically carried out by public school and district employees. While for many years discussions of privatization in schooling centered around the theoretically interesting potential for vouchers, the advent of SIGs point to an increased role for private vendors operating within what are still public schools. Burch (2006) describes how private suppliers increased following accountability reforms prior to SIGs; Forbes and Gordon (2012) show how competitive markets for private suppliers of intermediate goods in education markets may not lead to improvements in school quality.

The Race to the Top (RttT) program innovates by bringing a tournament model to federal education funds, while retaining the traditional flow of revenues from the federal government to state education agencies (or, in the most recent round, directly to local education agencies). While ESEA at its inception in 1965 offered the carrot of Title I funds to all agencies meeting its conditions (most bindingly, its desegregation requirements), RttT is explicitly a competition, laying out a menu of how agencies can accumulate points for their proposals in exchange for implementing policies in advance or including specific practices in their grant proposals. This appears quite cost-effective. The prospect of "winning" the race—as much as $700 million for large states like Florida and New York—prompted many states to change politically entrenched policies, though fewer than half the states have successfully won any of the three (to date) rounds of the race and ultimately received a grant.

Overall, the federal level has emerged as a policy force since the 1960s, more than doubling its share of education revenue and shaping local policies via civil rights protections and conditions of aid. Despite this increase, the magnitude of federal funds has remained low enough that they do not explain the massive growth in school spending witnessed over the full span of this period. For this, we turn next to state policies.

2.3.2 Changes in State Education Policy

Figure 2.3 also shows a climb in the share of total revenue coming from the states beginning around 1970. In many cases, these increases were prompted as part of school finance reforms that increased the progressivity of state formula aid (not visible within this figure), and were often in response to state-level judicial mandates. These court rulings have overturned the constitutionality of school finance systems in the majority of states to date, often multiple times within a state; see Corcoran and Evans (2008) for more details and a listing of cases. The first such ruling, with some of the most dramatic consequences, came in 1971's *Serrano v. Priest* decision by the California Supreme Court. This is marked on figure 2.3 as "Serrano I" to distinguish it from subsequent rulings in 1976 and 1977, known as Serrano II and III respectively, which sparked more dramatic reforms.

While the reforms to school finance following such rulings have differed substantively across states and over time (Hoxby 2001), Murray, Evans, and Schwab (1998) show that on average, these rulings have been associated with increased spending per pupil and increased progressivity of spending within states.[11] Card and Payne show that court-ordered school finance equalization (SFE) reforms increased the progressivity of spending within states and narrowed the gap in SAT scores by family income in affected states. SFEs could increase the observed progressivity of spending (where the district is the smallest unit observed) without necessarily affecting graduation rates if funds are disproportionately directed to higher-achieving students, such as future SAT takers, rather than students on the margin of dropping out.

States have exerted their influence over local districts historically through compulsory attendance laws (albeit with generally weak enforcement) and teacher credentialing requirements. More recently, states adopted curricular standards and subsequently imposed accountability systems with assessments at least nominally aligned to their standards, in many cases before they were required to do so by No Child Left Behind (which was modeled on existing state programs) if they wanted to continue to collect Title I funds. As new dimensions emerge in education policy, state regulations do so as well. For example, states are increasingly involved in homeschooling and online learning.

2.3.3   Local Policies and Practices

Traditionally, the local school district was the dominant political jurisdiction in determining total revenue and policy choices. The most readily identifiable changes in education policy in recent decades have been major state and federal initiatives, in part because of their inherent scale. This is not to say that school districts have not innovated; some large school districts have done so in highly visible ways, such as using value-added components in teacher assessments and compensation in Denver and Washington, DC. But local districts ultimately implement instructional programs and the effects of "big" federal and state programs depend critically on how school districts

---

11. California is a notable exception. See Fischel (1989) on the relationship between its school finance reform and the subsequent passage of Proposition 13, limiting growth in property tax revenues.

crowd out intergovernmental grants and use any net additional funds or work toward newly defined goals.

The extent to which school districts have crowded out state and federal intergovernmental grants by reducing local revenues appears to vary considerably, as discussed in the federal and state policy sections above. And while researchers have long acknowledged the importance of local implementation (McLaughlin 1976), we continue to know remarkably little about how most districts allocate resources across schools and how schools allocate resources across students (Roza 2010).

A series of studies by Marguerite Roza and colleagues (see Roza [2010] for a summary) is particularly illuminating of crowd out *within* school district budgets, when grants from state or federal governments nominally are allocated to typically disadvantaged schools meeting the relevant qualifications for different categorical programs, but unrestricted funds (e.g., from local revenue) are disproportionately allocated to schools receiving less aid from higher levels of government via categorical programs.

While it would be fascinating to look at the distribution of within-district allocations for a large sample of school districts and over time, this type of large sample school-level analysis is impossible based on existing data sources. Guin et al. (2007) use administrative data from the Texas Education Agency from 1994 to 2003—unusual in detailing district-level allocations to schools in dollars rather than full-time equivalent staff—and find that the variance in spending per pupil found *within* districts exceeds that measured *across* districts in Texas. School finance reform in Texas led to a system with a high degree of redistribution across districts, so other states likely have greater cross-district variance. There is no reason to expect, however, that extensive within-district variance in resources at the school level is specific to Texas or to this time period.[12]

Figure 2.4, reproduced from their study, shows how dollars from different funding streams are allocated across one anonymous Texas district. It shows how schools with low poverty rates get more state and local revenue than poor schools, which get a disproportionate share of their resources via federal funds. This violates the intention of Title I—to supplement resources for poor students, already equalized at the district level. Because of the comparability loophole discussed previously, however, it is technically legal. It is also quite difficult for districts to avoid given standard human resource policies. Districts typically open up new teaching positions first to teachers already working within the district. Teachers new to the district often enter through low SES schools, then transfer to higher SES schools as positions

---

12. The information systems are simply not in place, even administratively, to conduct such analyses for earlier time periods and in many other states. In the majority of cases, such analysis would require access to multiple administrative data systems at the district rather than state level (e.g., one database to determine individual teachers' salaries and another for their school placements).

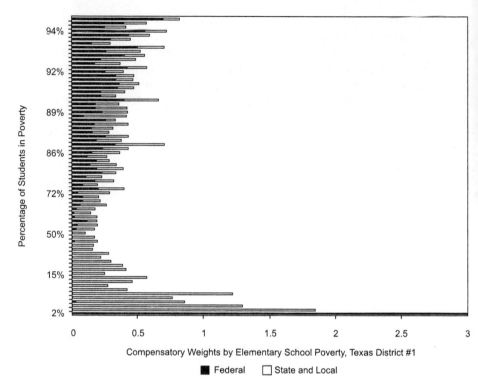

Fig. 2.4   **Allocation of revenue, by source, across schools within anonymous Texas district**

Source: CRPE School Finance Redesign Project. Roza, Guin, and Davis (2008). Data are from 2003/4 school year.

open. This leaves high poverty schools with a disproportionately inexperienced—and therefore cheap—workforce. Were districts to equalize spending in dollars, rather than FTEs, across schools, class sizes in low-poverty schools would so far exceed those in high poverty schools as to be politically infeasible.

I can only speculate on trends in within-district inequality of resources over time given the scarcity of data at the school level. If anything, policy changes in recent decades may have helped lower-performing schools, as the stakes and transparency of accountability systems might have pushed districts toward targeting low-achieving students and the schools in which they are disproportionately clustered.

2.3.4   Changes in the Labor Market for Teachers

The most recent direction for researchers studying education production functions is trying to identify teacher quality as an output-based measure. The main conclusion of the literature to date is that there is high variance in teacher quality, most of which is unexplained by observable characteristics, and therefore unfortunately does not yield clear policy implications for teacher selection or training. This literature prompts the question whether any stagnation in educational outcomes, such as graduation rates, might be attributed in part to stagnation or decline in teacher quality. A related literature examines the role of women's labor market conditions and the labor supply of teachers, and concludes that expansions of labor market opportunities for college-educated women in recent decades have resulted in a teaching workforce that looks considerably less competitive than it used to (see Bacolod 2007; Corcoran, Evans, and Schwab 2004; and Hoxby and Leigh 2004).

2.4   Income Inequality and High School Graduation

Duncan and Murnane (2011) set out a comprehensive model for how income inequality can affect educational outcomes, including its impact on home, community, and school environments. This model suggests that inequality could affect educational outcomes, including graduation rates, even conditional on the educational setting experienced by students, by, for example, depressing student expectations. Overall, the economics literature has contributed mainly to the mechanism in this larger model by which demographic heterogeneity, including income inequality, affects demand for public spending. Determining the existence and potential direction of this effect is not straightforward, theoretically or empirically.

The main theoretical ambiguity comes from two models with opposite predictions. Empirical work by Goldin and Katz (2008), Poterba (1997), Alesina, Baqir, and Easterly (1999), and Luttmer (2001), among others, supports a model in which fractionalization reduces support for public spending because voters do not wish to subsidize those outside of their own group. Alternatively, the median voter theorem, in the context of a uniform tax rate, predicts that as mean income rises relative to median income and lowers the tax price (or tax share) of public spending for the median voter, demand for public spending should rise. Two recent papers investigating the relationship between changes in income inequality at the local level and school spending in the United States in recent decades both find support for the latter theory dominating empirically (Corcoran and Evans 2010, henceforth CE; Boustan et al. 2013, henceforth BFWZ).[13]

It is likely that the relative importance of the two opposing theoretical forces varies with the historical policy context. Goldin and Katz (2008) find that high schools were established earlier—and graduation rates rose

13. Goldin and Katz face many more data constraints in studying the earlier part of the century, which they creatively work around. For example, in 1928, they use automobile registrations per capita as a way of inferring, conditional on mean income, the variance of income in a state.

earlier—in states with less inequality early in the twentieth century, while CE and BFWZ show greater income inequality within localities is associated with more demand for public spending in the latter part of the century.[14] This discrepancy could be due to measurement and aggregation issues. Those issues aside, it could also be resolved if salient major infrastructure investments—like establishing a public high school—require reaching a higher threshold of political consensus than do incremental increases in revenue used to fund continuous changes in the level of school spending.[15] CE examine the relationship between inequality and private school enrollment, which they note could reflect a perception of low quality public schools but also a desire to segregate. BFWZ's analysis is solely of fiscal variables.

I next examine correlations between state-level inequality and high school graduation rates from 1963 to 2007. These could operate through the spending increases CE and BFWZ attribute to inequality, or through other channels. For example, the positive established relationship between income inequality and income segregation combined with the residentially based school attendance policies of most districts could make increases in inequality translate into an increase in school segregation by income, which might independently affect graduation rates conditional on spending levels.

There are advantages and disadvantages to conducting this type of exercise at both the state and local levels. In this case, because I want a panel covering the universe of students in the United States as far back as possible, and construct my preferred graduation rate from the ratio of current graduates to eighth grade enrollment five years earlier, data requirements dictate that I conduct the analysis at the state level. In addition to being more readily available, state estimates of the graduation rate defined in this way will suffer only from measurement error due to mobility across states and the public or private sector, rather than also across districts.

Analysis at the state level yields more interpretable results when the median voter in the state, rather than the school district, drives the level of school spending; the trade-off is that analyzing local jurisdictions yields more interpretable results in states with more Tiebout-style finance systems (as in the earlier decades analyzed by Goldin and Katz). All states provide some funding to local districts, however, and local revenue toward school spending is determined in the context of state school finance systems that penalize or reward local contributions, to varying degrees.

The state level of analysis also has significant drawbacks: it obviously provides far fewer observations and masks the considerable within-state heterogeneity in both key independent and dependent variables. As CE and

14. The meaning of a purely income-based measure of inequality is changing over time, as well, given changes in taxes and transfer programs (Meyer and Sullivan 2012).

15. Establishing high schools in the early part of the century might be viewed as expanding access in a more meaningful way than increasing spending on schooling generally later in the century, and could correspondingly generate differences in political support.

BFWZ point out, there is more variation in inequality over time during these years within school districts than within states.[16] And while the presence or absence of a court-ordered school finance equalization is appropriately measured at the state level and may well affect mean educational inputs in a state, its impact within any given district is likely to vary from the state average depending on the extent to which the reform redistributes funds to that specific district—generally, a function of the property wealth per pupil in the district relative to the state average. Reforms that do not change state means could still change inputs in those districts with students disproportionately on the margin of high school.

I use data at the state-year level to describe correlations between high school graduation rates and income inequality, controlling for basic demographics (median income and percent nonwhite). I then apply the same framework to examine relationships between inequality and education spending per pupil. For both sets of analyses, I allow court-ordered school finance reforms to mediate the impact of inequality. The analysis is of state-level aggregates of current spending, so it reflects combined revenue decisions at federal, state, and local levels.

The major caveats to this empirical exercise also apply to decades of research on education policy: first, inputs are endogenous to the preferences of voters in the state and its districts (CE and BFWZ take considerable care with this issue); second, there is variation in inputs at the student level within states, districts, and schools, so the average level of school spending does not necessarily apply to the student on the margin of dropping out; and third, both the inputs and outputs analyzed are chosen for the ease with which they are quantified and systematically recorded over time and place, and may not map cleanly to the relevant concepts—the quality of education experienced (input) and human capital acquired (output)—even setting aggregation issues aside. To some extent, I can circumvent the first issue by considering the effects of court-ordered school finance equalizations, though the impact of such measures are mediated by political decisions regarding aggregate levels of resources for elementary and secondary education.

I define the graduation rate at the state (s) and year (t) level as the count of new graduates (excluding GED recipients) divided by the number of students enrolled in eighth grade five years earlier, as described by equation (1).

$$(1) \qquad graduation\ rate_{s,t} = \frac{graduates_{s,t}}{eighth\ grade\ enrollment_{s,t-5}}.$$

I begin with the general approach of Goldin and Katz's analysis (see their table 6.1, 2008) to correlate graduation rates, year by year, with baseline (in

16. Following Roza (2010), moreover, there is considerable variation in resources allocated to students even within the same schools, so the disaggregation problem is exceedingly difficult to solve given current data reporting systems, regardless of researcher access to data.

this case, 1963) state characteristics. Because each regression is estimated using only 48 state-level observations, I limit these characteristics to the inequality measures of interest—the 90/50 and 50/10 family income ratios, represented by $INEQ$ in equation (2) below—and control additionally only for median family income and percent nonwhite, in X below. I use decennial census data for income and race variables, which I impute for 1963, and use ACS data for 2007. I calculate these variables for families with school-aged children, as their characteristics will directly affect graduation rates. I also include regional fixed effects. Equation (2) below describes the specification.

(2) $$y_{s,t} = \alpha_t + INEQ_s \gamma_t + X_s \delta_t + REGION_s \eta_t + \varepsilon_{s,t}.$$

Because school quality can affect not only graduation, but also population characteristics, using fixed demographics from the baseline period helps mitigate endogeneity. The drawback is that I estimate each year's regression on only forty-eight observations, and miss the variation in inequality coming from the trends in decades to follow.

Table 2.1 provides summary statistics of the measures used, in both 1963 and 2007. Table 2.2 describes the results of the ordinary least squares specification above. In panel A, the dependent variable y is the graduation rate, and in panel B, it is current spending per pupil. All regressions control for median family income and percent nonwhite in 1963; the estimated coefficients are not shown but are often statistically significant and in the expected directions. Regional dummy variables are also not shown. Consistent with figure 2.2, the South experienced secular gains in graduation rates while the West lost. In later decades, all regions had significantly lower levels of school spending than the Northeast, even after controlling for race and income.

Both specifications, predicting graduation and spending, yield generally noisy estimates. Panel A of table 2.2 shows that the (1963) 50/10 ratio was negatively correlated with graduation rates in 1963 to a marginally statistically significant degree, but not in subsequent years; panel B shows no statistically significant relationship between inequality at the bottom and school spending.

The considerable literature demonstrating a strong correlation between family background and graduation suggests that the 90/50 ratio is less likely to reflect the individual circumstances of students on the margin of dropping out than is the 50/10 ratio. The 90/50 ratio could still affect graduation via changes to the tax price for education faced by the median voter, as emphasized by BFWZ and CE, and via changes in school peer group composition. The estimates of the 90/50 ratio on school spending, in panel B, quickly become quite imprecise, with confidence intervals including implausibly large positive and negative effects. The estimated relationship between the initial 90/50 ratio and graduation in panel A is generally positive and statistically significant in 1990 and 2000. Given the variability of the estimates over time, I do not emphasize this result, though it is possible that the growth of

Table 2.2   **Relationship between statewide income inequality in 1963 and subsequent education indicators**

	Levels						Change 1963 to 2007
	1963 (1)	1971 (2)	1980 (3)	1990 (4)	2000 (5)	2007 (6)	(7)
A. Dependent variable: High school graduation rate							
50/10 ratio in 1963	−0.0410*	−0.0361	0.00139	−0.00869	−0.0197	−0.0328	0.0205
	(0.0221)	(0.0228)	(0.0212)	(0.0142)	(0.0202)	(0.0199)	(0.0208)
90/50 ratio in 1963	0.108	0.0425	−0.0366	0.123**	0.140**	0.0197	0.077
	(0.0782)	(0.0863)	(0.0945)	(0.0545)	(0.0683)	(0.0790)	(0.0719)
R-squared	0.711	0.754	0.601	0.688	0.6	0.601	0.553
B. Dependent variable: Current elementary and secondary spending per pupil (in 1,000s of 2011$)							
50/10 ratio in 1963	0.1730	0.0316	0.137	0.186	0.238	0.531	0.0749
	(0.1520)	(0.3010)	(0.3360)	(0.4590)	(0.4560)	(0.5130)	(0.4960)
90/50 ratio in 1963	1.206*	1.131	1.906	2.027	0.14	3.086	−0.773
	(0.6510)	(1.2800)	(1.5590)	(1.8530)	(2.2380)	(2.8930)	(1.8200)
R-squared	0.756	0.624	0.565	0.766	0.726	0.695	0.68

Sources: All regressions include dummy variables for Midwest, South, and West regions and control for initial (1963) median family income and percent nonwhite. Each regression is estimated with forty-eight observations (the lower forty-eight states). Income and race data are from decennial censuses (Ruggles et al. 2010), linearly interpolated between years. Graduation rates are calculated as the count of graduates (in most states excluding GED recipients) divided by eighth-grade enrollment five years previously. Spending, graduate, and enrollment by grade data are from state educational agencies (as reported in *Statistics of State School Systems* and *Digest of Education*, various years).
***Significant at the 1 percent level.
**Significant at the 5 percent level.
*Significant at the 10 percent level.

accountability programs at the state level in these decades helped students at the bottom of the achievement distribution.

I also estimate a version of equation (2) predicting changes in outcomes over the entire 1960 to 2007 period, again with the baseline characteristics as predictors. Column (7) presents those results, which are again extremely imprecise. To interpret the magnitude of the statistically insignificant point estimate, holding median income and percent nonwhite constant, a state in which the 90/50 ratio increased from 1963 to 2007 by the national average (0.49) would experience a 3.7 percentage point increase in graduation rates over the time period, exceeding the mean observed actual increase in graduation over those years. In results not shown, these estimates are essentially unchanged when including an independent variable for whether a school finance reform has been judicially mandated in a state by that year. (That variable itself is positive and statistically significant for 1990.)

I next estimate a variant of this specification, described in equation (3), pooling annual data from 1963 to 2007 (the graduation and school spending data are annual; the inequality data are imputed from the decennial census data). This specification includes fixed effects for states and years. It differs significantly from the Goldin and Katz approach by including *concurrent* rather than baseline demographic independent variables: again, median family income and percent nonwhite, with the 50/10 and 90/50 family income ratios as the inequality variables of interest. These concurrent variables allow investigation of the full scope of changes in income inequality in the latter part of the century, and also better exploit the precise timing of school finance equalizations. Because school spending and high school graduation rates can affect income inequality within a state, I emphasize the descriptive nature of these correlations.[17]

$$(3) \qquad y_{s,t} = \alpha_t + INEQ_{S,T}\gamma + X_{s,t}\delta + \theta_s + \eta_t + \varepsilon_{s,t}.$$

Unlike baseline income inequality, current income inequality is robustly correlated with both graduation and spending (as in the 1963 estimation in table 2.2). Column (1) of table 2.3 controls only for median family income and percent nonwhite and reports the estimated coefficients on the 50/10 and 90/50 ratios. Applying these coefficients to the national average changes in inequality from 1963 to 2007 suggests that, all else equal, the average increase in inequality at the top correlates with a 5.5 percentage point increase in high school graduation rates (greater than the observed increase), and to a $1,200 per pupil increase in spending (about 10 percent of the actual increase). This positive correlation with spending is consistent with the lower tax price for education spending faced by the median voter. The average increase in inequality at the bottom correlates with a 1.8 percentage point reduction in high school graduation and a $1,070 per pupil increase in spending. There are several potential mechanisms consistent with these correlations: poor children are more costly to educate (for example, because of their disproportionate representation in special education programs); spending rises with poverty because of federal Title I funds (see Cascio and Reber 2012); or school finance reforms or state categorical programs require more funding for poorer districts. I examine the relationship with poverty in column (3).

I next turn to analysis of court-ordered SFEs. They are correlated with a 1.4 percentage point increase in the high school graduation rate, without significantly changing the correlations between inequality and graduation. The estimated positive correlations between SFEs and graduation nearly offset the negative ones between inequality at the bottom, again applying the national average increase, and graduation. They are also correlated with about a $330 increase in school spending per pupil. Including SFE as

---

17. My method is analogous to the OLS method of BFWZ. They address the endogeneity issues inherent in this approach by also applying national trends in income growth to initial local income distributions, creating instruments for subsequent local inequality levels.

Table 2.3   **Relationship between current statewide income inequality and education indicators**

	(1)	(2)	(3)
A. Dependent variable: High school graduation rate			
50/10 ratio	–0.0167***	–0.0173***	0.0058
	(0.0039)	(0.0039)	(0.0040)
90/50 ratio	0.0973***	0.0970***	0.0751***
	(0.0193)	(0.0191)	(0.0181)
SFE		0.0142***	0.0184***
		(0.0035)	(0.0033)
% poor			–0.0058***
			(0.0005)
nonwhite			–0.0019
medfaminc			0.0000
R-squared	0.822	0.824	0.835
B. Dependent variable: Current elementary and secondary spending per pupil (in 1,000s of 2009$)			
50/10 ratio	0.9449***	0.9027***	0.6227***
	(0.0790)	(0.0787)	(0.1197)
90/50 ratio	2.4833***	2.0885***	2.0329***
	(0.3647)	(0.3487)	(0.3516)
SFE		0.4652***	0.4558***
		(0.0775)	(0.0770)
% poor			0.0558***
			(0.0150)
nonwhite			(0.0347)
medfaminc			0.0002***
R-squared	0.950	0.950	0.952

Sources: All regressions include state and year dummy variables. Income, poverty, and race data are from decennial censuses (Ruggles et al. 2010), linearly interpolated between years. School finance equalizations (SFEs) are from Corcoran and Evans (2008). Graduation rates are calculated as the count of graduates (excluding GEDs where possible) divided by eighth-grade enrollment five years previously. Spending, graduate, and enrollment by grade data are from state educational agencies (as reported in *Statistics of State School Systems* and *Digest of Education*, various years).
***Significant at the 1 percent level.
**Significant at the 5 percent level.
*Significant at the 10 percent level.

an independent variable changes the correlations between inequality and graduation little; the correlations between spending and inequality at the top and bottom remain significant and positive, but are reduced somewhat by including SFEs as an independent variable.[18]

In column (3), I include the poverty rate. Though inequality at the bottom has increased over this period (primarily in the earlier decades) child

18. In analyses not shown, specifications including the interactions between SFEs and inequality yield highly imprecise estimates.

poverty has on net fallen. As anticipated, poverty is significantly negatively correlated with graduation rates; when it is included, the negative correlation between inequality at the bottom and graduation is eliminated.[19] Poverty is positively and significantly correlated with spending. It reduces the positive relationship between inequality at the bottom and spending, though that relationship remains statistically significant.

As with Altonji and Mansfield, which one could view as a microlevel analysis of these forces for two different points in time, this analysis is purely suggestive and does not support causal interpretation. State education policies and inputs likely respond to public opinion about school quality, whether actual or perceived. The income distribution in a state is determined in part by graduation rates in the state in earlier years, which could affect fertility, cross-state migration, and earnings of residents born and educated in the state.

2.4.1   Additional Determinants of Graduation Rates Excluded from This Analysis

This limited exercise neglects to empirically examine the role of several key factors potentially changing over the time period and shown by other research to affect the acquisition of human capital. The following discussion of such omitted forces is by no means complete, and rather is meant to touch on some of the most major forces. Perhaps most critically, research in the social and life sciences increasingly recognizes the importance of early life environment and experiences in shaping human capital, including cognitive and noncognitive skills as well as health outcomes. The now well-established fact that gaps in cognitive ability by socioeconomic status are present by the time children enter kindergarten (Duncan and Magnuson 2011) confirms that attempting to analyze variation in high school graduation solely as a factor of elementary and secondary education policies is necessarily limited, and suggests the potential for many policies to ultimately affect educational attainment. These could include policies affecting maternal exposure to a variety of environmental toxins and licit and illicit drugs (Currie 2011), prenatal and postnatal nutrition (Almond, Hoynes, and Schanzenbach 2011), and the quality of childcare environments prior to enrollment in elementary school, including the home environment (Phillips 2011).

2.5   Conclusion

The descriptive results presented raise an interesting question. If, as these results suggest (and CE and BFWZ show convincingly), the inequality in

---

19. Using microlevel data, Kearney and Levine (2012) find support for negative impacts of inequality at the bottom on youth outcomes: conditional on individual poverty status, inequality in a state is positively correlated with teen childbearing.

recent decades led to increased school spending, would a better-identified setting (e.g., one with exogenous changes in inequality) show a positive relationship between inequality and student outcomes? If so, would the benefits of inequality-induced additional resources reach students throughout the achievement distribution? There could be a positive impact of these funds on graduation rates, but one that is more than offset by other mechanisms through which inequality negatively affects attainment. Alternatively, little to none of the increases in spending at the district level may be making their way to those students on the margin of dropping out of high school, due to the nonuniform allocation of resources across schools within districts and within individual schools.

Research on school quality has been moving toward the more productive exercise of assessing returns to specific inputs, as opposed to dollars spent per pupil. As researchers have shown convincing correlations between specific inputs and educational outcomes, public policy has begun to embrace these findings. For example, consider the extent to which Race to the Top rewards the use of specific technologies in educational production, including those enabling the identification of teacher-specific contributions to achievement. Yet the role for policy is still limited as the most compelling input to school quality identified to date—teacher quality—has been identified essentially as a residual and it is not clear how policies can manipulate its level or distribution. Research into the production of *teacher* quality is an important next frontier for this literature. As recent efforts of the National Council on Teacher Quality reveal, this is a politically fraught endeavor, facing major resistance from schools of education and teachers' unions.

Another fruitful avenue for future research on education production functions is to consider the regulatory environments in which resources are allocated, at the state, district, and school levels. Regulation of federal Title I funds increased—both in terms of formal requirements and actual enforcement—in response to early reports of malfeasance (see Martin and McClure 1969), and other categorical programs, from federal and state sources, have followed suit with their own requirements. The initial push for greater regulation came about in response to a large volume of reports of school districts using federal funds to maintain a desired unequal distribution of total resources. The regulatory environment today has evolved such that critics fear it poses serious difficulties for districts genuinely attempting to equalize the quality of education across their schools (for detailed descriptions of particular regulations, see Junge and Krvaric [2011]; for discussion of the opaque and nonuniform allocation of resources within districts, see Roza [2010]). This allocation poses difficulties for researchers as well, who regularly implicitly view reported revenues and expenditures at the school district level as predictive of student-level resources throughout the district. The world of quantitative research in education has changed dramatically in the last decade. No Child Left Behind brought with it a push for "scientifically based research" emphasizing exogenous variation in educational inputs and large, quantitative data sets. Ideally this new orientation can be merged productively with careful attention to institutional detail, allowing for the creation of accessible data on the most relevant variables, and to produce the research necessary to guide investments in future generations of human capital.

References

Alesina, Alberto, Reza Baqir, and William Easterly. 1999. "Public Goods and Ethnic Divisions." *Quarterly Journal of Economics* 114 (4): 1243–84.

Almond, Douglas, Hilary Hoynes, and Diane Schanzenbach. 2011. "Inside the War on Poverty: The Effect of the Food Stamp Program on Birth Outcomes." *Review of Economics and Statistics* 93 (2): 387–403.

Altonji, Joseph G., and Richard K. Mansfield. 2011. "The Role of Family, School, and Community Characteristics in Inequality in Education and Labor-Market Outcomes." In *Whither Opportunity? Rising Inequality, Schools, and Children's Life Chances*, edited by Greg J. Duncan and Richard J. Murnane. New York: Russell Sage Foundation.

Autor, David H., Lawrence F. Katz, and Melissa S. Kearney. 2008. "Trends in US Wage Inequality: Revising the Revisionists." *Review of Economics and Statistics* 90 (2): 300–23.

Bacolod, Marigee. 2007. "Do Alternative Opportunities Matter? The Role of Female Labor Markets in the Decline of Teacher Quality, 1960–1990." *Review of Economics and Statistics* 89 (4): 737–51.

Balfanz, Robert, and Nettie Legters. 2004. "Locating the Dropout Crisis." Center for Research on Education of Students Placed At Risk, Report 70. http://www.csos.jhu.edu/crespar/techReports/Report70.pdf.

Boustan, Leah, Fernando Ferreira, Hernan Winkler, and Eric Zolt. 2013. "The Effect of Rising Income Inequality on Taxation and Public Expenditures: Evidence from US Municipalities and School Districts, 1970–2000." *Review of Economics and Statistics* 95 (4): 1291–1302.

Briffault, Richard. 2005. "The Local School District in American Law." In *Besieged: School Boards and the Future of American Politics*, edited by William G. Howell, 24–55. Washington, DC: Brookings.

Burch, Patricia. 2006. "The New Educational Privatization: Educational Contracting and High Stakes accountability." *Teachers College Record* 108 (12): 2582–610.

Card, David, and A. Abigail Payne. 2002. "School Finance Reform, the Distribution of School Spending, and the Distribution of SAT Scores." *Journal of Public Economics* 83 (1): 49–82.

Cascio, Elizabeth, Nora Gordon, Ethan Lewis, and Sarah Reber. 2008. "From *Brown* to Busing." *Journal of Urban Economics* 64 (2): 296–325.

———. 2010. "Paying for Progress: Conditional Grants and the Desegregation of Southern Public Schools." *Quarterly Journal of Economics* 125 (1): 445–82.

Cascio, Elizabeth, Nora Gordon, and Sarah Reber. 2013. "Local Responses to Federal Grants: Evidence from the Introduction of Title I in the South." *American Economic Journal: Economic Policy* 5 (3): 126–59.

Cascio, Elizabeth, and Sarah Reber. 2012. "The War on Poverty's K-12 Education

Battle: The History and Legacy of Title I." In *The Legacies of the War on Poverty*, edited by Bailey and Danziger. New York: Russell Sage Foundation.

Coleman, James S., Ernest Q. Campbell, Carl F. Hobson, James McPartland, Alexander M. Mood, et al. 1966. *Equality of Educational Opportunity.* Washington, DC: US Office of Education.

Corcoran, Sean P., and William N. Evans. 2008. "Equity, Adequacy and the Evolving State Role in Education Finance." In *Handbook of Research in Education Finance and Policy*, edited by Helen F. Ladd and Edward B. Fiske, 332–56. New York: Routledge.

———. 2010. "Income Inequality, the Median Voter, and the Support for Public Education." NBER Working Paper no. 16097, Cambridge, MA.

Corcoran, Sean P., William N. Evans, and Robert M. Schwab. 2004. "Changing Labor Market Opportunities for Women and the Quality of Teachers, 1957–2000." In *American Economic Review, Papers and Proceedings of the American Economic Association* 94 (2): 230–5.

Currie, Janet. 2011. "Inequality at Birth: Some Causes and Consequences." *American Economic Review* 101 (3): 1 22.

Dee, Thomas, and Brian Jacob. 2011. "The Impact of the No Child Left Behind Act on Student Achievement." *Journal of Policy Analysis and Management* 30 (3): 418–46.

Duncan, Greg J., and K. Magnuson. 2011. "The Role of Family, School, and Community Characteristics in Inequality in Education and Labor-Market Outcomes." In *Whither Opportunity? Rising Inequality, Schools, and Children's Life Chances*, edited by Greg J. Duncan and Richard J. Murnane. New York: Russell Sage Foundation.

Duncan, Greg J., and Richard J. Murnane, eds. 2011. "Introduction: The American Dream, Then and Now." In *Whither Opportunity? Rising Inequality, Schools, and Children's Life Chances*," New York: Russell Sage Foundation.

Evans, William, Craig Garthwaite, and Timothy J. Moore. 2012. "The White/Black Educational Gap, Stalled Progress, and the Long-Term Consequences of the Emergence of Crack Cocaine Markets." NBER Working Paper no. 18437, Cambridge, MA.

Ferguson, Ronald F. 2008. "What We've Learned about Stalled Progress in Closing the Black, White Achievement Gap." In *Steady Gains and Stalled Progress: Inequality and the Black-White Test Score Gap*, edited by Katherine Magnuson and Jane Waldfogel, p. 320–44. New York: Russell Sage Foundation.

Fischel, William. 1989. "Did *Serrano* Cause Proposition 13?" *National Tax Journal* 42:465–74.

Forbes, Silke, and Nora Gordon. 2012. "When Educators Are the Learners: Private Contracting by Public Schools." *B.E. Journal of Economic Analysis & Policy* 12 (1): 31. Berkeley Electronic Press.

Freeman, Richard B. 1976. *The Overeducated American.* New York: Academic Press.

Goldin, Claudia, and Lawrence F. Katz. 2008. *The Race between Education and Technology.* Cambridge, MA: Harvard University Press.

Gordon, Nora. 2004. "Do Federal Grants Boost School Spending? Evidence from Title I." *Journal of Public Economics* 88 (9–10): 1771–92.

———. 2008. "The Changing Federal Role in Education Finance and Governance." In *Handbook of Research in Education Finance and Policy*, edited by Helen F. Ladd and Edward B. Fiske, 295–313. New York: Routledge.

Guin, Kacey, Betheny Gross, Scott Deburgomaster, and Marguerite Roza. 2007. "Do Districts Fund Schools Fairly?" *Education Next* 7 (4): 68–73.

Guryan, Jonathan. 2004. "Desegregation and Black Dropout Rates." *American Economic Review* 94 (4): 919–43.

Hanushek, Eric A. 1997. "Assessing the Effects of School Resources on Student Performance: An Update." *Educational Evaluation and Policy Analysis* 19 (2): 141–64.

Heckman, James J., and Paul A. LaFontaine. 2010. "The American High School Graduation Rate: Trends and Levels." *Review of Economics and Statistics* 92 (2): 244–62.

Heuer, Ruth, and Stephanie Stullich. 2011. "Comparability of State and Local Expenditures among Schools within Districts: A Report from the Study of School-Level Expenditures." Office of Planning, Evaluation and Policy Development, US Department of Education.

Hoxby, Caroline M. 2001. "All School Finance Equalizations Are Not Created Equal." *Quarterly Journal of Economics* 116 (4): 1189–1231.

Hoxby, Caroline, M., and Andrew Leigh. 2004. "Pulled Away or Pushed Out? Explaining the Decline of Teacher Aptitude in the United States." *American Economic Review* 94 (2): 236–40.

Junge, Melissa, and Sheara Krvaric. 2011. "Federal Compliance Works against Education Policy Goals." *Education Outlook* 6, American Enterprise Institute. http://www.aei.org/article/education/k-12/federal-compliance-works-against-education-policy-goals/.

Kearney, Melissa, and Philip Levine. 2012. "Why Are Teen Birth Rates So High in the U.S. and Why Does It Matter?" *Journal of Economic Perspectives* 26 (2): 141–63.

Krueger, Alan. 1998. "Reassessing the View that American Schools are Broken." *Economic Policy Review* 4 (1): 29–46.

Luttmer, Erzo. 2001. "Group Loyalty and the Taste for Redistribution." *Journal of Political Economy* 109 (3): 500–28.

Martin, Ruby, and Phyllis McClure. 1969. *Title I of ESEA: Is it Helping Poor Children?* Washington, DC: National Association for the Advancement of Colored People and Washington Research Project.

McLanahan, Sara, and Gary D. Sandefur. 1994. *Growing Up with a Single Parent: What Hurts, What Helps.* Cambridge, MA: Harvard University Press.

McLaughlin, Milbrey. 1976. "Implementation of ESEA Title I: A Problem of Compliance." *Teachers College Record* 77 (3): 397–415.

Meyer, Bruce D., and James X. Sullivan. 2012. "Winning the War: Poverty from the Great Society to the Great Recession." *Brookings Papers on Economic Activity* 133–200. http://www.brookings.edu/~/media/Projects/BPEA/Fall%202012/2012b_Meyer.pdf.

Mishel, Lawrence, and Joydeep Roy. 2006. *Rethinking High School Graduation Rates and Trends.* Washington, DC: Employment Policy Institute.

Murnane, Richard. 2011. "US High School Graduation Rates: Patterns and Explanations." Working Paper, Harvard Graduate School of Education.

Murray, Sheila E., William N. Evans, and Robert M. Schwab. 1998. "Education-Finance Reform and the Distribution of Education Resources." *American Economic Review* 88:789–812.

Neal, Derek. 2006. "Why Has Black-White Skill Convergence Stopped?" In *Handbook of the Economics of Education*, edited by Eric Hanushek and Finis Welch, 511–76. Amsterdam: Elsevier.

Phillips, Meredith. 2011. "Parenting, Time Use, and Disparities in Academic Outcomes." In *Whither Opportunity? Rising Inequality, Schools, and Children's Life Chances*, edited by Greg J. Duncan and Richard J. Murnane. New York: Russell Sage Foundation.

Poterba, James. 1997. "Demographic Structure and the Political Economy of Education." *Journal of Policy Analysis and Management* 16:48–66.

Reardon, Sean. 2011. "The Widening Academic Achievement Gap between Rich and Poor: New Evidence and Possible Explanations." In *Whither Opportunity? Rising Inequality, Schools, and Children's Life Chances,* edited by Greg J. Duncan and Richard J. Murnane. New York: Russell Sage Foundation.

Reber, Sarah. 2010. "Desegregation and Educational Attainment for Blacks." *Journal of Human Resources* 45 (4): 893–914.

Rockoff, Jonah. 2004. "The Impact of Individual Teachers on Student Achievement: Evidence from Panel Data." *American Economic Review* 94 (2): 247–52.

Roza, Marguerite. 2010. *Educational Economics: Where Do School Funds Go?* Washington, DC: Urban Institute Press.

Roza, Marguerite, Kacey Guin, and Tricia Davis. 2008. "What Is the Sum of the Parts? How Federal, State, and District Funding Streams Confound Efforts to Address Different Student Types." Center on Reinventing Public Education, University of Washington.

Ruggles, Steven, J. Trent Alexander, Katie Genadek, Ronald Gocken, Matthew B. Schroeder, and Matthew Sobek. 2010. Integrated Public Use Microdata Series: Version 5.0 [Machine-readable database]. Minneapolis: University of Minnesota.

Swanson, Christopher B. 2004. "High School Graduation, Completion, and Drop out (GCD) Indicators A Primer and Catalog." Washington, DC: Urban Institute.

Vigdor, Jacob L., and Jens O. Ludwig. 2008. "Segregation and the Black-White Test Score Gap." In *Steady Gains and Stalled Progress: Inequality and the Black-White Test Score Gap*, edited by K. Magnuson and J. Waldfogel. New York: Russell Sage Foundation Press.

Watson, Tara. 2009. "Inequality and the Measurement of Residential Segregation by Income." *Review of Income and Wealth* 55:820–44.

Comment   Sarah J. Reber

Goldin and Katz (2008) document impressive increases in the accumulation of human capital in the form of a dramatic rise in high school graduation rates during the first half of the twentieth century. They tie these changes to an important policy development; namely, the American high school movement. The chapter by Nora Gordon documents how trends in high school completion have changed since then and then discusses what might explain those trends. Gordon focuses on high school completion, but it is worth noting that this story is not specific to that outcome. More than just documenting trends in high school graduation, she is asking why progress stalled after the high school movement ran its course.

Consistent with other related work, Gordon shows that high school graduation rates peaked in the late 1960s and declined since then. There has been an uptick recently, but in any case the trend since 1970 is at best flat. The lack of improvement in high school graduation rates occurred despite well-documented increases in the return to education as well as a num-

Sarah J. Reber is associate professor of public policy at the Luskin School of Public Affairs at the University of California, Los Angeles, and a research associate of the National Bureau of Economic Research.

For acknowledgments, sources of research support, and disclosure of the author's material financial relationships, if any, please see http://www.nber.org/chapters/c12899.ack.

ber of policy developments intended to improve educational outcomes in general and high school graduation in particular. This raises the question of what happened—and the chapter does a nice job of outlining the potential explanations and the evidence on each. In the end, however, none of those explanations go terribly far, and it is not really clear what the explanation is. This is, of course, not the fault of the author—it reflects the state of the literature. That raises the question of what academics and policymakers can do: what kind of research should we do and what policies should we pursue. I will focus my comments in this regard on school finance, though I note that the chapter covers much more territory.

I begin with the key empirical results presented by Gordon, which examine the relationship between inequality and school spending at the state level. Goldin and Katz show that income inequality was an impediment to the establishment of high schools, presumably because more heterogeneous communities had difficulty coming together to support public goods provision. In the same vein, one might worry that the recent rise in income inequality would undermine financial support for schools. Some recent papers suggest that this has not been the case at the level of the school district; if anything, increases in inequality are associated with small increases in school spending or simply a shift from state to local sources of revenue (Boustan et al. 2013; Corcoran and Evans 2010).

The existing literature focuses on revenue and spending at the level of local school districts. Gordon makes an important contribution to this discussion by looking at these relationships at the state level and examining the relationship between inequality and high school completion. This is an important contribution because state governments also make decisions that affect the level of school spending—and those decisions could be affected by inequality at the state level. Figure 2C.1 (adapted from Cascio and Reber [2013]) illustrates the substantial variation in average spending across states and how it relates to poverty over time. Panel A plots the relationship between the natural log of current expenditure per pupil in the 1963/64 school year against the 1960 child poverty rate at the state level; panel B shows the same relationship for the 2006/7 school year.[1] The variation in spending across states (the y-axis variation) is substantial and similar over time. In 1963, state-level poverty is highly negatively predictive of state-level school spending, with an R-squared of 0.69. The slope in panel A is -2.28, implying that a 10 percentage point increase in the state poverty rate was associated with a 23 log point reduction in average per-pupil spending. By 2006, the

1. Both panels use the 1960 child poverty rate calculated based on the number of students eligible for Title I on the horizontal axis. The key findings are quite similar if instead we use the contemporaneous poverty rate for panel B. That is, the declining explanatory power of the poverty rate over time is *not* due primarily to measurement error associated with using the 1960 child poverty rate in later years; this is because state-level poverty rates are highly correlated over time. See Cascio and Reber (2013) for details on the data used to make this figure.

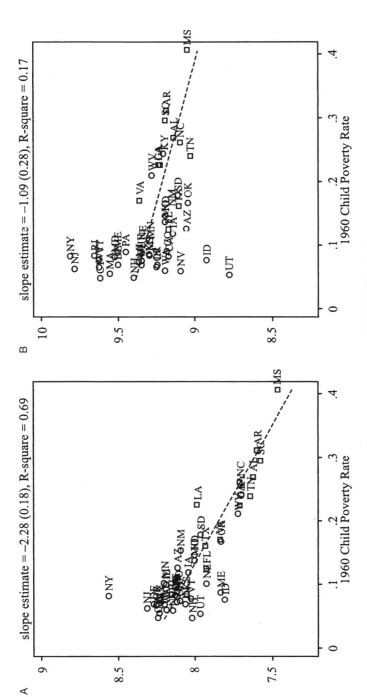

Fig. 2C.1   School spending and poverty: *A*, 1963–1964 school year; *B*, 2006–2007 school year.
Source: Cascio and Reber (2013).

R-squared was only 0.17, and the relationship between poverty and spending was less than half as steep—the slope in panel B is −1.09. The high-poverty states remain clustered closely around the regression line, but it is interesting to note that significant variation in spending among low-poverty states emerged. Cascio and Reber show that in later years, average income in the state is more predictive of school spending than poverty, but both income and poverty have become less predictive over time. States appear to be taking different approaches to school finance in a way that is less related to poverty and income than in the past.

Average school spending has increased dramatically and become less related to poverty over the last half century. At the same time, state governments have contributed a large share of the average dollar. Although it is important to consider the source of the *marginal* dollar—which does not follow directly from the state share of spending and may vary over time depending on the details of the state school finance regime and other factors—all of this suggests that states are an important player in school funding. We cannot necessarily extrapolate from the results of district-level analyses to predict how inequality might affect state governments' decisions since the tax bases, voting patterns, and political economy of school finance likely differ at different levels of government.

The new empirical findings presented in this chapter, together with the existing literature, suggest that inequality has probably not reduced education spending on average. Maintaining a similar level of spending may be insufficient if inequality increases social problems, in which case more money may be required to provide the same quality of education. But the lack of a decline in school funding suggests that the rise in inequality has not undermined support for school finance. The chapter also makes the very important point that, because of data constraints, virtually all of the research examines spending at the school district level. But there is significant heterogeneity of student characteristics across schools within districts (not to mention across classrooms within schools). We know little about how resources are distributed within districts and by extension how the rise in inequality and the policy changes outlined in the chapter have affected the resources to which students at the bottom of the income distribution have access. This is an important area for future research (and data collection).

So, in the last forty years or so, real per-pupil spending has nearly tripled, variation in spending across states was substantial and stable, but less related to poverty and income over time. Although we have little to no data on how resources are allocated within districts, the school finance equalization literature suggests that funding has become more equal and progressive across districts within states (Murray, Evans, and Schwab 1998; Hoxby 2001; Card and Payne 2002). Rising income inequality does not appear to be undermining school funding. Yet trends in educational outcomes—particularly the trends in high school graduation rates documented here—have not been favorable.

What should we make of this? One cannot help but ask if at least some of the new spending on K–12 education has been inefficient. Of course, we do not know what the counterfactual trend in high school graduation rates would have been, and there are offsetting trends: higher prices for skilled teachers as alternative labor market opportunities have opened up for high-ability women, and more children entering school at a disadvantage as the prevalence of single-parent, immigrant, and other socioeconomically disadvantaged families has grown. Schools may also be doing more than they used to, particularly with respect to special education, suggesting we need to consider a broad notion of what we mean by "educational output." Although test scores and high school graduation do not capture all of the relevant outputs, I believe that most people would consider high school graduates who are ready to attend college or participate meaningfully in the labor market to be one of the key outputs the K–12 system should be producing. And, despite the fact that the research base may not cover all the ground we would like, the evidence reviewed in this chapter, and the sheer magnitude of the increase in funding, suggest that demographic changes and other negative trends are unlikely to account for the apparent lack of output for all the new input.[2]

One possibility is that we have reached the "flat part" of the education production function—that is, spending has increased so much that we do not get much for our marginal dollar. That is certainly a possibility, but the literature discussed in the chapter showing well-identified positive effects of particular inputs—particularly the evidence on the effects of teacher quality in a variety of settings—suggests that money well spent could improve outcomes considerably. Taking this evidence together, it appears that we are not simply at the flat of the curve; we are off the efficient frontier. That is, the United States is not getting as much as we could from our education expenditures. It would be reassuring, particularly in the current fiscal environment, if this implied that cutting funding would not reduce outcomes. This is not the case, however, because there is no guarantee that cuts will be applied only to inefficient spending. In fact, we have pretty good evidence that, at least on average, very senior teachers are not that cost effective, since the return to experience flattens out after the first several years (or at most a decade), but pay does not. Similarly, research (not to mention common sense) suggests that the length of the school day and the length of the school year affect outcomes. Yet in response to recent cutbacks, teachers have been relieved of duty based on seniority rather than quality, and school years have been shortened. By a similar logic, increasing spending might not help, at

---

2. Although most of the vast literature looking at the relationship between school funding and educational outcomes (the "does money matter" literature) does not find a positive correlation, most of these studies are not well identified. A few better-identified studies have found evidence that money matters, but these have typically been in contexts where the marginal dollar goes to a poor, underfunded district (Guryan 2004; Reber 2010; Cascio, Gordon, and Reber 2013).

least not as much as it could, because there is no guarantee that new spending will be allocated to the most efficient uses.

The chapter and this discussion point to some potentially fruitful directions for policy and research on school finance. First, it suggests the potential value of shifting from a focus on equity of finance *across school districts* toward improving productive efficiency *everywhere*. This is not to say that the goal of reducing educational inequality, and especially increasing quality for those at the bottom, has become less important. To the contrary, it is arguably more important than ever in light of increasing returns to education and rising income inequality. But recent trends in spending are not sustainable, particularly in the current fiscal environment. And although there is still substantial inequality in funding, the system has become much more progressive in the last half century. It is also possible that poorer children could benefit more from policies that focus on how to get the highest return for each dollar spent on education, as their schools and districts are likely the most constrained in how they use funds and bear the brunt of, for example, inefficient human resources policies, such as last-in, first-out layoff rules.

Second, the chapter highlights the role of fiscal accountability and the distribution of resources (especially teachers) *across schools*. The chapter points to the many things we do not know about how resources are allocated, especially at the subdistrict level. It may not always be obvious how to spend money efficiently and fairly, but understanding how money is currently spent and distributed would provide a good starting place for these discussions. Better accounting of inequalities in the allocation of spending across schools will almost certainly reveal that the overrepresentation of young, less-expensive teachers in poor schools means that the poorest children receive the fewest resources within districts. We may not have policies at the ready to remedy this, but better data could do as much to shine a light on the issue as student testing has revealed persistent racial and socioeconomic gaps in achievement.

The chapter also points to important directions for future research. Yes, researchers should continue to try to understand better the education production function by looking for settings where we can identify whether (or under what conditions) money matters and how particular inputs do or do not affect outcomes. But if we are off the efficient frontier, it is probably because of "institutions," broadly construed—governance, unions, regulations, norms, the dissemination of information. Research on the political economy of the allocation of educational resources and educational institutions is likely to be informative for policy.

The federal government might play an important role in enhancing productive efficiency by improving educational institutions—and one could argue this is already happening. Historically, conditional federal grants have been quite effective at changing entrenched state and local policies in education and other domains. The threat of withdrawal of federal funds prompted recalcitrant southern districts to take their first steps toward desegregation (Cascio et al. 2010) and southern hospitals to open their doors to African Americans. The carrot of federal funding has convinced states to adopt accountability regimes under No Child Left Behind, reduce their speed limits, and increase their drinking ages. Most recently, many states (and some districts) have changed long-standing policies governing teacher evaluation and tenure as well as data use to compete for Race to the Top funds with no assurance of success at funding. This suggests that when a policy and research consensus forms around a particular idea, but state or local politics make it difficult to implement, tying federal dollars to the implementation of that idea is well worth considering.

To conclude, Gordon's chapter provides an excellent guide to researchers, policymakers, and students of education seeking a better understanding of how policies for primary and secondary education have evolved over the last half century.

References

Boustan, Leah, Fernando Ferreira, Hernan Winkler, and Eric Zolt. 2013. "The Effect of Rising Income Inequality on Taxation and Public Expenditures: Evidence from US Municipalities and School Districts, 1970–2000." *Review of Economics and Statistics* 95 (4): 1291–1302.

Card, David, and A. Abigail Payne. 2002. "School Finance Reform, the Distribution of School Spending, and the Distribution of SAT Scores." *Journal of Public Economics* 83:49–82.

Cascio, Elizabeth, Nora Gordon, Ethan Lewis, and Sarah Reber. 2010. "Paying for Progress: Conditional Grants and the Desegregation of Southern Public Schools." *Quarterly Journal of Economics* 125:445–82.

Cascio, Elizabeth, Nora Gordon, and Sarah Reber. 2013. "Local Responses to Federal Grants: Evidence from the Introduction of Title I in the South." *American Economic Journal: Economic Policy* 5 (3): 126–59.

Cascio, Elizabeth, and Sarah Reber. 2013. "The Poverty Gap in School Spending Following the Introduction of Title I." *American Economic Review* 103:423–7.

Corcoran, Sean, and William N. Evans. 2010. "Income Inequality, the Median Voter, and the Support for Public Education." NBER Working Paper no. 16097, Cambridge, MA.

Goldin, Claudia, and Lawrence F. Katz. 2008. *The Race between Education and Technology*. Cambridge, MA: Harvard University Press.

Guryan, Jonathan. 2004. "Desegregation and Black Dropout Rates." *American Economic Review* 94:919–43.

Hoxby, Caroline M. 2001. "All School Finance Equalizations Are Not Created Equal." *Quarterly Journal of Economics* 116:1189–231.

Murray, Sheila E., William N. Evans, and Robert M. Schwab. 1998. "Education-Finance Reform and the Distribution of Education Resources." *American Economic Review* 88:789–812.

Reber, Sarah. 2010. "Desegregation and Educational Attainment for Blacks." *Journal of Human Resources* 45:893–914.

3

The Role of Immigrant Children in Their Parents' Assimilation in the United States, 1850–2010

Ilyana Kuziemko and Joseph Ferrie

3.1 Introduction

The process of immigrant assimilation into the destination country's labor market fundamentally involves human capital: new arrivals often have to acquire a new language or learn new skills, and in many cases adapt to economic life in an environment vastly different from that in their home country. The view of migration as an investment in human capital has a long history (Schultz 1961; Becker 1962). More recently, the study of human capital formation by immigrants has been extended by considering the broader context in which that formation occurs. Rather than viewing each immigrant in isolation, immigrant husbands and wives are shown to make joint decisions regarding the accumulation and use of human capital (Baker and Benjamin 1997; Blau et al. 2003) and immigrants' decisions are influenced by the characteristics of the larger immigrant community in which they are located, particularly immigrant enclaves (Borjas 1995). The assimilation of parents has now been linked to the assimilation of their children once the children are adults (Abramitzky, Boustan, and Eriksson 2012; Portes and Rumbaut 2001; Perlmann and Waldinger 1997; Zhou 1997).

We examine immigrant assimilation in the United States, 1870–2010, but allow for a novel influence on the human capital accumulation and exploitation of immigrants: the presence of children who migrate along with their

Ilyana Kuziemko is the David W. Zalaznick Associate Professor of Business at Columbia Business School and a faculty research fellow at the National Bureau of Economic Research. Joseph Ferrie is the Household International Inc. Research Professor of Economics and professor of economics at Northwestern University and a research associate of the National Bureau of Economic Research.

For acknowledgments, sources of research support, and disclosure of the authors' material financial relationships, if any, please see http://www.nber.org/chapters/c12906.ack.

parents. Kuziemko (forthcoming) presents a model in which immigrant parents can both "learn" from their children as well as "lean" on them. That is, children might enhance adults' assimilation if, say, they can help teach their parents English. Conversely, if children learn English and serve as translators for the household, parents' incentives to learn the language themselves falls and their assimilation is thus retarded. Kuziemko finds that California's switch from bilingual education to English immersion in 1998 caused a significant increase in the English proficiency of immigrant children, but decreased proficiency of the adults with whom they lived. As such, leaning seems to outweigh learning in the context of recent California immigrants.

There is an extensive literature documenting the returns to English-language proficiency for immigrants, so the practical impact of the learning effect can be quite large, as can be the practical impact of the leaning effect where the children effectively substitute their own proficiency for their parents' proficiency. Ferrer, Green, and Riddell (2006) find that differences in English-language literacy alone explain two-thirds of the earnings gap between immigrants and natives. This effect of proficiency in the host country language is particularly large for higher-skilled workers (Berman, Lang, and Siniver 2003), and differs substantially by gender, with a lower penalty for females though their penalty rises more rapidly with education than the penalty for males (Mora and Dávila 1998). The importance of proficiency in the host country's language for immigrants' outcomes is underscored by the much lower rate of return earned on human capital acquired outside the host country (Friedberg 2000). Proficiency facilitates not just the acquisition of new skills specific to the host country but it also makes previously acquired skills more readily transferable. To address concerns that the relationship between language proficiency and outcomes might not be directly causal but instead run through another channel (for example, if immigrants proficient in the host country language have higher earnings because they are of higher ability), Bleakley and Chin (2004) examine immigrants who arrived as children. They compare those from English-speaking countries and non-English-speaking countries, and find a strong effect of English proficiency on earnings that appears to come through the proficiency's impact on education.

We extend the analysis of the role of children as teachers or helpers of their US immigrant parents and assess the relationship between immigrant children and outcomes for their parents in two eras (1850–1930 and 1970–2010).[1] We present several related empirical results. We first document a striking difference between the immigrants of the Great Migration and more recent immigrants—the latter were far less likely to arrive with their children or to later send for their children. These early immigrants were far more

---

1. See Goldin (1994) on the political economy of the decision to close borders to immigrants in the 1920s, effectively ending the Great Migration era.

likely to start families after arriving in the United States. Second, we show that assimilation appears slower for this more recent group of immigrants, though in both eras we find declining cohort quality that complicates estimates of assimilation.

Finally, we show that arriving with children during the early period appears to lead more to learning than to leaning, whereas today parents are more likely to lean on than to learn from their children. As children who migrate at very young or very old ages are unlikely to be relevant to their parents' decision to learn English or otherwise assimilate (as we will discuss in greater detail, a very young child cannot translate for the household and a very old child would have trouble learning the language herself), we use differences in the age of children at arrival as identifying variation for the leaning/learning effect. In the early period, arriving with a child of a "useful" age is associated with faster assimilation in terms of English language skills and wage growth of the household head, whereas in the current period it is associated with slower assimilation.

3.2   Immigrant Children and Their Parents' Assimilation

Kuziemko (forthcoming) provides a full description of a model of adult immigrants' human capital acquisition that takes account of the presence of these immigrants' children. As in the standard human capital model, investment decisions depend on the costs and benefits of additional units of human capital. In the present context, immigrant parents who come to the United States unable to speak English could invest in formal training to attain English proficiency (e.g., attending ESL classes). If they have children, however, they can learn English, perhaps at a lower cost, from those children. This is the "learning" effect. Here, children's human capital reduces the cost of parents' acquisition of human capital.

In some contexts, however, parents may choose to rely directly on the English-language skills of their children rather than transferring some of those skills to themselves. For example, the child may act as a translator. This is the "leaning" effect. In these cases, children's human capital acts as a substitute for the human capital of their parents. This substitution can take the form of acting as an intermediary in daily commercial transactions or helping parents seek employment.

The model does not predict whether the learning or leaning effect will dominate, but it does provide some insight into when the effect of children on adults' human capital is likely to be positive or negative. Specifically, the learning effect will be larger (the effect of children on adults' human capital will be positive and larger in magnitude) when adults have characteristics (e.g., basic literacy) that are complementary to acquiring human capital through tutoring by their children. When adults' utility from consumption goods is independent of their ability to speak English (e.g., if their own consumption consists of only food or clothing, or if the surrounding community provides a wide array of goods and services that the adult immigrants can consume in their native language), the leaning effect will be larger (the effect of children on adults' human capital will be negative and larger in magnitude). Conversely, if parents highly value the labor market returns to learning English or if children are especially adept English "tutors," the leaning effect will dominate.

3.3   Data

We use the 1850 to 2010 versions of the Integrated Public Use Microdata Series (IPUMS), though rely mostly on the years 1900 to 1930 and 1970 to 2010 as the variables related to immigration in these years are more detailed than in other years. These years also cover the high-immigration period of the "Great Migration" as well as the recent wave of immigration from Central America.

Over this long span of US history, there have been substantial changes to US immigration policy that should be kept in mind throughout the following analysis (Barde, Carter, and Sutch 2006). In the period from the early 1850s through the late 1910s, immigration to the United States was, with only a few minor exceptions, "free" in that anyone able to afford passage to the United States was unimpeded in entering the country, seeking employment, and eventually becoming a citizen. This unrestricted environment ended with the imposition of a literacy test for admission in 1917 and the imposition of quotas for each country of origin in 1921 and 1924. For immigrants arriving after 1917, the ability to read and write was crucial for admission, but there remained no requirement that the immigrant be literate in English.

Beginning in the 1950s (with further changes in 1965), however, policy came to favor immigrants with particular skills in demand in the United States, as well as close relatives already in the country. The first of these changes should have resulted in the admission of more immigrants with readily transferrable skills (and presumably greater English proficiency at arrival), while the second facilitated family reunifications from which we largely abstract below by focusing on immigrants who arrived at roughly the same time as their children.

Finally, with the imposition of the restrictions beginning in 1917, large numbers of immigrants fell into either of two broad categories for the first time: those who met the restrictions and were in the United States legally and those who were able to evade detection and entered the United States despite the restriction. The second group came to comprise mainly Mexican immigrants by the 1960s. The practical impact of this complex policy history for our analysis is that, for pre-1917 immigrants, the learning or leaning was likely important across the board; but by the late twentieth century, some groups (those selected on the basis of occupational qualifications or who entered the United States on student visas, for example) likely already possessed strong English skills, while numerous less skilled immigrants who entered the United States despite restrictions possessed little to no English proficiency. The effect of children as tutors or translators is likely to be more heterogeneous later than earlier.

In general, we focus on household heads between the ages of thirty and sixty, in their prime working years, and typically focus on those with at least one child in their household. Because we are interested in assimilation, we exclude those who immigrated as children (before the age of eighteen), given the well-documented differences in language acquisition between adults and children (see the recent survey in Singleton [2001]). We also generally focus on migrants from non-English-speaking countries, given that assimilation for those already speaking English is likely very different from that of the typical immigrant.

We generate several variables reflecting the household composition at the time of the household head's migration. First, we determine whether the eldest child is himself an immigrant, which indicates that the household head either immigrated with his children or sent for his children to immigrate after he settled. A related variable is whether the eldest child immigrated in the same year as the household head, which we use as a proxy for whether parent and child immigrated together. We also create similar variables for the household head's spouse, though we focus less on these measures in the later analysis.

The variables above likely categorize some individuals as not immigrating with their children when in fact they did, given that the IPUMS only records information about children *in the household*, not all children ever born to an individual. As such, we generally focus on households where either the householder or the spouse (almost always the wife) is no more than thirty-five years of age. This restriction reflects rather conservative bounds on when the mother likely had her first child (say, at age twenty) and the earliest point at which a child might leave the home (say, at age fifteen). As wives are generally four years younger than husbands in both periods, in most cases men in their late thirties will remain in the sample.

In figure 3.1, we graph the share of all individuals from our main analysis sample—those household heads between ages thirty and sixty who immigrated as adults from non-English-speaking countries, have at least one child in their household, and who is under age thirty-six or whose spouse is under age thirty-six—whose eldest child is also an immigrant. Figure 3.1 shows that this share has changed substantially over time. Among immigrant parents during the first Great Migration, their eldest child was very unlikely to have been born abroad. In 1920, for example, well over 70 percent of such householders' eldest recorded child was born in the United States. During

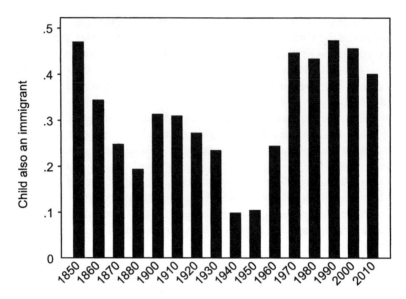

Fig. 3.1   Share of prime-age immigrant household heads with at least one child whose eldest child is also an immigrant

Notes: The sample includes all household heads born abroad who immigrated as adults (at least age eighteen) and who are at the time of the census between ages thirty and sixty. We also limit the sample to households where either the household head or the spouse are more than age thirty-five (to increase the probability that all children are still in the household).

the more recent immigration wave, nearly half of eldest children were born abroad, suggesting that householders had already begun their families in their homelands before moving to the United States.

Figure 3.2 graphs the share of our immigrant household sample whose eldest child immigrated in the same year (and thus presumably with) the householder. Year of immigration is only available for certain years in the IPUMS, and thus we plot this variable for only a subset of the years shown in figure 3.1. Again, the difference in family composition among immigrants in the Great Migration and recent years is striking. Between one-quarter and one-third of our main analysis sample immigrated with their eldest recorded child in recent years, whereas between 1900 and 1930 such an arrangement was the case only about 10 percent of the time.

Because we have far greater detail on the date of migration between 1900 and 1930 and from 1970 onward, we focus on these two periods in much of the regression analysis. Table 3.1 shows summary statistics for three groups in each of the periods. First, we show all prime-age immigrants who arrived as adults who have at least one child in the household. Second, we restrict this sample to those from non-English-speaking countries where either they or their spouse is under age thirty-six, so that readers can see the effect of our sampling restrictions. Finally, we show the sample of natives who meet all other regression-sample requirements outside of those referring specifically to immigration.

For both the immigrant and the immigrant-regression sample, ages at the time of the census are similar for both time periods. Not surprisingly, the immigrants in the regression sample are younger, given that we are restricting householders or spouses' age, but in both periods the average age for this sample is around thirty-seven, comparable to natives.

As we focus on household heads, all samples are disproportionately male, though less so in the recent period, consistent with the rise of female-headed households over the past several decades. Similarly, marriage rates decrease between the two time periods. In both time periods, the eldest child in the household is roughly ten years old in the regression samples.

We also examine ethnic isolation in the two periods, using county as the most detailed geographic unit available in both periods. In the early period, the average immigrant in our regression sample lived in a county with a 17.9 percent immigrant share. This share drops slightly to 16.6 percent in the recent period. Similarly, the average immigrant in the earlier period had a slightly higher share of immigrants from the same country in his county

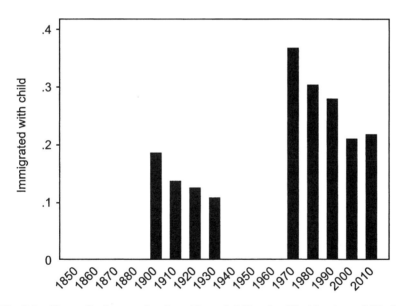

Fig. 3.2   Share of prime-age immigrant household heads with at least one child who immigrated with eldest child

Notes: The sample includes all household heads born abroad who immigrated as adults (at least age eighteen) and who are at the time of the census between ages thirty and sixty. We also limit the sample to households where either the household head or the spouse are more than age thirty-five (to increase the probability that all children are still in the household). Year of immigration is only available for selected years, so we can only determine whether a child immigrated with his parent for this subset.

Table 3.1   Summary statistics, immigrant parents from 1900 to 1930 versus 1970 to 2010

	1900–1930			1970–2010		
	(1) Immigr.	(2) Reg. samp.	(3) Native	(4) Immigr.	(5) Reg. samp.	(6) Native
Age	44.93	37.27	36.62	43.68	36.35	35.71
	(8.218)	(4.679)	(4.772)	(7.970)	(4.108)	(3.807)
Male	0.910	0.968	0.945	0.714	0.737	0.726
	(0.287)	(0.177)	(0.228)	(0.452)	(0.440)	(0.446)
Married	0.875	0.958	0.933	0.766	0.805	0.777
	(0.331)	(0.200)	(0.251)	(0.424)	(0.396)	(0.416)
Age of eldest child in household	15.49	9.247	9.672	14.88	9.443	10.20
	(7.700)	(5.074)	(5.143)	(7.792)	(5.537)	(5.404)
Immigrant share of county	0.174	0.179	0.134	0.172	0.166	0.0986
	(0.0763)	(0.0790)	(0.0729)	(0.105)	(0.103)	(0.0768)
Share of county from same	0.0464	0.0462		0.0376	0.0383	
homeland	(0.0513)	(0.0541)		(0.0530)	(0.0521)	
Age at arrival	25.99	24.05		28.91	25.95	
	(7.026)	(5.064)		(8.027)	(5.691)	
Years since migration	18.94	13.21		14.77	10.40	
	(8.956)	(5.748)		(8.793)	(5.873)	
Eldest child of HH head is an	0.280	0.241		0.437	0.382	
immigrant	(0.458)	(0.432)		(0.514)	(0.501)	
Eldest child immigrated same	0.136	0.102		0.248	0.219	
year as HH	(0.346)	(0.304)		(0.439)	(0.420)	
Spouse is also an immigrant	0.851	0.869		0.866	0.875	
(conditional on being married)	(0.356)	(0.337)		(0.341)	(0.330)	
Spouse immigrated same year	0.332	0.301		0.412	0.388	
(conditional on being married)	(0.471)	(0.459)		(0.492)	(0.487)	
Speaks English	0.875	0.827		0.925	0.923	
	(0.331)	(0.378)		(0.263)	(0.267)	
Occupational earnings score,	49.54	49.44	45.10	46.58	45.78	54.26
1950 basis	(26.25)	(24.61)	(31.08)	(28.49)	(28.49)	(27.06)
Share of all prime-age						
immigrants	0.252	0.0835		0.246	0.0977	
Observations	78,000	25,873	231,852	148,988	57,155	722,301

Notes: Columns (1) and (4) sample includes all immigrant parents between ages thirty and sixty who arrived as adults (at least age eighteen) and who are household heads. Columns (2) and (5) restrict this sample to those from non-English-speaking homelands and who are either under age thirty-six or whose spouse is under age thirty-six. Columns (4) and (6) include natives who otherwise meet the conditions in columns (2) and (5). The bottom of the table shows the share of all prime-age immigrants for which this group accounts. As in the regression tables, IPUMS person-weights are always used.

than does his counterpart today, which Lazear (1998) and others suggest could retard assimilation.[2] But the comparison to natives is instructive— immigrants in the early period were not more concentrated, there were just

2. Conversely, ethnic segregation might promote income growth, as Edin, Fredriksson, and Aslund (2003) find using random assignments of immigrants to different districts in Sweden.

significantly more numerous. The average *native* in the early period lived in a county that was 13.4 percent immigrant, compared to 9.8 percent today. Even though we restrict the sample to those who immigrated after age eighteen, there is a small difference in age at arrival between the two periods. In the earlier period, the average householder in our regression sample arrived at age twenty-four, whereas that age had climbed to twenty-six in the more recent sample. Not surprisingly, given the similarities in average age, the earlier arrival among immigrants in the earlier period translates to longer time since arrival—thirteen years versus ten years in the more recent period.

As demonstrated in figures 3.1 and 3.2, the eldest child is far less likely to be an immigrant or to have immigrated with the householder in the early years as in the more recent years. As noted above, householders are less likely to be married, but conditional on being married they are equally likely to be married to another immigrant (84 versus 86 percent in the early versus later period). As with children, in the more recent period the householder was also far more likely to have arrived with his spouse (39 percent did so as opposed to 30 percent earlier).

We tend to focus on two outcome variables in the regression analysis. Readers should note that we are somewhat limited in terms of finding outcome variables that are recorded in both periods—for example, wages and income are only recorded beginning in 1940. Our first outcome is the occupational score, based on the 1950 income distribution. As table 3.1 shows, immigrants have a higher score than natives in the earlier period, though this difference is completely accounted for by residential location—immigrants tend to live in urban areas where wages are higher—and once urbanicity controls are added immigrations have significantly lower scores than natives.

The second outcome variable is whether an immigrant reports speaking English. This variable was coded somewhat differently in 1900–1930 and in 1970–2010, with immigrants in the former group being asked only whether they speak at all and the latter group being asked whether they speak at all, speak well, or speak very well. To make both measures binary, we code "Speaks English" as one if an immigrant reports speaking English, regardless of how well. Our recoding suggests that immigrants today report better English skills. However, given how differently the question is asked in the two periods, we focus on within-time-period comparisons.

At the bottom of table 3.1, we show the share of all prime-age immigrants for which our samples account. The first set of restrictions (that an immigrant had come to the United States as an adult and that they have at least one child) leaves a sample that accounts for one-quarter of all immigrants in both periods. The additional assumptions (that an immigrant comes from a non-English-speaking family and be under age thirty-six or have a spouse under that age) leave a sample that accounts for roughly 9 percent of all prime-age immigrants in both periods. It is important to emphasize that our work obviously speaks to the subset of immigrants who arrive as adults and who eventually have children, and should not be generalized to other immigrant populations.

3.4   Regression Results on Assimilation

3.4.1   Basic Regression Results

Table 3.2 reports regression results on assimilation, separately for the two periods. All regressions include census-year fixed effects as well as the controls listed in the table.

Columns (1) to (5) examine the early period. The effect of being an immigrant on occupational score is strongly negative. Assimilation, as proxied by the coefficient on the years since migration (YSM) variable, is sizable. For example, taken literally, the coefficients in column (1) suggest that an immigrant who arrives at the age of twenty will have caught up with a native of similar demographic background by the age of forty-seven.

In column (2) we add birthplace fixed effects (which subsumes the main effect of being an immigrant). In this case, the coefficient on YSM is slightly smaller, though still positive and highly significant.

As the relationship between our outcomes and years since migration is unlikely to be linear over very large ranges, it is useful to make sure the relationship is not being driven by outliers. Moreover, immigrants who arrive with children are much more likely to be relatively recent arrivals (or else their children would be out of the household and thus not make our sampling restrictions), so not putting some restriction on the YSM variable means we are confounding the effect of YSM with having immigrant children in the household. As such, column (3) restricts the sample to those who arrived no more than fifteen years before the census record. This restriction substantially increases measured assimilation rates.[3]

Given that the gender composition of householders change between our two periods, it is useful to examine men in isolation (column [4]). Not surprising, given that men are the large majority of the sample in this period, the coefficient barely changes.

Column (5) examines English skills, so natives are no longer an appropriate control. The coefficient on years since migration suggests that the probability an immigrant reports speaking English increases by 2.3 percentage points a year.

Columns (6) through (10) perform the parallel analysis on the 1970–2010 sample and suggest far more limited assimilation—and in some specifications, regression—in the more recent period. In column (5), the coefficient

---

3. The effect of limiting the YSM variable is quite robust. The same drastic decrease in measured assimilation for the recent period occurs when the cutoff is twenty or ten as opposed to fifteen years.

Table 3.2   Measures of assimilation

| | 1900–1930 | | | | | 1970–2010 | | | | |
| | Occ. score | | | | Speaks Eng. | Occ. score | | | Speaks Eng. | |
	(1)	(2)	(3)	(4)	(5)	(6)	(7)	(8)	(9)	(10)
Immigrant	-6.579* [0.343]					-11.25* [0.176]				
Years since migration	0.240* [0.0176]	0.165* [0.0176]	0.241* [0.0679]	0.251* [0.0690]	0.0234* [0.00101]	0.189* [0.00992]	0.319* [0.0102]	-0.00388 [0.0305]	-0.00536 [0.0338]	0.00760* [0.000356]
Age	1.279* [0.119]	0.796* [0.116]	0.858* [0.123]	0.836* [0.125]	-0.00284 [0.00777]	2.870* [0.0855]	2.603* [0.0842]	2.544* [0.0880]	2.385* [0.0934]	-0.00901** [0.00400]
Age squared	-0.0191* [0.00151]	-0.0121* [0.00147]	-0.0127* [0.00156]	-0.0124* [0.00158]	-0.0000437 [0.000103]	-0.0364* [0.00114]	-0.0334* [0.00112]	-0.0323* [0.00118]	-0.0306* [0.00124]	0.0000797 [0.0000537]
Male	26.97* [0.317]	23.84* [0.311]	23.88* [0.327]		0.133* [0.0187]	17.32* [0.0762]	17.15* [0.0754]	17.62* [0.0777]		0.0693* [0.00320]
Urban	26.79* [0.130]	23.07* [0.134]	23.67* [0.145]	24.55* [0.148]	0.0118*** [0.00711]	-1.815* [0.100]	-1.872* [0.0997]	-1.700* [0.105]	-1.466* [0.129]	-0.00992* [0.00308]
Mean, dept. var.	44.59	44.59	43.69	44.65	0.757	54.25	54.25	54.71	59.25	0.915
Includes natives?	Yes	Yes	Yes	Yes	No	Yes	Yes	Yes	Yes	No
Yrs. since migration	All	All	Under 25	Under 25	Under 25	All	All	Under 25	Under 25	Under 25
Gender	Both	Both	Both	Men	Both	Both	Both	Both	Men	Both
Observations	214,590	214,590	189,899	182,484	14,633	675,231	675,231	638,916	481,447	39,250

Notes: All immigrant observations are household heads between the ages of thirty and sixty with at least one child in the household, who are under age thirty-six or whose spouse is under age thirty-six, who immigrated from non-English-speaking countries, and who immigrated as adults. Natives in the sample meet all these conditions as well, outside those related to immigration. "Occ. score" is the occupational earnings score using the 1950 income distribution. "Speaks Eng." is an indicator variable for speaking English at any level (in earlier years, there is only a yes/no answer allowed for this question, whereas in later years respondents are asked how well they speak). "Years since migration" is coded as zero for nonimmigrants. All regressions include fixed effects for census year. "Urban" is an indicator for living in a city large enough to be recorded in the census.

***Significant at the 1 percent level.

**Significant at the 5 percent level.

*Significant at the 10 percent level.

on years since migration is slightly smaller than that of column (1). Taking the results literally, it would take an immigrant today roughly sixty years to catch up with natives with similar background characteristics. Adding birth-place fixed effects in column (6) increases the YSM coefficient substantially.

However, the assimilation effects in this recent period appear entirely driven by outliers in the YSM variable. Excluding those who migrated more than fifteen years prior to the census record substantially affects the point-estimate, and it flips sign and becomes negative (though insignificant).[4] Because of our focus on assimilation while the child is ostensibly still in the house, we generally retain this restriction throughout the rest of the chapter, though we return later to why this restriction might be so consequential in the later years.

As in the earlier period, including only men in column (9) does not change the results appreciably.

In the final column of table 3.2 we examine English skills. While immi-grant household heads from this era appear to gain English skills each year in the United States, they do so at roughly one-third the rate of their coun-terparts from 1900 to 1930.

In summary, assimilation (either in earnings score relative to natives or in terms of English skills) for the earlier period is substantial and robust. In the later period, it is far more sensitive to specification and disappears when we restrict the sample to those who are relatively recently arrived. Our results on limited assimilation in the current period is consistent with Borjas (2013).

3.4.2   Controlling for Year-of-Arrival Effects

As noted by Borjas (2002) and others, years since migration can conflate two effects—time in the United States as well as differences in "cohort qual-ity" related to year of arrival. For example, a positive coefficient on years since migration could signify either the assimilation effects of time in the United States or higher quality of earlier cohorts (or, of course, some mix of both).

In table 3.3, we repeat the analysis in table 3.2 but add fixed effects for year of arrival. Natives are required to identify the census year effects and as such we only examine the earning score outcome, not English proficiency. Comparing the coefficients in the first four columns of tables 3.2 and 3.3 suggest that much of the positive effect attributed to years since migration may be coming from declining cohort quality. While the effect is still positive in the early period, it is reduced by about half, depending on the specifica-tion. These results are consistent with Abramitzky et al. (2012)—they find that once cohort quality and selective return migration are accounted for, assimilation during the Great Migration appears minimal.

---

4. This result is robust to choosing ten or twenty years instead of fifteen as the maximum value of YSM.

Table 3.3   Measures of assimilation (with year-of-arrival fixed effects)

	1900–1930				1970–2010			
	(1)	(2)	(3)	(4)	(5)	(6)	(7)	(8)
Years since migration	0.0846*	0.0712*	0.154***	0.168***	-0.0288**	0.183*	-0.156*	-0.169*
	[0.0221]	[0.0218]	[0.0879]	[0.0895]	[0.0138]	[0.0139]	[0.0478]	[0.0538]
Age	1.278*	0.795*	0.854*	0.832*	2.880*	2.599*	2.541*	2.379*
	[0.119]	[0.117]	[0.124]	[0.125]	[0.0854]	[0.0843]	[0.0880]	[0.0934]
Age squared	-0.0190*	-0.0121*	-0.0127*	-0.0124*	-0.0366*	-0.0334*	-0.0322*	-0.0306*
	[0.00151]	[0.00147]	[0.00156]	[0.00158]	[0.00114]	[0.00112]	[0.00118]	[0.00123]
Male	26.94*	23.82*	23.89*		17.39*	17.18*	17.64*	
	[0.317]	[0.311]	[0.327]		[0.0762]	[0.0754]	[0.0777]	
Urban	26.77*	23.04*	23.67*	24.55*	-1.783*	-1.937*	-1.755*	-1.495*
	[0.130]	[0.134]	[0.145]	[0.148]	[0.100]	[0.0999]	[0.105]	[0.130]
Mean, dept. var.	44.59	44.59	43.69	44.65	54.25	54.25	54.71	59.25
Includes natives?	Yes	Yes	Yes	Yes	Yes	Yes	Yes	Yes
Yrs. since migration	All	All	Under 25	Under 25	All	All	Under 25	Under 25
Gender	Both	Both	Both	Men	Both	Both	Both	Men
Observations	214,590	214,590	189,899	182,484	675,231	675,231	638,916	481,447

Notes: All immigrant observations are household heads between the ages of thirty and sixty with at least one child in the household, who are under age thirty-six or whose spouse is under age thirty-six, who immigrated from non-English-speaking countries, and who immigrated as adults. Natives in the sample meet all these conditions as well, outside those related to immigration. "Occ. score" is the occupational earnings score using the 1950 income distribution. "Speaks Eng." is an indicator variable for speaking English at any level (in earlier years, there is only a yes/no answer allowed for this question, whereas in later years respondents are asked how well they speak). "Years since migration" is coded as zero for nonimmigrants. All regressions include fixed effects for census year. "Urban" is an indicator for living in a city large enough to be recorded in the census.

***Significant at the 1 percent level.

**Significant at the 5 percent level.

*Significant at the 10 percent level.

We find similar evidence of declining cohort quality in the recent period. With year-of-arrival fixed effects, the coefficient on years since migration is close to zero or negative. Interpreted literally, the negative years since migration coefficients in columns (5), (7), and (8) of table 3.3 suggest that, as their time in the United States increases, these immigrants are not assimilating but are instead moving farther away from the native born. This finding likely results from our selection criteria: all of the immigrants in our sample arrived after age eighteen, so they are for the most part at ages when they arrive that are consistent with having received most, if not all, of their education prior to arrival. With human capital that is poorly matched to that in demand in the United States at arrival, they are running farther and farther behind natives as time in the United States increases, as the skills of the latter are more appropriate to the US labor market. Mora and Dávila (1998) find that years since migration has a similarly negative effect when they focus exclusively on immigrants who received all of their education abroad.

In summary, once cohort quality is controlled for, we find very slower assimilation in the earlier period and little if any assimilation in the current period. Note that because we cannot control for selective return migration, these results likely overstate the progress that immigrants make relative to similar natives.

3.5   The Role of Children in the Assimilation of Their Parents

3.5.1   Basic Results

Tables 3.4 and 3.5 explore how assimilation varies with whether the householder had started his family before immigrating. Table 3.4 is the analogue of table 3.2 in that it does not include cohort fixed effects and since it compares groups of immigrants to each other, we no longer use natives as a comparison group. Table 3.5 uses natives as a control in order to identify cohort effects (and thus drops regressions with speaking English as the outcome). The main difference between these tables and the ones in the previous section is that they now include controls for family composition as well as interacts those family composition controls with the *YSM* variable to examine how family composition covaries with assimilation.

Like the earlier tables, the first half of the columns in tables 3.4 and 3.5 focuses on the Great Migration period. Column (1) of table 3.4 suggests that, with respect to occupational score, immigrant parents who arrived with a child experienced similar assimilation patterns to immigrant parents who began their families in the United States. The main effect of arriving with a child is negative and marginally significant and the effect on the assimilation rate (the *Arrive with a Child* x *YSM* interaction term) is positive but insignificant. Assimilation with respect to English is potentially more affected—the main effect of arriving with a child is significantly negative but assimilation

Table 3.4   Relationship between assimilation and family composition

	1900–1930				1970–2010			
	(1) Score	(2) Speaks	(3) Score	(4) Speaks	(5) Score	(6) Speaks	(7) Score	(8) Speaks
Eldest child immigrated same year as HH	-2.203*** [1.191]	-0.0970* [0.0209]			-0.757 [0.539]	-0.0297* [0.00592]		
Eldest child of HH is an immigrant			-2.043*** [1.078]	-0.124* [0.0189]			-1.221** [0.553]	-0.0544* [0.00605]
Eldest child in household arrived same year x YSM	0.0719 [0.143]	0.00765* [0.00250]			-0.0985 [0.0706]	0.00275* [0.000764]		
Eldest also an immigrant x YSM			0.131 [0.115]	0.0103* [0.00202]			-0.198* [0.0632]	0.00368* [0.000683]
Years since migration	0.161** [0.0671]	0.0208* [0.00118]	0.132*** [0.0783]	0.0176* [0.00137]	0.0510 [0.0427]	0.00555* [0.000455]	0.0625 [0.0483]	0.00390* [0.000519]
Mean, dept. var.	48.66	0.761	48.66	0.761	46.16	0.925	46.16	0.925
Obs.	14326	14293	14326	14293	39142	36153	39142	36153

Notes: All observations are household heads between the ages of thirty and sixty with at least one child in the household, who are under age thirty-six or whose spouse is under age thirty-six, who immigrated from non-English-speaking countries, and who immigrated as adults and no more than fifteen years before the census record. All regressions include birthplace fixed effects. "Occ. score" is the occupational earnings score using the 1950 income distribution. "Speaks Eng." is an indicator variable for speaking English at any level (in earlier years, there is only a yes/no answer allowed for this question, whereas in later years respondents are asked how well they speak). All controls included in table 3.3 are included but not reported.

***Significant at the 1 percent level.

**Significant at the 5 percent level.

*Significant at the 10 percent level.

Table 3.5   Relationship between assimilation and family composition (adding natives and year-of-arrival fixed effects)

	1900–1930		1970–2010	
	(1)	(2)	(3)	(4)
Eldest child immigrated same year as HH	−1.860 [1.286]		−0.0746 [0.496]	
Eldest child of HH is an immigrant		−1.424 [1.045]		−0.464 [0.464]
Eldest child in household arrived same year x *YSM*	0.0694 [0.138]		−0.133** [0.0583]	
Eldest also an immigrant x *YSM*		0.0444 [0.0924]		−0.263* [0.0433]
Years since migration	0.0991** [0.0479]	0.0828 [0.0545]	−0.00793 [0.0310]	−0.00445 [0.0337]
Mean, dept. var.	44.14	44.14	54.44	54.44
Obs.	201,388	201,388	653,291	653,291

Notes: All immigrant observations are household heads between the ages of thirty and sixty with at least one child in the household, who are under age thirty-six or whose spouse is under age thirty-six, who immigrated from non-English-speaking countries within fifteen years of the census record, and who immigrated as adults. Natives in the sample meet all these conditions as well, outside those related to immigration. "Occ. score" is the occupational earnings score using the 1950 income distribution. "Speaks Eng." is an indicator variable for speaking English at any level (in earlier years, there is only a yes/no answer allowed for this question, whereas in later years respondents are asked how well they speak). "Years since migration" is coded as zero for nonimmigrants. All regressions include fixed effects for census year and birthplace fixed effects. "Urban" is an indicator for living in a city large enough to be recorded in the census. All controls included in table 3.3 are included but not reported.
***Significant at the 1 percent level.
**Significant at the 5 percent level.
*Significant at the 10 percent level.

is significantly faster. This effect could be consistent with the parent at first relying on his child to learn the language and broker for the family, but then later having the child teach the language to him. (Similarly, Baker and Benjamin [1997] argue that husbands rely on their wives to take paying jobs while the husbands invest in human capital). Similar patterns arise in columns (3) and (4) where instead of comparing parents who immigrated with their children to other parents, we compare parents whose children are also immigrants (but perhaps came to the United States later) to other parents.

As in tables 3.2 and 3.3, the patterns are quite different in the more recent period. Most notably, the interactions with years since migration are either negative or they are positive but substantially smaller in magnitude than in the earlier period. In column (5), while parents who arrive with children start out with an advantage when occupational score is the outcome, they assimilate at slower rates than other parents. In fact, while other parents make some progress (the coefficient on *YSM* is positive), parents with children regress. In column (6), while parents who arrive with children learn English slightly faster, the advantage is substantially smaller than in the 1900–1930 period. The same patterns emerge in the final two columns where, as in columns (3) and (4), we compare parents whose children are also immigrants (but perhaps came to the United States later) to other parents.

Table 3.5 repeats the analysis for occupational score, but includes natives and cohort-arrival fixed effects. The results are very similar—the presence of immigrant children retards assimilation much more in the recent period than during the Great Migration.

3.5.2   Can We Separate Treatment and Selection Effects?

An important question is whether the presence of children has a true treatment effect on their parents' assimilation, or whether parents arriving with children are differentially selected. We make an imperfect attempt to separate these two stories by using variation in the age of children at arrival.

The learning/leaning mechanism requires children to fall in a certain age range—too young, and they would be unable to perform any meaningful household functions involving translation; too old, and they would have no advantage over their parents in terms of learning the language. Newport (2002) reviews the research on the so-called "critical period"—after infancy but before puberty—when humans are best positioned to learn a second language. Bleakley and Chin (2004) use this idea to construct an instrument for language skills based on age at arrival and estimate a large wage premium for English language skills.

We thus make the rather arbitrary assumption that parents whose eldest child is between the ages of six and twelve at arrival have the greatest scope to either "lean" or "learn," though our results are not sensitive to changing the cutoffs by one year in either direction. Note that we choose a maximum age that is slightly above most "critical period" thresholds based on the idea that there would often be younger children who fall in the critical-period threshold if the eldest child is twelve. As such, our regression sample is now limited to those migrants who arrived with a child and the variable of interest is a dummy for arriving with an eldest child between six and twelve interacted with *YSM*. Our implicit assumption is that while arriving with children may be driven by differences in selection, their exact age has at least some random component.

Table 3.6 shows striking differences between the two time periods. In the Great Migration period, arriving with an eldest child in this specified age range promotes assimilation with respect to both the earnings score and English language skills, though only the language skills are statistically significant. Immigrants arriving with an eldest child in this age range gain English skills 49 percent more quickly than do immigrants arriving with an eldest child outside this range.

By contrast, arriving with an eldest child in this age range is associated with slower assimilation in the recent period. Again, the results on earnings score are not significant, but those arriving with an eldest child between ages

Table 3.6   Relationship between assimilation and immigrant children's ages

	(1) Score	(2) Speaks	(3) Score	(4) Speaks
Arrive with eldest child age 6–12 x *YSM*	0.124	0.0115**	−0.178	−0.00441*
	[0.298]	[0.00561]	[0.128]	[0.00154]
Years since migration	0.191	0.0234*	−0.0899	0.0127*
	[0.165]	[0.00313]	[0.0800]	[0.000958]
Observations	2300	2398	10353	10399

Notes: All observations are household heads between the ages of thirty and sixty with at least one child in the household, who are under age thirty-six or whose spouse is under age thirty-six, who immigrated from non-English-speaking countries the same year as their eldest recorded child, and who immigrated as adults and no more than fifteen years before the census record. All regressions include birthplace fixed effects. "Occ. score" is the occupational earnings score using the 1950 income distribution. "Speaks Eng." is an indicator variable for speaking English at any level (in earlier years, there is only a yes/no answer allowed for this question, whereas in later years respondents are asked how well they speak). All controls included in table 3.3 as well as a dummy for arriving with an eldest child between six and twelve years of age are included but not reported.

***Significant at the 1 percent level.
**Significant at the 5 percent level.
*Significant at the 10 percent level.

six and twelve acquire English 34 percent more slowly than adults arriving with an eldest child outside this age range.

3.5.3   Robustness Checks and Additional Specifications

One of the most significant differences between migrants today and in the earlier period is growth in immigration from Mexico. Fully one-quarter of our immigrant sample in the recent period are from Mexico, whereas that share was less than three percent during the Great Migration.

Table 3.7 replicates table 3.3 but excludes Mexicans (in both periods). The coefficients from the early period barely move, consistent with minimal Mexican migration during the period. More importantly, the coefficients in the recent period are also largely unaffected. Even after Mexicans are excluded, assimilation appears slower in the recent years (in every specification, the main effect of *YSM* is larger during the Great Migration) and the effect of children on assimilation is negative, or is positive, but smaller than that of the earlier period.

We experimented with additional specifications that we do not report but are available upon request. Family-composition effects might change as a function of the gender composition of children.[5] As such, the propensity

5. Goldin (1979) investigates the determinants of child labor in 1800s Philadelphia. She finds that immigrant and nonimmigrant parents in the 1800s were very similar with respect to sending their sons to work, but immigrant households were much more likely than their native counterparts to send their daughters to work as well (though these daughters were still less likely to work than their brothers).

Table 3.7   Relationship between assimilation and family composition (excluding Mexicans)

	1900–1930				1970–2010			
	(1) Score	(2) Speaks	(3) Score	(4) Speaks	(5) Score	(6) Speaks	(7) Score	(8) Speaks
Eldest child immigrated same year as HH	-2.578** [1.305]	-0.121* [0.0226]			-0.733 [0.640]	-0.0214* [0.00488]		
Eldest child of HH is an immigrant			-2.159*** [1.138]	-0.136* [0.0197]			-1.081 [0.665]	-0.0360* [0.00506]
Eldest child in household arrived same year x YSM	0.152 [0.157]	0.0117* [0.00271]			-0.161*** [0.0886]	0.00270* [0.000666]		
Eldest also an immigrant x YSM			0.146 [0.121]	0.0122* [0.00210]			-0.258* [0.0794]	0.00300* [0.000595]
Years since migration	0.222* [0.0696]	0.0222* [0.00120]	0.194** [0.0809]	0.0189* [0.00140]	C.0525 [C.0535]	0.00384* [0.000397]	0.0699 [0.0599]	0.00273* [0.000447]
Mean, dept. var.	49.69	0.786	49.69	0.786	51.69	0.963	51.69	0.963
Obs.	13,522	13,496	13,522	13,496	28,051	25,487	28,051	25,487

Notes: All observations are household heads between the ages of thirty and sixty with at least one child in the household, who are under age thirty-six or whose spouse is under age thirty-six, who immigrated from non-English-speaking countries *excluding Mexico*, and who immigrated as adults and no more than fifteen years before the census record. All regressions include birthplace fixed effects. "Occ. score" is the occupational earnings score using the 1950 income distribution. "Speaks Eng." is an indicator variable for speaking English at any level (in earlier years, there is only a yes/no answer allowed for this question, whereas in later years respondents are asked how well they speak). All controls included in table 3.3 are included but not reported.

***Significant at the 1 percent level.

**Significant at the 5 percent level.

*Significant at the 10 percent level.

of parents to learn or lean might depend in interesting ways on the gender composition of their children, and these differences may have changed over time with changing gender roles and expectations of daughters (see Goldin 2006). Somewhat surprisingly, there is no differential effect of the gender of the eldest child. In neither the Great Migration nor the recent period are parents more or less likely to lean or learn if they have a son as opposed to a daughter.

Neither are their differential effects based on the sex of the parent. Whereas women were very unlikely to be household heads in the Great Migration, there are enough female householders in the recent period to meaningfully compare men and women. We find no significant differences in how children affect assimilation measures for mothers versus fathers.

In summary, we draw three conclusions from this and the previous two sections. First, immigrant parents are substantially more likely to immigrate with their children today than they were during the Great Migration. Second, the correlation between years in the United States and assimilation outcomes such as occupational score and English skills was substantially more positive in the earlier period. In fact, for some samples and specifications, it appears that time in the United States is correlated with worse outcomes in the more recent period. Finally, the leaning tendency of immigrant parents appears to dominate today, whereas the learning tendency appears to have dominated earlier. In short, immigrants today are more likely to arrive with children and those children appear to retard the assimilation process more today than they did in 1900–1930.

It is important to emphasize that these relationships are correlations and not necessarily causal. We try to separate the selection effect of arriving with children and the treatment effect by using variation in the age of children, but as we discuss in the next section, important caveats to any causal interpretation remain.

3.6   Discussion

Why does assimilation among immigrant parents appear slower in the more recent period? We presented some suggestive evidence that children may retard the assimilation process, but here we emphasize some alternative explanations and limitations to our analysis (though surely many other caveats exist).

First, figure 3.2 shows not only that the share of immigrant parents who arrive with children is much lower in the earlier period (a fact we have been emphasizing) but that, in both periods, *it declines over time*. In 1900, the share of our immigrant sample arriving with children is about 20 percent, but falls to 10 percent by 1930. Similarly, in 1970 the share is 35 percent, falling to about 20 percent in 2010. If immigrants who arrive with children are of higher quality (that is, the "selection effect" of children is positive even if the "treatment effect" is negative), then this pattern might explain the declining cohort quality we find in both periods.

Second, the presence of children at arrival likely affects the ability of the immigrant householder to return to his native country. As noted earlier, our results cannot control for selective return migration, which Abramitzky, Boustan, and Eriksson (2012) have shown to be empirically important. It seems plausible that adults who arrive on their own would be more able to return to their homelands if, say, they have trouble finding work in the United States, and thus the coefficient on years since migration is positively biased for this group because of selective return migration. If adults that arrive with their families are more or less "stuck" in the United States, then comparing them to this first group, as our regressions do, might bias us toward finding that children seem to "retard" the assimilation process. If differential selective migration due to children was larger in the more recent period—as one might expect it would be, given that it is easier to return to Mexico today than, say, Poland in 1910—then it could also explain the much more negative effect of children in the recent period.

These caveats notwithstanding, in sum our evidence points to the possibility that while children once promoted their parents' assimilation, they now impede it. Taking the point-estimates literally and using the difference between arriving with children of a "useful" age versus arriving with children of other ages as our causal estimate of arriving with children, arriving with a child slows language acquisition by 1.59 percentage points per year in the current period relative to the earlier period (–0.44 to 1.15 percentage points, from table 3.6). Parents are 11.7 percentage points more likely to immigrate with children in the current period (0.219–0.102, from table 3.1). As such, taking both the difference in the effect of arriving with children from today versus earlier and the increased tendency to arrive with children today than earlier, our effects suggest a 1.59*0.117 = 0.186 percentage points per year slowing of language acquisition in the current period relative to the earlier one. From table 3.2, we see that the difference is 2.26 percentage points (0.234–0.0076), so our effects explain about 8.2 percent of the difference in language acquisition rates among immigrant parents between the two periods.

Section 3.3 suggested circumstances when parents might lean versus learn. One such circumstance is when the consumption value of the mother language is quite high—for example, if parents can have a high quality of life without learning English. It is interesting to consider how this factor may have changed over the two time periods.

One difference we note between the two periods is that immigration is much more concentrated with respect to country of origin or mother language than before. As noted, over one-fourth of our recent sample hails from Mexico, and an additional 13 percent from other parts of Latin America. The previous period has nowhere close the level of language concentration

(German being the largest group and less than half the concentration as we see today with Spanish) or country-of-origin concentration (the Herfindahl index, with respect to origin country in the current period, is larger by a factor of nine than that in the earlier period). It is also possible that, even for smaller language groups, technology facilitates consumption activities in the mother tongue (one can Skype with relatives back home, read online newspapers from the home country, etc.) compared to the options available during the Great Migration.

The model also suggests that the leaning versus learning tendency will depend on how much parents value labor market returns. Characterizations of the early immigration period tend to emphasize economic incentives as the main motivation for migration, and thus these migrants may have found leaning on their children and thus sacrificing their wage growth relatively unattractive. In contrast, policy changes suggest that the current period may be characterized more by noneconomic migration motives, such as family reunification and political asylum. This more recent period may have selected for migrants who are less motivated by labor market opportunities (and thus more likely to lean).

Finally, the model also predicts that parents are less likely to learn and more likely to lean when children's ability to teach them English declines. Indeed, there are reasons to believe that children's ability to teach their parents English may have diminished in the current period, making parents less likely to learn. We have documented that children in immigrant families in the current period are more likely to have been born in the origin country and arrive with their parents—thus they might tend to regard English as their second language, relative to children of immigrant parents who are themselves US-born. Children of the current generation of migrants may themselves have more challenges assimilating, and thus may be less useful as tutors to their parents.

3.7   Conclusion

In this chapter, we present evidence of the vastly different family composition at arrival between immigrant householders of the Great Migration and those today. To our knowledge, these differences have not been reported or analyzed by past research. We also document that assimilation among immigrant parents appears slower today than in 1900–1930, and that the presence of children at arrival appears to retard this process more today than it did then. In fact, children appear to have promoted their parents' assimilation in the early period but appear to impede it today. Put differently, parents used to learn from their children but not appear more inclined to lean on them.

We see these initial results as suggesting several areas for future work and we highlight two such areas below. First, as noted earlier, we found that limiting the sample to relatively recent arrivals (those who immigrated no more than fifteen years before their census record) had a large effect on measures of assimilation in the recent period. We speculate that two factors may explain this result. First, many of those who arrived more than fifteen years before their census record would have immigrated before 1965, when US immigration policy was based more on family connections. Even controlling for country of origin, that policy may have selected for individuals who could assimilate more quickly. Second, it might be the case that the tendency to lean on children in the later period means that much of parents' assimilation process is delayed until children leave the house, and thus, limiting the sample to adults who have recently arrived could have a large effect on the coefficient estimates.

Second, because educational data in the early years of the census is limited, it is difficult to investigate whether immigrants that arrive with children are positively or negatively selected relative to immigrants arriving without children during the Great Migration. Using data from the home countries, as in Abramitzky, Boustan, and Eriksson 2012, might help to document selection patterns with respect to family composition during this earlier period.

References

Abramitzky, R., L. P. Boustan, and K. Eriksson. 2012. "Europe's Tired, Poor, Huddled Masses: Self-Selection and Economic Outcomes in the Age of Mass Migration." *American Economic Review* 102 (5): 1832–56.

Baker, M., and D. Benjamin. 1997. "The Role of the Family in Immigrants' Labor-Market Activity: An Evaluation of Alternative Explanations." *American Economic Review* 87 (4): 705–27.

Barde, R., S. B. Carter, and R. Sutch. 2006. "International Migration." In *Historical Statistics of the United States, Earliest Times to the Present*, millennial ed., edited by S. B. Carter, S. S. Gartner, M. R. Haines, A. L. Olmstead, R. Sutch, and G. Wright. Cambridge: Cambridge University Press.

Becker, G. S. 1962. "Investment in Human Capital: A Theoretical Analysis." *Journal of Political Economy* 70 (5): 9–49.

Berman, E., K. Lang, and E. Siniver. 2003. "Language-Skill Complementarity: Returns to Immigrant Language Acquisition." *Labour Economics* 10 (3): 265–90.

Blau, F. D., L. M. Kahn, J. Y. Moriarty, and A. P. Souza. 2003. "The Role of the Family in Immigrants' Labor-Market Activity: An Evaluation of Alternative Explanations: Comment." *American Economic Review* 93 (1): 429–47.

Bleakley, H., and A. Chin. 2004. "Language Skills and Earnings: Evidence from Childhood Immigrants." *Review of Economics and Statistics* 86 (2): 481–96.

Borjas, G. J. 1995. "Ethnicity, Neighborhoods, and Human-Capital Externalities." *American Economic Review* 85 (3): 365–90.

———. 2002. "Self-Selection and the Earnings of Immigrants." *International Library of Critical Writings in Economics* 151:332–54.

———. 2013. "The Slowdown in the Economic Assimilation of Immigrants: Aging and Cohort Effects Revisited Again." NBER Working Paper no. 19116. Cambridge, MA.

Edin, P.-A., P. Fredriksson, and O. Åslund. 2003. "Ethnic Enclaves and the Economic Success of Immigrants–Evidence from a Natural Experiment." *Quarterly Journal of Economics* 118 (1): 329–57.

Ferrer, A., D. A. Green, and W. C. Riddell. 2006. "The Effect of Literacy on Immigrant Earnings." *Journal of Human Resources* 41 (2): 380–410.

Friedberg, R. M. 2000. "You Can't Take It with You? Immigrant Assimilation and the Portability of Human Capital." *Journal of Labor Economics* 18 (2): 221–51.

Goldin, C. 1979. "Household and Market Production of Families in a Late Nineteenth Century American City." *Explorations in Economic History* 16 (2): 111–31.

———. 1994. "The Political Economy of Immigration Restriction in the United States, 1890 to 1921. In *The Regulated Economy: A Historical Approach to Political Economy*, edited by Claudia Goldin and Gary D. Libecap, 223–58. Chicago: University of Chicago Press.

———. 2006. "The Quiet Revolution That Transformed Women's Employment, Education, and Family." NBER Working Paper no. 11953, Cambridge, MA.

Kuziemko, I. Forthcoming. "Human Capital Spillovers in Families: Do Immigrants Learn from or 'Lean on' Their Children?" *Journal of Labor Economics*.

Lazear, E. P. 1999. "Culture and Language." *Journal of Political Economy* 107 (S6): S95–S126.

Mora, M. T., and A. Dávila. 1998. "Gender, Earnings, and the English Skill Acquisition of Hispanic Workers in the United States." *Economic Inquiry* 36 (4): 631–44.

Newport, E. 2002. "Critical Periods in Language Development." In *Encyclopedia of Cognitive Science*, edited by L. Nadel. New York: Macmillan.

Perlmann, J., and R. Waldinger. 1997. "Second Generation Decline? Children of Immigrants, Past and Present–A Reconsideration." *International Migration Review* 31 (4): 893–922.

Portes, A., and R. G. Rumbaut. 2001. *Legacies: The Story of the Immigrant Second Generation*. Berkeley, CA: University of California Press.

Schultz, T. 1961. "Investment in Human Capital." *American Economic Review* 51 (1): 1–17.

Singleton, D. 2001. "Age and Second Language Acquisition." *Annual Review of Applied Linguistics* 21:77–89.

Zhou, M. 1997. "Segmented Assimilation: Issues, Controversies, and Recent Research on the New Second Generation." *International Migration Review* 31 (4): 975–1008.

4

Health, Education, and Income in the United States, 1820–2000

Hoyt Bleakley, Dora Costa, and Adriana Lleras-Muney

4.1 Introduction

The United States experienced large increases in educational attainment starting in the late nineteenth century and well into the twentieth century. Years of schooling among those in the labor force rose by about six years, from about 7.5 years in 1915 to 13.5 years in 2005 (Goldin and Katz 2008). Incomes also rose quite substantially, with real gross domestic product (GDP) per capita growing an average of 2.23 percent per year in the same period. A large amount of research has been devoted to understanding the factors that led to the rise in education, whether these increases in education led to the higher incomes we observe, or whether other factors led to the rapid increases in both (Card 2001).

Did improvements in health throughout the same period contribute to the observed changes in educational attainment and incomes? Health has improved dramatically: life expectancy at birth rose by about thirty years in the twentieth century—an unprecedented increase. Mortality decreases were mostly concentrated among children before 1950. These declines were mostly due to the eradication of infectious and parasitic diseases, which reduced morbidity in the population (Bleakley 2010a). However there were also substantial improvements in the health and mortality of the elderly,

Hoyt Bleakley is associate professor of economics at the University of Michigan and a research associate of the National Bureau of Economic Research. Dora Costa is professor of economics at the University of California, Los Angeles, and a research associate and director of the Cohort Studies Working Group at the National Bureau of Economic Research. Adriana Lleras-Muney is professor of economics at the University of California, Los Angeles, and a research associate of the National Bureau of Economic Research.

For acknowledgments, sources of research support, and disclosure of the authors' material financial relationships, if any, please see http://www.nber.org/chapters/c12900.ack.

particularly after 1950 (Cutler, Deaton, and Lleras-Muney 2006). Fogel estimates that improvements in health account for at least 20 percent and up to 30 percent of British economic growth between 1800 and 2000 (Fogel 1994; Floud et al. 2011, 127). In contrast, Easterlin (1996) is skeptical of the link between health and economic growth.

The main difficulty in establishing the effects of health improvements on education and productivity is to find variation in health that is not driven by the same factors that determine education and income. Additionally, exploring the long-term relationships between these factors requires comparable measures of health, income, and education and these are difficult to obtain. Using many individual data sets covering cohorts born between 1810 and 1990, we are the first to examine how the relationships between health, income, and education have changed over time in the United States. As our health measure, we use adult height, which has the advantage of being determined by early childhood, prior to obtaining schooling and entering the labor market.

Height is a good proxy for general health conditions in childhood. Height is a measure of *net* nutritional status during the growing years, including the fetal period. Differences in height across individuals are determined by environmental factors, such as the availability of food and the presence of disease, as well as by genetics (Steckel 1995). Most of the relative differences in height appear to be determined by age three: for example, the correlation between height at age three and height in adulthood is as large as 0.7 or larger (Case and Paxson 2008). Stunting starts in utero or in early childhood (before age three) and usually persists to give rise to a small adult. Based on extensive studies in Guatemala, Martorell, Rivera, and Kaplowitz (1990, 89) concluded that stunting is "a condition resulting from events in early childhood and which, once present, remains for life."[1]

Although height is a rough measure of health, short stature is associated with worse health later in life. Waaler (1984), using a sample of Norwegian males age forty to forty-nine in 1963–1979, was the first to show that mortality rises at a diminishing rate when height increases until height reaches 187cm. After that point, mortality rates begin to rise as height increases. Costa (1993) and Floud et al. (2011) report a similar functional relation between height and subsequent mortality among white American males

---

1. The extent to which catch-up is possible is not known, but it appears that full catch-up is not possible after age three. Rat pups and piglets that were malnourished for a period shortly after birth never caught up, suggesting that stunting in humans may be permanent (Widdowson and McCance 1960). Although there is usually definite catch-up growth in studies of adoptees, emigrants, or children treated for diseases, it is often not to the NCHS standards (Proos, Hofvander, and Tuvemo 1991). There may be a limitation imposed on an individual's maximum height by genetic imprinting in very early development. Full catch-up appears to take place at young ages (Barham, Macours, and Maluccio 2013) but is followed by an advanced puberty and early cessation of growth (Proos, Hofvander, and Tuvemo 1991).

in 1986–1992 and among Union Army veterans.[2] Height appears to be inversely related to heart and respiratory diseases and positively related to the hormonal cancers (Barker 1992).

Height is also strongly associated with wages and productivity in a variety of settings. Surveying the evidence from developing countries, Schultz (2002) concludes that an additional centimeter of adult male height is significantly associated with a higher wage of 1.5 percent in Ghana and 1.4 percent in Brazil. Historical data also shows that height was associated with productivity in now-developed countries. Data from the antebellum American South shows that height and weight were positively associated with slave value, suggesting that better-fed, healthier slaves were more productive (Margo and Steckel 1982). In the contemporary United States, taller individuals also earn higher wages (Case and Paxson 2008), although the "height premium" is higher in developing countries than in the United States (where one more centimeter raises wages by 0.45 percent). However, this evidence does not purely reflect the better physical health of taller individuals—improved conditions in childhood will often result in better health and cognitive abilities both, even in developed countries (Case and Paxson 2008; Schick and Steckel 2010; Barham, Macours, and Maluccio 2013).[3] For example, early life health interventions providing extra medical care in both Chile and Norway, two countries at very different stages of development, led to higher academic achievement in school (Bharadwaj, Løken, and Neilson 2013).

One of the implicit assumptions in the literature has been that in the Unites States' past, returns to height were as high as they are in developing countries today, thus suggesting that improvements in health account for a large fraction of productivity gains (e.g., Floud et al. 2011, 21–23; Costa and Steckel 1997). But improvements in nutritional status or health may not even lead to increases in education, which is widely viewed as a key determinant of economic growth in general and of twentieth-century US economic growth in particular (Goldin and Katz 2008; Acemoglu and Autor 2012). In the nineteenth-century economy where, prior to widespread mechanization, brawn relative to brain must have been of greater relative value, improvements in child health could even have raised the opportunity

2. A caveat is that the relationship between height and subsequent mortality only shows up in large samples and is sensitive to the choice of follow-up period. When we tried to reproduce Costa's (1993) results using a larger sample of Union Army recruits, we obtained suggestive evidence of a J-shaped relationship between height and mortality, but the height that minimized mortality was about ten centimeters shorter than in Waaler's (1984) Norwegian sample and the odds of death was greater at taller than at shorter heights.

3. An alternative explanation for the returns to height is that height is correlated with personal traits conducive to worker productivity, such as emotional skills and extraversion. For example, if the tall receive more investments and praise they become more optimistic and also have better communication skills (e.g., Persico, Postlewaite, and Silverman 2004; Mobius and Rosenblat 2006).

cost of schooling, particularly for adolescents, thus reducing the optimal time spent in school.

Formal education was often not a job requirement in the nineteenth century. Abraham Lincoln had roughly one year of formal education, taught by itinerant school teachers. As we later show, in climbing the occupational job ladder, the returns to formal education in the mid-nineteenth century were roughly 1 percent, whereas in the twentieth century they were up to 13 percent.[4] In this economy improvements in health may have increased the marginal cost of schooling. In contrast, in the twentieth century, when wage returns to education are high, if healthier students have a large advantage in learning the advanced concepts taught at higher educational levels, the marginal benefit of schooling is rising at higher educational levels. Yamauchi (2008), Bleakley (2010b), and Pitt, Rosenzweig, and Hassan (2012) present empirical examples of the ambiguity in the effect of childhood health on schooling.

We obtain correlations between height and educational attainment over a century and a half that are consistent with a model of human capital formation in which physical labor was more important in the nineteenth century, thus raising the opportunity cost of schooling and depressing the height-education relationship relative to the twentieth century. We find that the nineteenth century was characterized by low investments in height and education, a small correlation between height and education, and positive but small returns for both height and education. The relationship between height and education was stronger in the twentieth century and stronger in the first part of the twentieth century than later on (when both investments in education and height stalled), but never as strong as in developing countries. The labor market and wealth returns to height and education also were higher in the twentieth compared to the nineteenth century. Our findings are consistent with an increasing importance of cognitive abilities acquired in early childhood.

4.2   Theoretical Framework: Brain or Brawn?

We interpret height as a proxy for early-life health endowments that manifest themselves both in increased physical capability (brawn) as well as in improved cognitive ability (brain). The nineteenth-century economy, in which physical labor was used to do a variety of things that today would be done by machine, was one of brawn. The twentieth century, the human capital century, was a brain economy.

We can think of the effect of health on income as coming through three distinct channels:

---

4. We are not implying that the returns to skill, more broadly defined, were only 1.2 percent. Apprenticeships are not included in formal years of education. Neither is being self-taught.

1. An unskilled worker is more productive if he is healthier.

2. Better health helps a student learn, thus he obtains more value from his inframarginal (i.e., would have attended anyway) time in school.

3. Better health might motivate a student to spend more time in school.

A simple decomposition illustrates these points.[5] Let $y(e)$ be the lifetime income (in present discounted value) that accrues to a worker who has e years of schooling. Suppose the optimal choice of education is $e*$ and define $y* = y(e*)$. We are interested in the question of how a worker's productivity increases as his health endowment h changes: that is, the derivative $dy*/dh$. This full derivative of $y*$ w.r.t. h can be decomposed as

$$\frac{dy*}{dh} = \frac{\partial y}{\partial h}\bigg|_{e*} + \frac{de*}{dh}\frac{\partial y}{\partial e}\bigg|_{e*}.$$

The first term gives us the direct effect of health on income, holding education fixed. The second term values the reoptimized schooling choice at the marginal return to schooling. It is helpful to further decompose the direct effect of health on income into two components, which yields this expression for the full derivative:

$$\frac{dy*}{dh} = \frac{\partial y}{\partial h}\bigg|_{e=0} + \int_0^{e*} \frac{\partial^2 y}{\partial h\, \partial e}\, de + \frac{de*}{dh}\frac{\partial y}{\partial e}\bigg|_{e*}.$$

The first term (channel 1) is the effect of the health endowment on the productivity of an unskilled (unschooled, possibly illiterate if $e = 0$) worker. The complementarity between school and health is seen in both the second and third terms (channels 2 and 3, respectively), which measure the inframarginal and marginal effects, respectively, of health on income by way of schooling.

The first, "unskilled" channel arises disproportionately because of physical strength and stamina. This effect diminishes over time as machines replace humans for brute force and repetitive assembly. But even if there were cognitive returns to height in the nineteenth century, improved health could produce less education. We start with two plausible intuitions: (a) schooling is of less value when much of the labor is physical, and (b) a healthier child might be a better student, but is also a better unskilled worker, especially in an economy dominated by physical labor.

We explicitly model the effects of improved health on educational attainment. We augment the y function of lifetime income above to include both education and health (h) as arguments, and recall that it is a discounted sum of period-specific incomes, $\tilde{y}(e,h,t)$:

$$y(e,h) = \int_e^\infty \beta(t)\tilde{y}(e,h,t)\, dt - \hat{c}(e),$$

5. The theoretical presentation in this subsection borrows heavily from Bleakley (2010a, 292–94), who presents a simple version of the Ben-Porath model.

in which t is time, the $\beta(t)$ term reflects both discounting and wage growth that comes with age and/or economy-wide growth, and $\hat{c}$ are out-of-pocket costs of schooling.

To compute the optimal choice of education, we take the derivative of y with respect to e, which yields two groups of terms:

$$\frac{\partial y}{\partial e} = \underbrace{\int_e^\infty \beta(t)\frac{\partial \tilde{y}}{\partial e}\,dt}_{marginal\ benefits} - \underbrace{\left(\beta(e)\tilde{y} + \frac{d\hat{c}}{de}\right)}_{marginal\ costs}.$$

The marginal benefits (call them MB) are the appropriately discounted sum of gains in future earnings. The marginal costs (MC) are both direct and opportunity costs of schooling. The usual assumptions are that the marginal benefit of schooling declines with more time in school but that the marginal cost rises: $MC_e > 0$ and $MB_e < 0$, where subscripts denote partial derivatives. These assumptions turn the optimization problem into an "optimal stopping rule": stay in school as long as marginal benefits exceed marginal costs; when $MB = MC$, leave school and work. This is shown graphically in figure 4.1 (as the baseline model) and a dashed, vertical line denotes the optimal choice of time in school.

In this standard model, the effect of childhood health on years of schooling could be positive or negative. Taking full differentials of the condition for optimization ($MB = MC$), we derive the optimal response of schooling to health as

$$\frac{de^*}{dh} = -\left(\frac{MB_h - MC_h}{MB_e - MC_e}\right).$$

By assumption, the denominator is negative. If childhood health raises the marginal benefit of schooling, then $MB_h > 0$. Nevertheless, it might also be the case that $MC_h > 0$; that is, a healthier child is more productive (for reasons that we discuss below). Thus, the sign of the expression is ambiguous. We consider four cases here in our analysis of the health/education relationship. The associated MB and MC curves for each case are shown in figure 4.1. In each case, the baseline equilibrium is also shown in gray. The four cases are as follows:

CASE 1: *Healthier children get (relatively) stronger as they mature.* Height is associated with physical strength and stamina, which would have commanded a relatively higher wage premium in the era prior to mechanization. This raises the opportunity cost of school for healthy children, and especially when they are in adolescence and thus closer to physical maturity. This raises and rotates up the MC curve, depressing the optimal time in school.

CASE 2: *Healthier children learn more in school (parallel shift).* Learning more from the same time in school shifts up the MB curve. (In this and the remaining cases, $MB_h > 0$.) But yesterday's marginal benefits raise

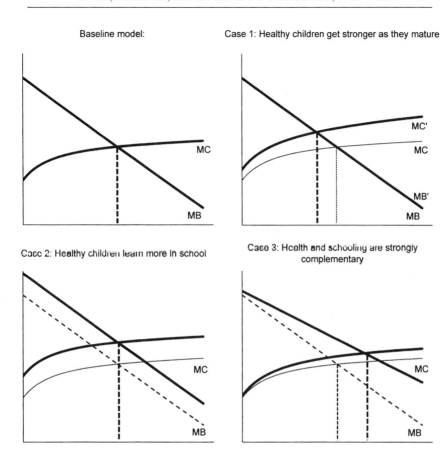

Fig. 4.1   **Health and the standard model of schooling**

Notes: This figure displays simulations of the Ben-Porath model of schooling choice under alternative assumptions about how childhood health affects the marginal benefits (*MB*) and marginal costs (*MC*) of time in school. The *x* axis is time in school (modeled as a time at which a child leaves school and starts working). The *y* axis measures present discounted value on a logarithmic scale. In Case 1, *MB* and *MB'* are identical. For further description of the model and cases, see section 4.2 of the chapter. An Excel spreadsheet containing these simulations is available from the authors upon request.

today's marginal costs.[6] Put another way, more education raises the worker's productivity and therefore raises the opportunity cost of getting even more education. If health raises the *MB* of schooling equally at all (infra-

6. One additional assumption, verified by Mincer and commonly used for this model, is that more education shifts up the $\bar{y}$ function in a manner that is essentially independent of *t*. In other words, more education raises period-specific productivity in roughly equal proportion across the working life. This imposes a good deal of structure on the model in that each point on the marginal-cost curve includes the (amortized) sum of earlier marginal benefits. The curves that we draw in figure 4.6 reflect this relationship. An Excel spreadsheet with supporting calculations is available from the authors upon request.

marginal) levels of schooling, then the MC curve shifts up in parallel, with little effect on the choice of time in school. Note that this is true even in an economy with no emphasis on physical labor, as long as health induces a parallel shift of the MB curve. In terms of the equations above, this neutral effect of health on the education choice obtains if $MB_{eh} = 0$. (This second derivative of MB is in reality a third derivative of the production function $\tilde{y}$. This is one more derivative beyond than the usual criterion for complements or substitutes because education is purchased with time rather than money, and education raises the value of time.)

CASE 3: *Health and school are strongly complementary.* Informed by the previous case, we see that the MB curve needs to shift up *more* at higher levels of schooling if optimal time in school is to increase: $MB_{eh} > 0$. This is to say that healthier children are not much better at learning basic school skills like literacy and numeracy, but do have an advantage at more advanced concepts.

CASE 4: *Health and school are less than strongly complementary.* For completeness, we consider this case as a counterpoint to cases 2 and 3. In this case, learning better basically equates to learning faster, allowing the child to get to the labor market earlier with the same amount of schooling human capital. This case is best understood with the example of child prodigies, where the cognitive endowment is sufficient to allow children to "blast through" school. Norbert Weiner (noted early-twentieth-century child prodigy and PhD in math at age seventeen) and Doogie Howser (noted 1980s-TV-fictional-character child prodigy and MD at age fourteen) could have obtained three doctoral degrees at an age before any of the coauthors of this chapter had obtained even one. But the opportunity cost of their time was apparently too high at the conclusion of their first doctorate. Bill Gates and Mark Zuckerberg, both Harvard dropouts who founded lucrative companies, might also be examples. For Case 4, $MB_{eh} < 0$. (We do not graph this case to save space.)

Whether Case 4 is mostly an intellectual curiosity (only holding in extreme cases) is debatable. But Cases 1–3 all seem pertinent to some aspects of the results from the nineteenth and twentieth centuries.

We hypothesize that in the nineteenth, relative to the twentieth century, the height/education gradient will be much weaker because of some combination of Case 1 and Case 2. The greater weight on physical labor in the nineteenth-century economy could have reduced or even flipped the relationship between height and education (Case 1). It may also be that the nature of the technology frontier was sufficiently different back then, such that one could acquire a high level of relative skill without having to delve into subjects that might be more cognitively taxing. This puts us closer to the realm of Case 2 in which the complementarity between health and education was not so strong.

We hypothesize that in the twentieth century the height/education gradient will be stronger than in the nineteenth century because the health endowment is strongly complementary with education (Case 3) in this period. Because the Mincerian returns to education were highest before World War II and in the last two decades of the twentieth century (Goldin and Margo 1992; Goldin and Katz 2000; Autor, Katz, and Kearney 2006), we also expect the height/education gradient to be lower for those cohorts in school in the several decades following World War II.

4.3   Data

We explore how health relates to education and income or wealth using many individual data sets spanning the 1860s to 2000. To obtain a picture of trends over the very long run in the United States, we make use of three data sets coming from army recruits prior to 1950 (the Union Army data, the Gould sample, and the World War II data) and combine them with data from the National Health and Nutrition Examination Surveys (1971 and later), the National Longitudinal Surveys (1966 and later), and the Health and Retirement Surveys (1992 and later). Together these data cover cohorts born between 1810 and 1990 and contain information on height, education, and productivity or income measures.

A challenge for this study is to construct measures of education that are comparable over time. Years of schooling (the standard measure used for education) are generally unavailable prior to the 1940 census in the United States. The World War II data allow us to look at years of schooling because it was collected of all enlisted men. The older Union Army samples do not contain comparable measures of education—therefore, we develop a measure to transform the information in these older data sets into units comparable to modern measures.

A second challenge is obtaining comparable productivity or income measures. Wages and income data are not available for the entire United States prior to the 1940 census. There are large numbers of sources describing wage rates and annual incomes for groups of people well before 1940, as well as sources allowing us to infer incomes. All the data we have contain measures of occupation, which we convert into a ranking reflecting the wages associated with each occupation in 1950.[7] We compare the occupation results to those we obtain using earnings in modern data sets. Finally, we also make use of the wealth measures available in various samples.

4.3.1   Union Army Sample

Our analysis will use two subsets of the roughly 39,000 white Union Army (UA) soldiers collected under the *Early Indicators* project.[8] At enlistment the

---

7. We use the occupational score created by IPUMS. Occupational score has been used by Sacerdote (2005) and Bleakley (2010b), and a modified version has been used by Angrist (2002).
8. (NIA AG10120, Robert Fogel, PI) and available for download at www.cpe.uchicago.edu.

white Union Army sample was representative not just of the Union Army but also of the northern population of military age in height, wealth, and literacy rates (Fogel 1993). Although men could purchase a substitute once the draft was imposed, more than 90 percent of soldiers were volunteers with the remainder evenly divided between substitutes and draftees. At older ages, these men experienced the same mortality rates seen in samples based on genealogies (Fogel 1993) and thus remain representative of their birth and nativity cohort.

The military service records provide information on height at enlistment. The full sample is linked to the 1850 and 1860 censuses (among others), which provides information on the school attendance of children and on the literacy of those age twenty-one and older, and a subset is linked to the 1870 census, which provides information on real estate and personal property wealth of $100 or more. We sum both real estate and personal property wealth and attribute zero wealth to those with less than $100 in wealth. The censuses also provide geographic, demographic, and socioeconomic information. In addition, we use occupational information in the 1870 census to construct an occupational income score based on the median income in that occupation in 1950.[9] The final sample covers the cohorts born between 1819 and 1850.

We construct several proxies for education using observations in the linked census manuscripts of the UA soldiers when they were of school age. Typically, the concept used for education is a stock variable: years of schooling. This presents a measurement difficulty in that the nineteenth-century censuses contain information on the flow of school attendance and not the stock of schooling.[10] School attendance is informative of time spent in school: if we observe a thirteen-year-old child in school in 1850, it should raise our expectation about the total years of schooling that he attains. Nevertheless, the variable only has information content during school ages; at other ages the attendance indicator is negligible and probably dominated by measurement error.

The definition of "school age" is complicated by the school-starting age having a large variance. We examined the fraction at school by age for the northern states in the 1850 and 1860 Integrated Public Use Microdata Series (IPUMS) data.[11] Rather than a spike at five or six years, the attendance rate slopes up gently and only peaks around ten years. We opted for a conservative approach and use the raw school-attendance variable only if that variable is observed sometime after the latest likely age at which someone would

9. The variable is constructed first by recoding the 1870 occupations into the 1950 coding scheme and then using the "occscore" classifications of income from ipums.org.
10. Using linked census samples, Long (2006) shows that childhood school attendance is predictive of higher occupational standing in the nineteenth-century United Kingdom. Bleakley and Ferrie (2012) show that this variable predicts both higher occupational score as well as higher wealth in nineteenth-century Georgia.
11. The IPUMS sample that we used was restricted to boys and excludes the three southern census regions.

have started school (say ten or eleven years) and before the age at which very few still attend school (say twenty-one years). So, we only include in the sample those who were linked to an antebellum census for which their ages were on the range [eleven, twenty-one] at the time of the census.

We impute years of schooling based both on attendance and on the age at which the boy was observed. Consider two examples. Observing a ten-year-old boy in school in these data imparts relatively little information about his eventual attainment in that he may have just started school and may drop out at the end of the year. In contrast, a twenty-year-old boy observed in school probably had above-average years of schooling. Following this logic, we construct the first measure of education, E_1, as follows,

$$E_1 = S_a * (a - a_0),$$

where a is age, a_0 is 10, E_1 is measure 1 for years of schooling, and S is the dummy variable for school attendance. This measure is an imputation of "years of school after turning 11" rather than simply total years in school. This measure is highly correlated with the dummy variable: the R^2 in a regression of measure 1 on the attendance dummy is 0.57 and the slope is 5.61.

We construct one additional imputation of years of schooling (measure 2) using three factors: school attendance, age when attendance status was observed, and contextual information on the rates of school attendance by age. One difficulty with the previous two measures is that they ignore the information in the overall distribution of attendance by age. To account for this information, we first treat flows of school attendance across the observed school ages as if they come from a single cohort. This is similar to work done by Margo (1986), who cumulates the flows of school attendance across ages within a particular year to compute years of schooling by cohort.[12]

We use the observed flows of schooling to adjust the imputed years of schooling for those observed out of school. Note that we assumed for measure 1 that the $S_a = 0$ boys got zero time in school, which is obviously extreme. If those in school at age a have been in school continuously since age a_0, it must be that

$$\underline{E}_a = q_a(a - a_0) + (1 - q_a)X_a,$$

where $\underline{E}_a$ is the (cumulated) stock of years in school at age a, q_a = the fraction in school at age a and X_a is the average years in school of those that dropped out before age a. We estimate q_a using aggregate data on school attendance by age in the antebellum IPUMS data.[13] Again maintaining the assumption of continuous schooling since a_0 if a boy is observed in school at age a, we

---

12. This method has been also used more recently by Hazan (2009) to construct school attendance by cohort over 150 years of cohorts in the United States and by Bleakley and Hong (2013) to examine changes in school quality by US region in the nineteenth century.

13. These flows of school attendance (the q measures) are computed by age, but not decomposed by area, except that the southern regions are excluded. The correlation between mea-

set measure 2 equal to measure 1 if $S_a = 1$. If $S_a = 0$, however, we set measure 2 equal to X_a. For example, for eleven-year-old boys, we impute an $E_2 = 1$ if they are in school and $E_2 = 0$ if not. For twenty-one-year-olds, however, we set $E_2 = 11$ if they are in school and $E_2 = 5.1$ if not, which keeps the average years of schooling consistent with what is implied by cumulating the flows of attendance over those ages.

4.3.2   The Gould Sample of Union Army Soldiers

In the early part of 1863 the United States Sanitary Commission began its inquiry into the physical and social condition of soldiers by sending sixteen examiners to specific locations, including Washington, where the armies of the Potomac and the West were concentrated. Examiners were instructed to measure as many men as possible. When necessary, additional examiners were sent to a location and then sometimes accompanied an army corps to obtain further measurements. Trained examiners armed with andrometers, spirometers, dynamometers, facial angle instruments, platform balances, calipers, and measuring tape measured men's body dimensions, weight, lifting strength, and vital capacity and obtained basic demographic and socioeconomic information. The data were first analyzed by Gould (1869) and the original forms were collected by Costa (2004) and include 15,866 white Union Army soldiers and sailors. Of these men, 11,710 are native born.

Compared to the Union Army as a whole, the location of the examiners increases the proportion of recruits who were born in the Middle Atlantic (especially New York City) relative to the Union Army. Therefore, the average recruit was shorter and the proportion of recruits who were farmers was smaller than in the Union Army. The average recruit in the Gould sample was also more likely to be native born.

We restrict ourselves to the native born and use the height and educational information in the Gould sample. After limiting the sample to men for whom education is available, we are left with 7,624 men born between 1793 and 1851. Education is described as none, limited common school, common school, college, or professional. We attribute 0.5 years to education to none, 4 years of education to limited common school, 8 years of education to common school, 10 years of education to high school, and 14 years of education to college or professional. There is quite a bit of variation in schooling. Among the native born of all ages (including those too young to have attended college), 5.3 percent had no years of education, 49.7 percent had limited common school, 39.2 percent had common school, 4.8 percent had high school, 0.6 percent had college, and 0.2 percent had a professional education.

---

sure 2 and a version constructed instead with region-specific schooling flows is 0.9719. We also constructed state-specific approximations, but concluded that the flow measures were too noisy. When the full-count files for the 1850 census becomes available, it may be possible to do state-specific imputations, but the existing IPUMS samples were too thin at the state x age level.

The limited information on apprenticeships in sample shows that years of education and the probability of ever having had an apprenticeship were positively correlated among the native born age twenty-one to forty-nine. Because we know apprenticeship status for only 154 native-born men age twenty-one to forty-nine (of which 104 were nonfarmers), we make no adjustment for skill beyond years of education.

4.3.3   World War II Enlisted Men

The World War II (WWII hereafter) data contain 9.2 million observations of individuals enlisted in the army between 1938 and 1946. The records contain the information reported at the time of enlistment, including measured height, educational attainment, and occupation prior to enlistment. A total of about sixteen million men served in all branches of the military, and a total of eleven million served in the army. About 60 percent were drafted and 40 percent volunteered. The records in the WWII data contain about 85 percent of those who served in the army (15 percent of the original records are unreadable). Thus, the data are likely to be representative of the men who served in the army.

However, because of drafting criteria, these men are not necessarily representative of the US population of men of drafting ages. To serve in WWII, a man had to be between five and six and a half feet tall, weigh at least 105 pounds, and have good vision and good teeth. Additionally, men had to be able to read and write. Those convicted of a crime were not eligible to serve. Finally there were exemptions based on occupation (men in a few agricultural and war-related production occupations were exempt), and initially, married men and fathers were exempt. Because of segregation relatively few blacks were drafted. Acemoglu, Autor, and Lyle (2004) and Goldin and Olivetti (2013) provide evidence that these exemptions generated substantial differences in the likelihood of serving in the war: blacks, farmers, and individuals of German descent were much less likely to have served.

To obtain a sample that is likely to be representative by cohort, we keep all white men born in the United States between 1898 and 1923 (other cohorts have very few observations), ages twenty to forty-five, with valid heights (between 60 and 78 inches), valid weight (over 105 pounds), and valid enlistment year (1938–1946). The final data we use contain about four million observations.

We construct years of schooling based on reported educational attainment. No individual is listed as having less than primary school—we impute those with exactly 8 years of schooling as having 4.5 years.[14]

We matched occupation to occupational scores using the 1950 occupation

---

14. We also experimented with coding them as illiterate, and all others as literate, under the assumption that the literacy requirement resulted in the education always being coded as at least eight years of schooling/primary grade.

categories. To each occupation in the WWII records we assign the occupational score associated with that occupation in the 1950 census. When multiple 1950 occupational categories were assigned to WWII civilian occupations we used the average occupational score for twenty-five to forty-eight-year-old white males across the listed occupations. We then compute the log of the occupation score, which is a positive value for everyone except for those that declared "no occupation" or "student" as their occupation prior to enlistment.

4.3.4   Commonly Used Contemporary Samples

We cover as many cohorts and time periods as possible by using several well-known recent data sets that contain standard measures of years of schooling, height, occupation, and earnings. The National Health and Nutrition Examination Surveys I (1971–1975), II (1976–1980), III (1988–1994), and 1999–2010 combine survey information on education and labor market outcomes with physical examination measurements, including height and death certificates. We use the 1961 wave of the National Longitudinal Survey of Old Men, the 1981 wave of the National Longitudinal Survey of Young Men, and the 1996 wave of the National Longitudinal Survey of Youth. Heights are self-reported, but the surveys have good information on incomes and wealth for individuals in their prime labor market years. We also use the Health and Retirement data—it contains excellent measures of wealth, but individuals are only sampled after age fifty-five and their heights are also self-reported. Finally, we include results from the National Health Interview surveys to examine the most recent cohort of men. These data do not contain wealth, heights are self-reported, and income is reported in categories only.

4.4   Trends in Height and Education

4.4.1   Height and Other Health Measures

Figure 4.2 illustrates the well-known long-term trend in heights in the United States, compiled from heights of native-born soldiers from the eighteenth through the twentieth centuries and of native-born men in the last decades of this century.[15] The data, which are arranged by birth cohort, show that troops who fought in the French and Indian War of the 1750s and the 1760s or who fought in the American Revolution of the 1770s nearly attained 1930s heights of 175 centimeters. Cohorts born from the early 1700s to those born in 1830 achieved a gradual increase in average stature of approximately

---

15. Since the sample sizes are substantial, particularly for those periods before the large wars, the major movements in the series are unlikely to represent sampling variation. In fact, the difference in average height between rejectees and those who served in the Union Army was 0.25 inches. The averages have been corrected for minimum height standards.

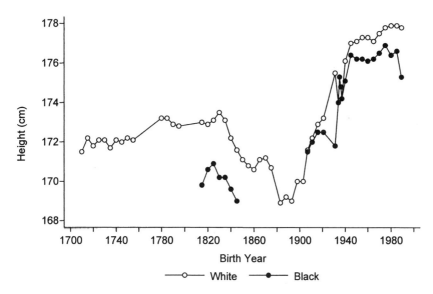

Fig. 4.2   Long-term trends in US heights

Notes: This figure updates the white height series in figure 2.1 in Costa and Steckel (1997) using the 1963–2010 NHIS and adds a height series for blacks using Union Army records, published WWII heights, and the NHIS. Year of birth is centered at the marks. Estimates using the NHIS were adjusted to account for biases resulting from self-reporting in the NHIS.

one centimeter. Average heights fell by approximately four centimeters in the ensuing half century, reaching a trough among births in the 1880s.[16] Corroborating evidence for the decline in stature among whites is found in mortality data from genealogies. Life expectancy at age twenty declined from approximately forty-seven years at the beginning of the century to slightly less than forty-one years in the 1850s and recovery to levels of the early 1800s was not attained until the end of the century (Pope 1992). The decline in black stature is consistent with Steckel's (1979) finding of a decline of two and a half to seven and half centimeters in the heights of slave children born in the two decades after 1830. Other work has documented that industrialization (and perhaps the accompanying urbanization) was associated with a mortality "penalty"—but the height decline is observed in both rural and urban areas and few Americans lived in urban areas.

After the 1880s, American men experienced the familiar secular increase in stature of recent times, gaining approximately six centimeters by the mid-twentieth century. This large increase in heights occurs at the same time that life expectancy and health are rising substantially.

The secular increase in heights continues in recent decades, although at

16. No national height series is available for the end of the nineteenth century. Interpolation was based upon the assumption that the time pattern for the country followed that for Ohio.

a much slower pace. As others have documented (Komlos and Lauderdale 2007), there is a stagnation in height growth, the causes of which are not understood.

We plot the height series we obtain from our data sets in figure 4.3. As in figure 4.2, we observe that heights steadily increased in the early period, and then reached a plateau for the post–World War II birth cohorts.

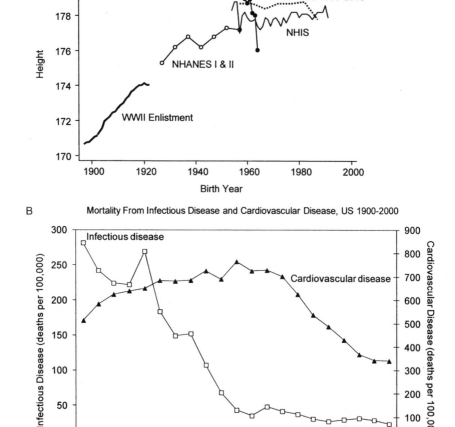

Fig. 4.3   Evolution of heights and mortality in the twentieth-century United States: *A*, trends in heights; *B*, mortality rates over time

Notes: In panel A, the means are centered at the mark. We do not have exact year of birth for NHANES 1999–2010. The surveys were done over a two-year period but the year of the survey was not recorded. Year of birth is not available for NHANES III. Figure 3 from Cutler et al. 2006.

Table 4.1	Brother-brother adult height correlations among whites	
Union Army, 1861–1865 (1812–1844 cohort)	World War II, 1939–1945 (1909–1924 cohort)	PSID (1959–1968 cohort)
0.394 (0.024)	0.462 (0.024)	0.492 (0.017)

Notes: All correlations are estimated using restricted maximum likelihood (REML). Standard errors are in parentheses. We thank John Parman for estimating the WWII correlation for us. The PSID estimates are from Mazumder (2004).

The increase in heights coincides with a decline in the variance of heights. The estimates in table 4.1 reveal that the correlation in adult heights between brothers has increased since the US Civil War. The most likely cause for the low correlation in the past is families' inability to protect themselves against disease and nutritional shocks. Among brothers in the Union Army heights were lower in more populous counties and the variability in height was greater, suggesting that the environmental contribution to variability in height is of greater relative importance in populations reared in worse environments (Lauderdale and Rathouz 1999). The US decline in brother-brother correlations is consistent with the increase in height heritability observed among Finnish twins born in the first half of the twentieth century and those born later (Silventoinen et al. 2000).

Finally the trend in height appears to follow the declines in infectious disease mortality: panel B of figure 4.3 shows that infectious disease mortality fell dramatically until about midcentury and then remained at a very low and stable level—cardiovascular mortality by comparison starts falling much later. This coincidence in the trend for height and for mortality is consistent with the notion that adult heights are most affected by conditions early in life, at least proxied by infectious disease mortality, which mostly kills children.

4.4.2   Trends in Education

Figure 4.4, which plots the average years of education by year of birth for various samples, shows that educational attainment steadily increases beginning in the nineteenth century and continuing up to about 1950, at which point education plateaus. The increase in years of schooling from 1900 to 1960 is about 5.5 years. These trends are consistent with the patterns that have been documented for the nation as a whole, although the stagnation for the very last few cohorts is atypical compared with other data for the population (however, our data for these later cohorts are noisy). The plateau in years of schooling coincides with the plateau in heights and in infant mortality.

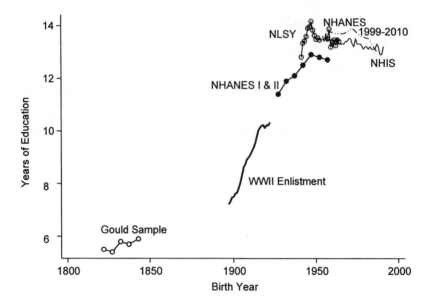

Fig. 4.4   Trends in educational attainment in some of our samples

Notes: The means are centered at the mark. We do not have exact year of birth for NHANES 1999–2010. The surveys were done over a two-year period but the year of the survey was not recorded. Year of birth is not available for NHANES III.

4.4.3   Summary

Our evidence on long-run trends implies that both childhood health and education improved substantially in the early twentieth century. We next look at the consequences of these improvements on long-term measures of labor market success. We start by assessing the extent to which education was determined by early childhood health, proxied by heights. Then we move on to examine how height and/or education affected our measures of labor market success and wealth.

4.5   The Effects of Height on Education

For each of our cross-sectional data sets we estimate ordinary least squares (OLS) regressions of the form

$$e_i = \beta_0 + \beta_1 h_i + \beta_2 C_i + u_i,$$

where e is years of education for individual i, h is height in centimeters, C is a vector of control variables, and u is an error term.

Table 4.2 shows that heights had little effect on educational attainment in either the Union Army or the Gould sample. The most that an extra centimeter of height contributed to years of education was 0.009, a 0.3 percent

Table 4.2   **The effect of height on schooling in the nineteenth century (birth cohorts)**

	Union Army, dummy = 1 if in school, 1850 or 1860	Union Army, years education, measure 1	Union Army, years education, measure 2	Gould sample, years education	Union Army, dummy = 1 if illiterate (age 21+)
Mean dependent Variable	0.652	3.322	4.072	5.766	0.026
Height (cm)	0.001	0.009*	0.005*	0.002	–0.000
	(0.001)	(0.004)	(0.003)	(0.003)	(0.000)
State FE	Y	Y	Y	Y	Y
Age census FE	Y	Y	Y		
Age enlistment FE	Y	Y	Y	Y	Y
Log population in town of enlistment	Y	Y	Y		Y
Population in town of enlistment > = 50,000				Y	
Year census dummy	Y	Y	Y		
Adjusted R-squared or pseudo R-squared	0.151	0.281	0.567	0.056	0.086
Observations	10,606	10,615	10,615	6,695	8,518

Notes: Standard errors clustered on state. The Gould sample is restricted to the native born. Because the first three columns of the Union Army sample (except for the last column) are restricted to children in 1850 or 1860, it consists predominately of the native born. The two education measures for the Union Army sample are constructed from the school attendance from linked antebellum censuses. See section 4.3.2 for further information.
***Significant at the 1 percent level.
**Significant at the 5 percent level.
*Significant at the 10 percent level.

increase relative to the mean. Heights had no effect on illiteracy rates. Recall that the main difficulty with these data is that we have to impute education based on enrollment and age. It is possible that our measures of education are too noisy. Nevertheless, the results suggest a small effect of height.

We find a small effect of height on education even under various sample restrictions. When we restricted height to men above five feet and below six feet, five inches (the restriction for WWII enlisted men) in the Gould sample, the coefficient rose only to 0.003 ($\widehat{\sigma}$ = 0.005) from 0.002. When we restrict to men who were younger than age twenty-five at enlistment the coefficient on the second measure of education in the Union Army sample rises from 0.005 to 0.008 ($\widehat{\sigma}$ = 0.036). When we restrict the sample to men who were older than age thirty-five at enlistment the coefficient falls to –0.031 ($\widehat{\sigma}$ = 0.322). So these results suggest that the effect of heights is larger among the more recent cohorts in the nineteenth-century sample.

Table 4.3, which presents results from identical models estimated with twentieth and twenty-first-century data, reveals that, relative to the nineteenth century, the effect of height on education is much larger in magnitude

Table 4.3   Effect of height on schooling in twentieth century (white native-born males [OLS])

Effect of height on years of schooling	Education mean (sd)	Height mean (sd)	N	Year data collected	Birth cohorts
Panel A: WWII sample					
Height (cms) 0.080 ***	9.8	175.4	3,862,228	1939–45	1897–1923
[0.000]	(3.6)	(6.62)			
Panel B: NLS Old Men					
Height (cms) 0.076***	10.16	177.20	1,266	1961	1904–21
[0.015]	(3.72)	(6.95)			
Panel C: NHANES I & II					
Height 0.074***	12.7	176.6	4,155	1971–76	1930–59
[0.006]	(3.03)	(6.79)			
Panel D: NLS Young Men					
Height (cms) 0.044***	13.64	179.86	1,597	1981	1941–52
[0.010]	(2.66)	(6.69)			
Panel E: NLSY79					
Height (cms) 0.047***	13.44	178.53	2,615	1996	1957–64
[0.007]	(2.56)	(7.31)			
Panel F: NHANES III					
Height (cms) 0.054***	12.8	175.9	1,566	1988–94	1943–74
[0.009]	(2.66	(6.99)			
Panel G: NHANES 1999–2010					
Height (cms) 0.037 ***	13.5	178.5	2,556	1999–2010	1954–90
[0.005]	[1.9]	(6.88)			
Panel H: NHIS samples					
Height (cms) 0.039 ***	13.4	178.3	43,190	2000–11	1955–91
[0.002]	[2.71]	(7.14)			

Notes: All samples are restricted to white native males between the ages of twenty and forty-five. NHANES I and II controls include state/place of birth dummies, year of survey dummies, age dummies, and ten-year cohort dummies. NHANES III only includes AGE dummies (neither survey year nor year of birth are given), region of residence dummies, and metro area. NHANES 1999–2010 includes age dummies and survey dummies. Sample weights were used. NHIS samples include age dummies, year of survey dummies, and region of residence dummies. NHIS uses sample weights.
***Significant at the 1 percent level.
**Significant at the 5 percent level.
*Significant at the 10 percent level.

and is statistically significant in all cases.[17] For cohorts born between 1897 and 1959 (Panels A–C) we find that a one centimeter increase in height is

17. An important caveat is that our results would change substantially in magnitude if we did not drop individuals with heights within enlistment parameters. If all height observations are included then the coefficients on height would be substantially smaller. However, the overall pattern would be similar.

associated with 0.08 more years of schooling.[18] But the coefficient of height on education is smaller in more recent cohorts: for the birth cohorts 1943 to 1974 the effect falls to 0.05 and then to 0.04 for the most recent cohorts.

We used the World War II sample to test for nonlinearities in the education-height relationship using height dummies. Although there is suggestive evidence that the relationship between years of education and height becomes weaker at tall heights, the effects are still positive for heights of 193.4 centimeters and over (more than six feet, three inches).

A caveat to our cross-sectional results is that unobserved family or environmental effects may lead us to overstate the cross-sectional height-education relationship. Case and Paxson (2008) find that controlling for mother fixed effects in the NLSY attenuates but still leaves statistically significant the relationship between test scores and children's height. By linking the WWII enlistment data to earlier censuses, Parman (2010) was able to identify brothers and also finds an attenuated but still statistically significant relationship between height and education among brothers.[19]

We assess the magnitude of our effects in table 4.3 by computing the fraction of the changes in education that can be "explained" by changes in heights. Height increased by about 1.2 centimeters across cohorts in panels A–C, thus the increase in education it is associated with is about 0.1 years of school, a small fraction of the increases in education across these cohorts (years of schooling increases by about 2.9 years). The decline in education in panels D through H is –0.02. Heights fell by 1.56 centimeters, and given the coefficient of –0.05, height accounts for about 0.0078 of the 0.02 decline, or about 40 percent.

The overall patterns suggest there are three periods. During the nineteenth century a large fraction of the sample is in farming occupations and average heights and education were low and tended not to be correlated with each other. From the late nineteenth century up to the 1940s, height and education increased rapidly and the correlation between them was high. Finally, from about 1940 onward average education levels and heights are falling, and the correlation between the two falls.

Our results raise multiple questions. What drove the tremendous improvements in education and health observed in the first part of the twentieth century? Were both driven by the same factors? A large number of policies were directed at improving maternal and child health as well as increasing

18. When we accounted for the left censoring of education in the WWII data we obtained a coefficient of 0.072 (.

19. Parman (2010) concluded that a one-inch difference in the height of brothers leads to 0.03 years of education compared to 0.07 years of education in a naïve regression that does not control for family effects. (An extra centimeter would lead to 0.01 years of education compared to 0.03 years in a naïve regression. Parman restricted his sample to privates but we do not find that this explains the difference between our results and his. His sample overrepresents men from large families.)

education during the progressive era. This era also saw large increases in incomes and nutrition, as well as increases in the returns to school. Finally, what explains the stagnation since 1940? Is it possible that declines in childhood investments have consequences for the labor market?

4.6 Height, Wealth, and Income

We estimate OLS regressions of the form

$$\ln(p_i) = \beta_0 + \beta_1 h_i + \beta_3 C_i + u_i$$

$$\ln(p_i) = \beta_0 + \beta_1 h_i + \beta_2 e_i + \beta_3 C_i + u_i,$$

where p is a measure of individual i's productivity, such as occupational score, wage, or wealth, h is height in centimeters, e is years of education, and C is a control variable. We estimate these regressions for each of our cross-sectional data sets with information on productivity.

4.6.1 The Nineteenth Century

We analyze the relationship between height and productivity measures in the nineteenth-century data using the Gould sample of Union Army soldiers and the Union Army enlistment records linked to the 1870 census. In both data sets, as a proxy for income, we use the "occupational income score," which combines the occupation reported in the nineteenth-century data with a tabulation of median income by occupation in 1950. Linkage of the Union Army enlistment records to the 1870 records provides us with a wealth variable, which is the sum of real estate and personal property wealth. We transform both variables into natural logarithms.

Figure 4.5 shows the basic results for the 1870 data for farmers, nonfarmers, and the pooled sample, respectively. Panel C of each of these figures displays the estimated distribution of heights. Panels A and B depict the estimated nonparametric regression of the relationship between height and outcomes. (In these figures, the estimated relationship is not adjusted for controls. We present regression-adjusted results below.)

In the data linked to 1870, the occupational score and the (natural logarithm of the) value of wealth increase almost linearly with height for most of the distribution, although apparently peaking a bit below six feet (see figure 4.5, panels A and B). In results not shown, the wealth gradient is steeper among farmers than among nonfarmers. The density of heights in the pooled sample is shown in figure 4.5, panel C.

Height is also associated with a higher occupational score among farming occupations. (The main two occupations in this category are farmers, who might own their farm, and farm laborers, who presumably do not.) In contrast, among nonfarmers height is negatively correlated with occupation. Occupational score and height are negatively related in the pooled

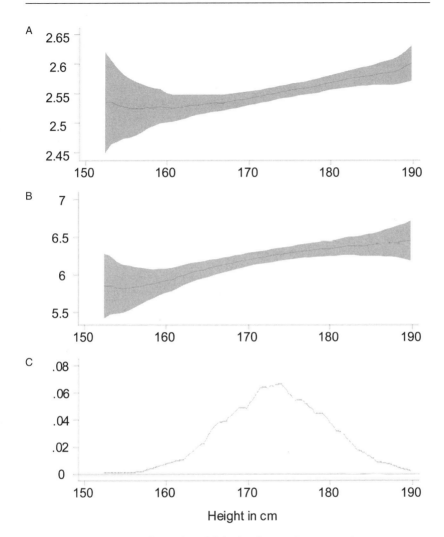

Fig. 4.5   Height, occupation and wealth in the nineteenth century: *A*, occupational income score, natural log; *B*, real and personal property, natural log; *C*, probability density

sample as well. The negative relationship is stronger in the pooled sample because farmers have low occupational scores and were on average taller because they were less exposed to disease. We therefore focus on the nonfarmer samples in looking at occupational scores in a regression framework.

The upper panels of table 4.4 show that although among nonfarmers height increased occupational score, the effect was modest. One additional centimeter in height among nonfarmers in the Gould sample was associated with a 0.2 percent increase in the occupation score, and this coefficient

Table 4.4　　　　**Effect of height and education on labor market outcomes, 1870–1996**

Dependent variable	log(occupational score)		log(annual wages)	
Panel A: UA Gould sample (nonfarmers)				
Height	0.002*	0.002*		
	[0.001]	[0.001]		
Years of school		0.012***		
		[0.003]		
Panel B: UA 1870 (nonfarmers)				
Height	0.001	0.001		
	[0.001]	[0.002]		
Years of school		0.013*		
		[0.006]		
Panel C: WWII sample				
Height	0.003***	0.001***		
	[0.000]	[0.000]		
Years of school		0.031***		
		[0.000]		
Panel D: NHANES I & II (1971–1976)				
Height	0.008***	0.004***		
	[0.001]	[0.001]		
Years of school		0.044***		
		[0.002]		
Panel E: NLS 1961				
Height (cms)	0.008***	–0.000	0.012***	0.004*
	[0.002]	[0.002]	[0.002]	[0.002]
Years of school		0.097***		0.084***
		[0.004]		[0.005]
Panel F: NLS 1981				
Height (cms)	0.009***	0.004**	0.011***	0.008***
	[0.002]	[0.002]	[0.002]	[0.002]
Years of school		0.129***		0.079***
		[0.005]		[0.006]
Panel G: NLS 1996				
Height (cms)			0.013***	0.008***
			[0.002]	[0.002]
Years of school				0.108***
				[0.006]

Notes: Occupational score is based on 1950 incomes. We imputed 1950 occupation codes and matched to occupational score in the 1950 census. When multiple 1950 occupation codes were imputed to an occupation, we took a population-weighted mean of income. The WWII sample is restricted to white males age twenty-five to forty-five with no missing values for education, height, and year of birth and within enlistment parameters. Those without occupation codes, or reporting their occupation as "student" or "none," are excluded in the occupation regressions. Regressions include state/place of birth dummies and year of birth dummies. Gould sample controls include age, whether the soldier was born in the United States, and whether he enlisted in a city with a population of 50,000+. Controls for the 1870 Union Army sample include age and region of birth dummies. Controls for NHANES I and II include age and whether the man was born in the United States.

Table 4.4   (continued)   ₹

NLS notes: Sample includes all white males with no missing values for education, height, and year of birth from the 1961 wave of the of National Longitudinal Survey of Old Men, the 1981 wave of the National Longitudinal Survey of Young Men, and the 1996 wave of the National Longitudinal Survey of Youth. Regressions include age dummies, year dummies, and a foreign-born dummy. We did not impute occupation scores for the NLSY79 because it uses 1960 occupation codes, which are not detailed enough. Individuals with zero or missing values for annual earnings are not included in the earnings regressions.
***Significant at the 1 percent level.
**Significant at the 5 percent level.
*Significant at the 10 percent level.

remains unchanged when we control for education. For the 1870 UA sample, the increase in occupation score with height was 0.1 percent and not significantly different from zero.

Table 4.4 also reveals that even among nonfarmers, returns to education, although positive, were low. An additional year of education increased the occupation score by only 1.2 percent circa 1860 and by 1.3 percent circa 1870. Recall that because education and apprenticeships were positively correlated, these low estimates of the positive effects of education are biased upward.

Table 4.5 reports that in 1870 a centimeter of height is associated with an additional 1 percent of wealth. This result is unchanged by controlling for education.[20] A similar pattern emerges from regressions that control for place of birth using alternative levels of geographic detail, use various sampling weights to make the sample more representative of the 1860 US population, drop outliers in height, or compute wealth in alternative ways.[21] We also found that while there is some evidence of nonlinearities in the height-wealth relationship, the nonlinearities are present only at heights of about 188 centimeters (six feet, two inches). Because few men are so tall, they have a minimal effect on our estimated wealth-height relationship.

The height-wealth relationship was stronger among the farm population (see table 4.5). When we split the sample between farmers and nonfarmers, we obtained coefficients on height of 0.009 and of 0.022 for the nonfarm and farm samples, respectively, with controls for education. The returns to height may have been greater for farmers because the physical demands of farming put a premium on health.

4.6.2   The Twentieth Century

The results for the twentieth century paint a different picture (see table 4.4). In the first two columns of table 4.4 we report the coefficient from a

---

20. However, the coefficient on education might be biased downward by measurement error; we note that the coefficient on height drops to 0.7 percent if we fix the coefficient on education to be 0.4, roughly in line with what is estimated in the twentieth-century data.
21. Results available upon request.

Table 4.5   Height, education, and wealth among Union Army veterans in 1870

Dependent variable: Logarithm of wealth		
All		
Height	0.010***	0.017**
	(.003)	(0.005)
Years of education		0.064***
		(0.014)
Nonfarmers		
Height	.001	0.009
	(.003)	(0.006)
Year of education		0.053**
		(0.018)
Farmers		
Height	0.012*	0.022*
	(.005)	(0.009)
Years of education		0.056**
		(0.021)

Notes: Total wealth is the sum of real estate and personal property wealth, as transcribed from the 1870 census manuscripts. The years of school are "measure 2" of education, imputed using the data on school attendance in 1850 or 1860 (depending on the census year in which the veteran was observed when age eleven to twenty-one). The regression includes controls for age in 1870, age at enlistment, and region of birth (all entering as dummy variables). All regressions include state fixed effects. Standard errors are in parentheses.
***Significant at the 1 percent level.
**Significant at the 5 percent level.
*Significant at the 10 percent level.

regression of the logarithm of the 1950 occupational score on height with and without controls for education, and with basic geographic and age controls. Several patterns emerge. The returns to height increased substantially throughout the century. Without education controls the returns to height increased from about 0.2 percent to 0.9 percent, and controlling for education they rose from 0.2 percent to 0.4 percent (panel A v. panel F). The returns to education also rose dramatically from 1.2 percent to 12.9 percent. In the twentieth-century samples (panels B–F) controlling for education substantially lowers the returns to height, unlike in the nineteenth-century samples, suggesting that the returns to height in the twentieth century are driven in part by cognitive improvements associated with both height and education.[22] Interestingly in the WWII enlistment data, we also observe positive and statistically significant effects of height and education for women and for black males.[23]

Results without farmers are very similar; for example, in the WWII data,

22. In the World War II data we also ran specifications controlling for compulsory schooling laws and child labor laws. Our results remained unchanged.
23. Results available upon request. Women who enlisted to serve in the army in WWII are unlikely to be representative of women at the time, and in previous research blacks were underrepresented (Acemoglu, Autor, and Lyle 2004).

the coefficient on height controlling for education is 0.0010 for the full sample (panel B of table 4.2), 0.0013 for nonfarmers, and 0.0002 for farmers. Farmers constituted at this point less than 20 percent of the labor force (Wyatt and Hecker 2006). The last two columns show that despite the coarseness of our occupation score measure, the same basic patterns are observed with wages. In fact, the returns to height are larger when we use wages—suggesting that within occupations there are substantial returns to height that are not accounted for when we use variation in income across occupations only.

Table 4.6 presents the results for wealth in the twentieth-century samples.

Table 4.6   **The relationship between height, education, and wealth measures, 1961–2004**

	White males			
Dependent variable	log (all observed wealth)		log(real estate and business wealth)	
Panel A: NLS 1961				
Height (cms)	0.053***	0.025**	0.061***	0.038**
	[0.012]	[0.012]	[0.017]	[0.017]
Years of school		0.318***		0.269***
		[0.024]		[0.034]
Panel B: NLS 1981				
Height (cms)	0.040***	0.024*	0.037*	0.022
	[0.013]	[0.013]	[0.020]	[0.020]
Years of school		0.368***		0.326***
		[0.034]		[0.051]
Panel C: NLS 1996				
Height (cms)	0.099***	0.075***	0.105***	0.081***
	[0.012]	[0.012]	[0.019]	[0.019]
Years of school		0.517***		0.505***
		[0.034]		[0.054]
Panel D: HRS samples 1992, 1998, and 2004				
Height (cms)	0.053***	0.032***	0.070***	0.045***
	[0.005]	[0.004]	[0.01]	[0.01]
Years of school		0.238***		0.276***
		[0.015]		[0.034]
X (1998 dummy)		0.095***		0.038
		[0.026]		[0.057]
X (2004 dummy)		0.084***		0.172***
		[0.026]		[0.057]

NLS notes: Real estate wealth is the sum of the reported value of house owned, farm owned, business or other real estate owned. All wealth is the sum of real estate wealth, savings, bonds, and stocks. Value of automobiles is never included as it was not collected prior to 1996. The data collection is, however, not identical over the years so the wealth measures are not exactly identical. Missing and nonreports are treated as zeros and set to 0.01 before taking logs.

***Significant at the 1 percent level.

**Significant at the 5 percent level.

*Significant at the 10 percent level.

Unfortunately, the WWII enlistment data contain no information on wealth. It also is substantially more difficult to construct comparable wealth measures over time. For instance, the NLS samples collected different information about wealth over time. Therefore it is more difficult to compare these coefficients and their evolution. However, in all of the samples we observe a very large and robust association between early investments and wealth. Both education and height are positively associated with wealth. The coefficients on height in these late twentieth-century samples range from 0.024 to about 0.04. In all of these samples height and education have larger coefficients than in the nineteenth-century samples. The wealth results are consistent with the occupation and wage results.

Overall a picture emerges with the nineteenth century having lower health and human capital (height and education), and positive but small wealth returns for both education and height. In the first part of the twentieth century, there are large increases in education and height, yet at the same time returns appear to have increased substantially.

4.6.3   Interpretation of the Results

Our productivity regressions have treated the causality as going from childhood health, proxied by adult height, to adult productivity. In our interpretation, adult height is a marker of both strength and cognition. But even the genetic return to height could have a productivity return if the tall receive more investments, which in turn makes them more outgoing, or if they are groomed for leadership roles simply by virtue of their height. In addition, height may be endogenous if unobserved variations in parents' endowments, prices, and preferences affect their children's early life height inputs and also enhance their adult health status and lifetime productivity. Instrumental variable estimates for Ghana, Brazil, and the United States are many times larger than the OLS estimates (Schultz 2002). Nonetheless, both OLS and IV estimates show that the wage returns to height are smaller in the United States than in Ghana and Brazil. Because our primary interest is in determining how the relationship between height and productivity has changed and because we do not have instruments for US heights over a century and half, reduced form estimates, estimated using similar specifications and sample restrictions, are used to establish long-run trends.

4.7   Comparisons with US Slaves and Developing Countries

Studies of the effects of health on long-run economic growth commonly cite the relationship between US slave height and prices and the height and productivity relationship in developing countries as evidence of the importance of health to productivity (e.g., Floud et al. 2011, 21–23; Costa and Steckel 1997). Floud et al. (2011, 132) use the estimated effect of height and weight on slave prices to estimate the effect of changes in height and weight on earnings and therefore of changes in body size on British economic growth. How do our height and productivity results compare to those for slaves and for developing country populations?

4.7.1   Comparisons with US Slaves

The only other study examining the relationship between height and wealth in the nineteenth-century United States is Margo and Steckel's (1982) examination of the relationship between height and slave prices. Their table 6 reports a coefficient of log slave price on height of 2.1 percent per centimeter. Although this coefficient is similar to the height-wealth relationship we observe for farmers in table 4.6, slave prices exhibit a steeper gradient for height than those for all free men. Throughout this chapter we interpret the returns to height being returns to both broader health and cognition. But this cognition interpretation does not seem consistent with the returns to height being higher for slaves than free men. Slaves were not being purchased for their cognitive skills, by and large. The labor services provided by slaves circa 1860 were likely more physical than cognitive, especially relative to circa 1870 free whites in the North. We argue that there is no inconsistency, however, for both theoretical and econometric reasons.

Why would the measured return to some endowment be higher in the slave price than in the wealth accumulation of a free person? We suggest two relevant distinguishing characteristics:

1. Is the variable forward or backward looking?
2. What is the endowment effect if the labor endowment belongs to someone else?

The first point (1) is that the slave price is an asset value, and thus forward looking, while a free man's wealth is the result of an accumulation process, and thus backward looking. This indicates that we should compare the gradient among young (adult) slaves with that of older free men. Indeed, if we reestimate the height/wealth model with an interaction term between age and height, it is strongly positive and statistically significant. Evaluating the coefficient at age twenty-five, we find a return to height of .01 per centimeter.[24] Evaluating instead at age fifty-five, we obtain .04, which is double the Margo/Steckel number for slaves.

Now consider the endowment effect (point 2). If the taller free man has, in effect, a more valuable labor endowment, he might work less (and thus accumulate less wealth) because of the endowment effect (some might call this a wealth effect instead). Whether this effect is strong enough to generate backward-bending labor supply is not the point. The point is that the endowment effect is weaker for slaves, *who did not own their own labor endow-*

---

24. We also found evidence of increasing age profiles for occupation in the WWII data and for wealth in the NLS data. Results available upon request.

ment. Thus, we would expect that the marginal value of height to be higher for slaves. (Note that this difference would disappear if we could control for labor effort, but the price or wealth data is not adjusted for hours worked.) Furthermore, combining points (1) and (2), we note that the slave price also incorporates the productive value of their progeny, which might be higher for taller men.

Further, the gradient in slave prices with height becomes considerably smaller than the estimated wealth/height gradient in 1870 if we account for two important differences between our specification and the one used by Margo and Steckel. First, their specification included weight as well as height, while ours above does not. Those authors sought to relate observed anthropometric measures to slave prices, and thus it was appropriate to control for height and weight simultaneously. For the purposes of the present study, however, we are interested in height as a proxy of early-life endowments. We are therefore cautious about overcontrolling for too many physical attributes. Fortunately, the data employed in their study was conserved as ICPSR study no. 9427 (Margo 1979), and therefore we can estimate comparable specifications using their original data.[25] When we reestimate their model dropping both weight and the interaction of weight and height from the specification, we obtain a coefficient on height of .005 per centimeter. This is considerably smaller than our results above using 1870 wealth. At first glance, this was perplexing because our intuition was that the coefficient on height would rise after dropping the weight controls, because height and weight are positively correlated. But this brings us to a second issue in their specification: namely, the construction of the interaction term. Their interaction between height and weight appears to be the simple product of the two variables. Constructing the interaction term this way forces the main effect of height to be evaluated at a weight equal to zero. For the present purposes, this is not an interesting point in the distribution at which to evaluate productivity/height gradient. With an interaction term constructed by first removing the means from height and weight, the coefficient on height is now evaluated at the mean of the weight distribution. When estimating their equation with this alternative construction of the interaction term, we obtain a coefficient on height of .004 per centimeter.[26] This is two to four

---

25. In our attempt to replicate their results in table 6, we drop females, those with age less than eighteen, and those with height or weight coded to zero. Light skin complexion is coded as stated in the data documentation. Nevertheless, the sample that we obtain is substantially larger (871 versus 523 observations) and the coefficient of log slave price on height in inches is 0.043 rather than their reported estimate of 0.053. The pattern of statistical significance across variables is similar to their results. Most of the other coefficients are smaller in magnitude in our estimates than those reported by Margo and Steckel. Note that our focus here is on how much the price/height gradient attenuates when adjusting the specification to match ours, and we suppose that the comparative values of coefficients would be similar if we were able to match their sample exactly.

26. We found some suggestive evidence of nonlinearities at heights of 188 centimeters (six feet, two inches) and above, but few men were in this height range.

times lower than what we estimate in section 4.7.1 above for height and 1870 wealth, suggesting that the cognitive channel plays a role in interpreting these results, even in the nineteenth century. If the wealth return to brawn is 0.004 then the wealth return to cognition is 0.005 (= 0.009 − 0.004) for nonfarmers and 0.018 (= 0.022 − 0.004) for farmers, suggesting that a good part of the return to height was via cognitive human capital rather than physical strength, even in the nineteenth century.

4.7.2   Comparisons with Developing Countries

Findings from developing countries on the relationship between education and health include work by Glewwe and Jacoby (1995) on Ghana, which finds that the shorter sibling receives less schooling, and work by Paxson and Schady (2007) showing that taller children in Ecuador have better cognitive outcomes.

One of the difficulties, however, in comparing our results with those from developing countries is that specifications and sample restrictions differ, and more importantly large representative samples of adult males with height measures are uncommon. We therefore use the 2005–2006 Indian Demographic and Health Survey (hereafter DHS) to examine the relationship between height, education, and wealth among Indian men age twenty to forty-five. The DHS is a unique data set for our purposes: it sampled all men age fifteen to fifty-four (regardless of marital status), and the sample is very large. The survey covered 99 percent of the population and was designed to be representative of the nation and of both rural and urban areas. It contains years of schooling, occupation, and a measure of wealth. Height and weight were measured by interviewers.[27] Although wealth is difficult to measure in agrarian societies, the wealth index provided by the DHS survey is an excellent measure of resources.[28] We restrict attention to men ages twenty to forty-five, with nonmissing values for height and education and use survey weights. The final sample has about 48,000 observations. On average these men have about eight years of school and measure 164 centimeters.

Panel A of table 4.7 shows that the relationship between height and education in India was 0.15 for all men with slightly smaller effects for farmers. The effects, as measured by the height coefficients, were larger than for the twentieth-century United States. The effects of a standard deviation increase in height were also larger than for the United States (see table 4.8). Interestingly, the Mincerian wage returns to education are also higher in developing than in developed countries (Psacharopoulos 1994).

Panel B of table 4.7 shows that the wealth returns to height in India are 0.018 without controls for education and 0.008 controlling for education. The returns are thus similar to those observed in the nineteenth-century

27. http://www.measuredhs.com/pubs/pdf/FRIND3/00FrontMatter00.pdf.
28. http://www.measuredhs.com/pubs/pdf/CR6/CR6.pdf.

Table 4.7   Height, education, and wealth among Indian males, age twenty to forty-five, in 2005–2006

A. Dependent variable = years of education

	All	Farmers	Nonfarmers
Height	0.151***	0.114***	0.161***
	[0.003]	[0.006]	[0.004]
State and age FE	Y	Y	Y
Observations	48,670	11,978	36,692
R-squared	0.115	0.131	0.102

B. Dependent variable = logarithm of wealth index

	All		Farmers		Nonfarmers	
Height	0.018***	0.008***	0.015***	0.009***	0.018***	0.008***
	[0.000]	[0.000]	[0.001]	[0.001]	[0.000]	[0.000]
Years of education		0.063***		0.049***		0.060***
		[0.000]		[0.001]		[0.000]
State and age FE	Y	Y	Y	Y	Y	Y
Observations	48,670	48,670	11,978	11,978	36,692	36,692
R-squared	0.193	0.447	0.210	0.370	0.184	0.440

Notes: Estimated from the Indian DHS 2005–2006. The mean of years of education is 7.97 and mean height is 164.73 centimeters.
***Significant at the 1 percent level.
**Significant at the 5 percent level.
*Significant at the 10 percent level.

United States and lower than those observed in the twentieth-century United States.

Comparing our results for the occupational score and wage returns to height with studies of the wage returns to height for various developing countries suggests that returns are higher in developing countries.[29] Using data from Colombia (the ENH), Ribero and Nuñez (2000, table 5, column [6]) report a coefficient of log wages on height of 0.008 when controlling for education, which is identical to the estimate from India just reported. Vogl (2011, table 2, column [4], and table 4, column [1]) finds in Mexican data (the MxFLS) that an additional centimeter of height is associated with 0.023 higher log wages and 0.16 extra years of schooling. Controlling for education, Schultz's OLS estimates of the coefficients on height in a log wage regression are 0.015 for Ghana and 0.014 for Brazil. With the exception of

29. Our review of the developing-country literature is selective, however, because the heterogeneity in specifications makes it difficult to compare results from all of the studies we found. As we saw above in the comparison with slave prices, seemingly small differences in the specifications can make major differences in comparability of the coefficients. We restrict ourselves here to a few cases where it seemed clear that we are making an apples-to-apples comparison.

Table 4.8   **Comparisons of effects of standard deviation increase in height on years of education**

Sample	Coefficient height	Std. dev. height	Increase in years of education	% increase in years of education
Gould	0.002	6.36	0.01	0.21
Union Army	0.009	6.57	0.06	1.79
WWII	0.080	6.62	0.53	5.40
NHANES I & II	0.074	6.62	0.49	3.82
NHANES III	0.054	6.98	0.38	2.92
NHANES 1999–2010	0.037	6.87	0.25	1.88
India, 2005–2006	0.151	6.75	1.02	12.98

Sources: Estimated from tables 4.2, 4.3, and 4.7.

the height coefficient for Colombia, all of these coefficients are larger than for the twentieth-century United States, and therefore for the nineteenth-century United States as well.

Why are the returns to height and education so much stronger in developing countries than in the United States, both in recent data and in the past? One tempting hypothesis is that the returns to education are generally higher in contemporary developing economies. But this explanation raises a puzzle. The difference in height coefficients in the log-wage-height relationships between developing countries and the United States is about 0.01. The difference in height coefficients in the education-height relationship between India and the United States is about 0.07. Asssuming that the return to education is about 0.05 and 0.10, then the decomposition of the effects of health on education

$$\frac{dy^*}{dh} = \frac{\partial y}{\partial h}\bigg|_{e=0} + \int_0^{e^*} \frac{\partial^2 y}{\partial h\, \partial e}\, de + \frac{de^*}{dh}\frac{\partial y}{\partial e}\bigg|_{e^*}$$

implies that all of the effects of height on education are working through the third term (better health increases years of education). The puzzle is why there are no first-term effects given the continued presence of brawn-intensive jobs in the developing world and why, if health is a complement with education at the margin, it does not complement inframarginal education (the second term). For the moment, we leave this inconsistency for future research.

4.8   Education and Mortality

We have focused thus far on the effect of early life investments on economic success. We finish this chapter by considering how education affects adult mortality—another welfare measure. We examine the effects of education on mortality among native-born Union Army veterans alive and on the pension rolls in 1900 and age fifty-five to seventy-four, and men of the same age in the second and third NHANES surveys. To ensure comparability across the surveys we examine twelve-year mortality rates. We run Gompertz hazard models of the form,

$$h(t) = h_0(t)e^{x\beta}, h_o(t) = e^{\gamma t}.$$

We control for age at time of observation, population (size of city of enlistment for Union Army veterans and whether in a metro area for NHANES), state of enlistment or residence fixed effects, and, for Union Army veterans, a dummy for census year used and age in 1850 or 1860 fixed effects.

Table 4.9 shows that education was not a statistically significant predictor of twelve-year middle- and older-age mortality rates among native-born Union Army veterans. When we use our first measure we obtain a coefficient of 0.994 ($\hat{\sigma} = 0.030$). When we instrument using our first measure of education we obtain a coefficient of 0.991 ($\hat{\sigma} = 0.050$). We also performed additional robustness tests. The results were similar even controlling for occupation in 1900 (or past occupation if retired). We also obtained similar results using a Cox proportional hazards model. When we looked at cause of death, we found that the more educated were less likely to die of stroke but were more likely to die of ischemic heart disease.

Education was a statistically significant predictor of mortality rates in all

Table 4.9   Effect of education on twelve-year mortality rates

	Hazard ratio			
	Union Army	NHANES I (1971–1975)	NHANES II (1976–1980)	NHANES III (1988–1994)
Without controls for smoking				
Years education	0.989	0.969***	0.956***	0.948***
	(0.025)	(0.007)	(0.010)	(0.008)
With controls for ever and current smoker				
Years education		0.977*	0.965***	0.964***
		(0.013)	(0.010)	(0.009)
With controls for ever and current smoker and years smoked				
Years education				0.979**
				(0.010)

Notes: Hazard ratios are from Gompertz models examining twelve-year mortality rates among Union Army veterans age fifty-five to seventy-four in 1900 and men of the same age first observed in the NHANES surveys. Additional controls for the Union Army sample are age in 1900, log of population in the city of enlistment, an 1860 census dummy, and state of enlistment fixed effects. Additional controls for NHANES are age at the time of the survey, a metro dummy, region of residence fixed effects in NHANES I and II, and state of residence fixed effects in NHANES III. Sample weights were used for NHANES III.

***Significant at the 1 percent level.
**Significant at the 5 percent level.
*Significant at the 10 percent level.

three late twentieth-century samples, and its effect appears to be increasing, largely because of differential educational responses to smoking information. Without smoking controls the hazard ratios suggest that the relative risk of death for a year of education fell from 0.989 in the Union Army to 0.969 in NHANES I to 0.956 in NHANES II and then to 0.948 in NHANES III. (A caveat is that only the differences between the Union Army sample and NHANES II and III were statistically significant in a pooled sample.) With controls for past smoking history, the effects of education become smaller and there is no longer an obvious trend.

These results are consistent with the labor market and wealth results—the returns to early investments appear to have increased substantially in the twentieth century, and this is also true for mortality.

4.9   Conclusion

We document trends in early childhood investments measured by height and educational attainment for cohorts born in the United States between 1820 and 1990 and the extent to which height and education were correlated over time. We then relate the heights and education to various measures of labor market success and wealth. To investigate these relationships we make use of a large number of data sets containing the highest-quality comparable measures of height and economic success.

Overall a picture emerges with the nineteenth century having low investments in height and education, and positive but small returns for both education and height in nonfarm occupations. Height was a significant predictor of wealth in the population; however, height was negatively associated with occupational scores among farmers.

In the first part of the twentieth century, there are large increases in education and height but these investments stall in the second part of the twentieth century. At the same time returns to height and education, though not as large as in developing countries today, appear to have increased substantially all throughout the twentieth century and appear to be at their highest today. Investments in both health and education are thus even more potentially valuable today. Interestingly, investments in college education seem to have stalled despite persistently high returns the second half of the twentieth century (Goldin and Katz 2008; Oreopolous and Petronijevic 2013). Understanding the determinants of investments in early human capital investments and why these investments slowed down significantly after WWII but started increasing after 2000 (*New York Times*, June 29, 2013)[30] is an important topic for future research.[31]

<hr>

30. http://www.nytimes.com/interactive/2013/06/12/us/across-the-board-growth-in-college-degrees.html?ref=education&_r=0.
31. Unfortunately our data sets are not well suited to investigate the determinants of education and height over time since the WWII records and the UA data contain very little information on parental or family background.

We speculate that the greater importance of physical labor in the nineteenth-century economy, which raised the opportunity cost of schooling, may have depressed the height-education relationship relative to the twentieth century. Technological change, leading to a move from a brawn- to a brain-based economy, and the rise in publicly funded education (Goldin and Katz 2008) lowered the opportunity cost of schooling and increased the marginal benefit of time spent in schooling. Taking full advantage of the returns to health may thus require both a modern brain-based economy and the availability of education.

References

Acemoglu, Daron, and David H. Autor. 2012. "What Does Human Capital Do? A Review of Goldin and Katz's *The Race Between Education and Technology.*" NBER Working Paper no. 17828, Cambridge, MA.

Acemoglu, Daron, David H. Autor, and David Lyle. 2004. "Women, War, and Wages: The Effect of Female Labor Supply on the Wage Structure at Midcentury." *Journal of Political Economy* 112 (June): 497–551.

Angrist, Joshua. 2002. "How Do Sex Ratios Affect Marriage and Labor Markets? Evidence from America's Second Generation." *Quarterly Journal of Economics* 117 (3): 997–1038.

Autor, David H., Lawrence F. Katz, and Melissa S. Kearney. 2006. "The Polarization of the US Labor Market." *American Economic Review* 96 (2): 189–94.

Barham, Tania, Karen Macours, and John A. Maluccio. 2013. "Boys' Cognitive Skill Formation and Physical Growth: Long-Term Experimental Evidence on Critical Ages for Early Childhood Interventions." *American Economic Review* 103 (3): 467–71.

Barker, D. J. P. 1992. *Fetal and Infant Origins of Adult Disease.* London: British Medical Publishing Group.

Bharadwaj, Prashant, Katrine Velleson Løken, and Christopher Neilson. 2013. "Early Life Health Interventions and Academic Achievement." *American Economic Review* 103 (5): 1862–91.

Bleakley, Hoyt. 2010a. "Health, Human Capital, and Development." *Annual Review of Economics* 2:283–310.

———. 2010b. "Malaria in the Americas: A Retrospective Analysis of Childhood Exposure." *American Economic Journal: Applied Economics* 2 (2): 1–45.

Bleakley, Hoyt, and Joseph Ferrie. 2012. "Shocking Behavior: The Cherokee Land Lottery of 1832 in Georgia and Outcomes Across the Generations." Unpublished manuscript, University of Chicago. September.

Bleakley, Hoyt, and Sok Chul Hong. 2013. "When the Race between Education and Technology Goes Backwards: The Postbellum Decline of White School Attendance in the Southern US." Unpublished manuscript, University of Chicago. April.

Card, David. 2001. "Estimating the Return to Schooling: Progress on Some Persistent Econometric Problems." *Econometrica* 69 (5): 1127–60.

Case, Anne, and Christina Paxson. 2008. "Stature and Status: Height, Ability, and Labor Market Outcomes." *Journal of Political Economy* 116:491–532.

Costa, Dora L. 1993. "Height, Weight, Wartime Stress, and Older Age Mortality: Evidence from Union Army Records." *Explorations in Economic History* 30:424–49.

———. 2004. "The Measure of Man and Older Age Mortality: Evidence from the Gould Sample." *Journal of Economic History* 64 (1): 1–23.

Costa, Dora L., and Richard H. Steckel. 1997. "Long-Term Trends in Health, Welfare, and Economic Growth in the United States." In *Health and Welfare during Industrialization*, edited by R. H. Steckel and R. Floud, 47–89. Chicago: University of Chicago Press.

Cutler, David, Angus Deaton, and Adriana Lleras-Muney. 2006. "The Determinants of Mortality." *Journal of Economic Perspectives* 20 (3): 97–120.

Easterlin, Richard A. 1996. *Growth Triumphant: The Twenty-First Century in Historical Perspective*. Ann Arbor: University of Michigan Press.

Floud, Roderick, Robert W. Fogel, Bernhard Harris, and Sok Chul Hong. 2011. *The Changing Body: Health, Nutrition, and Human Development in the Western World since 1700*. Cambridge: Cambridge University Press.

Fogel, Robert W. 1993. "New Sources and New Techniques for the Study of Secular Trends in Nutritional Status, Health, Mortality, and the Process of Aging." *Historical Methods* 26 (1): 1–44.

———. 1994. "Economic Growth, Population Theory, and Physiology: The Bearing of Long-Term Processes on the Making of Economic Policy." *American Economic Review* 84 (3): 369–95.

Glewwe, P., and H. G. Jacoby. 1995. "An Economic Analysis of Delayed Primary School Enrollment in a Low Income Country: The Role of Early Childhood Nutrition." *Review of Economics and Statistics* 77 (1): 156–69.

Goldin, Claudia, and Lawrence F. Katz. 2000. "Education and Income in the Early Twentieth Century: Evidence from the Prairies." *Journal of Economic History* 60 (3): 782–818.

———. 2008. *The Race between Education and Technology*. Cambridge, MA: The Belknap Press of Harvard University Press.

Goldin, Claudia, and Robert A. Margo. 1992. "The Great Compression: The Wage Structure in the United States at Mid-Century." *Quarterly Journal of Economics* 107 (1): 1–34.

Goldin, Claudia, and Claudia Olivetti. 2013. "Shocking Labor Supply: A Reassessment of the Role of World War II on US Women's Labor Supply." NBER Working Paper no. 18676, Cambridge, MA.

Gould, Benjamin Apthorp. 1869. *Investigations in the Military and Anthropological Statistics of American Soldiers*. New York: Published for the US Sanitary Commission by Hurd and Houghton.

Hazan, Moshe. 2009. "Longevity and Lifetime Labor Supply: Evidence and Implications." *Econometrica* 77 (6): 1829–63.

Komlos, John, and Benjamin Lauderdale. 2007. "Underperformance in Affluence: The Remarkable Relative Decline in US Heights in the Second Half of the 20th Century." *Social Science Quarterly* 88 (2): 283–305.

Lauderdale, Diane S., and Paul J. Rathouz. 1999. "Evidence of Environmental Suppression of Familial Resemblance: Height among US Civil War Brothers." *Annals of Human Biology* 26 (5): 413–26.

Long, Jason. 2006. "The Socioeconomic Return to Primary Schooling in Victorian England." *Journal of Economic History* 66 (4): December.

Margo, Robert A. 1979. *Union Army Slave Appraisal Records from Mississippi, 1863–1865*. Ann Arbor, MI: Inter-university Consortium for Political and Social Research [distributor]. doi:10.3886/ICPSR09427.v1.

————. 1986. "Race, Educational Attainment, and the 1940 Census." *Journal of Economic History* 46 (March): 189–98.

Margo, Robert A., and Richard Steckel. 1982. "The Heights of American Slaves: New Evidence on Slave Nutrition and Health." *Social Science History* 6 (4): 516–38.

Martorell, R., J. Rivera, and H. Kaplowitz. 1990. "Consequences of Stunting in Early Childhood for Adult Body Size in Rural Guatemala." *Annales Nestlé* 48:85–92.

Mazumder, Bhaskar. 2004. "Sibling Similarities, Differences and Economic Inequality." Federal Reserve Bank of Chicago, Working Paper no. 2004-13.

Mobius, Markus M., and Tanya S. Rosenblat. 2006. "Why Beauty Matters." *American Economic Review* 96 (1): 222–35.

National Archives and Records Administration. *U.S. World War II Army Enlistment Records, 1938–1946* [database online]. Provo, UT, USA: Ancestry.com Operations Inc., 2005. Original data: Electronic Army Serial Number Merged File, 1938–1946 [Archival Database]; World War II Army Enlistment Records; Records of the National Archives and Records Administration, Record Group 64; National Archives at College Park, College Park, MD.

Oreopoulos, Philip, and Uros Petronijevic. 2013. "Making College Worth It: A Review of Research on the Returns to Higher Education." NBER Working Paper no. 19053, Cambridge, MA.

Parman, John. 2010. "Childhood Health and Human Capital: New Evidence from Genetic Brothers in Arms." Unpublished manuscript, Williams College. http://wmpeople.wm.edu/asset/index/jmparman/childhoodhealthandeducational attainment.

Paxson, C., and N. Schady. 2007. "Cognitive Development among Young Children in Ecuador: The Roles of Wealth, Health, and Parenting." *Journal of Human Resources* 42 (1): 49–84.

Persico, Nicola, Andrew Postlewaite, and Dan Silverman. 2004. "The Effect of Adolescent Experience on Labor Market Outcomes: The Case of Height." *Journal of Political Economy.* 112:1019–53.

Pitt, Mark M., Mark R. Rosenzweig, and Nazmul Hassan. 2012. "Human Capital Investment and the Gender Division of Labor in a Brawn-Based Economy." *American Economic Review* 102 (7): 3531–60.

Pope, C. L. 1992. "Adult Mortality in America before 1900: A View from Family Histories." In *Strategic Factors in Nineteenth-Century American Economic History,* edited by C. Goldin and H. Rockoff, 267–96. Chicago: University of Chicago Press.

Proos, L. A., Y. Hofvander, and T. Tuvemo. 1991. "Menarcheal Age and Growth Pattern of Indian Girls Adopted in Sweden. Catch-up Growth and Final Height." *Indian Journal of Pediatrics* 58 (1): 105–14.

Psacharopoulos, George. 1994. "Returns to Investment in Education: A Global Update." *World Development* 22 (9): 1325–43.

Ribero, Rocío, and Jairo Nuñez. 2000. "Adult Morbidity, Height, and Earnings in Colombia." In *Wealth from Health: Linking Social Investments to Earnings in Latin America,* edited by W. D. Savedoff and T. P. Schultz. Washington, DC: Inter-American Development Bank.

Sacerdote, Bruce. 2005. "Slavery and the Intergenerational Transmission of Human Capital." *Review of Economics and Statistics* 87 (2): 217–34.

Schick, Andreas, and Richard H. Steckel. 2010. "Height as a Proxy for Cognitive and Non-Cognitive Ability." NBER Working Paper no. 16570, Cambridge, MA.

Schultz, T. Paul. 2002. "Wage Gains Associated with Height as a Form of Health Human Capital." *American Economic Review* 92 (2): 349–53.

Silventoinen, K., J. Kaprio, E. Lahelma, and M. Koskenvuo. 2000. "Relative Effect of Genetic and Environmental Factors on Body Height: Differences across Birth Cohorts among Finnish Men and Women." *American Journal of Public Health* 90 (4): 627–30.

Steckel, Richard. 1979. "Slave Height Profiles from Coastwise Manifests." *Explorations in Economic History* 16:363–80.

———. 1995. "Stature and the Standard of Living." *Journal of Economic Literature* 33:1903–40.

Vogl, Tom. 2011. "Height, Skills, and Labor Market Outcomes in Mexico." Unpublished manuscript. May.

Waaler, Hans T. 1984. "Height, Weight, and Mortality: The Norwegian Experience." *Acta Medica Scandinavia Supplement* 679:1–51.

Widdowson, E. M., and R. A. McCance. 1960. "Some Effects of Accelerating Growth. I. General Somatic Development." *Proceedings of the Royal Society, Ser. B* 152 (947): 188–206.

Wyatt, Ian D., and Daniel A. Hecker. 2005. "Occupational Changes during the 20th Century." *Monthly Labor Review* March:35–57.

Yamauchi, F. 2008. "Early Childhood Nutrition, Schooling and Sibling Inequality in a Dynamic Context: Evidence from South Africa." *Economic Development and Cultural Change* 56:657–8.

5

The Female Labor Force and Long-Run Development
The American Experience in Comparative Perspective

Claudia Olivetti

5.1 Introduction

The nature and extent of segmentation of economic activity across genders and its changing roles during the course of economic development has been a central topic of inquiry since Ester Boserup's pioneering work on *Woman's Role in Economic Development*. This is, of course, a complex phenomenon and its systematic analysis is complicated by measurement issues. Goldin's work greatly contributed to its understanding and inspired much of the subsequent work on the topic. In a series of seminal papers, Goldin establishes the existence of a U-shaped labor supply of women across the process of economic development, and the important roles played by education and the emergence of a white-collar sector in fostering the paid employment of married women.

The absence of a clear distinction between market production and work for the family affects the measurement of labor force participation in early phases of economic development, especially for women. Goldin's extensive work to fill the gaps in the historical record on women's work in the United States reveals that female labor force participation was U-shaped: it declined

Claudia Olivetti is associate professor of economics at Boston University and a research associate of the National Bureau of Economic Research.

This chapter was prepared for the "Human Capital in History: The American Record" conference in Cambridge, Massachusetts, December 2012. I thank Francine Blau for her insightful discussion of the chapter. Comments from Carola Frydman, Robert Margo, and two anonymous referees are also gratefully acknowledged. Many thanks to Marric Buessing for her invaluable research assistance and to Sharon D'souza for her help with data collection. I am also grateful to Berthold Herrendorf, Richard Rogerson, and Akos Valentinyi for sharing their historical data on structural transformation. For acknowledgments, sources of research support, and disclosure of the author's material financial relationships, if any, please see http://www.nber.org/chapters/c12892.ack.

during the nineteenth century, reached the bottom sometimes in the 1920s, and then it steadily increased during the twentieth century.

Goldin (1986, 1990) argues that, until the late nineteenth century, women in the United States worked almost exclusively in the home or as unpaid labor in family enterprises. This work involved not only the care of children and the upkeep of the house, but also goods production activities such as the cultivation and preparation of food and the manufacture of many of the goods used in the home or sold in the marketplace (clothing, canned food, etc.). Women, both on farms and in cities, were active participants in the labor force when the home and work activities could be performed in the same place. But their participation declined as the nature of the production process changed and production moved from the household to factories and offices.

Official statistics, however, might not capture the full extent of female participation in the labor market going back in time, especially for married women. According to census data, the labor participation for white women was 16.3 percent in 1890 and it increased to 24.5 percent by 1940, when the census established its labor force construct. As shown in Goldin (1990), the figure for 1890 heavily underestimates women's work, especially for married white women, whose participation rate was particularly low, 2.5 percent (data are from Goldin [1990], table 2.1). Based on her calculations, adding paid and unpaid farm labor of married women and boardinghouse keepers would imply a labor force participation rate for white women in 1890 similar to that observed in 1940. Moreover, Goldin (1986) shows that female labor force participation in 1890 might have been considerably lower than earlier in the nineteenth century and in the late eighteenth century. Thus, more inclusive measures of labor supply trace a U-shaped function: after declining for about a century, the female labor force participation rate was as high in 1940 as it was in 1890 and kept rising thereafter. The bottom of the U must have occurred somewhere between 1890 and 1940.

Goldin (1995) finds further evidence of a U-shaped female labor supply function with economic development (as measured by gross domestic product [GDP] per capita) using a large cross section of countries observed in the first half of the 1980s. Goldin also establishes that increasing women's education and the emergence of the white-collar sector are important determinants of this pattern, both historically and across countries. Subsequent work by Mammen and Paxson (2000), Lundberg (2010), and Luci (2009) provides additional evidence of a U-shaped labor supply based on larger panels of economies observed in the 1970s and 1980s, 2005, and for the years 1965 to 2005, respectively.[1]

---

1. See Blau, Ferber, and Winkler (2014, chs. 17 and 18) for a comparative discussion of a recent cross section of world economies. This work includes an insightful discussion of the experience of the former Soviet countries as well as differences among African economies.

This chapter builds on this work by providing additional evidence on the relationship between the process of economic development and women's labor force participation. Specifically, it investigates whether the United States experience was exceptional historically and whether the timing of a country's transition to a modern path of economic development affects the shape of women's labor supply.

First, the experience of the United States is studied in a comparative perspective relative to a sample of economically advanced economies. Pre–World War II data on labor force participation rates and sectoral employment by gender from the International Historical Statistics (IHS; Mitchell 1998a, 1998b, 1998c) are combined with comparable post–World War II data from the International Labour Organization (ILO) to construct a sample of sixteen developed economies for which data are consistently available for most of the 1890 to 2005 period. The sample includes: Australia, Belgium, Canada, Denmark, France, Finland, Germany, Ireland, Italy, the Netherlands, Norway, Portugal, Spain, Sweden, the United Kingdom, and the United States.[2] The analysis confirms the existence of a U-shaped female labor supply function, coming from both cross-country and within country variation.

Next, ILO data for the years 1950 to 2005 are used to study the link between female labor force participation and income in a large cross section of countries. The analysis of this long panel confirms the findings of Goldin (1990), Mammen and Paxson (2000), Luci (2009), and Lundberg (2010). In addition, it shows that the U-shape is more muted when early Organisation for Economic Co-operation and Development (OECD) economies are not included in the sample. One possible explanation of this evidence is that the stigma toward married women's participation in the labor market, or women's dislike for factory production, might be lower when manufacturing production is cleaner or less brawn-intensive than it was in the nineteenth century. For example, if, as it is the case with electronics in Asia, industrialization is associated with an increased demand for fine motor skills (in which women have a comparative advantage), then industrialization would generate an increase in women's relative wages that, by counteracting the income effect for married women, could potentially lead to a smaller drop in female labor supply. Alternatively, women's labor force participation would not drop as much if economic development is driven by a rapid expansion of the service economy in which women have a comparative advantage and whose wealth of jobs do not share the same stigma as work in factories.[3]

2. Far from being perfect, these data are as close as possible to being harmonized in terms of the definition of the employment construct. See section 5.3.1 and the data appendix for a detailed discussion.
3. It would be interesting to quantify the relative importance of these two alternative explanations. This analysis, which would require a more structural approach, is behind the scope of this chapter and is thus left for future work.

Last, the evolution of women's employment is linked to the process of *structural transformation*. This process is defined in the growth literature as the reallocation of labor across the three main sectors of production: agriculture, manufacturing, and services.[4] The typical process of sectoral reallocation over the course of economic development involves a systematic fall in the share of labor allocated to agriculture, a hump-shaped change in the share of labor in manufacturing, which increases in the early stages of the reallocation process and then declines, and a steady increase in the share of labor in services. This chapter establishes gender differentials in the process of sectoral reallocation. The share of women employed in the agricultural sector drops more rapidly than that of men. The employment share in manufacturing exhibits the distinct hump-shaped profile for both genders, but women's profile is much flatter than men's. The employment share in services increases much more rapidly for women than for men. Interestingly, the gender differentials are smaller in emerging economies.

Taken together, these findings seem to suggest that the timing of a country's transformation from agriculture to manufacturing and services determines whether female labor force participation experiences the first, downward portion of the U. The U-shaped association between economic development and female labor force participation seems to be a feature of economies that went through the transition from agriculture to manufacturing in the nineteenth century and whose service sector significantly expanded decades later. The cleaner, precision manufacturing of the present time and the rapidly expanding service economy in some developing countries may be less likely to trigger norms against women's work.

5.2   Background

The relationship between gender equality and economic development has been widely investigated. On the one end, gender equality contributes to economic development, particularly when the well-being of children is involved. On the other end, economic development might foster gender equality. Among the many useful indicators of women's economic status, including women's educational attainment, health, role in politics, and legal rights, labor force participation is arguably the most fundamental to the evolution of gender roles. However, in the early stages of economic development growth initially lowers female participation to the (formal) labor market, and only subsequently is associated with higher female employment. For this reason, Goldin (1995) points out that the positive relationship

---

4. This process has been extensively documented starting with the work by Kuznets (1966). Recent work by Herrendorf, Rogerson, and Valentinyi (2013) provides systematic evidence about the "facts" of structural transformation for a large cross section of countries and going back in time as far as possible.

between women's status and economic development might be camouflaged, and opposing views on whether economic growth enhances gender equality might arise.

What do we know about the U-shaped female labor supply function and its determinants outside the United States?

A rich literature analyzes this phenomenon with reference to supply and demand factors that played an important role in the evolution of female labor force participation, and can explain the observed cross-country variation.[5] Here, the discussion is organized around the link between female labor force participation and structural transformation.

Women's influence on production across phases of economic development depends on the degree of substitution between their own labor in agricultural production and other activities, on the degree of substitution between labor and capital, and between male and female labor inputs under different production, organizational, and social conditions.

For example, the declining portion of the U-shape can be explained by the change in the nature of agricultural work as an economy moves away from subsistence agriculture. This change typically involves a shift from very labor-intensive technologies, where women are heavily involved as family workers, to capital-intensive agricultural technologies where men tend to have a comparative advantage because of the physical strength these technologies require (Boserup 1970).[6]

The early transition to a mostly industrial economy is characterized by conflicting forces affecting women's work. For instance, in the United States, the expansion of the manufacturing sector was accompanied by a process of de-skilling as the factory system began to displace the artisanal shop in the 1820s (Goldin and Sokoloff 1982). De-skilling became rapidly more marked as production increasingly mechanized with the adoption of steam power after 1850 (Atack, Bateman, and Margo 2008). Goldin and Sokoloff (1984) argue that the United States agricultural areas, where the marginal products of females and children were low relative to those of adult men, were the first to industrialize. This "relative productivity hypothesis" predicts that the lower the relative productivity of females and children in the preindustrial agricultural economy, the earlier manufacturing is likely to evolve.

Thus, it seems that with the increasing industrialization happening during

---

5. See Goldin (1990, 2006), Blau, Ferber, and Winkler (2014, chap. 2), Blau (1998), and Blau and Kahn (2007) for a comprehensive discussion of the factors affecting the trends in the United States at different points in time; Blau, Ferber, and Winkler (2014, chaps.17 and 18) for international comparisons; and Lundberg (2010) for a discussion of the changing sexual division of labor with economic development.

6. Boserup (1970) offers plough cultivation as an example. She argues that plough agriculture might originate traditional gender role attitudes that affect the gender division of labor, potentially lowering female labor force participation. Recent work by Alesina, Giuliano, and Nunn (2013) proves Boserup's hypothesis right.

the nineteenth century there was initially a greater demand for (relatively unskilled) female labor. Why, then, did female labor force participation decrease during early industrialization?

First, as shown by Katz and Margo (this volume, chapter 1), the demand for unskilled female workers was probably not exceedingly high. They show that the share of female workers was positively correlated with the use of steam and water power, and with capital deepening. However, the positive correlation largely disappears (and even becomes negative for steam) once they control for establishment size, which is positively associated with the percent of unskilled workers, as in Goldin and Sokoloff (1982). Moreover, "the evidence on size and relative use of female and child labor does not reflect the full extent of division of labor in nineteenth-century manufacturing, because many establishments did not hire women or children, and yet were relatively large." (Katz and Margo, this volume, p. 32)

Second, there was some kind of redistribution of employment across groups, as single women, who began to leave the house to work in factories, displaced widows handling the artisanal shop of their deceased husbands (Goldin 1986).

Third, as emphasized in Goldin (1990), production processes in the early phases of industrialization were characterized by dirty, noisy, and often physically demanding jobs. While it might be acceptable for a single woman to work in such conditions, the expectation was that a single woman would work only until her marriage. Stated differently, there was a stigma against married women working as manual laborers in factory-type work.[7] Because of the changing nature of agricultural production, as well as the stigma attached to women's employment in manufacturing, the "income effect" dominated during this phase of development, and female labor force participation declined.

The increasing portion of the U during the transition from the industrial to the postindustrial phase of economic development is unambiguously associated with increasing female labor force participation and changing gender roles. The expansion of the service sector with its attendant white-collar jobs and/or the pervasive skilled-biased technological change in the economy (see Goldin and Katz 2008; Katz and Margo, this volume, chapter 1) greatly facilitated this transformation (Goldin 1990, 2006). As intellectual skills grew in importance in market production relative to physical power, increasing relative wages lowered fertility and increased labor force par-

---

7. In August 1936, a Gallup poll asked: "Should a married woman earn money if she has a husband capable of supporting her?" A resounding 82 percent answered no. A similar question was asked in October 1938 and November 1945. In both instances 78 percent of Americans disapproved of a "woman earning money in business or industry if she has a husband capable of supporting her." Given the changes in the economic outlook and female labor force participation across these years, it seems reasonable to interpret these sentiments as evidence of a strong stigma toward a working married woman.

ticipation (Galor and Weil 1996).[8] Other types of technological progress reinforced this process by affecting women's investment in human capital and fertility choices.[9]

5.3 The American Experience in Comparative Perspective: Developed Economies

I use data from sixteen high-income countries over the period 1890 to 2005 to trace the relationship between economic development and women's labor force participation. The data set is constructed using information reported from the International Historical Statistics (Mitchell 1998a, 1998b, 1998c) and, for the post-1950 period, the International Labour Organization (ILO).[10] The past experience of economically advanced countries is interesting. While they are similar to the United States in many ways, they transitioned across stages of economic development at different points in time. Table 5.1 summarizes statistics on GDP per capita expressed in 1990 international dollars (column [2]), sectoral employment shares (columns [3] to [5]) and value-added shares (columns [6] to [8]), for a subset of developed economies at three points in time: 1890, 1950, and 2000. The first panel in the table reports statistics for the United States followed by Belgium, the Netherlands, France, Spain, Sweden, and the United Kingdom.[11]

The range of experiences spanned by these countries is quite heterogeneous. The United Kingdom had the highest GDP per capita in 1890, only 16 percent of its workers were employed in agriculture and the agricultural value-added share was below 10 percent, a relatively "postindustrial" value. The manufacturing sector employed 44 percent of its workers (value-added share of 41 percent). The broad service sector employed 40 percent of its workers and had the highest value-added share, 50 percent.

The other countries were well behind in the process of structural transformation. In the United States, the country with the third highest GDP per capita in 1890, the employment share in agriculture was still quite high (42 percent), although the size of the sector as measured by its value-added

---

8. Most models in this vein predict a monotonic relationship between growth and female labor force participation. Galor and Weil (1996, 384–85) is an exception. They propose extensions of their model that can generate the U-shaped labor supply. For example, by adding a technology for producing market goods that is not fully a rival with raising children at home and does not require capital.

9. For example, progress in medical technologies related to motherhood (Albanesi and Olivetti 2009), progress in contraceptive technology (Goldin and Katz 2002; Bailey 2006), and progress in household technologies in new domestic appliances (Greenwood, Seshadri, and Yorukoglu 2005). Changing cultural norms and attitudes toward gender roles might also have played a role (see, for example, Fernandez, Fogli, and Olivetti 2004; Fogli and Veldkamp 2011; Fernandez 2013).

10. See data appendix for details about data sources and measurement issues.

11. Data on GDP per capita are from Maddison (2010). Sectoral data are constructed and discussed in Herrendorf, Rogerson, and Valentinyi (2013).

Table 5.1   **GDP per capita and sectoral shares: Selected countries, 1890–2000**

Year (1)	GDP per capita (2)	Employment shares			Valued-added shares		
		Agriculture (3)	Manufacturing (4)	Services (5)	Agriculture (6)	Manufacturing (7)	Services (8)
		United States					
1890	3,391	0.427	0.272	0.301	0.190	0.350	0.460
1950	9,557	0.109	0.340	0.551	0.068	0.357	0.575
2000	28,481	0.024	0.204	0.772	0.010	0.218	0.773
		Belgium					
1890	3,429	0.321	0.415	0.264	0.110	0.440	0.451
1947	4,798	0.140	0.517	0.343	0.082	0.415	0.503
2000	20,661	0.023	0.220	0.757	0.013	0.244	0.743
		France					
1886	2,237	0.470	0.257	0.273	0.273	0.390	0.337
1954	5,914	0.263	0.355	0.382	0.130	0.480	0.390
2000	20,415	0.039	0.212	0.749	0.028	0.229	0.743
		Netherlands					
1889	3,502	0.365	0.316	0.319	0.208	0.321	0.471
1947	5,049	0.187	0.356	0.458	0.130	0.370	0.500
2000	22,159	0.034	0.194	0.771	0.026	0.249	0.724
		Spain					
1887	1,586	0.694	0.160	0.147	0.336	0.280	0.384
1950	2,189	0.496	0.255	0.249	0.287	0.270	0.443
2000	15,615	0.063	0.294	0.642	0.044	0.292	0.664
		Sweden					
1890	1,769	0.581	0.234	0.184	0.304	0.271	0.424
1950	6,768	0.208	0.420	0.372	0.112	0.425	0.463
2000	20,702	0.032	0.285	0.683	0.012	0.306	0.681
		United Kingdom					
1891	3,976	0.157	0.436	0.407	0.090	0.410	0.500
1950	6,940	0.053	0.454	0.493	0.050	0.470	0.480
2000	20,353	0.017	0.221	0.762	0.010	0.270	0.715

Sources: GDP per capita in 1990 dollars (PPP adjusted) from Maddison (2008) Employment and value-added shares from Herrendorf, Rogerson, and Valentinyi (2013).

share was already less than 20 percent, an indication of low labor productivity in agriculture. The rest of the economically active population was equally distributed in the manufacturing sector (27 percent) and in services (30 percent), but the service sector had the largest value-added share (46 percent). The remaining economies were still prevalently agricultural at the turn of the twentieth century. At least half of the economically active population in France, Spain, and Sweden, the three countries with the lowest GDP per capita in 1890, was employed in agriculture. However, by 1950 most of these countries had industrialized and were on the verge of a phase of rapid economic growth. In all countries, except for Spain, the employment share in agriculture had dropped to less than 30 percent (with a value-added share around or below 10 percent), and the log of GDP per capita was around 9, a level that is associated with the onset of the decline of the manufacturing sector and the rise of the so-called service economy (Herrendorf, Rogerson, and Valentinyi 2013). By 2000, all the countries in the table are in a mature phase of economic development. The employment and value-added shares are 5 percent or lower in agriculture, approximately 20 percent in manufacturing, and 70 percent or higher in the service sector.

Table 5.1 shows that, although these countries are comparable in terms of standards of living (and have been for the past few decades), they still display substantial cross-country variation in the timing of economic development and industrial transformation. Consequently, looking at the past experience of currently developed economies can contribute to our understanding of the U-shaped relationship between economic development and female labor force participation.

5.3.1   Data and Measurement Issues

The history of women's participation in market work is complicated by measurement issues. The concept of being in the labor force is often ambiguous, and its definition can vary substantially across countries and time periods as well as over time within a country. I developed a panel data set for sixteen high-income countries that contains comparable data on labor force participation for the population age fifteen and older and the sectoral distribution of workers for the period 1890 through 2005. This sample of "developed economies" includes: Australia, Belgium, Canada, Denmark, France, Finland, Germany, Ireland, Italy, the Netherlands, Norway, Portugal, Spain, Sweden, the United Kingdom, and the United States. The year 1890 is the first for which a starting data point is available for almost all countries. In Australia and Denmark the first available year is 1900. The end date is the latest year for which International Labour Organization (ILO) statistics are available. The data are available at ten- or five-year intervals for most of the countries in the sample. Starting with 1990, data at five-year intervals are available for all countries.[12]

The United States

Prior to 1940, only workers who reported an occupation were classified as "gainfully employed" and thus included in the labor force in the United States. Starting in 1940, and consistent with the ILO construct of "economically active" population, the definition of labor force participation was revised to include all individuals working for pay, unpaid family workers,

---

12. Keeping only the statistics at ten-year intervals or changing the start and end point of the sample does not significantly alter the main findings of the analysis.

and also the unemployed seeking work during the survey week. It is not surprising then that the International Historical Statistics (IHS), which uses the ILO definition of labor force participation, does not report data for the United States prior to 1940. To circumvent this problem, this chapter combines 1890 to 1930 female labor force participation rates from Goldin (1990, table 2.1, first row), with 1940 to 2005 data from the IHS and the ILO, in the same way as for the other countries in the sample.[13] Note that when they overlap (that is, between 1940 and 1980), the labor force participation statistics from the IHS and the ILO are almost identical to those from table 2.1 in Goldin (1990). This perfect overlap is also noted in Goldin (1990, 43). She argues that the 1940 change in the definition of employment has no effect on the participation rate of women: "Applying the labor force concept to the pre-1940 data produces approximately the same numbers as obtained by the gainful worker definition." Goldin (1990, 44) also shows that the most important source of bias for female labor force participation comes from the undercounting of people working as boardinghouse keepers, unpaid family farm workers, and manufacturing workers in homes and in factories. This is because women were disproportionately engaged in these activities. Section 5.3.2 returns to this point.

Other Countries

It is difficult to construct somewhat comparable female labor force statistics going back to the second half of the nineteenth century for a relative large cross section of countries. Goldin's discussion centers on US statistics; however, similar concerns about undercounting women working in family enterprises or working for very few hours generally applies. For example, Costa (2000) discusses the existence of similar measurement issues related to historical data on female participation for France and Great Britain. Here, pre–World War II data on economically active populations by gender and by industrial group, as well as population counts by gender from the IHS (Mitchell 1998a, 1998b, 1998c) are combined with similar post–World War II data from the ILO. Based on this data, a long time series of labor force participation rates for women and men age fifteen and older can be constructed.[14] Although imperfect, these data are probably as close as possible to being harmonized in terms of the ILO definition of the employment construct. The ILO definition classifies an individual as economically active if he/she is working for pay or profit at any time during the specific reference period, *whether he/she receives wages or not.* This definition of employment varies across countries, but it generally includes unpaid family farm workers, those in family businesses, and own-account traders. Accord-

13. Labor force participation rates for men age fifteen and above for years prior to 1940 were gathered from Pencavel (1986, table 1.1). See the data appendix for further details.
14. See the data appendix for additional details. Unfortunately, the data do not allow the construction of historical labor force statistics by age.

ing to Mitchell (1998a, 161), the statistics prior to 1968 were unified across different countries and different time periods to adhere to this definition as much as possible. Post-1968 IHS data were pulled directly from the ILO tables, and thus should be harmonized using sophisticated estimation and imputation procedures.[15] Recent versions of the ILO labor statistics report data start with the 1940s. This overlap between the available ILO and IHS statistics is exploited to detect and fix inconsistencies in the data (see the data appendix for details). As a consequence of this further check, some of the nineteenth-century data points had to be dropped from the sample. The resulting panel of sixteen countries is analyzed below.[16] Comparisons between countries, however, must still be made with some caution owing to remaining potential differences in classification, including differences in the definition of "economically active."

5.3.2 Long-Run Trends in Female Labor Force Participation

Figure 5.1 displays female labor force participation rates for each of the sixteen countries in the sample. Based on the figure, it is possible to loosely identify two alternative patterns for the evolution of female labor supply.

Female labor force participation grew monotonically in the United States and Canada. Only 18 percent of women in the United States worked for pay in 1890 and the figure had risen to around 26 percent in 1940, when the definition of the employment construct changed. By the year 2000, women's participation rate in the United States was around 60 percent. However, as argued by Goldin (1990), the 1890 figure is artificially low because it undercounts the paid and unpaid work of married women within the home and on the farm. Goldin estimates a 7 percentage point adjustment in female labor force participation for 1890, mostly stemming from unpaid employment of family members in agriculture and from widespread boarding in late nineteenth-century cities (see Goldin 1990, table 2.9, 44). The adjustment implies that female labor force participation in 1890 was in the vicinity of 26 percent and, therefore, is as high as in 1940.[17] Goldin (1990, 45) argues that the "obvious implication is that the labor force activity of adult and married women must have reached a minimum point sometime just after the turn of the century, falling before that time and rising after. Thus the

15. See ILO report (2011) for a discussion of the difficulties collecting high-quality data for women's labor force participation.

16. For a few of these countries, namely Belgium, the Netherlands, and the United Kingdom, it is possible to calculate labor force participation rates by gender going as far back as 1840–1850. The trade-off is that the statistics for the earlier decades of the nineteenth century, especially pre-1870, are only available for a very small subset of countries. Using 1890 as a start date delivers the most balanced panel of countries going as far back in time as possible. The results of the analysis are basically unchanged if the sample starts in 1870 or 1880.

17. Most of the adjustment comes from white married women. Goldin (1990) estimates a rate of omission of 10 percentage points for this group. This implies a 12.5 percent labor force participation rate for white married women in 1890, as opposed to the 2.5 percent figure from the census.

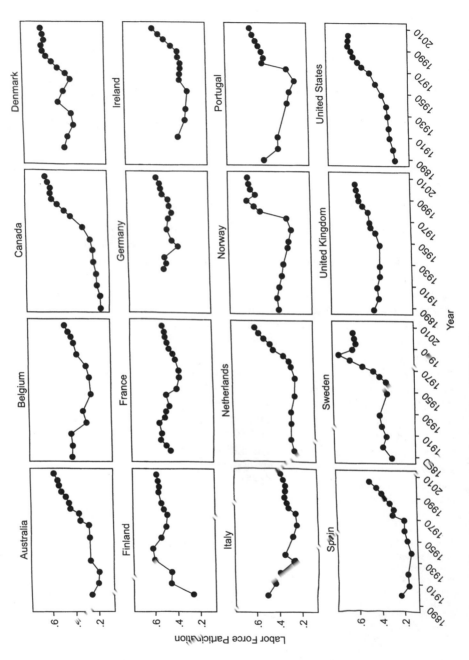

Fig. 5.1 Trends in female labor force participation, 1890–2005

participation of married women in the labor force may well be somewhat U-shaped over the course of economic development."[18] Although the monotonicity of female labor supply might be genuine for Canada, it is reasonable to think that undercounting of women's paid or unpaid work at home and on the farm might be also be plaguing these estimates.

In most of the remaining countries, the trends in female labor force participation are U-shaped, although in some cases the U is more muted than in others. Women's participation rates in Great Britain were the same in the early 1960s as they were in the past two decades of the nineteenth century. This pattern is consistent with the analysis in Costa (2000). In Belgium female labor force participation hovers around 41 percent from 1890 to 1910, and then drops substantially and starts increasing again in the 1950s, reaching 41 percent again only by the mid-1990s. Ireland's trend is very similar to that observed for Belgium. Spain, Portugal, and Italy also exhibit a U-shaped female labor supply, although at lower levels of female labor force participation. The female participation rate in Spain was the same, around 23 percent, in 1890 as in 1970. In Italy women's labor force participation in year 2000 was still 13 percentage points lower than in 1900.[19] The time path of female labor supply is also U-shaped in Australia, the Netherlands, and Sweden, although the U is more muted in these countries. Finally, France and Finland both display a slightly N-shaped pattern for female labor supply. Female labor force participation in France was around 44 percent at the turn of the twentieth century, peaked at 53 percent in 1920, and then dropped and rose again during the course of the twentieth century. Yet, by year 2000 female labor force participation was still lower than in 1920.[20] Finland's trend is very similar to France's, although the peak of the N occurs twenty years later, in 1940.[21]

---

18. In other work, Goldin (1986) shows that female labor force participation might have been even higher at the turn of the nineteenth century, thus implying an even stronger U-shape. Using data from twenty-six cities and business directories for Philadelphia, she estimates that in 1800 the labor force participation rate for female head of households (mostly widows) was around 65 percent, dropping to approximately 45 percent by 1860.

19. Denmark's female labor supply is also U-shaped. The apparent W-shape observed in figure 5.1 is due to a blip in 1940. This "deviation from trend" in the labor force participation series is observed both for men and for women. This suggests that it might be driven by factors other than gender. In any case, the 1940 data point for Denmark should be used with caution.

20. Costa (2000, figure 2) documents the same pattern for France using a different data source. She argues that the N-shape can be explained by the fact that the French agricultural sector was large and employed many women (more than in Great Britain or in the United States) and that France industrialized very slowly. Costa also observes that this could be a common feature of economic development across countries. That is, if we go back in time, women's participation may have more of an N-shape.

21. Similar to France, Finland's experience is associated with a larger and more female-intensive agricultural sector and a slower rate of industrialization (than in Britain or the United States).

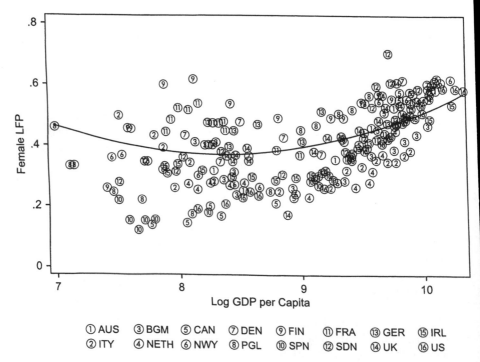

| ① AUS | ③ BGM | ⑤ CAN | ⑦ DEN | ⑨ FIN | ⑪ FRA | ⑬ GER | ⑮ IRL |
| ② ITY | ④ NETH | ⑥ NWY | ⑧ PGL | ⑩ SPN | ⑫ SDN | ⑭ UK | ⑯ US |

Fig. 5.2   Female labor force participation and economic development, 1890–2005

5.3.3   Female Labor Force Participation and Economic Development

Having discussed the trends, figure 5.2 plots the relationship between female labor force participation and log GDP per capita. The distinct U-shaped relationship between the two series is apparent. Female participation rates tend to be high, above 40 percent, both at low and at high levels of income per capita, and dip below 40 percent in between.

Table 5.2 reports the results of a quadratic regression of labor force participation against log GDP per capita and its square term. Columns (1) to (3) report the results obtained for women as we progressively add year and country fixed effects. Column (4) displays the estimates for men based on the full specification.

Column (1) displays the estimates for the fitted U-shaped line shown in figure 5.2. All coefficients are statistically significant at the 1 percent level. This result is based on comparing women's labor force participation in a set of countries observed over multiple time periods and it could be driven by some other (common) aggregate factors that are changing over time. Thus the specification in column (2) adds year fixed effects, something akin to comparing repeated cross sections of countries by year. The estimates are

Table 5.2   Female labor force participation and economic development: Sixteen developed economies, 1890–2005

	Female		Male	
	(1)	(2)	(3)	(4)
Log GDP per capita	−1.178***	−1.030**	−0.846*	−0.192
	(0.251)	(0.388)	(0.460)	(0.478)
Log GDP per capita squared	0.072***	0.064**	0.053*	0.013
	(0.014)	(0.023)	(0.026)	(0.027)
Constant	5.159***	4.431**	3.699*	1.661
	(1.107)	(1.637)	(1.971)	(2.074)
N	240	240	240	230
R²	0.449	0.518	0.725	0.784
Country effects	No	No	Yes	Yes
Year effects	No	Yes	Yes	Yes

statistically significant at the 5 percent level, though the U becomes slightly more muted in this case. Column (3) reports the results when instead we add both year and country fixed effects. This specification shows the relationship within countries over time while controlling for differences across years that are common to all countries. The main finding is confirmed, although the U-shape is slightly more muted than in the previous cases and the point estimates on log GDP per capita and its square are now statistically significant only at the 10 percent level. Finally, column (4) reports the estimates for males using the same specification as in column (3). Males can be seen as a placebo group since almost all men age fifteen or older work, and this is true at all levels of economic development spanned by this panel of countries.[22] Consistent with this hypothesis, I find no clear relationship between male labor force participation and economic development. The coefficient estimates are very small and not statistically significant.[23]

To ease the interpretation of the results in table 5.2, figure 5.3, panel A, graphs the implied relationship between labor force participation and income based on the estimates in columns (2) and (3).[24] The figure shows that the country fixed effects estimates produce a slightly more muted U-shape,

22. With the caveat that in all countries there is a declining trend in male labor supply driven by increasing years of education and early retirement.
23. To mitigate concerns that the results in table 5.2 might be driven by cross-country differences in employment classification, a specification is also run where the dependent variable is the female-to-male labor force participation ratio (mismeasurement should be, at least in part, common across genders within a country). The results confirm the main findings based on levels.
24. Because the level of the U in the country and year effect specification differs across countries, the vertical position of the function is scaled so that it lies at the average position of the curve across all countries.

but the two curves are not substantially different from each other. Thus, a quadratic can capture equally well the evolution of female labor force participation across countries and for individual countries as they grow. This is not surprising in light of the finding that in many of the countries in this sample female labor force participation traces a U-shape *over time* (see figure 5.1) but, as shown in the next section, this is not a pattern that generally holds for the post–World War II period.

As discussed in section 5.2, one of the regularities established in the literature on structural transformation is that the manufacturing share peaks when log GDP per capita is around nine (Herrendorf, Rogerson, and Valentinyi 2013). This peak corresponds to the onset of the expansion of the so-called service economy. Based on the estimates in table 5.2, we can compare the trough of the U-shaped labor supply function to the peak of the manufacturing share. The lowest female labor force participation rate is 29 percent for the regression with year effects and 32 percent for the country effect specification, corresponding to a log GDP per capita of 8.04 and 7.98, respectively (equivalent to 1990 international dollars 2,900 and 3,100). These estimates indicate that the growth in female labor force participation precedes the acceleration in the growth of the service sector. Men may gain from the shift away from agriculture initially, with more robust manufacturing growth, but women who concentrate in service sector jobs are well positioned in what will eventually be the leading sector.

5.4   Female Labor Force Participation and Economic Development, 1950–2005

Next I analyze a full sample of advanced and emerging economies for the period 1950 to 2005.[25] The purpose of repeating the analysis for this larger sample is twofold. First, it enables the further investigation of the relationship between female labor force participation and economic development by using information on education and labor force participation rates by age group that is not available for the longer data series. Second it enables to study whether the findings in the previous section apply more generally.

Table 5.3 presents the results of this analysis. Column (1) reports the coefficients for the basic regressions with no controls, columns (2) and (3) include year effects, and columns (4) to (6) include both year and country fixed effects. Following Goldin (1995), columns (3) and (5) add the log gender differential (male-female) in years of schooling. Finally, column (6) reports the results for males. The concept of labor force participation in

25. Labor force participation data were pulled directly from the ILO web page, see the data appendix for details. Note that the analysis in this chapter is consistent with that by Goldin (1995) and Mammen and Paxson (2000) based on the United Nations WISTAT collection. This is because the labor statistics in WISTAT are taken from the ILO. Data on educational attainment by gender are from Barro and Lee (2010).

Table 5.3 Female labor force participation, education gap, and GDP per capita: Full sample, 1950–2005

	Females			Males		
	(1)	(2)	(3)	(4)	(5)	(6)
15–64 years old						
Log GDP per capita	−1.025***	−0.797***	−1.126***	−0.336*	−0.351**	−0.034
	(0.224)	(0.216)	(0.195)	(0.178)	(0 167)	(0.057)
Log GDP per capita squared	0.063***	0.049***	0.066***	0.020*	0.021**	0.004
	(0.013)	(0.013)	(0.012)	(0.010)	(0.010)	(0.003)
Log of male to female yrs. school			−0.171***		−0.010	
			(0.036)		(0.032)	
Constant	4.596***	3.592***	5.146***	1.264*	1.340**	1.027***
	(0.935)	(0.907)	(0.827)	(0.719)	(0.673)	(0.229)
N	871	871	871	871	871	871
*R*²	0.116	0.290	0.375	0.863	0.863	0.744
45–59 years old						
Log GDP per capita	−1.328***	−1.072***	−1.437***	−0.436**	−0.354*	0.110**
	(0.257)	(0.250)	(0.232)	(0.184)	(0.181)	(0.051)
Log GDP per capita squared	0.080***	0.064***	0.083***	0.025**	0.020*	−0.006*
	(0.015)	(0.015)	(0.014)	(0.011)	(0.011)	(0.003)
Log of male to female yrs. school			−0.197***		0.051	
			(0.045)		(0.054)	
Constant	5.930***	4.763***	6.488***	1.620**	1.208	0.523**
	(1.070)	(1.047)	(0.983)	(0.752)	(0.753)	(0.204)
N	824	824	824	824	824	824
*R*²	0.137	0.298	0.367	0.893	0.894	0.744
Country effects	No	No	No	Yes	Yes	Yes
Year effects	No	Yes	Yes	Yes	Yes	Yes

Sources: International Labour Organization; see data appendix for a full description. Education data, Barro and Lee (2010).
Notes: Robust standard errors in parentheses are clustered at the country level. Years are at five-year intervals. If multiple data points exist the values are averaged over the five-year period.
***Significant at the 1 percent level.
**Significant at the 5 percent level.
*Significant at the 10 percent level.

the first panel is the fraction of economically active women age fifteen to sixty-four. The second panel reports the results for women age forty-five to fifty-nine. Fertility is higher in countries with a lower living standard and, at the same time, it is inversely related to female labor force participation in a cross section of developed and developing economies (Feyer, Sacerdote, and Stern 2008). The forty-five to fifty-nine age restriction, also used by Goldin (1995) and Mammen and Paxson (2000), helps minimize the confounding effect that cross-country differences in fertility might have on the correlation between female labor force participation and GDP per capita.

Entries in table 5.3 confirm the results obtained for the historical sample of developed economies. Every specification shows a statistically significant U-shaped relationship between female labor force participation and log GDP per capita, though the U is more muted once we control for country fixed effects. This effect holds controlling for the gender gap in years of schooling and for both measures of female labor force participation. However, as predicted by the theory, the U-shape is more marked for women past their childbearing age. At any level of economic development, female labor force participation is lower when women have fewer years of schooling relative to men (column [3]), although the coefficient is not significant when adding country effects (column [5]). There is no evidence of a U-shaped labor supply for men. If anything, consistent with trends in early retirement, labor force participation of men age forty-five to fifty-nine declines at higher levels of economic development.

Table 5.4 reports the results when countries that joined the OECD before 1973 are excluded from the sample (see notes to table 5.4 for the list of countries). The results in columns (1) to (3) are broadly similar to those observed in table 5.3, except for the fact that the U-shape is now more muted, especially when we use labor force participation of women age fifteen to sixty-four. However, unlike in the previous two tables, the U-shape disappears once we control for country effect (columns [4] and [5]). In other words, for non-OECD economies, female labor force participation does not drop as much as in the full sample as income per capita increases. In contrast to the full sample and the sample for developed countries, the labor supply of older men does not decline with GDP (column [6]). This indicates that early retirement is not a staple of emerging economies, although it is common in more advanced economies.[26]

To ease the comparison of the results across samples, figure 5.3, panels B and C, illustrates how the U-shape varies, within and across countries, based, respectively, on the estimates for the 1950–2005 full sample (columns [2] and [4], table 5.3), and for the sample that excludes early OECD economies (columns [2] and [4], table 5.4). The figure highlights differences in the predicted relationship between female labor force participation and income, both across panels B and C and relatively to the results in panel A. For all samples, the solid line traces a significant U-shape that becomes more muted once we keep only countries that were not part of the OECD as of 1973. In both panels B and C, participation rates are at least 50 percent, both at low and high levels of income. The trough in the U occurs when log GDP per capita is 8.1 (in panel B) and 8.4 (panel C). The corresponding female labor force participation rate is around 35 percent and 38 percent, respectively. Differences across samples emerge once we add country fixed effects.

26. The results of a series of nonparametric regressions show that female labor supply is U-shaped in all decades. For the pre-1980 period, the estimates are not statistically significant; this is due to sample imbalance: there are fewer observations for the earlier years and they are skewed toward relatively richer economies.

Table 5.4   **Female labor force participation, education gap and GDP per capita, 1950–2005 (excludes early OECD countries)**

	Females			Males		
	(1)	(2)	(3)	(4)	(5)	(6)
	15–64 years old					
Log GDP per capita	−0.755**	−0.539*	−0.901***	−0.039	−0.057	0.023
	(0.321)	(0.288)	(0.263)	(0.231)	(0.217)	(0.068)
Log GDP per capita squared	0.045**	0.032*	0.051***	0.002	0.003	0.000
	(0.020)	(0.018)	(0.016)	(0.014)	(0.013)	(0.004)
Log of male to female yrs. school			−0.172***			−0.015
			(0.038)			(0.032)
Constant	3.544***	2.648**	4.320***	0.135	0.233	0.789***
	(1.287)	(1.175)	(1.081)	(0.910)	(0.850)	(0.270)
N	669	669	669	669	669	669
R^2	0.052	0.260	0.355	0.879	0.879	0.770
	45–59 years old					
Log GDP per capita	−1.026***	−0.754**	−1.150***	−0.150	−0.092	0.043
	(0.375)	(0.334)	(0.312)	(0.241)	(0.243)	(0.065)
Log GDP per capita squared	0.061**	0.043**	0.064***	0.008	0.004	−0.002
	(0.023)	(0.021)	(0.019)	(0.014)	(0.015)	(0.004)
Log of male to female yrs. school			−0.195***			0.050
			(0.047)			(0.056)
Constant	4.753***	3.585***	5.398***	0.550	0.240	0.796***
	(1.496)	(1.358)	(1.285)	(0.954)	(0.963)	(0.252)
N	627	627	627	627	627	627
R^2	0.093	0.298	0.372	0.910	0.911	0.756
Country effects	No	No	No	Yes	Yes	Yes
Year effects	No	Yes	Yes	Yes	Yes	Yes

Sources: International Labour Organization. See data appendix for a full description. Education data, Barro and Lee (2010).

Notes: Robust standard errors in parentheses are clustered at the country level. Years are at five-year intervals. If multiple data points exist the values are averaged over the five-year period. Excluded OECD countries are Australia, Austria, Belgium, Canada, Denmark, France, Finland, Germany, Greece, Iceland, Ireland, Italy, Japan, Luxemborg, the Netherlands, New Zealand, Norway, Portugal, Spain, Sweden, Switzerland, Turkey, the United Kingdom, and the United States.

***Significant at the 1 percent level.
**Significant at the 5 percent level.
*Significant at the 10 percent level.

For the full sample (panel B), the U-shape predicted by the regression with country effect is flatter relative to the specification with only year effects.[27] Moreover, the difference between the solid and the dashed line is larger than that observed for the sample of developed countries. For the sample of

27. Mammen and Paxson (2000, figure 2) show a similar pattern for a panel of ninety countries observed in 1970, 1975, 1980, and 1985.

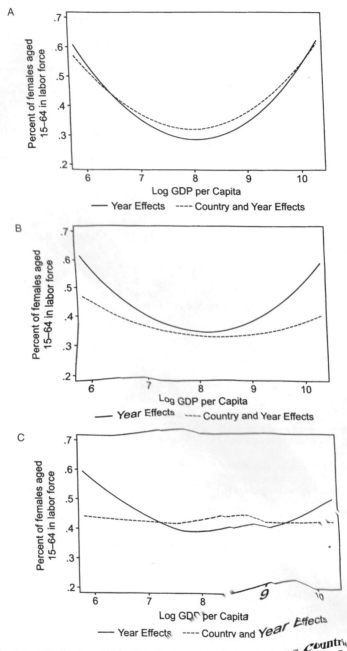

Fig. 5.3   The U-shaped female labor supply within and across countries: *A*, 1890–2005, developed economies; *B*, 1950–2005, full sample; *C*, 1950–2005, excludes OECD countries

non-OECD economies (panel C), the line predicted by the regression with country effect is flat. If anything it declines slightly. For the specification with country and year effects, the bottom of the U corresponds to a female labor force participation rate of 34 percent observed when log GDP per capita is equal to 8.4 (in panel B), and to a 42 percent female labor force participation rate when log GDP per capita equals 9.4 (panel C). Interestingly, for the sample that drops OECD economies the GDP level corresponding to the trough of female labor force participation roughly coincides with the peak of the manufacturing employment share.

The findings are summarized in figure 5.3, which suggests that the presence of a U-shaped female labor supply might depend on the specifics of the process of structural transformation of an economy. One possibility is that the nature of manufacturing production might be cleaner or less brawn-intensive for countries that industrialize in the twentieth century relative to developed economies that went through the transition in the nineteenth century. For example, industrialization could be associated with an increased demand for fine motor skills, in which women have a comparative advantage, as is the case with electronics in Asia. Alternatively, in some countries, like India, the process of economic development could be associated with the expansion of the service economy in which women have a comparative advantage. In either case industrialization would generate an increase in women's relative wages that, by counteracting the income effect for married women, could potentially lead to a smaller drop in female labor supply with economic development.[28]

Before turning to the sectoral analysis, it is interesting to study the interplay between income, occupational composition, and women's participation to the labor market. Goldin (1995) suggests that one reason for the existence of a U-shaped female labor supply function is the relationship between female education, increased white-collar employment, and economic development. At low levels of economic development, education increases for males far more than for females, and women are underrepresented in the clerical sector. Goldin argues that in these cases, women's absence as clerical workers might be explained by their own extremely low level of educational attainment rather than by their education gap relative to men. This conjecture finds support in the data (see Goldin 1995, table 1, 77). Table 5.5 reproduces this analysis for the subsample of countries for which ILO data on occupation are available (see data appendix for details). The results confirm Goldin's findings. The ratio of female-to-male clerical workers is positively

---

28. A valid concern, raised by the discussant, is that there might not be enough within-country variation to identify the U in this sample. This legitimate concern is partly mitigated by the fact that for *all* the non-OECD countries there are at the very least four data points spanning 1990 to 2005 (in many cases one can go back to the 1980s). Further investigation of this pattern with a longer data series and including a larger set of controls is left for future work.

Table 5.5   Clerical work and education: Population age forty-five to fifty-nine

	F/M clerical workers		
	(1)	(2)	(3)
Log of male to female years school	−0.700***	−0.683***	−0.837***
	(0.188)	(0.206)	(0.301)
Percent women with secondary educ.	0.020***	0.025***	0.005
	(0.005)	(0.005)	(0.006)
Constant	0.759***	0.368*	0.686***
	(0.170)	(0.201)	(0.242)
[1em]			
N	354	354	354
R^2	0.111	0.190	0.925
Country effects	No	No	Yes
Year effects	No	Yes	Yes

Sources: International Labour Organization. See data appendix for a full description.

Notes: Robust standard errors in parentheses are clustered at the country level. Years are at five-year intervals. If multiple data points exist the values are averaged over the five-year period.

***Significant at the 1 percent level.
**Significant at the 5 percent level.
*Significant at the 10 percent level.

correlated with the percentage of women with secondary education and negatively correlated with the ratio of male-to-female total years of education. As pointed out by Goldin (1995, 74) this is consistent with Boserup's observation that competition from men serves to force women out of clerical employment. The coefficient on female education loses significance once we control for country effects, indicating that the level of female education is an important determinant of cross-country differences in women's work outcomes.

5.5   Gender and Structural Transformation

The relationship between the process of structural transformation and women's involvement in the labor market has been noted by several authors, especially in relation to the increasing importance of the service sector in the economy. The idea is that production of goods is relatively intensive in the use of "brawn" while the production of services is relatively intensive in the use of "brain." Since men and women may have different endowments of these factors, with women having a comparative advantage in "brain" activities, the historical growth in the service sector may impact female participation in the labor market.

Goldin (1995, 2006) notes that service jobs tend to be physically less demanding and cleaner, thus more "respectable" for women entering the labor force, than typical jobs in factories. Thus the expansion of the service sector is well positioned to generate the rising portion of the U. Insofar as the decline in manufacturing and the parallel rise in services are staggered across countries, this development can explain the international variation in women's labor market outcomes. Only a handful of papers in the recent literature have made this connection explicitly (see Blau and Khan 2003; Rendall 2014; Akbulut 2011; Olivetti and Petrongolo 2011; Ngai and Petrongolo 2012). All these papers are concerned with recent trends in female labor force participation in economically advanced economies and suggest that industry structure affects women's work.[29] Other authors have studied the role of home production in explaining the shift toward services but do not explicitly focus on the link with female labor force participation (see Ngai and Pissarides 2008; Rogerson 2008; Buera and Kaboski 2011, 2012).

Far less has been written about the transition from agriculture to manufacturing. The declining portion of the U can be linked to the change in the nature of agricultural work as an economy moves away from subsistence agriculture. This change typically involves a shift from very labor-intensive technologies, where women are heavily involved as family workers, to capital-intensive agricultural technologies (such as the plough) where men tend to have a comparative advantage because they require physical strength. De Vries (1994) argues that market production increased (also for women) during the early stages of the Industrial Revolution but home production gained importance as female labor market participation declined. As discussed in section 5.2, Goldin and Sokoloff's (1984) "relative productivity hypothesis" predicts that the manufacturing sector would develop earlier in agricultural areas where the relative productivity of females and children is especially low relatively to men. According to this hypothesis, we should see an increase in the demand of female (unskilled) workers but, based on the evidence in Katz and Margo (this volume, chapter 1), this increase should be limited. They show that although the share of female workers was positively correlated with firm size in the nineteenth century, many relatively large establishments did not hire women or children. Moreover, since production in manufacturing was arduous and relatively intensive in the use of brawn, especially in the early phases of industrialization in the nineteenth century, women, especially married women, were more likely to drop out of the market.

To date, no study has proposed a mechanism that can simultaneously generate structural transformation and the full U-shaped pattern for female labor force participation, at least to the author's knowledge. One notable

29. Of course, supply-side factors might be driving the change, although work by Lee and Wolpin (2006) suggests that demand-side factors associated with technical change are likely to be the prevailing force underlying these changes.

exception, although the link to female labor supply is not explicit, is Buera and Kaboski (2012). Their theory emphasizes the scale of the productive unit as being important to understand both movements among broad sectors (agriculture, manufacturing, technology) and movements between home and market production. Among other things, scale technologies can generate the movement of services from the market sector to the home sector, and vice versa. To the extent that the division of labor between home and market activities is gendered, this mechanism has the potential to generate a declining female labor supply, associated with the phase of greatest expansion of the manufacturing sector, as well as the increasing portion of the curve associated with the manufacturing sector decline and the acceleration in the expansion of the service sector.

This is a promising area of research. This chapter contributes to it by documenting gender differentials in the relationship between the process of structural transformation and economic development, both historically and in a modern cross section of countries. Note that using sectoral shares to study the evolution of women's work mitigates some of the issues related to the measurement of female labor force participation, especially for the sample of developed economies. This is because it does not require matching population counts with data about the economically active population.

5.5.1   Developed Economies

As discussed in Herrendorf, Rogerson, and Valentinyi (2013), increases in GDP per capita have been associated with decreases in employment share in agriculture and increases in the employment share in services. The manufacturing share of employment behaves somewhat differently from the other two sectors: its employment share follows an inverted-U shape. At low levels of development the employment share in manufacturing increases with more development. It then reaches a peak and then begins falling as development continues.[30]

The first column in figure 5.4 confirms these findings based on the historical sample of developed economies. The vertical axis in each of the horizontal panels reports the share of economically active population working in agriculture (panel A), manufacturing (panel B), and services (panel C), respectively.[31] The next two columns show how this relationship varies by gender. Specifically, the vertical axis represents the share of economically active women (column [2]) and men (column [3]) employed in each of the three sectors. The trends by gender do not differ from those in the aggregate. That is, for both genders the correlation between GDP per capita and

---

30. The same patterns are observed when using nominal value-added shares.
31. Following the definition of the three sectors in Herrendorf, Rogerson, and Valentinyi (2013), I include mining as well as the utilities sector in the manufacturing sector.

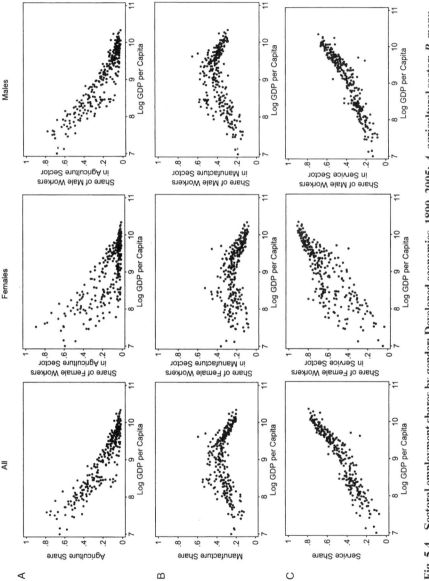

Fig. 5.4 Sectoral employment shares by gender: Developed economies, 1890–2005: *A*, agricultural sector; *B*, manufacturing sector; *C*, service sector

sectoral employment shares is negative in the agricultural sector, positive in the service sector, and it has an inverted-U shape in the manufacturing sector. However, the graph reveals some interesting differences. The female employment share in agriculture seems to drop somewhat less rapidly with log GDP per capita, the inverted-U shape in manufacturing is more muted for women than for men, and the employment share of women in services seems to grow more rapidly.

To investigate whether these gender differentials are statistically significant, table 5.6 reports the results of pooled regressions, by industry, of employment shares against a female dummy, log GDP per capita (entering both linearly and as a quadratic polynomial), and interaction terms between the two. Columns (1) to (3) report the results for the linear specification, columns (4) and (5) those for the quadratic specification. As in earlier tables, controls for year effects (columns [2] and [4]), as well as country effects (columns [3] and [5]), are progressively added.

For the agricultural sector, as shown in panel A, the employment shares drop for both genders but the rate of decline is smaller for women than for men. This finding might be surprising in light of the discussion in section 5.2, but it stems from the fact that both shares are converging to zero as GDP per capita increases. Since men's employment share in agriculture is initially higher than women's, its drop is also larger. The results of the quadratic regressions in columns (4) and (5) confirm this pattern, although the gender differential is not statistically significant in this case.

Panel B reveals strong gender differentials in the manufacturing sector. In the linear specification, male employment shares in manufacturing substantially increase with log GDP per capita, even when we control for both year and country effects, but the increase is much smaller, by about 8 log points, for females. The estimates for the quadratic specification substantially differ by gender. Consistent with Goldin and Sokoloff (1982) and Katz and Margo (this volume, chapter 1), the employment share in manufacturing initially rises more rapidly for women than for men, but it flattens out much earlier so that the inverted-U shape is much more pronounced for men than for women.

The last panel in table 5.6 reports the results for the service sector. Columns (1) to (3) show that the employment share in the service sector increases at a higher rate for women than for men, but the difference is not statistically significant (at standard levels of significance). The results of the quadratic regressions (columns [4] and [5]) reveal the existence of important gender differentials. The increase in the share of women working in services is steeper than men's at low levels of log GDP per capita, but it increases at a decreasing rate as GDP per capita grows. This is not surprising since the share is bounded by 1 and, in all the countries in our sample, 90 percent of all working women are in services. On the other end, the share of men employed in the service sector increases somewhat linearly, or with a slightly convex

Table 5.6   **Sectoral employment shares by gender and GDP per capita: Sixteen developed economies, 1890–2005**

	(1)	(2)	(3)	(4)	(5)
	Agriculture				
Log GDP per capita	−0.221***	−0.330***	−0.359***	−1.091**	−0.810*
	(0.012)	(0.047)	(0.073)	(0.481)	(0.438)
Female x log GDP	0.047**	0.047**	0.047**	−0.137	−0.137
	(0.020)	(0.020)	(0.021)	(0.312)	(0.317)
Log GDP per capita squared				0.045	0.029
				(0.026)	(0.027)
Female x log GDP squared				0.010	0.010
				(0.018)	(0.018)
Female	−0.494**	−0.494**	−0.494**	0.313	0.313
	(0.198)	(0.202)	(0.205)	(1.362)	(1.384)
Constant	2.217***	3.053***	3.363***	6.255**	5.113**
	(0.120)	(0.353)	(0.595)	(2.159)	(1.788)
N	510	510	510	510	510
R^2	0.719	0.766	0.838	0.777	0.841
	Manufacturing				
Log GDP per capita	0.049***	0.122***	0.265***	1.402***	0.844***
	(0.014)	(0.039)	(0.045)	(0.315)	(0.214)
Female x log GDP	−0.087***	−0.087***	−0.087***	−0.564***	−0.564***
	(0.009)	(0.009)	(0.010)	(0.125)	(0.127)
Log GDP per capita squared				−0.074***	−0.035**
				(0.017)	(0.014)
Female x log GDP squared				0.027***	0.027***
				(0.007)	(0.007)
Female	0.624***	0.624***	0.624***	2.718***	2.718***
	(0.089)	(0.091)	(0.092)	(0.539)	(0.548)
Constant	−0.061	−0.630**	−1.857***	−6.081***	−4.253***
	(0.129)	(0.293)	(0.373)	(1.428)	(0.848)
N	510	510	510	510	510
R^2	0.546	0.669	0.844	0.713	0.851
	Services				
Log GDP per capita	0.172***	0.208***	0.094*	−0.311	−0.033
	(0.008)	(0.034)	(0.047)	(0.255)	(0.301)
Female x log GDP	0.040**	0.040**	0.040**	0.701**	0.701**
	(0.017)	(0.018)	(0.018)	(0.266)	(0.271)
Log GDP per capita squared				0.030*	0.006
				(0.015)	(0.018)
Female x log GDP squared				−0.037**	−0.037**
				(0.015)	(0.015)
Female	−0.130	−0.130	−0.130	−3.031**	−3.031**
	(0.172)	(0.176)	(0.179)	(1.155)	(1.173)
Constant	−1.156***	−1.423***	−0.506	0.826	0.140
	(0.067)	(0.254)	(0.386)	(1.061)	(1.256)
N	510	510	510	510	510
R^2	0.820	0.835	0.900	0.838	0.903
Country effects	No	No	Yes	No	Yes
Year effects	No	Yes	Yes	Yes	Yes

Sources: International Historical Statistics, Mitchell (1998a, 1998b, 1998c), and International Labour Organization.

Notes: Robust standard errors in parentheses are clustered at the country level. Years are at five-year intervals. If multiple data points exist the values are averaged over the five-year period.

***Significant at the 1 percent level.

**Significant at the 5 percent level.

*Significant at the 10 percent level.

profile with economic development (being slow at first and then accelerating once the manufacturing sector starts rapidly shrinking).[32]

5.5.2   Full Sample

Figure 5.5 and table 5.7 report the result of the sectoral analysis for the full sample. The results are similar to those observed for the sample of developed economies with a few exceptions. The share of working women employed in agriculture drops more abruptly relative to men (at least for the quadratic specification); the gender gap in service sector shares (favorable to women) is larger; and the manufacturing share of female employment is higher than in the sample of developed economies at all levels of economic development. Once again, this evidence indicates that the nature of manufacturing work might matter for the declining part of the U. Excluding early OECD economies from the sample does not substantially alter this picture. The most notable difference is that both the female service sector share and the gender differential grow more rapidly than in the full sample.

5.6   Conclusions

This chapter shows that there is a consistent U-shaped relationship between women's role in the labor market and the process of economic development, both within and across countries, although the U-shape is more muted for countries developing post-1950. The chapter is purely descriptive and, among the other things, does not discuss the potential determinants for the observed differences in female labor supply across countries and over time. However, differences in taxation, childcare availability, maternity leave policies, institutions, and culture are obviously important.

Although this chapter focuses on female labor force participation, there are other dimensions of women's status that might not vary linearly with economic development. Alesina, Giuliano, and Nunn (2013) confirm the U-shaped relationship for female participation to the labor market (even after controlling for cultural differences across countries), but not for indicators of female participation in politics and entrepreneurial activities. Further investigation using alternative indicators of economic status, such as women's rights or maternal health, could potentially uncover other interesting nonlinear relationships.

One interesting avenue for future research is to use the cross-state variation within the United States to gain a deeper understanding of the determinants of the U-shaped female labor supply: there was (and still is) a substantial

---

32. Additional regressions (not shown) using the female share of total sector employment (that is a measure of female input intensity) as a dependent variable have also been run. The results show that while in the manufacturing sector female intensity declines as its relative importance in the overall economy increases, the female intensity in the service sector is positively correlated with the size of the sector.

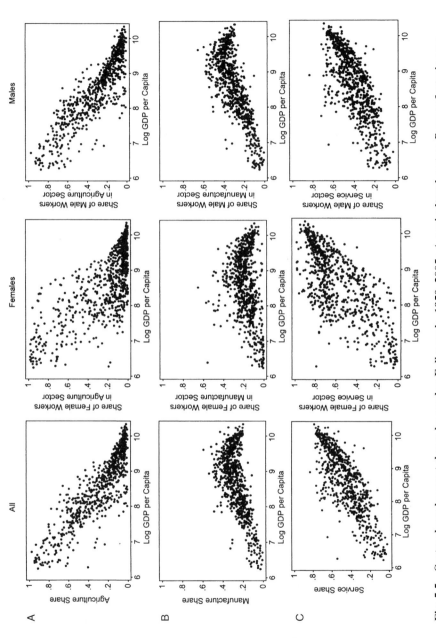

Fig. 5.5 Sectoral employment shares by gender: Full sample, 1950–2005: *A*, agricultural sector; *B*, manufacturing sector; *C*, service sector

Table 5.7　　　　Sectoral employment shares by gender and GDP per capita: Full sample, 1950–2005

	(1)	(2)	(3)	(4)	(5)
		Agriculture			
Log GDP per capita	–0.219***	–0.214***	–0.106***	–0.606***	–0.408**
	(0.007)	(0.008)	(0.024)	(0.123)	(0.183)
Female x log GDP	0.008	0.008	0.008	–0.524***	–0.524***
	(0.012)	(0.012)	(0.013)	(0.175)	(0.182)
Log GDP per capita squared				0.024***	0.017*
				(0.007)	(0.010)
Female x log GDP squared				0.032***	0.032***
				(0.010)	(0.011)
Female	–0.123	–0.123	–0.123	2.076***	2.076***
	(0.116)	(0.117)	(0.122)	(0.713)	(0.744)
Constant	2.179***	2.164***	1.283***	3.787***	2.596***
	(0.066)	(0.069)	(0.170)	(0.528)	(0.801)
N	1360	1360	1360	1360	1360
R^2	0.649	0.654	0.828	0.683	0.837
		Manufacturing			
Log GDP per capita	0.099***	0.107***	0.095***	0.448***	0.688***
	(0.005)	(0.005)	(0.014)	(0.082)	(0.090)
Female x log GDP	–0.073***	–0.073***	–0.073***	0.155*	0.155*
	(0.006)	(0.006)	(0.006)	(0.081)	(0.085)
Log GDP per capita squared				–0.020***	–0.035***
				(0.005)	(0.005)
Female x log GDP squared				–0.014***	–0.014***
				(0.005)	(0.005)
Female	0.509***	0.509***	0.509***	–0.434	–0.434
	(0.049)	(0.050)	(0.052)	(0.331)	(0.345)
Constant	–0.546***	–0.579***	–0.468***	–1.987***	–2.999***
	(0.043)	(0.045)	(0.101)	(0.341)	(0.392)
N	1360	1360	1360	1360	1360
R^2	0.509	0.549	0.754	0.598	0.790
		Services			
Log GDP per capita	0.120***	0.107***	0.011	0.159*	–0.280*
	(0.005)	(0.007)	(0.018)	(0.090)	(0.154)
Female x log GDP	0.065***	0.065***	0.065***	0.369**	0.369**
	(0.011)	(0.011)	(0.011)	(0.163)	(0.170)
Log GDP per capita squared				–0.003	0.017*
				(0.005)	(0.009)
Female x log GDP squared				–0.018*	–0.018*
				(0.010)	(0.010)
Female	–0.386***	–0.386***	–0.386***	–1.642**	–1.642**
	(0.100)	(0.100)	(0.104)	(0.662)	(0.691)
Constant	–0.633***	–0.585***	0.185	–0.800**	1.403**
	(0.047)	(0.054)	(0.137)	(0.376)	(0.669)
N	1360	1360	1360	1360	1360
R^2	0.600	0.630	0.825	0.634	0.827
Country effects	No	No	Yes	No	Yes
Year effects	No	Yes	Yes	Yes	Yes

Sources: International Labour Organization; see data appendix for a full description.

Notes: Robust standard errors in parentheses are clustered at the country level. Years are at five-year intervals. If multiple data points exist the values are averaged over the five-year period.

***Significant at the 1 percent level.

**Significant at the 5 percent level.

*Significant at the 10 percent level.

amount of regional variation in economic structure that can be exploited for identification (see Kim 1998, 1999; Kim and Margo 2004), as well as a substantial variation in married women labor force participation and earnings (Olivetti and Petrongolo 2011). This could be a promising identification strategy because, historically, for married women the geographic location of the household was arguably determined by the husband and thus, at least to a first approximation, can be thought of as exogenous.

Data Appendix

All data sets were merged with historical data on GDP per capita from Maddison (2010). (See http://www.ggdc.net/maddison/maddison-project /home.htm for data and documentation.)

Developed Country Sample

There are reasonable concerns about data comparability, especially for the early period in our sample. Fortunately for developed economies, there is an overlap between the labor force statistics from IHS and those from ILO. Data sources by year are listed in the following section. Countries for which the IHS statistics are inconsistent with the ones from the ILO have been dropped from the sample. In all cases the inconsistency was due to compatibility issues between the numerator (economically active population) and the denominator (population counts). For example, for some of the countries' geographical boundaries were redesigned after wars. The IHS statistics usually refer to a country's boundaries for the year the information was reported; however, there are instances in which the geographical unit at the numerator is not consistent with that at the denominator (for example, Lombardia and Veneto and Austria pre-1890). In other cases the numerator and denominator represented a different age universe or referred to different populations.[33] The next subsection provides more details about this process. For the years of overlap between IHS and ILO statistics, the data source selection rule was to switch to the ILO statistics for the first year they became available, 1950 in most cases. Alternative data source selection rules have also been explored; for instance, using IHS as the main data source and ILO data to "fill the blanks." The overall results of the analysis were unchanged.

Developed Country Sample: Data Sources

Data for the developed countries sample come from the following sources: International Historical Statistics (IHS), Mitchell (1998a, 1998b, 1998c);

---

33. See Mitchell (1998a), notes to "B1 Economically Active Population by Major Industrial Groups."

International Labour Organization (ILO). Pre-1940 data for the United States are from Goldin (1990) and Pencavel (1986). Specifically, I use the following data source/year combinations: Australia: 1900–1920 (IHS), 1960–2005 (ILO); Belgium: 1890–1930 (IHS), 1945, 1960–2005 (ILO); Canada: 1890–1940 (IHS), 1950–2005 (ILO); Denmark: 1890–1940 (IHS), 1950–2005 (ILO); Finland: 1900–1950 (IHS), 1960–2005 (ILO); France: 1895–1955 (IHS), 1960–2005 (ILO); Germany: 1925–1945 (IHS), 1950–2005 (ILO); Ireland: 1910–1935, 1950 (IHS), 1960–2005 (ILO); Italy: 1900–1935 (IHS), 1950–2005 (ILO); Netherlands: 1890–1930 (IHS), 1945, 1960–2005 (ILO); Norway: 1890–1930 (IHS), 1945–2005 (ILO); Portugal: 1890–1910, 1940 (IHS), 1950–2005 (ILO); Spain: 1900–1920, 1940 (IHS), 1950–2005 (ILO); Sweden: 1890–1930, 1950 (IHS), 1960–2005 (ILO); United Kingdom: 1890–1930, 1950 (IHS), 1960–2005 (ILO); United States: 1890–1930 (Goldin 1990 and Pencavel 1986), 1940 (IHS), 1950–2005 (ILO).

Developed Country Sample: Assumptions and Corrections

Economically active data and sectoral data were combined within the International Historical Statistics (IHS) as one table (Mitchell 1998a, 1998b, 1998c). The following set of notes are thus relevant for both the analyses on overall labor force participation and sectoral shares. The sector classification in agriculture, manufacturing, and services is described in a later section. The below list provides all the assumptions and corrections made to the data that was compiled from the IHS.

Economically Active Population—Europe

- France: For the male population, the year 1866 was listed twice. It was assumed that the second 1866 was meant to be 1886 based on the corresponding year listed for women.
- Germany: East and West Germany were combined in the IHS for consistency with the other data sources.

  - Observation for the period 1882 to 1939 in Germany includes statistics for the area considered part of Germany from 1882 to 1939.
  - East Germany includes statistics for the respective territory from 1946 to 1971. Only years 1960 and 1971 include statistics for East Berlin.
  - West Germany includes statistics for the respective territory from 1946 to 1980. Only years 1961, 1970, and 1980 include statistics for West Berlin.
  - Germany includes statistics for the respective territory from 1992.

- Ireland: Northern Ireland was included in the United Kingdom and Southern Ireland is listed as Ireland following 1926 to be consistent with how the ILO reports data for Ireland.

Total Population—Europe

- Denmark: Starting in 1921, Schleswig, which was acquired in that year, is included.
- Germany:

  - Germany: Areas ceded to Germany by Austria, Denmark, and France in 1860–1871 are excluded until 1864.
  - Germany: From 1910 the territories ceded after World War I are excluded.
  - East Germany: Statistics include East Berlin.
  - West Germany: Statistics include West Berlin. The last year following 1970 for West Germany was 1950. This year was changed to 1987 as that was the next census conducted after 1970.[34]

- Italy:

  - The year 1921 was listed twice, the second observation includes territories acquired after World War I.
  - The year 1951 was listed twice, the second observation and all subsequent observations are for the resident population.

- Portugal: Years prior to 1841 do not include Azores and Maderia.
- Sweden: The year 1890 was included twice, consecutively. Based on the Department of National Archives, it was assumed the first observation was in fact 1880 and was adjusted accordingly.[35]

United States

Labor force participation rate for men and women age fifteen and older in the United States for periods prior to 1940 were gathered from Pencavel (1986, table 1.1) and Goldin (1990, table 2.1).

Sector information for the United States prior to 1940 comes from the author's calculations using Integrated Public Use Microdata Series (IPUMS) data for the years 1900 and 1910, and 1920 comes from table Ba670-687 and table Ba688-705 contributed by Matthew Sobek in Carter et al. (2006).

The above data were combined with the EAPEP and ILO data for the 1950 to 2005 period (see below for a full description).

34. *Wall Street Journal*, http://online.wsj.com/article/SB10001424052702303982504576423814268469244.html, and http://www.faqs.org/faqs/genealogy/german-faq/part2/section-4.html\#b.
35. http://www.svar.ra.se/winder.asp?uidObjectGUID=6587EEF0-3E98-4BE3-A404-E1938D3AEA68\&uidRedirectGUID={9BCE8D60-1DC2-43AD-A33C-B758BAE5ACEE}&strType=.

Full Sample

Labor Force Participation Data

Data for 1990–2005 came from the sixth edition of the Economically Active Population, Estimates and Projections (EAPEP) published by the International Labour Organization (ILO). The data provide labor force participation by age group for a harmonized panel of 196 countries.[36]

Labor force data for the full sample prior to 1990 were pulled directly from the Economically Active Population 1A tables from the ILO website.[37]

Sector Data

Sector shares were calculated using data from the ILO Economically Active Population 1C tables. This data source has employment information by industry that can be broadly categorized into agriculture, manufacturing, and services. Data was generally available over the period 1945–2005 but was not consistently gathered for all countries. The International Standard Industrial Classification (ISIC) also changed over time.

Occupation Data

The analysis on clerical work utilized the ILO data discussed above, but limited the sample to women age forty-five to fifty-nine. The labor force participation data was then merged with the ILO Economically Active Population 1E tables, which contains information on occupation by industry and gender.

Classification of Broad Sectors of Production

Sectors were assigned as follows:

- Agriculture corresponds to the sum of ISIC-Rev.3, sections A and B. If ISIC classification was not available, industries were assigned to agriculture if the source table heading said "Agriculture" or "Agriculture, Forestry, and Fishing."
- Manufacturing corresponds to the sum of ISIC-Rev.3, sections C, D, and F and includes mining, manufacturing, and construction. If ISIC classification was not available, industries were assigned to manufacturing if the source table heading said "Mining" or "Extraction Industries" or "Manufacturing" or "Construction" or "Electricity, Gas, and Water Supply" or "Utilities."
- Services corresponds to the sum of ISIC-Rev.3, sections E, G–P, and includes wholesale, retail trade, hotels and restaurants, transport, stor-

36. For a complete write-up of the methodology used see http://laborsta.ilo.org/applv8/data /EAPEP/v6/ILO_EAPEP_methodology_2011.pdf.
37. See http://laborsta.ilo.org/STP/guest.

age and communication, finance, insurance, real estate, business services, and community, social, and personal services. If ISIC classification was not available, industries were assigned to service if the source table heading said "Commerce" or "Finance" or "Trade" or "Transport" or "Communication" or "Services."

The following economically active individuals were classified as missing sector information:

- For 1950 and 1960: ISIC-Rev. 1, code "9 Activities not adequately described."
- For 1970–1990: ISIC-Rev. 2, code "0 Activities not adequately defined."
- For years 2000–2005: ISIC-Rev. 3, section "Q Extra-territorial organizations and bodies" and "X Not classifiable by economic activity."

References

Akbulut, Rahşan. 2011. "Sectoral Changes and the Increase in Women's Labor Force Participation." *Macroeconomic Dynamics* 15:240–64.

Albanesi, Stefania, and Claudia Olivetti. 2009. "Gender Roles and Medical Progress." NBER Working Paper no. 14873, Cambridge, MA.

Alesina, Alberto, Paola Giuliano, and Nathan Nunn. 2013. "On the Origins of Gender Roles: Women and the Plough." *Quarterly Journal of Economics* 128 (2): 469–530.

Atack, Jeremy, Fred Bateman, and Robert A. Margo. 2008. "Steam Power, Establishment Size, and Labor Productivity Growth in Nineteenth Century American Manufacturing." *Explorations in Economic History* 45:185–98.

Bailey, Martha J. 2006. "More Power to the Pill: The Impact of Contraceptive Freedom on Women's Lifecycle Labor Supply." *Quarterly Journal of Economics* 121:289–320.

Barro, Robert, and Jong-Wha Lee. 2010. "A New Data Set of Educational Attainment in the World, 1950–2010." NBER Working Paper no. 15902, Cambridge, MA.

Blau, Francine D. 1998. "Trends in the Well-Being of American Women, 1970–1995." *Journal of Economic Literature* 36 (1): 112–65.

Blau, Francine D., Marianne A. Ferber, and Anne E. Winkler. 2014. *The Economics of Women, Men, and Work*, 7th ed. Upper Saddle River, NJ: Prentice-Hall.

Blau, Francine D., and Lawrence M. Kahn. 2003. "Understanding International Differences in the Gender Pay Gap." *Journal of Labor Economics* 21:106–44.

———. 2007. "Changes in the Labor Supply Behavior of Married Women: 1980–2000." *Journal of Labor Economics* 25:393–438.

Boserup, Ester. 1970. *Woman's Role in Economic Development*. London: George Allen and Unwin Ltd.

Buera, Francisco J., and Joseph P. Kaboski. 2011. "Scale and the Origins of Structural Change." *Journal of Economic Theory* 147 (2): 684–712. doi:10.1016/j.jet.2010.11.007.

———. 2012. "The Rise of the Service Economy." *American Economic Review* 102 (6): 2540–69.
Carter, S. B., S. Gartner, M. Haines, A. Olmstead, R. Sutch, and G. Wright. 2006. *Historical Statistics of the United States: Earliest Times to the Present.* Cambridge: Cambridge University Press.
Costa, Dora. 2000. "From Mill Town to Board Room: The Rise of Women's Paid Labor." *Journal of Economic Perspective* 14:101–22.
De Vries, Jan. 1994. "The Industrial Revolution and the Industrious Revolution." *Journal of Economic History* 54 (2): 249–70.
Fernández, Raquel. 2013. "Culture as Learning: The Evolution of Female Labor Force Participation over a Century." *American Economic Review* 103 (1): 472–500.
Fernández, Raquel, Alessandra Fogli, and Claudia Olivetti. 2004. "Mothers and Sons: Preference Development and Female Labor Force Dynamics." *Quarterly Journal of Economics* 119 (4): 1249–99.
Feyrer, James, Bruce Sacerdote, and Ariel D. Stern. 2008. "Will the Stock Return to Europe and Japan? Understanding Fertility within Developed Nations." *Journal of Economic Perspectives* 22 (3): 3–22.
Fogli, Alessandra, and Laura Veldkamp. 2011. "Nature or Nurture? Learning and Female Labor Force Participation." *Econometrica* 79 (4): 1103–38.
Galor, Oded, and David N. Weil. 1996. "The Gender Gap, Fertility and Growth." *American Economic Review* 86:374–87.
Goldin, Claudia. 1986. "The Economic Status of Women in the Early Republic: Quantitative Evidence." *Journal of Interdisciplinary History* 16 (3): 375–404.
———. 1990. *Understanding the Gender Wage Gap: An Economic History of American Women.* Oxford: Oxford University Press.
Goldin, Claudia. 1995. "The U-Shaped Female Labor Force Function in Economic Development and Economic History." In *Investment in Women's Human Capital and Economic Development*, edited by T. P. Schultz, 61–90. Chicago: University of Chicago Press.
———. 2006. "The Quiet Revolution that Transformed Women's Employment, Education, and Family, Ely Lecture." *American Economic Review, Papers and Proceedings* 96:1–21.
Goldin, Claudia, and Lawrence Katz. 2002. "The Power of the Pill: Oral Contraceptives and Women's Career and Marriage Decisions." *Journal of Political Economy* 100:730–70.
———. 2008. *The Race between Education and Technology.* Cambridge, MA: The Belknap Press of Harvard University Press.
Goldin, Claudia, and Kenneth Sokoloff. 1982. "Women, Children, and Industrialization in the Early Republic: Evidence from the Manufacturing Censuses." *Journal of Economic History* 42:741–74.
———. 1984. "The Relative Productivity Hypothesis of Industrialization: The American Case, 1820 to 1850." *Quarterly Journal of Economics* 99 (3): 461–87.
Greenwood, Jeremy, Ananth Seshadri, and Mehmet Yorukoglu. 2005. "Engines of Liberation." *Review of Economic Studies* 72:109–33.
Herrendorf, Berthold, Richard Rogerson, and Akos Valentinyi. 2013. "Growth and Structural Transformation. NBER Working Paper no. 18996, Cambridge, MA.
International Labour Organization. 1990. *Economically Active Population Estimates and Projections, 1950–2025*, vol. 6. http://laborsta.ilo.org/applv8/data/EAPEP/v6/ILO_EAPEP_methodology_2011.pdf.
———. 2011. "Methodological Description." In *ILO Estimates and Projections of the Economically Active Population*, 6th ed. http://laborsta.ilo.org/applv8/data/EAPEP/v6/ILO_EAPEP_methodology_2011.pdf.

Kim, Sukkoo. 1998. "Economic Integration and Convergence: US Regions, 1840–1990." *Journal of Economic History* 58 (3): 659–83.

———. 1999. "Regions, Resources and Economic Geography: The Sources of US Regional Comparative Advantage, 1880–1987." *Regional Science and Urban Economics* 29 (1): 1–32.

Kim, Sukkoo, and Robert A. Margo. 2004. "Historical Perspectives on US Economic Geography." In *Handbook of Urban and Regional Economics*, Volume 4: Cities and Geography, edited by V. Henderson and J. Thisse, 2982–3019. Amsterdam: North-Holland.

Kuznets, Simon. 1966. *Modern Economic Growth*. New Haven, CT: Yale University Press.

Lee, Donghoon, and Ken Wolpin. 2006. "Intersectoral Labor Mobility and the Growth of the Service Sector." *Econometrica* 74:1–46.

Luci, Angela. 2009. "Female Labour Market Participation and Economic Growth." *International Journal of Innovation and Sustainable Development* 4 (2/3). doi: 10.1504/IJISD.2009.028065; ISSN 1740-8822.

Lundberg, Shelly. 2010. "The Sexual Division of Labour." In *The Shape of the Division of Labour: Nations, Industries and Households*, edited by Robert M. Solow and Jean-Philippe Touffut, 122–48. Cheltenham, UK: Edward Elgar.

Maddison, Angus. 2010. *Statistics on World Population, GDP and Per Capita GDP, 1–2008 AD*. Groningen, Netherlands: University of Groningen.

Mammen, Kristin, and Christina Paxson. 2000. "Women's Work and Economic Development." *Journal of Economic Perspectives* 14 (4): 141–64.

Mitchell, Brian. 1998a. *International Historical Statistics; Europe 1750–1993*. 3rd edition. New York: Macmillan, Stockton.

———. 1998b. *International Historical Statistics; The Americas 1750–1993*, 3rd ed. Basingstoke, England: Macmillan.

———. 1998c. *International Historical Statistics; Africa, Asia & Oceania 1750–1993*, 3rd ed. New York: Macmillan, Stockton.

Ngai, L. Rachel, and Barbara Petrongolo. 2012. "Structural Transformation, Marketization and Female Employment." Unpublished manuscript, London School of Economics.

Ngai, L. Rachel, and Cristopher Pissarides. 2008. "Trends in Hours and Economic Growth." *Review of Economic Dynamics* 11 (2): 429–43.

Olivetti, Claudia, and Barbara Petrongolo. 2011. "Gender Gaps across Countries and Skills: Supply, Demand and the Industry Structure." NBER Working Paper no. 17349, Cambridge, MA.

Pencavel J. 1986. "Labor Supply of Men." In *Handbook of Labor Economics*, vol. 1, edited by Orley C. Ashenfelter and Richard Layard, 3–102. Amsterdam: Elsevier.

Rendall, Michelle. 2014. "The Service Sector and Female Market Work." IEW Working Paper no. 492, University of Zurich.

Rogerson, Richard. 2008. "Structural Transformation and the Deterioration of European Labor Markets." *Journal of Political Economy* 166:235–58.

Comment   Francine D. Blau

Claudia Olivetti's excellent chapter revisits the fundamental issue of the relationship between women's labor force participation and economic development first probed in econometric analyses by Goldin (1990, 1995). In these path-breaking contributions, Goldin builds on the work of Boserup (1970) to advance the hypothesis that the relationship between women's labor force participation and economic development is U-shaped. In the early stages of economic development, women's participation is high since women tend to be heavily involved as family workers in family farms or businesses, or otherwise working for pay or producing for the market within the household. Women's labor force participation initially falls in the course of economic development, along the declining portion of the U, as the locus of production moves out of household and family enterprises and into factories and offices. According to Goldin, this decrease is due both to the negative income effect on women's participation of rising family income and the stigma of women's, particularly married women's, employment as wage workers in manufacturing. The latter, in turn, partially reflects the dirty and unpleasant nature of early manufacturing employments, given which, the employment of a wife is taken as an extremely negative reflection on her husband's ability to provide for his family. As economic development progresses, however, women's education and their consequent opportunities for white-collar employment rise. Women's labor force participation then increases along the rising portion of the U both because the higher wages available to women lead to a substitution effect, increasing their labor force participation, and because white-collar employment does not share the same stigma as factory work and wage labor on farms.

Goldin found strong empirical support for this U-shaped relationship, using both a cross section of international comparative data, as well as historical evidence from the course of economic development in the United States. The latter required painstaking efforts on her part to correct the measured statistics on women's participation for the undercounting of women's activities in earlier periods, including work performed for income in the home (e.g., taking in boarders or doing piecework), unpaid work in family farms and businesses, and even wage work in manufacturing. Goldin's findings regarding the U have been strongly confirmed in subsequent research exploiting international data by Mammen and Paxson (2000), Luci (2009), and Lundberg (2010).

In her impressive contribution to this volume, Olivetti has assembled a

Francine D. Blau is the Frances Perkins Professor of Industrial and Labor Relations and professor of economics at Cornell University and a research associate of the National Bureau of Economic Research.

For acknowledgments, sources of research support, and disclosure of the author's material financial relationships, if any, please see http://www.nber.org/chapters/c12893.ack.

prodigious amount of cross-sectional and time-series data that enables her to substantially raise the bar of the empirical test of the U, as well as to pose a number of new questions. Olivetti finds resounding support for the U, both in international cross sections of early developed countries for the 1890–2005 period and of all countries for the 1950–2005 period. In addition, and of particular interest, her *within country* analysis of early developed economies over the 1890–2005 period also strongly supports the U. This is the first effort that I am aware of to test the U-shape hypothesis controlling for country fixed effects, and hence this finding is especially notable in subjecting the U hypothesis to a particularly stringent test. However, for the 1950–2005 period, Olivetti finds that the U-shape is more muted when the early OECD economies are not included in the cross-sectional sample. Further, she finds no support for the U in within-country analyses that exclude the early OECD countries.

In addition to her econometric exploration of the U, Olivetti provides new evidence regarding the relationship between the evolution of women's employment and the process of structural transformation in the course of economic development. As Olivetti states, the typical process of reallocation of employment across sectors involves redeployment of the labor force, initially, from agriculture to manufacturing and services; and then, as development continues, this is followed by a decline in the share of employment in manufacturing but a continued increase in the share in services. She finds a broad similarity in this experience for both men and women, but with significant gender differences. Women move out of agriculture and into services more rapidly than men do, while men's employment share in manufacturing initially rises more steeply than women's. These gender differences also appear to be smaller in emerging economies.

Taking her findings together, Olivetti suggests that, in the more recent context, the declining portion of the U is less in evidence because, in contrast to the experience of early developing economies, service employments are more plentiful in the earlier stages and manufacturing employments are cleaner and less brawn intensive. She speculates that such employments will not only encounter less stigma but also that the robust demand for women workers in service and less brawn-intensive manufacturing, including manufacturing work that requires fine motor skills, will create a more favorable market for female employment and generate higher relative wages for women than was the case under early industrialization.

Olivetti's analysis is insightful and carefully done, and her new results on emerging economies are provocative and interesting. I am sure this work will garner considerable well-deserved attention and stimulate additional research on the nature of the relationship between women's participation and economic development and the possibility that it has changed over time. My own view is that, while her findings for emerging economies are extremely interesting and certainly not implausible, they would benefit from additional probing in future work. My concern is that there may not be enough variation to identify the U in the emerging economies sample, particularly in the within-country estimates (Hamermesh 2000). The U traces out a long-term relationship between economic development and female labor force participation, using GDP per capita as an indicator of economic development. The international cross section, particularly the version that includes the full sample of countries, is well designed to test the U hypothesis since the included countries span the full course of economic development, from the relatively primitive to the most advanced economies. Similarly, there is considerable within-country variation among the sample of early developed countries, which are observed starting at relatively early stages of industrialization through their emergence as economically advanced nations. Thus, it is not surprising that these samples yield the strongest evidence supporting the U-shaped relationship.

In contrast, some of the countries in the 1950–2005 emerging economies sample experienced relatively modest increases in GDP per capita for considerable periods of time during the window in which they were observed; changes that were likely not substantial enough to be associated with significant economic development. Moreover, even countries experiencing fairly robust growth in GDP per capita may not have experienced a substantial enough increase to trace out a portion of the U during the time period for which data on them are available. For these reasons, it may be difficult to detect a U-shape in a within-country analysis for the emerging economies sample, and this may also explain why the U is more muted when the international cross section is restricted to the emerging economies. Olivetti correctly points out in a footnote that my concern is partly mitigated by the fact that the 1950–2005 data set includes at the very least four data points spanning fifteen years for all the non-OECD countries in the sample. However, this is not sufficient to fully allay my concerns. Thus, I believe Olivetti's findings on emerging economies could use further probing. This might include, not only further investigation using a longer data set and including a larger set of controls, as suggested by Olivetti in a footnote, but also case studies of individual countries, comparable to Goldin's study of the United States for the earlier period.

To the extent that Olivetti's story of a more muted U in emerging economies is borne out, I would add an additional factor militating against a decline in women's participation with early economic development in the current climate. The broad acceptance of women's employment in most of the advanced economies likely has an impact on gender roles and norms in the emerging economies. Much of the literature on the impact of culture focuses on the influence on current behavior of traditional beliefs and norms of an earlier period (e.g., Alesina, Giuliano, and Nunn 2013) or different country of origin (e.g., Blau 1992; Antecol 2000; Fernández and Fogli 2009; Blau, Kahn, and Papps 2011; Blau, Kahn, Liu, and Papps 2013). But our world of increasingly global economic activity and communications likely impacts not only the economic opportunities of women in developing countries, but also the gender roles and norms in those countries. For example, Jensen (2012) finds broad-ranging effects on women in a developing country of new job opportunities in the business process outsourcing industry. In his experimental study, young women in randomly selected Indian villages were provided with three years of recruiting services (e.g., information about job openings, assistance with interview skills) to help them get back office jobs in this new industry. Jensen found that women who received the recruiting services were less likely to marry and have children during this period, and instead obtained more schooling or entered the labor market. As another example, a recent study by Jensen and Oster (2009) suggests the potential broad-reaching effects of increased communications. They identified a number of cultural shifts resulting from the introduction of cable television in rural India, including decreases in the reported acceptability of domestic violence toward women, reduced son preference, lower fertility, and increases in women's autonomy.

Moving to Olivetti's results for the early developed economies, let me begin by noting that she has done an incredible job assembling the data that permit her to trace women's participation patterns over a long period for these economies. Her results highlight some issues that could be addressed in future research. For example, she finds some different patterns within the individual countries—including the classic U-shape, but also monotonically increasing female participation rates in two countries and even a slightly N-shaped pattern in some countries. It would be interesting to know whether the different patterns she uncovered reflect measurement issues or real differences across countries; and, if the latter, how we might explain these patterns. Monotonically increasing female participation is obtained for Canada and the United States. We already know from Goldin's work that the US result is due to measurement issues; however, it is unclear whether or not this is the case for Canada. Olivetti speculates that it is and I am inclined to agree with her but it would be interesting to see further work on this. What the N-shaped pattern represents is a more open question. Addressing these questions would probably entail more detailed historical research of the type that Goldin did for the United States.

Regarding the sectoral patterns by gender that Olivetti uncovers, she makes the interesting point that she and others have examined whether international differences in industrial structure help to explain international differences in women's wage outcomes. A related point I would like to make is that the sectoral pattern she uncovers suggests that women were well positioned in what would eventually become the leading sector in most advanced economies—services. This location of women underlies the evidence for the United States that sectoral demand shifts favoring women help to explain the narrowing of the gender wage gap since 1980 (e.g., Blau and Kahn 1997,

2006; Welch 2000; Bacolod and Blum 2010). Thus, it is interesting to contemplate that what was a disability to women compared to men in earlier stages of economic development, that is, the less robust increase in demand for women than for men in early manufacturing, became an advantage at a later time in the form of women's greater concentration in services.

Let me close by noting one more fruitful area for future research. My suggestion here echoes an especially innovative use of econometric analysis in Goldin (1990). One criticism that is sometimes made of economic modeling is that it abstracts from historical and institutional factors. However, Goldin turns this feature of economic models to her advantage. She estimates an econometric model of married women's labor force participation using decennial US Census data for the period 1890–1980. She finds that the model overpredicts married women's labor force participation for 1930, 1940, and 1950. She presents this discrepancy as evidence in support of her thesis that the process of change in participation for married women was retarded by institutional barriers like marriage bars (i.e., prohibitions against employing married women that were particularly prevalent in teaching and clerical work) and the lack of availability of part-time employment.

My suggestion points to how estimates of the econometric relationship between economic development and female participation, like those Olivetti has produced in this comprehensive analysis, might be used in an analogous fashion to highlight the role of noneconomic factors in accounting for international differences in female labor force participation. Findings reported by Lundberg (2010) suggest that this would be a useful direction. In a cross-sectional graph of the U, where the data points (countries) are labeled, she notes that communist countries (China and Vietnam) lie above the U, suggesting that they have higher than expected female participation rates, given their levels of economic development, while "Muslim countries in the Middle East with many sequestered women drag down the center of the 'U'" (127). This could be formalized in future work, with the estimated U used to develop a measure of expected versus actual participation, given the level of economic development. The difference between the two might make for an interesting shorthand summary measure of the role of political and cultural factors.

References

Alesina, Alberto, Paola Giuliano, and Nathan Nunn. 2013. "On the Origins of Gender Roles: Women and the Plough." *Quarterly Journal of Economics* 128:469–530.

Antecol, Heather. 2000. "An Examination of Cross-Country Differences in the Gender Gap in Labor Force Participation Rates." *Labour Economics* 7:409–26.

Bacolod, Marigee, and Bernardo S. Blum. 2010. "Two Sides of the Same Coin: US 'Residual Inequality' and the Gender Gap." *Journal of Human Resources* 45:197–242.

Blau, Francine D. 1992. "The Fertility of Immigrant Women: Evidence from High Fertility Source Countries." In *Immigration and the Workforce: Economic Consequences for the United States and Source Areas*, edited by G. Borjas and R. Freeman, 93–133. Chicago: University of Chicago Press.

Blau, Francine D., and Lawrence M. Kahn. 1997. "Swimming Upstream: Trends in the Gender Wage Differential in the 1980s." *Journal of Labor Economics* 15 (1, pt. 1): 1–42.

———. 2006. "The US Gender Pay Gap in the 1990s: Slowing Convergence." *Industrial and Labor Relations Review* 60:45–66.

Blau, Francine D., Lawrence M. Kahn, and Kerry L. Papps. 2011. "Gender, Source Country Characteristics and Labor Market Assimilation among Immigrants." *Review of Economics and Statistics* 93:43–58.

Blau, Francine D., Lawrence M. Kahn, Albert Yung-Hsu Liu, and Kerry L. Papps. 2013. "The Transmission of Women's Fertility, Human Capital, and Work Orientation across Immigrant Generations." *Journal of Population Economics* 26:405–35.

Boserup, Ester. 1970. *Woman's Role in Economic Development*. London: George Allen and Unwin, Ltd.

Fernández, Racquel, and Alessandra Fogli. 2009. "Culture: An Empirical Investigation of Beliefs, Work, and Fertility." *American Economic Journal: Macroeconomics* 1:146–77.

Goldin, Claudia. 1990. *Understanding the Gender Wage Gap: An Economic History of American Women*. Oxford: Oxford University Press.

———. 1995. "The U-Shaped Female Labor Force Function in Economic Development and Economic History." In *Investment in Women's Human Capital and Economic Development*, edited by T. Paul Schultz, 61–90. Chicago: University of Chicago Press.

Hamermesh, Daniel S. 2000. "The Craft of Labormetrics." *Industrial and Labor Relations Review* 53:363–80.

Jensen, Robert. 2012. "Do Labor Market Opportunities Affect Young Women's Work and Family Decisions? Experimental Evidence from India." *Quarterly Journal of Economics* 127:753–92.

Jensen, Robert, and Emily Oster. 2009. "The Power of TV: Cable Television and Women's Status in India." *Quarterly Journal of Economics* 124:1057–94.

Luci, Angela. 2009. "Female Labour Market Participation and Economic Growth." *International Journal of Innovation and Sustainable Development* 4:97–108.

Lundberg, Shelly. 2010. "The Sexual Division of Labour." In *The Shape of the Division of Labour: Nations, Industries and Households*, edited by R. M. Solow and J. Touffut, 122–48. Cheltenham, UK: Edward Elgar.

Mammen, Kristin, and Christina Paxson. 2000. "Women's Work and Economic Development." *Journal of Economic Perspectives* 14:141–64.

Welch, Finis. 2000. "Growth in Women's Relative Wages and in Inequality Among Men: One Phenomenon or Two?" *American Economic Review* 90:444–9.

6

The Origin and Persistence of Black-White Differences in Women's Labor Force Participation

Leah Platt Boustan and William J. Collins

The twentieth-century rise in women's labor force participation was one of the most important social changes in American history. The growth in women's market work was precipitated by and, in turn, contributed to a shift in industrial composition from agriculture and manufacturing to services; a revolution in norms and expectations about women's careers; and changes in marriage, fertility, and human capital investment. Writing this complex story—documenting it, analyzing it, and placing it into its social context—has been one of Claudia Goldin's great contributions to scholarship.

As with many other social trends, the levels and changes in female labor force participation have been notably different for black and white women in the United States. Goldin (1977, 1990) proposes that these long-standing racial differences can, in part, be traced back to a "double legacy" of slavery. The widespread poverty and low levels of education in the black population after the Civil War may have had a direct effect on the labor force participation of black women relative to white women. In addition, slavery may have had an indirect effect by shaping prevailing social norms in the black community about women's work. In particular, Goldin hypoth-

Leah Platt Boustan is associate professor of economics at the University of California, Los Angeles, and a research associate of the National Bureau of Economic Research. William J. Collins is the Terence E. Adderley Jr. Professor of Economics and professor of history at Vanderbilt University and a research associate of the National Bureau of Economic Research.

We thank Nayana Bose, Francisco Haimovich, Mike Moody, and Greg Niemesh for research assistance. Members of the KALER group at UCLA provided useful comments on our initial draft. We also appreciate suggestions made by our discussant, Richard Freeman, at the "Human Capital in History" conference; by the conference organizers, Robert Margo and Carola Frydman; and by two referees. For acknowledgments, sources of research support, and disclosure of the authors' material financial relationships, if any, please see http://www.nber.org/chapters/c12902.ack.

esizes that because black women worked intensively under slavery, African Americans developed norms and expectations about women's work that were different from those of most whites and that were carried into the post-Emancipation era.[1] Goldin (1977) demonstrates that observable economic and demographic characteristics cannot account fully for black-white differences in women's labor force participation in the immediate postbellum period, which is consistent with the idea of disparate social norms about women's work by race.

In this chapter we explore how initial gaps in labor force participation, coupled with the intergenerational transmission of work behavior from mother to daughter, may have contributed to racial differences in women's labor force participation well into the twentieth century. We begin by describing trends in labor force participation rates for black and white women from 1870 to 2010. Participation in market work is the outcome of a labor supply decision that is influenced by nonlabor income, market wage offers, and nonpecuniary aspects of employment, including social stigma against women's work in particular kinds of jobs that may vary by race. The market wage offers and work conditions available to women, in turn, reflect evolving patterns of labor demand and discrimination, which again may vary by race. Guided by this framework, we document the presence of a large racial gap in participation rates even after controlling for proxies for income and wages. This unexplained gap is consistent with the hypothesis that racial differences in norms concerning women's work may have played some role in determining differences in labor market activity.

We then present new evidence that daughters who were raised by working mothers are themselves more likely to work. This intergenerational correlation may reflect the transmission of norms about women's work outside of the home from mother to daughter, although it could also be explained by the development of skills, information, or networks that are conducive to their subsequent work activity. Higher labor force participation rates for black mothers, along with the intergenerational correlation in work behavior between mother and daughter, can explain one-third of the racial gap in female labor force participation in the early twentieth century and around 10 percent of the remaining gap in the mid-twentieth century. This aspect of our chapter contributes to the growing literature on the role of "culture" in explaining variation in female labor force participation across groups

---

1. Weiss (1999) estimates an overall participation rate for black women (free and slave, over age fifteen) of about 82 percent in 1860. The high rate of LFP for female slaves is well documented in the historical literature. Wayne (2007) summarizes this view: "At cotton-picking time everyone, including children and the elderly, worked in the fields. A male slave from South Carolina remembered: 'Women worked in de field same as de men. Some of dem plowed jes' like de men and boys. Couldn't tell 'em apart in de field, as dey wore pantalets or breeches.' Besides working in the field, women might be used as housekeepers, nannies for white children, laundresses, cooks, personal servants, caregivers for slave children (usually elderly women), or sexual mistresses for the master" (130). See also Jones (1985).

(e.g., Reimers 1985; Farré and Vella 2007; Fernández and Fogli 2009; Blau et al. 2013).

6.1   Trends in Female Labor Force Participation by Race

We begin by presenting trends in labor force participation (henceforth "LFP") among black and white women. We confirm and extend patterns that are familiar to readers of Goldin (1990, chapter 2). Our data are drawn from the Integrated Public Use Microdata Series (IPUMS; Ruggles et al. 2010), which are based on the federal census of population manuscripts.[2] Some of our analysis will focus specifically on participation by married women, for whom the changes for whites have been largest, but for the most part we present data for all women regardless of marital status to give a wider perspective on the range of women's activities.

The characterization of changes in LFP over such a long period is, of course, accompanied by some caveats. The modern concept of labor force participation was first implemented in the 1940 census, whereas earlier censuses collected occupational information for "gainful workers." Complete consistency between these two concepts is impossible due to inherent differences in their definitions and year-to-year variation in enumerator instructions and practices. In addition to these conceptual differences, the late nineteenth-century censuses appear to undercount female workers relative to later years, particularly among married white women living on farms and those taking in boarders in urban areas. Goldin (1990, appendix to chapter 2) explores this issue in depth, drawing on a variety of sources to adjust figures for 1890. She concludes that the LFP for married women was understated by at least 10 percentage points in that year; for all women (single and married), the undercount is at least 7 percentage points. Most of our description and analysis relies on the IPUMS-based labor force variable without modification, but we have attempted some adjustments to get a sense of the potential magnitude of miscounting.[3]

---

2. The 2010 data are from the American Community Survey. See dissertations by Sobek (1997) and Roberts (2007) for detailed discussion of the census data on women's work.

3. Our attempts to account for underenumeration of women's work, particularly on farms or in boarding houses, are reported in appendix table 6A.2. In the microdata, we simply reassigned LFP for women who lived on farms or had boarders present (and were "head of household" or "spouse-of-head"), substituting the LFP rate observed in the same race/region/farm/married /boarder-status cells for later census years (1920, 1940, or 1960), all of which had more careful enumerator instructions about how to count female workers. For white women between 1870 and 1900, the adjusted rates are between 1 and 15 percentage points higher than their unadjusted counterparts, depending on the year chosen as the basis for the adjustment. Because within-cell rates are substantially higher in 1960 than previously (particularly on farms), using 1960 as the base year leads to the largest adjustments. For black women, however, the modifications lead to relatively small differences in LFP. Thus, the magnitude of the racial gap at any point in time is sensitive to adjustments for differential undercounting of white women, but it remains in all cases a sizable difference.

■Married and In Labor Force   ⬚Not Married and In Labor Force
⬚Not Married and Not In Labor Force   □Married and Not In Labor Force

Fig. 6.1   White women's labor force participation, 1870–2010
Notes: The sample includes women age twenty-five to fifty-four. From 1870 to 1930, "partici-pation" is determined by whether the person reported a "gainful occupation." See the text for discussion of this issue. The 1910 census counted gainful occupations (especially for black women in agriculture) in a manner that appears to be inconsistent with earlier or later practice and is therefore omitted here. We define "married" as "married and spouse present." In 1870, the IPUMS does not include a marital status variable, and so "married" is determined by whether the relation to household head is "spouse."

Figures 6.1 and 6.2 show participation rates in samples of black and white women, ages twenty-five to fifty-four from 1870 to 2010, taking the IPUMS coding of LFP at face value. In each census year, women are in one of four mutually exclusive categories: in the labor force and married (with spouse present); in the labor force and not married (or spouse not present); not in the labor force and not married; and not in the labor force and married. The combination of the first two groups yields the overall share of women in the labor force. Appendix table 6A.1 provides the data that underlie figures 6.1 and 6.2, along with some additional summary statistics.

A few key facts are clear from figures 6.1 and 6.2. First, the convention-ally measured participation rate among black women was much higher than among white women in the late nineteenth and early twentieth centuries. From 1870 to 1900, black LFP was around 40 percent, whereas white LFP was below 15 percent, with the vast majority of white workers consisting of unmarried women. Even in our upward-adjusted LFP rates, reported in appendix table 6A.2, the overall white participation rate did not reach 40 percent until 1960, almost a full century later than for blacks.[4]

---

4. For perspective, it is important to recognize that the LFP rate for black women was *much* higher before Emancipation. As mentioned above, Weiss (1999) estimates an overall participa-

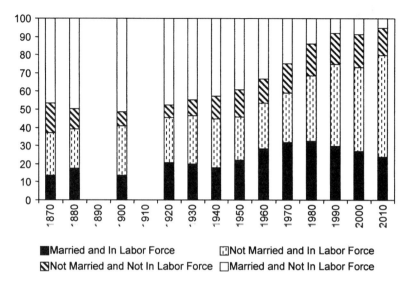

Fig. 6.2   Black women's labor force participation, 1870–2010
See notes to figure 6.1.

Second, the twentieth-century rise in white women's participation was primarily driven by an increase in the number of *married* workers, whereas most of the rise in black women's participation, especially after 1970, can be explained by an increase in the number of *unmarried* workers.[5] This is not because the participation rate within the group of married black women fell or stagnated (to the contrary it increased), but rather because the share of black women who were married (with spouse present) declined sharply, from more than 60 percent through 1960 to just 29 percent in 2010. Focusing exclusively on married women would miss this important aspect of black women's labor market participation. Although selection into marriage is outside the focus of this chapter, the trend among black women is likely to be connected in complex ways to the declining share of black men in the labor force (Wilson 1990).

---

tion rate for black women (free and slave, over age fifteen) of about 82 percent in 1860, compared to 35 percent in 1870. The sharp postwar decline reflects the end of coercion under slavery (Ransom and Sutch 1977) and may also reflect a fall in southern wages and labor productivity (Margo 2004). Whether the remaining black-white gap is attributable to differences in observable socioeconomic variables is explored in the next section.

5. The overall LFP among whites increased by 61 percentage points from 1900 to 2000, of which 47 points can be attributed to higher participation by married women (subject to caveats about undercounts of married women's work circa 1900). Among blacks, the overall LFP increased by 32 percentage points from 1900 to 2000, of which only 13 points can be attributed to married women. From 1970 to 2010, the share of married-and-working women *declined* among blacks by 8 points (despite rising participation within the married group), but this was more than offset by the growth of the not-married-and-working group in driving an increase in overall participation.

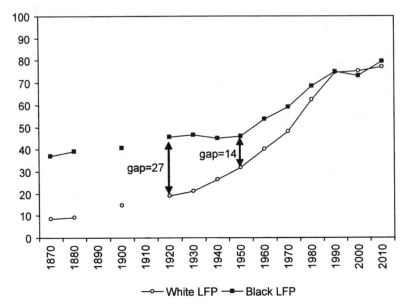

Fig. 6.3   Levels and gaps in overall LFP among women, 1870 to 2010
See notes to figure 6.1.

Third, and shown directly in figure 6.3, the racial gap in women's LFP narrowed significantly between 1920 and 1950 (from 27 to 14 percentage points), due almost entirely to an increase in the white LFP. As we discuss below, the rise in LFP among white women reflects both a shifting demand for clerical workers, as firms and the federal government grew larger and more complex, and a shifting supply of high school–educated white women. Black women, on the other hand, were generally barred from the expanding clerical sector during this period, and relatively few had had the opportunity to attend high school.[6] After 1950, both black and white rates rose steeply and almost in parallel until 1970. Over the next few decades, the overall racial gap narrowed again and was nearly eliminated by 1990.

6.1.1   Racial Differences in the Female Occupational Distribution

Standard models of labor supply suggest that women's entry into the labor market is influenced by both income and substitution effects. A higher market wage for women, perhaps associated with higher levels of (or returns to) education or experience, or improving nonpecuniary job characteristics would tend to pull women into the labor force. On the other hand, a higher level of family income due, for example, to higher husband earnings, would

6. There were remarkably few public high schools for black students in the South in the early decades of the twentieth century.

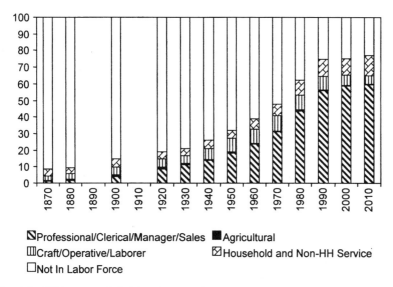

☒Professional/Clerical/Manager/Sales ▪Agricultural
⊞Craft/Operative/Laborer   ☒Household and Non-HH Service
☐Not In Labor Force

Fig. 6.4   White women's LFP and occupational distribution, 1870–2010

lower the likelihood of a wife's participation in the labor market because the utility gain from her marginal income would be low.

Goldin (1995) adds that women's labor supply decisions are also influenced by prevailing social norms about market work. In the late nineteenth century, "the social stigma against wives working in paid manual labor outside the home [was] apparently widespread and strong. . . . The stigma is a simple message. Only a husband who is lazy, indolent, and entirely negligent of his family would allow his wife to do such labor" (Goldin 1995, 71). In this framework, a higher level of stigma would lead to a lower rate of labor force participation for married women, all else the same. The key idea is simply that a woman will not enter the labor force when the household's utility loss from the stigma is greater than the utility gain from working outside the home.[7]

For white women, rising levels of education and the growing availability of "clean jobs" offered both higher wages and the opportunity to work without incurring the stigma associated with physically demanding or dirty tasks. Figure 6.4 shows the occupational distribution for white women, including a category for not-in-labor-force to provide a broad view of the range of women's activities. It is striking that white women's participation increased almost in lockstep with the rise in white-collar work (professional, clerical,

---

7. A goal of Goldin (1995) is to explain not only the twentieth-century rise in women's LFP, but also the apparent decline in the late nineteenth century. The model with stigma attached to women's manual labor predicts that, as average income rises in the late nineteenth century, women's LFP will fall, thereby explaining the downward portion of the U-shaped pattern.

manager, and sales occupations). Clerical work was a key component of this growth up to 1970 (appendix table 6A.3), and clerical sector experience early in a woman's career was relatively conducive to persistent labor force participation (Goldin 1989). Women who left the workforce to raise children found that they could reenter clerical jobs later in life.

The rise of black women's labor force participation over the twentieth century was associated with some of the same forces that influenced white women, but it differed in key respects. One important difference is that black women completed high school in large numbers a full generation after white women. This educational delay was due, in large part, to the black population's concentration in the South, which lagged behind the rest of the country in education in general and undersupplied schools for black children (Collins and Margo 2006). As a result, a relatively small share of black women was prepared for office work in the early twentieth century. In addition, on the demand side of the market, discrimination against black women in clerical work delayed the rise in black women's work in this sector until the 1960s even as their educational attainment increased (Sundstrom 2000).[8]

Figure 6.5 shows that the rise in black women's LFP began to coincide with a rise in white-collar work only after 1960. The jump in black women's clerical employment from 4 percent of all black women in 1960 to 18 percent by 1980 is especially noteworthy (appendix table 6A.4); this includes a sizable increase in government employment from 1.6 to 5.3 percent of all black women. A second salient feature of figure 6.5 is that black women were heavily concentrated in agriculture and domestic service until the latter part of the twentieth century, exactly the kind of low-paying, arduous labor that was heavily stigmatized for married white women.

Not only were black women far more likely to be in the labor force than white women, especially before 1980, but they were also more likely to hold low-paying manual jobs once in the labor force. This pattern is likely explained by a combination of demand-side and supply-side forces. First, black families were poorer than white families, implying that the marginal income from female employment was more valuable. In combination with low levels of human capital and hiring discrimination in the clerical sector, high rates of black poverty would lead to a concentration of black women in "dirty jobs." Second, the stigma associated with married women's work applied to a smaller share of black women because fewer black women were married. Third, even among married women, work in manual tasks may have been less subject to stigma in the black community, perhaps because, as Goldin hypothesized, the historically high rates of women's work under

8. Goldin (1990, 147) cites the prevalence of racial discrimination in clerical employment revealed in a Women's Bureau survey of firms in 1940. Collins (2003) finds that antidiscrimination laws implemented at the state level in the 1940s and 1950s had positive effects on black women's labor market outcomes.

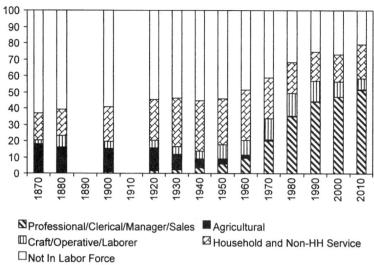

Fig. 6.5   Black women's LFP and occupational distribution, 1870–2010

slavery shaped attitudes toward married women's work. We explore this hypothesis in more detail in the next two sections.

6.2   Personal Characteristics and Racial Differences in Women's LFP, 1870–2010

This section investigates the extent to which differences in observable characteristics can account for the racial gap in female LFP over the last 140 years. In a simple model of labor supply, an individual's decision to enter the labor force depends on a comparison of the available market wage and her reservation wage. The reservation wage, in turn, depends on the level of nonlabor income, wealth, costs associated with taking up work, and preferences. Therefore, one might expect large racial differences in women's labor force participation to be accounted for by differences in education, location, family composition, and household economic characteristics. The portion of the gap in LFP that cannot be explained by these socioeconomic factors may be due to unobservable black-white differences in norms concerning market work.[9]

9. Interpreting the residual gap in LFP as evidence of racial differences in attitudes toward women's work depends on having high-quality measures of nonlabor income and wealth and good proxies for reservation wages. Given the available census data, we are missing wealth information after 1870 and cannot produce accurate measures of husband's earnings before 1940. Therefore, we urge caution in interpreting the residual gap as a true measure of racial differences in norms, but we do think it is useful to see whether the quantitative evidence that does exist in the census records is consistent with Goldin's interpretation.

The 1870 census of population is an especially interesting place to start our investigation. It is, of course, the first post-Emancipation census. Furthermore, unlike all subsequent censuses, it includes information about the value of personal and real property (i.e., wealth). Goldin (1977) collected a random sample of census manuscripts from seven southern cities in 1870 and 1880, and found that large black-white differences in LFP remained after adjusting for differences in observable characteristics. We use the national IPUMS 1 percent sample for 1870 to present simple regressions that confirm Goldin's conclusion in a broader data set, yield some additional insights, and dovetail with our analysis for later years.

Given the scarcity of individual wage and nonwage income data in this period, we do not attempt to estimate a standard labor supply equation.[10] Rather, our goal is simply to determine whether an extensive set of personal and household observables can account for the large difference in black and white LFP rates. These observables may control for a large part of slavery's "direct effect" on labor market behavior, operating through low family income, wealth, place of birth, education, and family structure. The residual difference in LFP may then reflect differences in norms or expectations about women's work outside the home, potentially an indirect product of slavery. Of course, given the scope for omitted variables and endogeneity bias, interpreting the residual requires caution and qualification. For example, black women may have been more likely to work than white women (controlling for observables) because they expected a higher likelihood of marital instability or believed that their husbands had a higher risk of unemployment or mortality, expectations that we cannot observe in census data.

Table 6.1 reports coefficients from separate linear probability model regressions of LFP on an indicator for race (black = 1) in 1870.[11] The base sample in panel A includes all women age twenty-five to fifty-four; panel B presents results for a subsample of married women. Within each panel, we estimate separate regressions for the entire United States, the South, and the nonfarm South to see if narrowing the basis of comparison affects the main

10. In addition to Goldin (1990), see Fraundorf (1979) and Rotella (1980) for efforts to estimate women's labor supply equations with historical data. A large literature on the topic emerged in the 1960s, including notable contributions from Mincer (1962) and Bowen and Finegan (1969). See Killingsworth and Heckman (1986) for a review of this literature and Blau and Kahn (2007) for more recent evidence.

11. The analyses in tables 6.1 and 6.2 are pooled regressions (black and white women) with a race indicator and controls for observables. The coefficient on the race indicator can be interpreted as the "unexplained" portion of a version of the Blinder-Oaxaca decomposition in which the intercepts for each group are constrained to be equal but opposite. See Fortin (2008) for elaboration. In this setting, we see that the unexplained portion of the gap is large relative to the overall gap in LFP. We have implemented a version of this decomposition with a detailed breakdown within the explained and unexplained categories such that the breakdown is invariant to the choice of omitted categories (Jann 2008). Much of the unexplained portion of the gap is located in the differences in the constant terms, as opposed to differences in responsiveness to observables.

Table 6.1   Race and labor force participation in 1870

	1	2	3
A. All women 25–54			
All US	0.284 (0.0289)	0.284 (0.0233)	0.249 (0.0222)
All South	0.320 (0.0279)	0.303 (0.277)	0.274 (0.0218)
Nonfarm South	0.330 (0.0343)	0.306 (0.0317)	0.291 (0.0295)
B. Married women, 25–54			
All US	0.221 (0.0374)	0.198 (0.0340)	0.158 (0.0268)
All South	0.240 (0.0383)	0.220 (0.0376)	0.149 (0.0258)
Nonfarm South	0.273 (0.0422)	0.235 (0.0393)	0.177 (0.0290)
Controls for age and birthplace	no	yes	yes
Additional controls	no	no	yes

Source: Data are from the IPUMS (Ruggles et al. 2010) sample for 1870.
Notes: The IPUMS coding of labor force participation is taken at face value. Standard errors are clustered by state of birth. The base sample includes all white and black women age twenty-five to fifty-four. Column (1)'s specification includes only the race dummy, giving the unadjusted difference in participation rates. Column (2) adds fixed effects for state of birth and age. Column (3) adds controls for several other observables, including literacy, the number of own children under five, the number of own children over five (in household), marital status, city-resident status (based on IPUMS "metro" variable), farm-resident status, household wealth (four categories), and (if married with spouse present) husband's occupation. Wealth is the combination of real and personal property value. Dependent variable = 1 if in labor force.

results. The specification in column (1) includes only the race dummy, reflecting the unadjusted racial difference in participation rates. Column (2) adds fixed effects for state of birth and age, our limited set of exogenous background variables. Column (3) adds controls for several other observables, including literacy, the number of own children in the household (separate categorical variables for children under and over five years of age), city-resident status, farm-resident status, household wealth (four categories), and husband's status (nine occupational categories and a no-husband-present category).

Among women in the South, the racial difference in LFP is approximately 32 percentage points in 1870. Our extensive set of control variables and fixed effects account for very little of the racial difference, approximately 5 percentage points out of 32. The levels are slightly different in the other rows of panel A (all United States and nonfarm South), but the basic story is unchanged: observables account for little of the large racial gap in women's labor force participation in the wake of the Civil War.

Among married women who reside with their spouse, the magnitude of the base racial gap is smaller (panel B, column [1]) than in panel A. This sample composition effect reflects both the relatively high level of participation among unmarried black women and the relatively large share of unmarried women among blacks. Adjusting for observables can explain more of the racial LFP gap for married women in panel B than for all women in panel A. Nonetheless, the residual gap in women's LFP is still greater than 15 percentage points, more than half of the unadjusted gap. The large residual gap is notable because the 1870 data provide a measure of household wealth, which is typically an omitted variable in contemporary studies of women's labor force participation.[12] The presence of a large residual gap in women's LFP, as Goldin (1977) found, is consistent with differences in social norms or stigma associated with women's work by race, which may be an indirect legacy of slavery.

The "unexplained" gap in women's labor force participation persisted for more than 100 years, although this residual narrowed alongside the overall gap. Figure 6.6 plots three sets of coefficients from regressions that are similar to those described above for a national sample of black and white women: one plot simply shows the difference in black-white LFP at each census date (unadjusted), whereas the other two show adjusted differences in LFP rates (i.e., the coefficient on black, conditional on observables). One of the adjusted plots begins in 1940 because that year is the first in which we can observe women's educational attainment in detail (as opposed to just "literacy" in earlier years).[13] Censuses after 1870 do not provide measures of wealth, but husband's occupation and the other covariates should capture wealth differences to some extent.[14]

Consistent with earlier depictions of LFP rates, figure 6.6 documents a large but declining unadjusted difference in black-white LFP. The novel information in this graph is conveyed by the plots showing the size of the racial gap conditional on observables. Until 1930, controlling for observables makes little difference in the size of the racial gap. Around midcentury (1940–1970), observable differences begin to account for a larger portion of the gap, both absolutely and relative to the gap's unadjusted size. By 1990, however, the overall black-white gap is very small by historical standards, and, in contrast to the earlier years, adjustments for observables tend to *increase* the racial gap.[15]

12. Relative to households with zero wealth (about one quarter of the sample) and controlling for other observables (including husband's status), women from wealthier households were more likely to be in the labor force, although the coefficients vary across the subsamples of table 6.1. This pattern might reflect the endogeneity of household wealth with respect to women's past work.

13. For the "adjusted" plot that runs from 1880 to 2010 we have a literacy variable in all specifications. Up to 1930, this is based on the ability to read and write, as reported by the census enumerator. From 1940 onward, when the census did not inquire about literacy but did inquire about educational attainment, we code women as literate if they went beyond fourth grade.

14. Results from the fully specified regressions for married women in 1870 are not much different if the categorical wealth controls are omitted.

15. Starting in 1940, we are able to add more detailed educational attainment variables as controls (up to this point, literacy is the only human capital variable). Higher educational attainment is associated with higher labor force participation rates. In each year, black women lower educational attainment (on average) than white women. Therefore, adjusting for educational attainment tends to increase the coefficient on the black indicator variable.

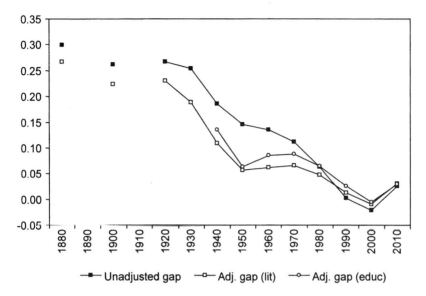

Fig. 6.6   Regression-adjusted black-white gap in labor force participation, all women

For reference, at twenty-year intervals, coefficients for key variables from linear probability models of LFP are reported in table 6.2. By 1940, there is a strong positive link between educational attainment and women's LFP, even after controlling for husband's occupation. The omitted "husband category" consists of women who were "single, never married." Relative to never-married women, LFP for married women declines from 1880 to 1920 across all categories of husbands' occupations, but then the pattern reverses, such that by 2000 the differences between married and unmarried women are small by historical standards.[16] Blinder-Oaxaca decompositions corresponding to the regression specifications in table 6.2 are reported in appendix table 6A.5.[17] In this setting, differences in husband's presence and

16. Table 6.2 documents few differences in the propensity of married women to work based on their husband's occupation, with the exception of the wives of farmers, farm laborers and domestic servants, all of whom were more likely to work for pay than were their other married counterparts, especially in the late nineteenth and early twentieth centuries. Recall that the omitted husband category is never married women. Our coefficients suggest that, in 1880 for example, the wives of professional workers, craftsmen, operatives, laborers and nonhousehold service workers were all between 36 and 39 percentage points less likely to work than were never married women. Over time, the gap between married and unmarried women declines, but, conditional on being married, the effect of husband's occupation remains small.

17. The usual caveats about decompositions apply here, as well. See Fortin, Lemieux, and Firpo (2011) for an extended discussion. In addition to the mechanical (but important) issues related to the choice of coefficient vectors, omitted categories, and linear versus nonlinear methods, we note that some of the variables in our regressions are likely endogenous to women's labor force participation. We present the decomposition results for descriptive purposes.

Table 6.2 Linear probability models of women's LFP, 1880–2000

	1880	1900	1920	1940a	1940b	1960	1980	2000
Black	0.267	0.223	0.230	0.112	0.120	0.076	0.054	0.001
	(0.019)	(0.011)	(0.009)	(0.008)	(0.008)	(0.008)	(0.009)	(0.011)
Husband categories								
Absent spouse	-0.091	-0.133	-0.176	-0.179	-0.165	-0.236	-0.101	-0.097
Separated	—	—	—	—	—	-0.013	0.016	0.017
Divorced	-0.012	0.033	0.016	0.007	0.019	0.080	0.109	0.047
Widowed	-0.087	-0.055	-0.110	-0.129	-0.115	-0.031	-0.017	-0.064
Professional	-0.359	-0.501	-0.574	-0.497	-0.501	-0.311	-0.097	-0.051
Farmer	-0.261	-0.440	-0.482	-0.452	-0.439	-0.319	-0.159	-0.015
Craftsmen	-0.362	-0.500	-0.572	-0.507	-0.490	-0.288	-0.087	-0.020
Operatives	-0.363	-0.494	-0.550	-0.468	-0.448	-0.233	-0.056	-0.015
Service (hh)	0.015	-0.206	-0.292	-0.206	-0.189	-0.126	0.092	0.015
Service (non-hh)	-0.386	-0.510	-0.535	-0.455	-0.438	-0.197	-0.015	-0.010
Farm laborer	-0.297	-0.461	-0.501	-0.446	-0.426	-0.224	-0.084	-0.010
Laborer	-0.365	-0.496	-0.538	-0.490	-0.468	-0.230	-0.048	-0.010
Does not work	-0.336	-0.453	-0.497	-0.403	-0.389	-0.253	-0.136	-0.146
Literate	-0.016	-0.009	0.001	0.049	—	—	—	—
Years of school								
N/A or none	—	—	—	—	-0.131	-0.347	-0.366	-0.299
1–4 years	—	—	—	—	-0.070	-0.182	-0.216	-0.206
5–8 years	—	—	—	—	-0.049	-0.095	-0.175	-0.257
9 years	—	—	—	—	-0.036	-0.051	-0.148	-0.214
10 years	—	—	—	—	-0.026	-0.035	-0.113	-0.173

	(1)	(2)	(3)	(4)	(5)	(6)	(7)	(8)
11 years	—	—	—	—	-0.026	-0.016	-0.081	-0.160
12 years (omitted)	—	—	—	—	—	—	—	—
1 year college	—	—	—	—	0.012	0.012	0.041	0.063
2–3 years college	—	—	—	—	0.040	0.028	0.050	0.103
4 years college	—	—	—	—	0.068	0.074	0.077	0.110
5+ years college	—	—	—	—	0.123	0.179	0.161	0.170
1 child under 5	-0.022	-0.026	-0.061	-0.138	-0.139	-0.221	-0.223	-0.129
2 child under 5	-0.032	-0.040	-0.075	-0.162	-0.162	-0.303	-0.383	-0.253
3+ child under 5	-0.036	-0.042	-0.087	-0.173	-0.171	-0.341	-0.462	-0.333
1 child over 4	-0.021	-0.016	-0.034	-0.076	-0.071	-0.057	-0.038	0.011
2 children over 4	-0.021	-0.013	-0.041	-0.106	-0.099	-0.105	-0.075	-0.012
3+ children over 4	-0.029	-0.011	-0.034	-0.111	-0.101	-0.124	-0.105	-0.056
N	81,662	131,920	198,743	277,727	277,727	342,983	423,501	537,356

Source: Data are from IPUMS (Ruggles et al. 2010), and we take the IPUMS coding of labor force participation at face value.

Notes: The sample includes all women, age twenty-five to fifty-four. All regressions include fixed effects for state of birth and age, city-resident status (based on IPUMS "metro" variable), and farm-resident status. The omitted "husband category" consists of single, never-married women. Occupation categories are based on the IPUMS "occ1950" codes. The omitted educational attainment category (highest grade completed) is twelve years. Standard errors clustered by state of birth are reported under the coefficient for "black"; others are omitted to save space but the full results are available on request. Dependent variable = 1 if in labor force.

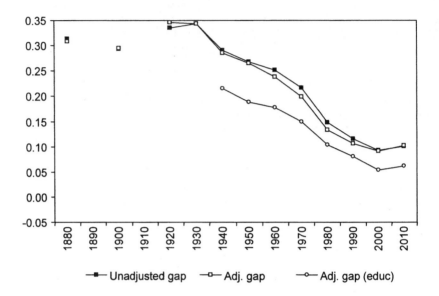

Fig. 6.7   Regression-adjusted black-white gap in "dirty jobs," all women

Notes: "Dirty jobs" are defined as craft, operative, laborer, household service, and nonhousehold service (e.g., janitors, cleaners, hospital attendants, cooks, waitresses), as opposed to "clean jobs" in the categories of professional, clerical, managerial, and sales, and the not-in-labor force category.

occupation account for some portion of the racial difference in women's LFP, which is consistent with the expectation that for most of US history single women and women married to men in relatively low-earning occupations are more likely to work for pay than others. The estimated contribution ranges from 4 percentage points in the early twentieth century to 7 percentage points in 1960, but differences in other observables tend to have little explanatory power. As noted earlier, given that education is positively associated with LFP, racial differences in educational attainment cannot explain the relatively high level of black women's participation.

Figure 6.7 shows that the racial gap in the likelihood of working "dirty jobs" was large throughout most of the twentieth century, even with controls for marital status, husband's occupation, number of children, birthplace, and literacy or highest grade of education. From 1940 onward, we see that controlling for years of educational attainment accounts for a sizable share of the gap, though a nontrivial share remains unexplained despite a pronounced decline in agricultural and household-service employment as a share of all women's work (Bailey and Collins 2006).[18]

In sum, for at least 100 years after Emancipation, black women partici-

18. Restricting the sample to non-Hispanic whites has little impact on the size of the conditional gap in the late twentieth century relative to what is shown in figure 6.7.

pated in the labor force at significantly higher rates than white women. Prior to 1950, observable characteristics fail to account for a large share of this gap, suggesting that something else that is correlated with race mattered, and that it mattered more in the decades immediately after the Civil War than later in the twentieth century. Racial differences in the probability of being raised by a working mother, an indirect legacy of the high rates of women's work under slavery, might help account for this pattern. The next section shows that daughters of working mothers were more likely to work themselves.

6.3   Evidence on Intergenerational Transmission

Thus far, we have presented indirect evidence that racial differences in social norms about women's work may have contributed to the generation and perpetuation of the racial gap in female LFP. In particular, we interpreted the presence of a residual in a regression of women's LFP on a set of socioeconomic traits as suggestive evidence that other factors, including perhaps social norms, are needed to explain the racial participation gap. In this section, we present more direct evidence about the role of historical differences in women's work in sustaining the racial gap in women's work behavior over time. Specifically, we demonstrate a strong association between the work activity of mothers and daughters in both the late nineteenth century, a generation after Emancipation, and in the mid-twentieth century. The link between mothers' and daughters' behavior is large enough to explain up to a third of the black-white gap in female LFP a generation or more after slavery.

Racially distinct attitudes and expectations about women's work outside the home provide one explanation for the observed correlation in work behavior between mothers and daughters. Social norms about women's work (and many other social phenomena) are transmitted to children, in part, through interactions with their parents (Moen, Erickson, and Dempster-McClain 1997). These norms may be transmitted tacitly, as young women observe the work behavior of their mother, or they may be actively conveyed through conversation and exhortation. Alternatively, an intergenerational correlation between mothers and daughters may reflect other means by which parents influence their children. For example, working mothers may provide their daughters with skills or a labor market network, which could increase their economic return to market work. Although we cannot econometrically distinguish between the transmission of attitudes and norms, on the one hand, or of skills and information on the other, estimating the reduced-form relationship between the work behavior of mothers and daughters is interesting in its own right and may help account for racial differences in the propensity to work outside of the home.

Our analysis is related to a series of recent papers that has investigated the role that "culture," broadly defined as beliefs or preferences, plays in explaining differences in women's market work across groups (Fernandez and Fogli 2009; Blau et al. 2013; Farré and Vella 2007). Because attitudes about women's work are formed in a particular economic context, it is an empirical challenge to disentangle the effects of culture from those of economic conditions. For this reason, the recent literature has focused on the work behavior of immigrants. Immigrants leave the economic environment in which their preferences were first formed but may still carry with them specific attitudes or norms shaped in their source country. Consistent with this hypothesis, Fernandez and Fogli (2009) show that the LFP of immigrant women is correlated with lagged female LFP in their source country, and Blau et al. (2013) find an association between the LFP of first- and second-generation immigrant women from the same country of origin.

6.3.1   Nineteenth-Century Data

We begin our analysis of the intergenerational correlation of women's work behavior by investigating the generation of daughters born immediately after Emancipation. We focus on the birth cohorts of 1866 to 1884, all of whom were old enough to participate in the labor force in 1900. For this group, we ask whether women whose mothers were born into slavery were themselves more likely to engage in market work in adulthood. Data are drawn from the 5 percent IPUMS sample of 1900. Although mother's slave status is unknown, we assume that black daughters whose mothers were born in the South are the direct descendants of slaves (see also Sacerdote 2005).[19]

In particular, we estimate

(1) $I(\text{daughter works}) = \alpha + \beta_1 I(\text{black}) + \beta_2 I(\text{mother born in South})$
$+ \beta_3 [I(\text{mother born in South}) * I(\text{black})]$
$+ \gamma_1 I(\text{born in South})$
$+ \gamma_2 [I(\text{born in South}) * I(\text{black})] + (X')\Delta + \varepsilon.$

The dependent variable is an indicator equal to 1 if the daughter participates in the labor force in 1900. The coefficient β_1 identifies the racial gap in labor force participation. Coefficient β_2 compares the work behavior of all women, both white and black, whose mothers were born in the South. The coefficient of interest is β_3, which isolates any additional effect of having a mother who was born in the South for black women. We interpret β_3 as reflecting the effect of being a descendant of slaves. Daughters of former slaves differ from daughters of free blacks both in the likelihood that their own mothers worked, which may have influenced their own attitudes about the value and

19. The youngest daughter in the sample was sixteen years old in 1900. As long as her mother was at least twenty years old at the time of her birth, her mother would have been born under slavery.

Table 6.3   Mother's slave status and daughter's LFP, 1900

Gender Birth cohort Region	Women After 1865 Full South	Women After 1865 Deep South	Women Before 1865 Deep South	Men After 1865 Deep South
Mother south * black	0.045	0.092	0.004	0.004
	(0.014)	(0.012)	(0.013)	(0.008)
Mother born in south	−0.092	−0.105	−0.002	−0.004
	(0.003)	(0.004)	(0.003)	(0.002)
Born south * black	0.186	0.113	0.046	0.045
	(0.013)	(0.011)	(0.013)	(0.007)
Born in south	−0.054	−0.044	0.029	0.011
	(0.003)	(0.004)	(0.003)	(0.002)
Black	0.094	0.134	0.234	−0.017
	(0.010)	(0.006)	(0.007)	(0.004)
N	440,177	440,177	220,497	445,387
Ages in 1900	16–34	16–34	45–64	16–34

Source: Estimates from 1900 IPUMS 5 percent sample.

Notes: Columns (1) and (2) include daughters born after Emancipation (birth cohorts of 1866 to 1884). Column (3) contains daughters born before Emancipation (birth cohorts of 1836 to 1855). Column (4) contains sons born after Emancipation. In column (1), the South includes all states in the three southern census regions. In columns (2) to (4), the South excludes the border states of DC, DE, MD, MO, OK, and WV. All regressions include a quadratic in son's or daughter's age and an indicator for literacy. Dependent variable = 1 if in the labor force.

suitability of women's work, and also, perhaps, in other aspects of family background such as accumulated wealth. The coefficient β_3 estimates the net effect of these various differences between the descendants of slave and free blacks.

Daughters of southern-born mothers are themselves more likely to live in the South. We therefore control for the daughter's own place of birth (alone and interacted with race) to account for contemporaneous regional differences in industrial composition or agricultural practice that may influence women's labor force participation. We also include a quadratic in age and a dummy variable for literacy in the vector X.

Results for this estimation are reported in table 6.3. The first column uses an expansive definition of the South, while the second column excludes the "border states."[20] In both cases, we find that black daughters whose mothers spent their first few decades (or more) under slavery are themselves 5 to 9 percentage points more likely to be in the labor force, even after controlling for daughter's region. The relationship is stronger if we contrast daughters

20. The expansive definition of the South includes all states in the three southern census regions. The narrower definition excludes the District of Columbia, Delaware, Maryland, Missouri, Oklahoma, and West Virginia. Despite the fact that slavery was legal in the border states, the slave population in these areas was unlikely to work on large plantations or in the cultivation of cotton where the norm of women's work was the most well developed (Jones 1985).

whose mothers grew up in the Deep South to mothers who grew up either under freedom or in a border state. In both cases, we find that white daughters whose mothers came of age in the antebellum South were *less* likely to work outside the home, perhaps because they absorbed a white southern attitude that work outside of the home was fit only for slaves.[21]

In the early twentieth century, black women were 27 percentage points more likely than white women to be in the labor force (see figure 6.3). Therefore, our estimates imply that up to 33 percent of the black-white gap in female LFP may be attributed to the intergenerational effects of slavery, which include both the direct effect of slavery on household wealth as well as the indirect effect of slavery on attitudes toward women's work (= 9/27).

Columns (3) and (4) provide suggestive evidence that mother's slave status influences daughter's work behavior through transmission of attitudes, skills, or networks between mother and daughter, rather than through the direct effect of slavery on later socioeconomic status. Column (3) considers an older cohort of daughters born between 1836 and 1855. Members of this cohort were old enough to have worked as slaves and absorbed the bundle of norms about the skills related to women's work inherent in the slave system on their own. Therefore, after controlling for daughter's own place of birth, we do not expect mother's place of birth to have an additional effect on daughter's work behavior due to transmission between mother and daughter—and, indeed, we find no association between mother's slave status and daughter's labor force participation in this older cohort. Column (4) looks instead at sons born after Emancipation. We do not expect a mother's slave status to influence her son's propensity to work given the strong norm of near-universal male LFP in both the slave and nonslave economy. Reassuringly, mother's slave status has no effect on son's behavior either.

6.3.2 Mid-Twentieth-Century data

The nineteenth-century data allow us to observe work behavior of the descendants of slaves and free people in the first generation after Emancipation. Through the intergenerational transmission of work behavior, the higher female participation rates under slavery may have persisted into the second and third generations after slavery. To assess this possibility, we examine data from the first cohort of young women in the National Longitudinal Survey (NLS), which was initiated in 1968. These women (the daughters, in our analysis) were born between 1944 and 1954; their mothers were typically born between 1910 and 1930. In other words, many of their mothers belonged to the second generation after Emancipation, while the daughters belong to the third (or fourth) generation.

---

21. In the antebellum South, white women primarily engaged in home production. "Southern white women of all classes managed farms, homes, children, and sometimes slaves . . . they were responsible for tasks such as organizing the household, food production, attending to the medical needs of their families, and educating their own children" (Wayne 2007, 135).

At the survey's inception, women were asked a series of questions about their family background, including whether or not their mother worked for pay during their own teenage years. Women were then resurveyed and asked to report on aspects of their own work and family life every three years until the early 1990s. We investigate a series of associations between the work behavior of mothers and daughters, asking: Does growing up with a working mother change a daughter's expectations about working for pay? Are women whose mothers worked during their formative years more likely to work themselves? And is this relationship equally strong for all women or is it particularly powerful for black women, perhaps because the values transmitted by a working mother are reinforced by more affirming attitudes toward women's work in the wider black community?

We address these questions in a set of regressions relating a daughter's work behavior to an indicator for whether or not her mother worked when she was fourteen years old. In particular, we estimate

$$(2) \quad \text{Daughter's behavior}_{iy} = \alpha + \beta I(\text{black})_i + \gamma_1 I(\text{mother worked at age } 14)_i$$
$$+ \gamma_2 [I(\text{mother worked})_i * I(\text{black})_i] + (X_{1i}') \Delta$$
$$+ (X_{2iy}') \Theta + \varepsilon_{iy}.$$

Our main dependent variable is an indicator variable equal to 1 if daughter i works for pay in calendar year y. We estimate this relationship in six separate years, beginning in 1977 when the typical respondent was twenty-eight years old and ending in 1993, when she was forty-four years old. We also consider other aspects of a daughter's work and family life that could be influenced by her mother's work behavior, including her expectations about engaging in market work later in life (elicited at the modal age of nineteen) and her marital and fertility history.

The explanatory variable of interest is an indicator for whether a respondent's mother worked for pay when she was fourteen years old (in the modal year of 1963). We interact this indicator with a race variable equal to 1 for black respondents to test whether the association between mother's and daughter's work behavior was stronger in the black community. In some specifications, we also include vectors of family background characteristics (X_{1i}) or contemporaneous measures of a daughter's economic circumstance (X_{2iy}). The family background characteristics include mother's and father's educational attainment, father's occupation (in four categories), a dummy variable for whether the daughter lived with both of her parents at age fourteen, and an indicator for whether the daughter had a library card at age fourteen, a common measure of family resources and commitment to education.[22] Contemporaneous economic measures consist of the daughter's

---

22. We classify father's occupation into four categories as follows: high white collar (professional, managerial), low white collar (clerical, sales), high blue collar (craftsmen, operatives), low blue collar (service, labor).

educational attainment, her marital status, and the presence of children in her household. All regressions are weighted to account for the fact that the NLS oversampled poor households.

Table 6.4 reports characteristics for the 3,565 daughters in our sample, 24 percent of whom are black. In 1977, at the average age of 28, 55 percent of the white women and 61 percent of the black women were in the labor force, a 6-percentage-point gap in participation by race. By 1991, when the typical respondent was 42 years old, the labor force participation rate rose to 72 percent for whites and 74 percent for blacks.

The racial gap in LFP was larger among mothers of sample women: 36 percent of white mothers and 50 percent of black mothers worked for pay when their daughters were fourteen, in the modal year of 1963. These figures, which are derived from daughters' recollections in the first survey period (1968), match labor force participation rates for married women for this year reasonably well (according to interpolations between the 1960 and 1970

Table 6.4   **Summary statistics for NLS sample**

Variable	Whites	Blacks
Age in 1977	27.71	27.63
	(3.13)	(3.11)
	2731	*834*
LFP in 1977	0.55	0.61
	(0.50)	(0.49)
LFP in 1991	0.72	0.74
	(0.45)	(0.44)
	2236	*592*
Mother worked at age 14	0.36	0.50
	(0.48)	(0.50)
Years of education (1982)	13.37	12.36
	(2.42)	(2.48)
	2,421	*718*
Any children in 1977	0.66	0.73
	(0.47)	(0.44)
Any children in 1991	0.73	0.74
	(0.44)	(0.44)
Currently married in 1977	0.76	0.50
	(0.43)	(0.50)
Currently married in 1991	0.74	0.40
	(0.44)	(0.49)
Library card at age 14	0.79	0.50
	(0.41)	(0.50)
Mother's years of education	11.23	9.25
	(2.74)	(3.03)
	2530	*701*

Notes: Cells report sample means with standard deviations in parentheses. The number of observations used to calculate means for selected variables are reported in italics to demonstrate attrition over time.

census years, 35 percent of white married women and 45 percent of black married women were in the labor force in 1963).

Our family background measures reveal large differences in the socioeconomic status of the households in which white and black respondents were raised. Only 50 percent of black women held a library card at age fourteen, compared to 79 percent of white women, and the mothers of black women had two fewer years of education than their white counterparts (9.2 versus 11.2 years). By the daughters' generation, the racial gap in educational attainment had declined but had not disappeared. Black daughters completed one fewer year of schooling than white daughters (12.4 versus 13.4 years). In addition, black daughters were more likely to have children in their twenties (despite little difference in the probability of ever having a child), and were less likely to be married both in their twenties and in their thirties.

Table 6.5 investigates the relationship between a daughter's labor force participation in 1977 at the average age of twenty-eight and her mother's work behavior during the daughter's childhood. Model 1 contains only dummy variables for race and for having a working mother during one's teenage years, and the interaction between the two. We find that daughters of working mothers are 3.4 percentage points more likely to be working themselves at age twenty-eight; this relationship is statistically significant at the 10 percent level. Having a working mother has an even stronger effect on one's own propensity to be in the labor force for black women although the interaction between race and mother's work cannot be statistically distinguished from zero.

These estimates suggest that nearly 10 percent of the black-white labor force participation gap in 1977 can still be explained by intergenerational transmission of labor force behavior from mother to daughter. Black mothers were 14 percentage points more likely than white mothers to be in the labor force in 1963, and, by our estimate, women with working mothers are 3.4 percentage points more likely to be in the labor force themselves.[23] Together, these figures imply that intergenerational transmission can explain 8 percent of the black-white participation gap in 1977 (= [0.14 mother's gap * 0.034 effect of mother's work] / 0.06 gap).[24]

Model 2 controls for our family background measures to account for the fact that growing up with a working mother may be an indication of a

23. In Model 1, which contains limited controls, it appears that the effect of mother's work may be stronger for black daughters. However, after controlling for family background in Model 2, this interaction disappears.

24. Another way to assess the economic significance of this intergenerational correlation is to ask: How many more daughters would have been in the labor force in 1977 if their mothers had worked to the same degree as mothers work today? In the data, 56 percent of the daughter's generation worked in 1977 (properly weighted for racial composition). If 75 percent of their mothers had worked in 1963, rather than only 37.5 percent, our estimate implies that the daughter's LFP rate would have increased to 57.3 percent (= 37.5 additional points of mother's work * 0.034 effect of mother's work).

Table 6.5 **Mother's work and daughter's LFP in 1977 (at average age = 28)**

	Model 1	Model 2	Model 3	Model 4
Mother worked (*R* age 14)	0.034*	0.036*	0.033*	0.054***
	(0.018)	(0.020)	(0.020)	(0.018)
Mother worked *x* black	0.031	0.007	0.006	0.014
	(0.056)	(0.064)	(0.063)	(0.058)
Black	0.041	0.087*	0.078*	0.034
	(0.039)	(0.046)	(0.046)	(0.042)
Library card at 14		0.041*	0.009	−0.009
		(0.024)	(0.024)	(0.022)
Mother's education 9–12		−0.003	−0.031	−0.028
		(0.026)	(0.026)	(0.024)
Mother's education >12		0.005	−0.056	−0.063*
		(0.036)	(0.036)	(0.033)
Father's education 9–12		0.037	0.017	0.000
		(0.024)	(0.024)	(0.022)
Father's education > 12		0.078**	0.034	−0.003
		(0.033)	(0.033)	(0.031)
Lives w/ both parents (age 14)		0.011	−0.016	−0.010
		(0.040)	(0.039)	(0.036)
Own education = 12			0.124***	0.112***
			(0.031)	(0.029)
Own education >13			0.258***	0.165***
			(0.033)	(0.031)
Any children				−0.360***
				(0.021)
Previously married				0.251***
				(0.027)
Never married				0.133***
				(0.027)
Constant	0.487***	0.319***	0.237***	0.594***
	(0.030)	(0.059)	(0.060)	(0.044)
Dummies for father's occup.	N	Y	Y	Y
Observations	3,565	2,994	2,994	2,990

Notes: Cells report coefficients from a regression of daughter's labor force participation in 1977 on mother's work and other covariates for the NLS sample. Standard errors are reported in parentheses. In addition to the reported covariates, all regressions include dummy variables for daughter's age in 1977 (average = 28 years old). Mother's work activity and other family background characteristics are reported by the daughter in 1968 and refer to the year in which the daughter was fourteen years old. The daughter characteristics added in Models 3 and 4 are measured in 1977. Dependent variable = 1 if in labor force.

***Significant at the 1 percent level.
**Significant at the 5 percent level.
*Significant at the 10 percent level.

family's socioeconomic circumstances, which could itself influence a daughter's propensity to work, either through attitudes or through a daughter's acquisition of human capital. Daughters from families of higher socioeconomic status—those with a library card or those whose father graduated from high school—are more likely to work, perhaps because they have more skills and thus can earn higher wages for doing so. However, these factors have no effect on the core relationship between mother's and daughter's propensity to work.[25]

Model 3 controls for a daughter's own educational attainment to assess whether mother's work behavior has a direct effect on a daughter's LFP beyond any indirect effects it may have on a daughter's human capital acquisition.[26] Daughters who have graduated from high school (college) are 12 (24) percentage points more likely to be in the labor force than are high school dropouts. Yet, adding daughter's educational attainment to the model does not weaken the relationship between mother's work behavior and daughter's labor force attachment. However, we do note that accounting for a daughter's educational attainment eliminates any association between our family background measures and a daughter's propensity to be in the labor force, suggesting that the relationship between socioeconomic status and labor force participation operates through investments in human capital.

Model 4 demonstrates that a daughter's labor force participation is strongly related to her own family circumstance. Daughters with children in the household are 36 percentage points less likely to be currently in the labor force. Daughters who never married (or who are widowed or divorced) are 13 (25) percentage points more likely to be in the labor force than are those who are currently married. Somewhat surprisingly, accounting for a daughter's domestic situation *increases* the association between a daughter's and her mother's labor force participation by 60 percent. This pattern is consistent with findings below demonstrating that daughters of working mothers are more likely to be currently married and to have a child living at home.

Thus far, we have considered the effect of a mother's work behavior on her daughter's outcomes in 1977 when daughters were in their mid to late twenties. The influence of one's mother's example may be strongest in these years because daughters are still relatively young and thus turning to their parents for guidance. In addition, women's labor force participation tends to increase over the life cycle as their children age, leaving less scope for individual factors (like differences in mother's work behavior) to generate differences in outcomes (Goldin 1990).

Figure 6.8 graphs the estimated effect of having a working mother on

25. Model 2 requires us to drop the 557 women who do not report one or more of the family background items. Results are nearly unchanged if we rerun Model 1 for this reduced sample.

26. A daughter's educational aspirations could be directly influenced by her mother's work behavior; in this sense, educational attainment is an endogenous variable (as are marital and fertility history in Model 4).

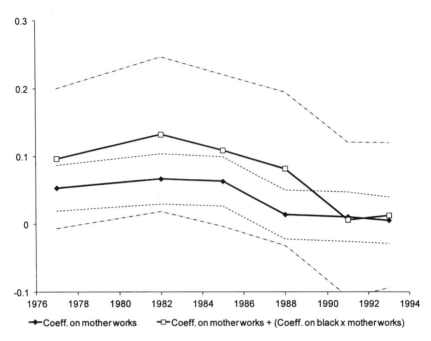

Fig. 6.8   Relationship between work behavior of mothers and daughters, coefficients from regressions using NLS data, 1977–1993

Notes: Coefficients on "mother works" and the interaction of "mother works" and a dummy variable for "black." Estimates of regression reported in table 6.5, Model 4, for each survey wave between 1977 and 1993. Modal daughter is twenty-eight years old in 1977 and forty-four years old in 1993.

a daughter's propensity to be in the labor force according to the baseline specification (Model 1) in six survey years: 1977, 1982, 1985, 1988, 1991, and 1993. We find a strong and stable association between a mother's work behavior and her daughter's labor force attachment in the 1970s and early 1980s. In these years, daughters in the NLS cohorts are still likely to have young children at home (average ages of 28, 33, and 36). However, in the late 1980s and 1990s, when the daughters are older, we no longer find that a daughter's labor force participation is related to her mother's work behavior. The coefficient on mother's work at age fourteen, as well as the interaction between mother's work and race, fall nearly to zero for daughters between the ages of thirty-nine and forty-five. Because we are only able to follow a single cohort in the NLS, we cannot identify whether the declining association between mother's and daughter's work behavior is a period or an age effect. Our data are consistent with the possibility that the example set by one's own mother has become less relevant over time as female LFP became more commonplace. Alternatively, it could be that having a working mother as a role model is particularly important to a woman's decision to couple work with child rearing but is less relevant for women without children or women with older children, many more of whom work outside of the home. Table 6.6 explores the channels through which a mother's work behavior influences her daughter's own labor force attachment. Following Goldin (2006), we suspect that having a working mother changes daughters' expectations about the course of their own lives. Rather than presuming that they will marry and specialize in home production, daughters of working mothers may expect that they too will work outside of the home, as their mothers did. As a result, they may be more likely to invest in human capital

Table 6.6   **Mother's work and other daughter outcomes**

	Dependent variables					
	Expectation housewife	Highest grade	College degree	Ever married	Age at first marriage	Age at first birth
Mother worked	–0.049**	0.017	–0.006	0.017*	–0.637***	–0.491**
	(0.019)	(0.091)	(0.017)	(0.010)	(0.187)	(0.243)
Mom work x black	0.015	0.005	0.042	0.009	–0.290	0.028
	(0.064)	(0.300)	(0.056)	(0.031)	(0.647)	(0.770)
Black	–0.237***	0.145	0.007	–0.096***	1.695***	–0.520
	(0.046)	(0.218)	(0.041)	(0.023)	(0.476)	(0.561)
Library card at 14	0.005	0.891***	0.064***	–0.011	0.585***	0.825***
	(0.023)	(0.110)	(0.021)	(0.011)	(0.223)	(0.287)
Mother's edu. 9–12	0.052**	0.602***	0.050**	0.021*	–0.227	0.925***
	(0.026)	(0.120)	(0.023)	(0.012)	(0.246)	(0.315)
Mother's edu. > 12	0.035	1.641***	0.240***	0.024	0.583*	2.679***
	(0.035)	(0.165)	(0.031)	(0.017)	(0.342)	(0.440)
Father's edu. 9–12	–0.006	0.432***	0.053**	–0.029**	1.140***	0.521*
	(0.023)	(0.110)	(0.021)	(0.011)	(0.225)	(0.288)
Father's edu. > 12	–0.001	1.122***	0.184***	–0.043***	1.659***	1.585***
	(0.032)	(0.153)	(0.029)	(0.016)	(0.315)	(0.407)
Lived with 2 parents	–0.028	0.770***	0.101***	–0.004	0.072	1.049**
	(0.039)	(0.182)	(0.034)	(0.019)	(0.373)	(0.477)
Constant	0.588***	11.348***	0.088*	0.972***	20.102***	20.369***
	(0.057)	(0.274)	(0.052)	(0.029)	(0.561)	(0.705)
Observations	2,735	2,636	2,636	2,913	2,720	2,608

Notes: Regression follow the format of Model 2 in table 6.5, with the exception of the dependent variables. "Expectation housewife" is measured from a survey question of what the daughters expect to be doing at age thirty-five. The question is asked in 1968, when the daughters were, on average, nineteen years old. "Highest grade" and "ever married" are measured in 1982 when the daughters were, on average, thirty-three years old. "College degree" is constructed from "highest grade" and is equal to one for women who completed sixteen years or more of schooling.

***Significant at the 1 percent level.
**Significant at the 5 percent level.
*Significant at the 10 percent level.

to increase the return to this market work and may delay marriage until after completing their schooling.

We find some evidence consistent with these conjectures but other patterns that are quite contrary to them. As expected, column (1) demonstrates that daughters of working mothers are 4.9 percentage points less likely to expect that they would be housewives when they reach the age of thirty-five, even after controlling for other family background measures. These expectations are elicited in the first survey wave when the daughters are, on average, nineteen years old. Yet despite expecting a higher rate of future labor force participation, daughters of working mothers do not attain more years of education on average and are no more likely to graduate from college or attain a postbaccalaureate degree (last result not shown). Even more surprisingly, mother's work is associated with a *higher* probability of ever marrying and, among those who do marry, with *earlier* ages of first marriage and first child birth (by 0.5 to 0.6 of a year).[27] In contrast, having a father or mother who graduated from high school raises the age of first marriage and first birth by one to two years, respectively; similarly, living with both parents in childhood and having a library card at age fourteen are also associated with delay of childbearing.

The positive association between mother's work and early marriage is somewhat of a puzzle. Perhaps daughters whose mothers worked outside of the home have adopted a more equitable view of marriage and do not associate marriage with specialization in home production. In that case, the cost of marrying in terms of foregone earnings or independence would be lower and, therefore, these daughters would be more likely to marry and to do so at younger ages. Alternatively, this early marriage may simply reflect the fact that poorer families are more likely to have two working parents and that daughters from a lower socioeconomic status background are more likely to marry and engage in childbearing at younger ages.

6.4   Conclusion

Large racial differences in women's labor force participation persisted for more than 100 years after the Civil War. Following Goldin (1977), we hypothesize that these differences might, in part, reflect an indirect legacy of slavery that operated through differences in social norms about women's work in arduous occupations. We find that well into the twentieth century only a portion of the racial difference in women's LFP (or in their work specifically in physically demanding jobs) can be attributed to differences in observable characteristics, which is consistent with the presence of some

---

27. That daughters of working mothers marry at younger ages (and, for this reason, are less likely to be in the labor force) explains why controlling for marital status *augments* the relationship between mother's work and daughter's labor force participation in table 6.5.

persistent propensity toward work outside of the home that initially derived from the institution of slavery.

Any legacy of slavery on any subsequent work behavior must be transmitted across generations. We present two separate analyses that further test the intergenerational transmission of female labor force participation. In 1900, it appears that women born to ex-slaves were significantly more likely than other black women to be in the labor force. Later in the twentieth century, the NLS data reveal that daughters of working mothers were more likely to work themselves even when controlling for a number of background characteristics. Both patterns are consistent with the possibility that the higher rates of female LFP under slavery persisted into the second and third generation after Emancipation through a process of intergenerational transmission.

The structural transformation of the US economy and rapid gains in educational attainment greatly expanded the scope for women's work in relatively "clean" jobs. White women started moving into such jobs in the early decades of the twentieth century, but black women did not make large inroads in white-collar work until after World War II. Thereafter, participation rates for both white and black women increased as white-collar jobs became more prevalent, such that by the end of the twentieth century, the racial gap in women's labor force participation had greatly narrowed. A small residual difference remained in terms of employment in less prestigious occupations, perhaps a last trace of a long-standing difference in social norms with respect to such work.

Appendix

Table 6A.1 Women's labor force participation by race, 1870–2010

	1870	1880	1900	1920	1930	1940	1950	1960	1970	1980	1990	2000	2010
A. White women, age 25–54													
In LF and married	0.60	1.27	1.58	4.15	6.42	10.09	17.99	27.62	34.48	43.04	49.53	48.29	44.71
In LF and not married	7.93	8.05	13.02	14.72	14.66	16.15	13.88	12.31	13.60	19.22	25.22	26.90	32.32
Not in LF and married	20.52	17.08	13.77	9.76	8.88	8.70	6.53	4.90	5.25	4.96	4.93	6.14	7.86
Not in LF and not married	70.96	73.61	71.63	71.36	70.03	65.06	61.60	55.17	46.66	32.78	20.32	18.68	15.11
Overall LFP	8.52	9.31	14.60	18.88	21.08	26.24	31.87	39.93	48.08	62.26	74.75	75.18	77.03
Percent of married in LF	0.83	1.69	2.16	5.50	8.40	13.43	22.60	33.36	42.50	56.77	70.91	72.11	74.74
Percent of not married in LF	27.87	32.02	48.60	60.14	62.26	64.99	68.01	71.55	72.13	79.49	83.64	81.41	80.44
Share of married in pop.	71.55	74.88	73.21	75.52	76.46	75.16	79.59	82.79	81.15	75.83	69.84	66.96	59.82
B. Black women, age 25–54													
In LF and married	13.81	17.59	13.68	20.61	19.84	17.72	21.90	28.39	31.97	32.51	29.56	26.89	23.89
In LF and not married	23.10	21.66	27.12	24.89	26.56	27.15	23.98	25.01	27.14	36.09	45.35	46.19	55.68
Not in LF and married	16.60	11.01	7.78	6.97	8.71	12.38	14.80	13.35	16.22	17.33	17.14	18.23	15.19
Not in LF and not married	46.49	49.74	51.42	47.53	44.89	42.75	39.31	33.26	24.67	14.07	7.95	8.69	5.24
Overall LFP	36.91	39.25	40.80	45.50	46.40	44.87	45.88	53.40	59.11	68.60	74.91	73.08	79.56
Percent of married in LF	22.90	26.12	21.02	30.25	30.65	29.30	35.78	46.05	56.44	69.80	78.80	75.57	82.00
Percent of not married in LF	58.20	66.30	77.70	78.13	75.30	68.68	61.83	65.21	62.59	67.56	72.57	71.70	78.56
Share of married in pop.	60.30	67.33	65.10	68.14	64.74	60.47	61.21	61.64	56.64	46.58	37.51	35.58	29.13
C. US-born white women, age 25–54													
In LF and married	0.47	1.01	1.47	3.85	6.37	9.94	18.02	27.61	34.65	43.43	50.04	49.17	45.63
In LF and not married	6.40	6.96	12.86	15.26	15.24	16.66	13.86	12.16	13.55	19.32	25.36	27.32	32.80
Not in LF and not married	23.22	18.88	14.70	10.38	9.20	8.62	6.29	4.83	5.13	4.67	4.78	5.83	7.67
Not in LF and married	69.91	73.15	70.97	70.51	69.19	64.77	61.84	55.39	46.67	32.58	19.82	17.68	13.90
Overall LFP	6.87	7.97	14.33	19.11	21.61	26.60	31.87	39.77	48.20	62.75	75.40	76.49	78.43
Percent of married in LF	0.67	1.36	2.03	5.18	8.43	13.31	22.56	33.26	42.61	57.13	71.63	73.56	76.66
Percent of not married in LF	21.60	26.93	46.65	59.51	62.35	65.89	68.78	71.57	72.53	80.54	84.15	82.41	81.05
Share of married in pop.	70.38	74.17	72.44	74.36	75.56	74.71	79.85	83.00	81.32	76.01	69.86	66.85	59.53

Source: Microdata are from IPUMS (Ruggles et al. 2010).

Notes: "Overall LFP" is the sum of "In LF and married" and "In LF and not married" categories. Participation rate conditional on marital status are reported in row labeled "Percent of married in LF" and so on.

Table 6A.2   Alternative series of women's labor force participation by race, 1870–1920

	1870	1880	1900	1910	1920	1930	1940
		Based on 1920 cell-specific rates					
White women	11.47	12.14	15.75	17.80	18.88	20.77	25.51
Married	2.79	3.11	3.24	4.78	5.50	8.09	12.48
Single	37.16	39.04	49.94	55.52	60.14	61.93	64.94
Black women	40.39	41.86	43.95	49.52	45.50	47.65	47.66
Married	28.05	29.06	25.92	33.80	30.25	32.16	31.80
Single	62.81	68.23	77.60	81.54	78.13	76.08	71.93
		Based on 1940 cell-specific rates					
White women	13.07	13.72	17.09	19.07	19.94	21.69	26.24
Married	4.91	5.24	5.08	6.49	6.88	9.27	13.43
Single	37.21	39.00	49.90	55.55	60.21	62.02	64.99
Black women	38.37	38.71	39.73	45.60	41.39	44.45	44.87
Married	26.72	26.20	22.06	30.09	26.51	29.37	29.30
Single	59.53	64.50	72.68	77.19	73.20	72.13	68.68
		Based on 1960 cell-specific rates					
White women	22.48	23.13	25.04	26.00	26.08	26.71	30.69
Married	15.58	15.98	14.23	14.47	13.93	14.94	18.52
Single	42.89	44.45	54.59	59.45	63.54	64.96	67.51
Black women	40.25	42.06	43.18	49.22	45.02	47.42	47.29
Married	30.69	32.26	29.09	36.88	33.34	35.21	34.45
Single	57.62	62.26	69.46	74.35	70.00	69.82	66.93

Source: Microdata are from IPUMS (Ruggles et al. 2010).

Notes: To create an alternative LFP series back to 1870, we first estimate within-cell participation rates for all women (25–54) in 1920, 1940, and 1960 categorized by interactions of race, farm, south, married, and has-boarders status. "Has boarders" is 1 for women who are household heads or spouses of household heads who reside with at least one person whose relation is coded "other nonfamily" in the IPUMS. Then, for women who lived on farms or had boarders in each census year, we replaced their IPUMS reported LFP with the cell-specific rate observed in 1920, 1940, or 1960.

Table 6A.3   Women's LFP and occupational distribution by race, 1870–2010

	1870	1880	1900	1920	1930	1940	1950	1960	1970	1980	1990	2000	2010
					A. White women, 25–54								
Professional/clerical/manager/sales	1.12	1.66	3.87	8.60	11.46	14.00	18.37	23.59	31.12	43.74	56.04	58.77	59.46
Agricultural	0.53	0.76	1.32	1.05	0.79	0.49	0.84	0.56	0.35	0.51	0.44	0.35	0.39
Craft/operative/laborer	2.67	3.49	4.71	5.07	4.36	6.41	8.05	8.62	9.38	9.20	8.00	6.35	5.00
Household and non-HH service	4.21	3.40	4.70	4.16	4.48	5.11	4.51	5.95	7.14	8.69	10.19	9.65	12.05
Not in labor force	91.48	90.69	85.40	81.12	78.92	74.00	68.23	61.28	52.01	37.87	25.34	24.88	23.10
					B. Black women, 25–54								
Professional/clerical/manager/sales	0.09	0.22	0.74	1.64	2.43	3.40	5.97	9.48	20.17	34.84	43.95	47.04	51.51
Agricultural	17.98	15.96	14.70	14.13	9.40	5.63	3.22	1.80	0.79	0.29	0.24	0.09	0.08
Craft/operative/laborer	2.21	6.77	4.09	4.47	4.68	4.86	8.27	9.01	12.83	14.41	12.64	9.28	6.90
Household and non-HH service	16.64	16.30	21.27	25.25	29.89	30.76	28.27	30.99	25.15	18.73	17.73	16.43	20.81
Not in labor force	63.09	60.75	59.20	54.50	53.60	55.34	54.26	48.71	41.06	31.73	25.45	27.15	20.70
					C. US-born white women, 25–54								
Not in labor force	93.13	92.03	85.67	80.89	78.39	73.64	68.22	61.45	51.89	37.37	24.67	23.55	21.66
Professional/clerical/manager/sales	1.10	1.69	4.38	9.84	12.85	14.97	18.89	23.93	31.65	44.91	57.18	60.61	62.58
Agricultural	0.67	0.92	1.52	1.18	0.88	0.51	0.88	0.57	0.35	0.49	0.41	0.32	0.27
Craft/operative/(nonfarm) laborer	2.50	3.27	4.77	4.61	4.01	6.08	7.70	8.24	9.01	8.64	7.74	6.15	4.55
Household and non-HH service	2.59	2.09	3.67	3.47	3.87	4.80	4.30	5.81	7.09	8.60	9.99	9.37	10.93

Source: Data are from the IPUMS (Ruggles et al. 2010).

Notes: A small number of women who are counted as "in labor force" but without an occupation are omitted from this sample. Therefore, the "not in labor force" row does not necessarily match results in appendix table 6A.1. Occupation codes are based on the IPUMS "occ1950" coding scheme.

Table 6A.4   Women's detailed occupational distribution, 1870–2010

	1870	1880	1900	1920	1930	1940	1950	1960	1970	1980	1990	2000	2010
A. White women, 25–54													
0 Not in labor force	91.48	90.69	85.40	81.12	78.92	74.00	68.23	61.28	52.01	37.87	25.34	24.88	23.10
1 Professional	0.73	1.06	2.01	3.03	3.83	4.12	4.57	5.62	8.71	13.79	20.04	23.77	25.36
1.5 Teacher	*0.57*	*0.80*	*1.32*	*1.77*	*2.24*	*2.26*	*2.03*	*2.44*	*3.34*	*4.78*	*5.62*	*5.54*	*5.81*
1.6 Other professions	*0.16*	*0.27*	*0.68*	*1.26*	*1.59*	*1.86*	*2.54*	*3.18*	*5.37*	*9.02*	*14.42*	*18.23*	*19.55*
2 Clerical	0.03	0.05	0.73	3.37	4.80	6.45	9.15	12.73	16.73	21.21	22.19	20.01	18.92
3 Craft	0.32	0.30	0.39	0.44	0.37	0.45	0.65	0.61	0.98	1.49	1.70	1.47	1.13
4 Operative	2.31	3.04	4.11	4.25	3.65	5.71	7.19	7.81	7.97	6.99	5.36	4.20	3.17
4.5 Manufacturing	*0.87*	*1.19*	*1.54*	*2.71*	*2.55*	*4.53*	*5.90*	*6.68*	*6.61*	*5.51*	*3.66*	*2.62*	*1.64*
4.6 Laundry	*0.01*	*0.05*	*0.09*	*0.20*	*0.31*	*0.35*	*0.44*	*0.36*	*0.23*	*0.12*	*0.12*	*0.09*	*0.07*
4.7 Other operatives	*1.43*	*1.80*	*2.48*	*1.34*	*0.79*	*0.83*	*0.84*	*0.77*	*1.13*	*1.36*	*1.59*	*1.50*	*1.45*
5 Laborer	0.04	0.15	0.21	0.37	0.33	0.25	0.22	0.20	0.42	0.72	0.94	0.67	0.70
6 Service household	3.80	2.76	3.20	2.31	2.15	2.20	0.91	0.93	0.61	0.40	0.41	—	—
7 Service nonhousehold	0.41	0.65	1.50	1.85	2.32	2.91	3.60	5.02	6.52	8.29	9.78	9.65	12.05
8 Manager	0.25	0.39	0.53	0.73	0.96	1.29	1.65	1.73	1.87	4.68	9.01	10.29	10.48
9 Sales	0.10	0.16	0.60	1.46	1.87	2.14	3.01	3.51	3.80	4.05	4.80	4.71	4.69
10 Farmers and farm laborers	0.53	0.76	1.32	1.05	0.79	0.49	0.84	0.56	0.35	0.51	0.44	0.35	0.39
B. Black women, 25–54													
0 Not in labor force	63.09	60.75	59.20	54.50	53.60	55.34	54.26	48.71	41.06	31.73	25.45	27.15	20.70
1 Professional	0.02	0.12	0.43	0.95	1.53	2.12	2.77	4.13	7.92	12.23	14.76	17.11	19.46
1.5 Teacher	*0.02*	*0.10*	*0.37*	*0.76*	*1.15*	*1.69*	*1.72*	*2.36*	*3.52*	*4.72*	*4.44*	*3.81*	*4.09*
1.6 Other professions	*0.00*	*0.01*	*0.06*	*0.20*	*0.38*	*0.44*	*1.04*	*1.77*	*4.39*	*7.52*	*10.32*	*13.30*	*15.37*
2 Clerical	0.00	0.01	0.05	0.25	0.31	0.50	1.90	3.97	9.96	18.40	21.54	20.15	19.99
3 Craft	0.00	0.06	0.05	0.07	0.14	0.21	0.32	0.42	0.93	1.65	2.09	1.69	1.25
4 Operative	0.54	0.85	1.65	3.02	3.54	4.02	7.10	8.00	11.07	11.43	9.27	6.66	4.81
4.5 Manufacturing	*0.12*	*0.15*	*0.15*	*1.04*	*1.13*	*1.85*	*3.71*	*4.58*	*7.97*	*9.16*	*6.73*	*4.37*	*2.47*
4.6 Laundry	*0.00*	*0.06*	*0.43*	*0.62*	*1.45*	*1.21*	*2.35*	*2.26*	*1.53*	*0.51*	*0.38*	*0.25*	*0.15*
4.7 Other operatives	*0.42*	*0.63*	*1.06*	*1.36*	*0.96*	*0.95*	*1.04*	*1.16*	*1.57*	*1.77*	*2.17*	*2.04*	*2.18*
5 Laborer	1.67	5.87	2.38	1.38	1.00	0.64	0.84	0.59	0.84	1.33	1.27	0.93	0.85
6 Service household	14.30	12.91	15.01	21.02	24.85	26.07	19.24	18.82	9.70	2.40	1.00	—	—
7 Service nonhousehold	2.34	3.39	6.26	4.23	5.04	4.69	9.04	12.17	15.45	16.34	16.73	16.43	20.81
8 Manager	0.03	0.07	0.15	0.32	0.41	0.43	0.71	0.60	0.72	2.39	5.03	6.48	8.18
9 Sales	0.04	0.03	0.11	0.13	0.18	0.35	0.60	0.78	1.58	1.81	2.62	3.31	3.87
10 Farmers and farm laborers	17.98	15.96	14.70	14.13	9.40	5.63	3.22	1.80	0.79	0.29	0.24	0.09	0.08

Table 6A.5   **Decompositions of differences in women's LFP, 1880–2000**

	1880	1900	1920	1940A	1940B	1960	1980	2000
White	0.0931	0.1460	0.1888	0.2624	0.2624	0.3993	0.6226	0.7518
Black	0.3925	0.4080	0.4550	0.4487	0.4487	0.5340	0.6860	0.7307
Difference	-0.2994	-0.2620	-0.2663	-0.1863	-0.1863	-0.1347	-0.0634	0.0211
Explained (due to differences in Xs)								
Literacy or education	-0.0109	-0.0044	0.0002	0.0119	0.0236	0.0384	0.0278	0.0238
Children	0.0018	0.0005	-0.0046	-0.0119	-0.0115	-0.0033	0.0062	-0.0015
Husband	-0.0229	-0.0385	-0.0422	-0.0547	-0.0591	-0.0712	-0.0345	-0.0111
Age	-0.0063	-0.0028	-0.0039	-0.0074	-0.0070	-0.0011	-0.0033	-0.0030
Farm and metro	0.0006	0.0090	0.0192	0.0092	0.0085	-0.0072	0.0026	0.0036
Birth states	0.0055	-0.0025	-0.0046	-0.0217	-0.0206	-0.0145	-0.0083	0.0101
Total explained	-0.0321	-0.0387	-0.0358	-0.0746	-0.0661	-0.0590	-0.0095	0.0220
Total unexplained	-0.2673	-0.2233	-0.2304	-0.1117	-0.1202	-0.0757	-0.0539	-0.0009

Notes: In this context "explained" refers to the differences in LFP accounted for by racial differences in observables weighted by a vector of coefficients that corresponds to the regressions in table 6.2. Negative values in the "explained" rows imply that racial differences in that set of characteristics contribute to the racial gap (e.g., differences in husband's presence and occupation tend to explain part of the LFP gap). The subcategories under "explained" each represented several variables. For instance, "children" captures the influence racial differences summed across all the relevant "child" variables in table 6.2. The decomposition method follows Fortin (2008) and is implemented with Stata's "Oaxaca" command with "pooled" and "categorical" options applied, as described by Jann (2008). This approach dovetails with table 6.2, but of course other decomposition methods could be chosen.

References

Bailey, Martha J., and William J. Collins. 2006. "The Wage Gains of African-American Women in the 1940s." *Journal of Economic History* 66 (3): 737–77.

Blau, Francine D., and Lawrence M. Kahn. 2007. "Changes in the Labor Supply Behavior of Married Women: 1980–2000." *Journal of Labor Economics* 25:393–438.

Blau, Francine D., Lawrence M. Kahn, Albert Yung-Hsu Liu, and Kerry L. Papps. 2013. "The Transmission of Women's Fertility, Human Capital and Work Orientation Across Immigrant Generations." *Journal of Population Economics* 26 (2): 405–35.

Bowen, William G., and T. Aldrich Finegan. 1969. *The Economics of Labor Force Participation.* Princeton, NJ: Princeton University Press.

Collins, William J. 2003. "The Labor Market Impact of State-Level Antidiscrimination Laws, 1940–1960." *Industrial and Labor Relations Review* 56 (2): 244–72.

Collins, William J., and Robert A. Margo. 2006. "Historical Perspectives on Racial Differences in Schooling in the United States." In *Handbook of the Economics of Education*, vol. 1, edited by E. Hanushek and F. Welch, 107–54. Amsterdam: North-Holland.

Farré, Lidia, and Francis Vella. 2007. "The Intergenerational Transmission of Gender Role Attitudes and Its Implications for Female Labor Force Participation." IZA Discussion Paper no. 2802, Institute for the Study of Labor.

Fernández, Raquel, and Alessandra Fogli. 2009. "Culture: An Empirical Investigation of Beliefs, Work, and Fertility." *American Economic Journal: Macroeconomics* 1 (1): 146–77.

Fortin, Nicole M. 2008. "The Gender Wage Gap among Young Adults in the United States: The Importance of Money versus People." *Journal of Human Resources* XLIII (4): 884–918.

Fortin, Nicole M., Thomas Lemieux, and Sergio Firpo. 2011. "Decomposition Methods." In *Handbook of Labor Economics*, vol. 4A, edited by O. Ashenfelter and D. Card, 1–102. Amsterdam: North-Holland.

Fraundorf, Martha Norby. 1979. "The Labor Force Participation of Turn-of-the-Century Married Women." *Journal of Economic History* 39:401–18.

Goldin, Claudia. 1977. "Female Labor Force Participation: The Origin of Black and White Differences, 1870 to 1880." *Journal of Economic History* 37 (1): 87–108.

———. 1989. "Life-Cycle Labor Force Participation by Married Women: Historical Evidence and Implications." *Journal of Labor Economics* 7:20–47.

———. 1990. *Understanding the Gender Gap: An Economic History of American Women.* New York: Oxford University Press.

———. 1995. "The U-Shaped Female Labor Force Function in Economic Development and Economic History." In *Investment in Women's Human Capital*, edited by T. Paul Schultz. Chicago: University of Chicago Press.

———. 2006. "The Quiet Revolution That Transformed Women's Employment, Education, and Family." *American Economic Review* 96 (2): 1–21.

Jann, Ben. 2008. "The Blinder-Oaxaca Decomposition for Linear Regression Models." *Stata Journal* 8 (4): 453–79.

Jones, Jacqueline. 1985. *Labor of Love, Labor of Sorrow: Black Women, Work, and the Family from Slavery to the Present.* New York: Basic Books.

Killingsworth, Mark R., and James J. Heckman. 1986. "Female Labor Supply: A Survey." In *Handbook of Labor Economics*, vol. 1, edited by O. Ashenfelter and R. Layard, 103–204. Amsterdam: Elsevier.

Margo, Robert A. 2004. "The North-South Wage Gap before and after the Civil

War." In *Slavery in the Development of the Americas*, edited by D. Eltis, F. Lewis, and K. Sokoloff, 324–51. New York: Cambridge University Press.

Mincer, Jacob. 1962. "Labor Force Participation of Married Women." In *Aspects of Labor Economics*, A Conference of the Universities-National Bureau Committee for Economic Research. Princeton, NJ: Princeton University Press.

Moen, Phyllis, Mary Ann Erickson, and Donna Dempster-McClain. 1997. "Their Mother's Daughters? The Intergenerational Transmission of Gender Attitudes in a World of Changing Roles." *Journal of Marriage and the Family* 59 (2): 281–93.

Ransom, Roger L., and Richard Sutch. 2001 [1977]. *One Kind of Freedom: The Economic Consequences of Emancipation*. New York: Cambridge University Press.

Reimers, Cordelia W. 1985. "Cultural Differences in Labor Force Participation among Married Women." *American Economic Review*, Papers and Proceedings 75 (2): 251–5.

Roberts, Evan Warwick. 2007. "Her Real Sphere? Married Women's Labor Force Participation in the United States, 1860–1940." PhD. diss., University of Minnesota.

Rotella, Elyce. 1980. "Women's Labor Force Participation and the Decline of the Family Economy in the United States." *Explorations in Economic History* 17:95–117.

Ruggles, Steven, Trent Alexander, Katie Genadek, Ronald Goeken, Matthew B. Schroeder, and Matthew Sobek. 2010. *Integrated Public Use Microdata Series: Version 5.0* [Machine-readable database]. Minneapolis, MN: University of Minnesota.

Sacerdote, Bruce. 2005. "Slavery and the Intergenerational Transmission of Human Capital." *Review of Economics and Statistics* 87 (2): 217–34.

Sobek, Matthew Joseph. 1997. "A Century of Work: Gender, Labor Force Participation, and Occupational Attainment in the United States, 1880–1990." PhD. diss., University of Minnesota.

Sundstrom, William A. 2000. "From Servants to Secretaries: The Occupations of African-American Women, 1940–1980." Unpublished manuscript, Santa Clara University.

Wayne, Tiffany K. 2007. *Women's Roles in Nineteenth Century America*. Santa Barbara, CA: ABC-Clio.

Weiss, Thomas. 1999. "Estimates of White and Nonwhite Gainful Workers in the United States by Age Group, Race, and Sex: Decennial Census Years, 1800–1900." *Historical Methods* 32:21–35.

Wilson, William Julius. 1990. *The Truly Disadvantaged: The Inner City, the Underclass, and Public Policy*. Chicago: University of Chicago Press.

Cohabitation and the Uneven Retreat from Marriage in the United States, 1950–2010

Shelly Lundberg and Robert A. Pollak

7.1 Introduction

Since 1950 there have been dramatic changes in patterns of marriage and divorce in the United States. Americans now marry later and are more likely to divorce. More men and women, though still a small minority, do not marry at all. Cohabitation as a precursor or an alternative to marriage has become commonplace. A growing fraction of births now take place outside marriage. This decoupling of marriage and parenthood has received a great deal of scholarly and public attention, particularly focused on differences in nonmarital childbearing across racial and ethnic groups. Within each racial and ethnic group, however, there are dramatic differences in marriage and childbearing behavior across education and income strata. But these differences, which also have potentially important implications for investments in

Shelly Lundberg is the Broom Professor of Demography at the University of California, Santa Barbara, and professor II at the University of Bergen. Robert A. Pollak is the Hernreich Distinguished Professor of Economics in the Faculty of Arts and Sciences and in the Olin Business School at Washington University in St. Louis and a research associate of the National Bureau of Economic Research.

Prepared for the NBER-Spencer conference on "Human Capital in History: The American Record," Cambridge, Massachusetts, December 2012. Pollak's research was supported in part by the University of Bergen and the Research Council of Norway as part of the AGEFAM project. Earlier versions of this chapter were presented at the NBER Cohort Studies conference in Chicago, SOLE in Boston, and at the University of Bergen. We are especially grateful to Andrew Cherlin, Paula England, and Valerie Ramey for their perceptive comments on an earlier version of this chapter. We also wish to thank the editors, Leah Boustan, Carola Frydman, and Robert Margo, for very helpful comments; Jarrett Gorlick, Jenna Stearns, and Xinyi Zhang for excellent research assistance; and Joanne Spitz for excellent editorial assistance. For acknowledgments, sources of research support, and disclosure of the authors' material financial relationships, if any, please see http://www.nber.org/chapters/c12896.ack.

children and intergenerational income mobility, have received less attention than racial and ethnic gaps.

In this chapter, we make two claims about marriage. First, we claim that intertemporal commitment is central to understanding marriage as an economic institution. Second, we claim that in early twenty-first-century America intertemporal commitment is valuable primarily because it facilitates investment in children. These claims are distinct, but together they imply that the desire to invest in children as a joint project has become a primary motive for marriage. Differences in the expected returns to these investments across socioeconomic groups explain the uneven retreat from marriage.

We revisit the literature on the economics of marriage, distinguishing between explanations that involve intertemporal commitment and those that do not. What Claudia Goldin has called the "quiet revolution" in women's economic status since 1970 has led to a wholesale redefinition of men's and women's roles in the household. Commitments between wage-earning men and their stay-at-home wives that were central to marriage in the first half of the twentieth century became obsolete as the labor force participation of married women increased. Changes in family law and social norms weakened the strength of the marriage commitment by making divorce easier to obtain and blurring the social distinction between cohabitation and marriage. Once cohabitation became a socially and legally acceptable way to achieve the benefits of coresidential intimacy and economic cooperation, the advantages of living in a multiple-person household no longer provided a rationale for marriage. Marriage must be based on gains compared with cohabitation as well as gains compared with living alone.[1] Sociologists have emphasized the cultural significance of marriage as the source of its persistence as a goal and ideal. An economic approach to understanding the persistence of marriage, once cohabitation is recognized as an alternative, emphasizes the potential returns to intertemporal commitment.

Investment in children is clearly not the only reason couples have ever made intertemporal commitments, nor do we claim it is the only reason couples do so now. In particular, not all couples that marry intend to have children, and some married couples have other motives for commitment.[2] Women who marry after menopause generally do not intend to have additional children; for many older couples, the relevant marital commitment may be to provide care for each other in old age. The current debate over

1. By "living alone" we mean living in a one-adult household; thus, living alone includes lone parents. The not entirely satisfactory rationale for this is the fiction that the adult is the sole decision maker in a one-adult household.

2. Abma and Martinez (2006) find that only 4 percent of married women age thirty-five to forty-four in the 2002 National Survey of Family Growth are voluntarily childless, and that rates of voluntary childlessness are lower in the 2002 wave of the National Survey of Family Growth (NSFG) than in the 1988 and 1992 waves.

same-sex marriage is best understood as primarily a contest over social recognition and acceptability, with considerations involving children playing a secondary role. We argue, however, that during the last half of the twentieth century the importance of investment in children has increased, particularly for the most advantaged families, while the importance of other reasons for making intertemporal commitments has diminished.

7.2   The Retreat from Marriage, 1950–2010

The family in the Western world has been radically altered, some claim almost destroyed, by the events of the last three decades.
—Becker, *A Treatise on the Family* ([1981] 1991)

In her 2006 Ely Lecture, Claudia Goldin traces the "quiet revolution" in American women's careers, education, and family arrangements that began in the 1970s, and the "evolutionary" changes in labor force participation that preceded it (Goldin 2006). Evolving patterns of marriage and divorce in the United States are linked to these changes in women's status and identity, as well as historic changes in fertility rates and in women's participation in the paid workforce. As the postwar baby boom came to an end and fertility rates fell in the 1960s, and as women's intermittent employment turned into lifetime commitments to market work and careers, marriages changed as well. Marriage was delayed to accommodate higher education and smaller families, divorce rates rose rapidly, and for many, coresidence without marriage became an acceptable precursor if not a replacement for marriage.

The median age at first marriage was at a historic low during the height of the baby boom in the 1950s—just over age twenty for women, and about age twenty-three for men. A modest delay in first marriage during the 1960s was followed by a rapid increase in marriage age that continued for the next four decades (figure 7.1). Part of this delay was due to additional years spent in school: the college attendance of young men and women rose steadily until the 1980s, when improvements in men's educational attainment stalled but women's continued to rise. The proportion of young adult women with college degrees equaled, and then exceeded, that of men in the 1990s. Beginning in the 1980s, increases in premarital coresidence by young couples become another important driver of marriage timing—stabilizing the age at which households are first formed while further delaying age at marriage (Bailey, Guldi, and Hershbein, this volume, chapter 8).

Marriage delay alone tended to reduce the fraction of young men and women who were currently married (or ever married) in their twenties, but in the 1970s the prevalence of marriage began to decline even for older groups of men and women. Figure 7.2 shows this decline for men and women age thirty to forty-four, much of it accounted for by an increase in cohabita-

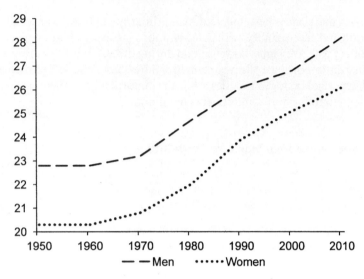

Fig. 7.1   Median age at first marriage
Source: US Bureau of the Census.

tion.[3] The National Survey of Family Growth (NSFG) permits the tracking of trends in cohabitation from the first wave in 1982 to the most recent in 2006–2010. Over this period, the 8 percent decline in the fraction of fifteen- to forty-four-year-old women currently married (from 44 to 36 percent) is exactly offset by the increase in the proportion cohabiting (from 3 to 11 percent).[4]

The gap between the proportion of thirty- to forty-four-year-olds currently married (now about 60 percent) and the proportion ever married (80 percent for women, 74 percent for men) has widened due to increases in divorce (figure 7.2). The annual divorce rate (the number of divorces per thousand married couples) more than doubled between 1960 and 1980— from less than ten to more than twenty. In part a transitory response to liberalized divorce laws, the divorce boom has since subsided, falling by more than 25 percent since the peak in 1979. Stevenson and Wolfers (2007) argue that current rates are consistent with a long-term prewar trend of rising divorce.[5]

---

3. Much of the family structure literature combines cohabitation and marriage into a single category (i.e., two-parent families) rather than distinguishing between cohabitation and marriage. Ginther and Pollak (2004) and Gennetian (2005) distinguish between families that include stepchildren (e.g., blended families) and traditional nuclear families (i.e., households in which all of the children live with both biological parents).

4. Copen et al. (2012) find, not surprisingly, similar trends for men.

5. Taking a different approach, Rotz (2011) shows that, given the strong negative relationship between the probability of divorce and age at marriage, the delay in marriage age since 1980 may be a major proximate cause of the decrease in divorce propensity during that period.

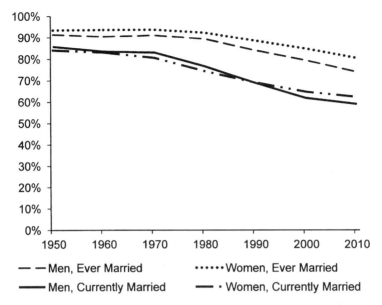

Fig. 7.2   Proportion of men and women ever married and currently married, age 30–44
Sources: US Census 1950–2000 and American Community Survey 2010.

In recent decades, the social and legal significance of the distinction between marriage and nonmarriage has eroded. Spells of cohabitation have become longer and more likely to involve children (Kennedy and Bumpass 2008). Supreme Court decisions in the 1960s and 1970s increased the rights of children born out of wedlock to financial support and inheritance.[6] Marriage also became less important as a determinant of obligations for paternal child support as the introduction of in-hospital voluntary paternity establishment programs by states (following a federal mandate) during the 1990s reduced the costs of legal paternity establishment. By 2005, the ratio of paternities established to nonmarital births had risen to nearly 90 percent (Rossin-Slater 2012). The costs of exiting marriage fell as unilateral divorce became, in one form or another, universal across the United States.[7] Changes in social norms that accompanied these changes have also played a role: the stigma associated with nonmarital sex, cohabitation, nonmarital fertility, and divorce have declined dramatically (Thornton and Young-DeMarco 2001).

Rising rates of nonmarital fertility in the United States and the pro-

6. Stevenson and Wolfers (2007) provide a summary of these rulings.
7. Grossman and Friedman (2011) describe these changes as well as changes in the rules governing the division of property, spousal support, and alimony. To a first approximation, however, these rules affect distribution between the ex-spouses, not the cost of exiting marriage.

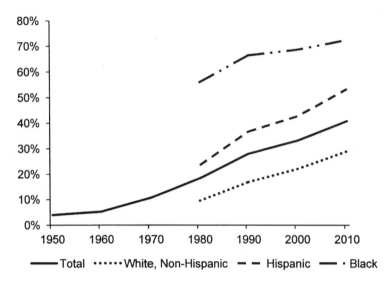

Fig. 7.3   Nonmarital births as a proportion of all births, by race and ethnicity
Source: Child Trends Data Bank.

nounced race/ethnic gaps in these rates (figure 7.3) have received a great deal of attention from researchers and policymakers. The median age at first marriage has been rising more rapidly than the median age at first birth and in 1991 the two trends crossed and continue to diverge. In 2009, the median age at first birth was more than one year lower than the median age at first marriage (Arroyo et al. 2012). The circumstances in which nonmarital births take place have been changing, however. England, Wu, and Shafer (2013) show that, for women who reached childbearing age in the 1950s through the mid-1960s, the primary cause of rising premarital births was an increase in premarital pregnancies that were brought to term (and, in all probability, an increase in premarital sex). During the subsequent two decades, however, the principal driver of the trend in premarital childbearing was a reduction in the probability of marriage following a premarital conception—a decrease in "shotgun" marriages.[8] The proportion of nonmarital births that are to lone mothers has also been decreasing: 52 percent of nonmarital births now occur within cohabiting unions, many of them the outcome of a "shotgun cohabitation" (Manlove et al. 2010; Lichter 2012).

8. Akerlof, Yellen, and Katz (1996) attribute this change to endogenous norms regarding nonmarital sex and responsibility for unintended pregnancies. They argue that the increasing availability of the birth control pill in the 1960s and the nationwide legalization of abortion in 1973 led to a new equilibrium in which nonmarital sex was more readily available because competition for the attention of men increased the pressure on unmarried women to have sex and responsibility for contraception (and unintended pregnancies) shifted to women.

Compared with other wealthy countries, the United States is an outlier in many dimensions of family dynamics. The level of fertility that occurs outside any union—marital or cohabiting—is relatively high, and both marital and cohabiting unions are very unstable (Cherlin 2009). In many northern European countries, cohabitation has progressed further in the direction of becoming a replacement for marriage: a much smaller proportion of the population ever marries, rates of cohabitation and proportions of births within cohabiting unions are much higher, and these unions are much more durable than in the United States. In most southern European countries, levels of nonmarital fertility are much lower, but in both northern and southern Europe there are substantial differences within countries (e.g., between eastern and western Germany, and between northern and southern Italy).[9] There is a socioeconomic gradient in family structure in most European countries, with low levels of education associated with more cohabitation and higher rates of nonmarital childbearing,[10] but these discrepancies are less pronounced than in the United States.

Focusing on whites with different levels of education, we can see that the retreat from marriage has been much more rapid for men and women with lower levels of education (figures 7.4 and 7.5). We use a threefold classification, distinguishing among college graduates (the "college educated"), individuals with some college, and those with a high school education or less.[11] The proportion of men age thirty to forty-four who are currently married (reflecting both marriage and divorce behavior) has been almost flat for men with a college degree, but has declined substantially for men with less education. Women with college degrees were less likely to be married than women with less education until 1990, and more likely to be married thereafter. Both marriage and remarriage rates have risen for women with college degrees relative to women with less education, and the fall in divorce rates since 1980 has been much larger for the college educated (Isen and Stevenson 2011). This implies that long-term marital stability also has an education gradient: the probability that a first marriage will remain intact for twenty years is sharply higher for women with a college degree (78 percent)

---

9. Klüsener, Perelli-Harris, and Sánchez Gassen (2013) document the differences in nonmarital fertility between and within European countries since 1960.

10. Perelli-Harris et al. (2010) also find that the negative educational gradient of childbearing within cohabitation is significantly steeper than that of marital births in four of the eight countries they study.

11. The literature often uses a different threefold classification, combining college graduates and individuals with some college into a single category, but distinguishing between high school graduates and high school dropouts. We have chosen our categorization because the high school dropout group has become increasingly dominated by immigrants with distinctive family patterns and the some college group behaves very differently from college graduates. According to census figures in 2012, 43.7 percent of non-Hispanic white women between twenty-five and twenty-nine were college graduates; the comparable figure for Hispanics is 17.5 percent and for non-Hispanic blacks is 26.2 percent.

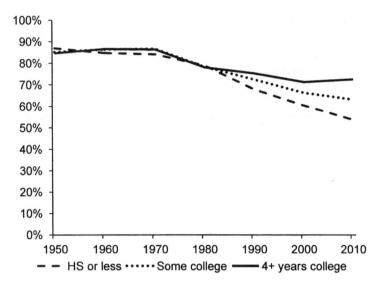

Fig. 7.4 Proportion of white men currently married, age 30–44
Sources: US Census 1950–2000 and American Community Survey 2010.

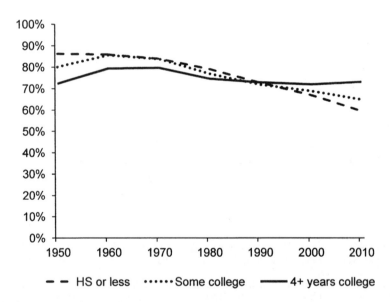

Fig. 7.5 Proportion of white women currently married, age 30–44
Sources: US Census 1950–2000 and American Community Survey 2010.

Table 7.1   Current union status among women age 15–44 years, 2006–2010

	First marriage	Second or higher marriage	Cohabiting	Never in a union	Formerly married
No high school diploma or GED	36.6	7.7	20.2	19.1	16.5
High school diploma or GED	39.5	9.2	15.5	20.3	15.6
Some college	42.1	7.4	11.6	26.4	12.6
Bachelor's degree	58.3	3.3	6.8	25.5	6.1
Master's degree or higher	63.0	4.4	5.5	20.1	7.0

Source: Copen et al. (2012), from the National Survey of Family Growth.

than for women with a high school diploma (41 percent) or some college (49 percent) (Copen et al. 2012).[12]

The prevalence of cohabitation is strongly decreasing in education (table 7.1), and cohabitation tends to play different roles in the life cycles of women with high and low levels of education. For high-education couples, cohabitation is usually a precursor to marriage—a part of courtship or a trial marriage that rarely includes childbearing. Serial cohabitation[13] is much more prevalent among economically disadvantaged men and women and, for low-income and low-education groups, cohabiting unions are less likely to end in marriage than in dissolution (Lichter and Qian 2008). Though serial cohabitation increased in the late 1990s and first decade of the twenty-first century along with cohabitation more generally, a substantial majority of women only cohabit with the men they eventually marry (Lichter, Turner, and Sassler 2010).

The growing divergence in marriage, cohabitation, and fertility behavior across educational groups has potentially important implications for inequality and the intergenerational transmission of economic disadvantage. In her presidential address to the Population Association of America, Sara McLanahan (2004) showed how the rise in single-parent families and widening gaps in maternal age and divorce rates were leading to growing disparities in the parental resources, both time and money, received by the children of more- and less-educated mothers. The sociologist Andrew Cherlin (2009) also emphasizes the costs imposed on children, and particularly the children of the noncollege educated, by the instability in living arrangements and parental ties inherent in what he calls the American "marriage-go-round." Focusing on non-Hispanic whites, Charles Murray's 2012 book on the class divide in family arrangements and economic status makes a similar point from a conservative social and political perspective.

12. They also find that the education gradient in divorce probability is much less steep for men than for women.
13. Serial cohabitation is defined as multiple premarital cohabiting relationships (Lichter, Turner, and Sassler 2010).

The causes of postwar changes in cohabitation and marriage patterns, both the general retreat from marriage and its education and income gradient, are more difficult to establish than their likely consequences. The question we address here is how to reconcile these changes with an economic model of marriage.

7.3   Economic Models of Cohabitation and Marriage: The Role of Commitment

From an economic point of view, marriage is a voluntary partnership for the purpose of joint production and joint consumption.
—Weiss, *The New Palgrave Dictionary of Economics* (2008)

The standard economic model of marriage ignores cohabitation as a possible living arrangement and recognizes only two alternatives: marriage and living alone. Marriage is treated as a choice by individuals who evaluate the gains to a specific marriage relative to other marriages and to living alone. According to this approach, divorce is the only route to lone parenthood and, hence, never-married individuals will be childless.[14] For example, in Becker's *Treatise on the Family* (Becker [1981] 1991) and in Weiss's important survey article on the formation and dissolution of families (Weiss 1997), the feasible set contains exactly two elements, marriage and living alone without children. In the mid-twentieth century, when cohabitation and nonmarital childbearing were rare and stigmatized, this truncation of the feasible set bought analytical simplicity at a relatively low cost. In recent decades, however, changes in technology, social norms, and laws have increased the attractiveness and prevalence of alternative family arrangements including cohabitation and lone parenthood.[15]

The economics of the family has recognized two broad categories of potential gains from marriage: joint production and joint consumption. Production gains arise in household production models and reflect the "division of labour to exploit comparative advantage or increasing returns" (Weiss 2008). Consumption gains come from the joint consumption of household public (nonrival) goods (Lam 1988). Stevenson and Wolfers (2007) expand the joint consumption category to include shared leisure activities as well as household public goods and coined the phrase "hedonic marriage" to describe modern marriages in which there is little gender-based division of labor and consumption benefits are paramount.

The presence of children affects both the production and consumption gains to marriage, and the economics of the family has long acknowledged

---

14. And possibly celibate—for the most part, family economics is silent about sex.
15. The few theoretical papers in economics that model nonmarital fertility do so in the context of lone parenthood, rather than cohabitating parents (Willis 1999; Neal 2004).

the centrality of children. For example, Becker ([1981] 1991, 135) writes, "The main purpose of marriage and families is the production and rearing of own children." Similarly, Weiss (1997, 82) writes, "The production and rearing of children is the most commonly recognized role of the family" (also see Weiss 2008). The presence of children enhances the gains to marriage in two ways: children are themselves household public goods that generate utility for each of their parents, and the coresidence of their caring parents permits the efficient coordination of child care and investment in children (Weiss and Willis 1985).

How can the standard model of marriage explain the retreat from marriage over the past sixty years? As long as the family economics literature continues to assume that unmarried men and women face a two-element feasible set—{marriage (i.e., living together), living alone}—it must explain the delay and increased instability of marriage in terms of the increasing relative attractiveness of living alone.

Though much of the increase in the age at first marriage for very recent cohorts can be attributed to increases in premarital cohabitation, the pronounced delay in marriage between 1970 and 1990 was associated with an extended period of living alone. Advances in contraceptive technology and changes in state laws in the 1970s regarding access to oral contraceptives made reliable fertility control readily available to young single women. These changes in technology and law, together with the weakening of norms stigmatizing premarital sex, reduced the risk and increased the availability of sex outside marriage or cohabiting unions. As a result, delaying "union formation" no longer required choosing between abstinence and the risk of unwanted pregnancy.[16] Goldin and Katz (2002) show that these changes in technology and law accelerated the entry of women into careers that required extended periods of tertiary education.

The relative attractiveness of living alone was also enhanced by the greater availability of market substitutes for commodities that used to be produced within the household and by improvements in household technology. The availability of market substitutes led to the outsourcing of functions that were traditionally regarded as central to the family such as cooking and child care. Improvements in household technology such as electric washing machines and microwaves not only reduced the time needed to perform the remaining household tasks but also reduced the level of skill required to feed and clothe oneself (Greenwood, Seshadri, and Yorukoglu 2005). This emergence of market substitutes and developments in applied technology were, to a considerable extent, endogenous—responding to the growing

---

16. Sex does provide a rationale for marriage if sex outside marriage is strongly stigmatized. For example, those who believe that sex outside marriage is a sin may marry early, especially in communities that readily accept divorce and remarriage. Cherlin (2009) argues that the acceptance of divorce and remarriage by religious communities, especially evangelical Protestants, has been an important factor in the instability of American children's living arrangements.

number of single-person households as well as to increased market work by women. This is one way that living alone creates positive externalities for others who live alone; the increased density in single social networks is undoubtedly another.

As conditions for one-adult households improved and women entered the workforce, the incremental value of specialization and exchange in multiple-person households fell. Gender specialization in married couple households has decreased dramatically during the past sixty years (Lundberg and Pollak 2007).[17] The labor force participation rate for women age twenty-five to fifty-four has increased from 37 to 75 percent between 1950 and 2010, while the participation rate for prime-age men has fallen from 97 to 89 percent. Though married women still report more weekly hours of housework than married men, women's housework hours have fallen by ten hours per week since 1965 and men's have increased by about four hours per week (Aguiar and Hurst 2007). As women's educational attainment, wages, and hours of market work have risen relative to men's, the opportunities for gains from trade within a household, which depend to a large extent upon the segregation of men and women in separate home and market sectors, have diminished—and so have the potential gains to marriage.

The expansion of the feasible set to include cohabitation, with or without children, substantially changes the economic analysis of marriage. Cohabitation provides many, but not all, of the sources of marital surplus identified in standard economic models of marriage. In particular, a cohabiting couple can exploit many of the joint production advantages (e.g., specialization and the division of labor, economies of scale) and the joint consumption advantages (e.g., shared leisure and household public goods, including children). Many of the gains that economists usually ascribe to marriage are, in fact, gains to multiple-person households that coordinate production. For some couples, living together can be simply a solution to the problem of finding a compatible roommate or housemate, unrelated to children or to marriage, but for others cohabitation can be a precursor to marriage or a substitute for it. What distinguishes marriage from cohabitation in an economically meaningful way?

Marriage is more costly to exit than cohabitation, and this higher exit cost enables marriage to act as a commitment device that fosters cooperation between partners. Some degree of commitment is valuable in any shared household because of transactions costs—even roommates must rely on one another to pay a share of next month's rent—and all commitments,

---

17. By "gender specialization" in a married couple household, we mean that the husband's allocation of time between market work and household work differs substantially from the wife's. In contrast, the "specialization theorems" in Becker's *Treatise on the Family* concern extreme patterns of specialization in which one spouse (and perhaps both spouses) work in only the market sector or in only the household sector (see Pollak 2013).

including marriage, are limited. Marriage represents a stronger commitment because the social and legal costs of exit are greater than the costs facing roommates or cohabitants, even though the legal costs of marital exit have decreased as fault-based or mutual consent grounds for divorce have been replaced by state laws permitting unilateral divorce. The social costs of marital dissolution have also fallen as divorce has become commonplace. Nevertheless, a theme of much of the sociological literature on the retreat from marriage is that divorce is seen as a personal failure to be avoided, if necessary, by delaying or avoiding marriage (Edin and Kefalas 2005; Gibson-Davis, Edin, and McLanahan 2005). The cultural significance of marriage in America and the public commitment to a permanent and exclusive relationship that marriage entails distinguishes marriage from cohabitation, which often begins informally and without an explicit discussion of terms or intentions (Manning and Smock 2005).

Divorce costs enable marriage to serve as a commitment device that fosters cooperation and encourages marriage-specific investments, and models of marriage emphasize this high cost of exit. For example, Matouschek and Rasul (2008) construct alternative models of marriage and cohabitation with differential exit costs. They show that, if marriage facilitates commitment, a decrease in divorce costs may lead to an improvement in the average match quality of married couples (lower divorce costs weaken marriage as a commitment device, leading low-match-quality couples to cohabit instead of marrying). Their empirical evidence supports this commitment theory of marriage over an alternative model in which the willingness to marry acts as a signal that expected match quality is high. A plausible theory of marriage, however, must explain not only why commitment is valuable in generating a demand for marriage rather than cohabitation but also, given the substantial heterogeneity in marriage patterns across education/income groups, why couples with more education and income value it more than others. Such an explanation requires that we specify the types of investments that marriage can foster.

Long-term intertemporal commitments are required to support the production benefits of specialization and exchange. Becker ([1981] 1991, 30–31) provides a clear statement of this aspect of the marital contract: "Since married women have been specialized to childbearing and other domestic activities, they have demanded long-term 'contracts' from their husbands to protect them against abandonment and other adversities. Virtually all societies have developed long-term protection for married women: one can even say that 'marriage' is defined by a long-term commitment between a man and a woman." In its strongest form, the standard model assumes and rationalizes a traditional marriage with strong sector specialization: the wife works exclusively in the household sector and the husband works exclusively in the market sector. This pattern of sector specialization leaves the wife vulnerable because she fails to accumulate market human capital. Marriage, and in particular the costs of exiting marriage, protects her.[18] Specialization and vulnerability provide a plausible account of most marriages in the nineteenth and early twentieth centuries but they are less and less plausible as a rationale for contemporary American marriage in the face of the converging economic lives of men and women.

It is clear that one-period models are not well suited to explaining marriage. Once cohabitation is recognized as a socially and legally acceptable alternative, then cohabitation is as good as marriage in a one-period model except to the extent that marriage has direct "consumption" value to one or both spouses or associated tax and transfer advantages. For example, increasing returns to scale in household production provides a rationale for multiple-person living arrangements (e.g., marriage, cohabitation, roommates) rather than living alone, but cannot explain the choice among alternative multiple-person living arrangements.[19] Household production can provide a rationale for intertemporal commitment only in the context of a multiperiod model that includes physical or human capital.

After discussing "the division of labor to exploit comparative advantage or increasing returns," Weiss (1997) discusses two sources of gains from marriage that are necessarily intertemporal: providing credit that facilitates investment (one partner works while the other is in school) and risk pooling (one works while the other is sick or out of work). Credit and investment activities require intertemporal commitment, but one spouse investing in the other's human capital has become less common as student loans have become more important and age at marriage has increased.[20] Risk pooling also requires intertemporal commitment and often involves extended families as well as marital partners. Other benefits (and costs) of marriage depend on policy structures and laws that are conditional on legal marital status, including the tax code (e.g., joint taxation vs. individual taxation), eligibility for social security (e.g., spousal and survivor benefits), and eligibility for employer benefits (e.g., health insurance).

Hedonic/consumption theories of marriage focus on shared leisure and household public goods. Their starting point is the recognition that production theories, with their emphasis on specialization and the division of labor, fail to provide a satisfactory account of contemporary marriage. Stevenson

18. Cigno (2012) argues that the effectiveness of marriage as a commitment device depends, not on the exit cost per se, but upon the property division regime, which can be designed to compensate domestic specialists.

19. For discussions of the perfect substitutes assumption, see Becker ([1981] 1991, ch. 2), Lundberg (2008), and Pollak (2012, 2013).

20. Because marriage is a limited commitment with divorce always an outside option, such investments are risky. How risky depends on the divorce laws of the state. Stevenson (2007) finds that spouses are less likely to invest in each other's human capital in states where the investing spouse has less legal protection. For a discussion of the optimal treatment of human capital in divorce, see Borenstein and Courant (1989).

and Wolfers (2007, 2008) sketch a hedonic/consumption theory that can be extended to a multiperiod theory in order to provide a rationale for commitment and, hence, for marriage. If shared leisure requires the purchase of physical capital (e.g., ski equipment) or investment in activity-specific human capital (e.g., skiing human capital), then intertemporal commitment may be useful. Shared leisure, however, seems too insubstantial a motive for intertemporal commitment to provide a plausible account of marriage.[21]

Lam's notion of household public goods provides a more promising rationale for intertemporal commitment. Weiss (1997, 86) observes that "some of the consumption goods of a family are nonrival and both partners can share them. Expenditures on children or housing are clear examples." With household public goods, multiple-person living arrangements may dominate living alone. When the household public good is housing, intertemporal commitment is valuable only in the presence of market imperfections, transaction costs, or search frictions. If the rental market for housing were frictionless, an individual could share housing with one person today and another tomorrow. If the market for owner-occupied housing were perfect, an individual could buy a house in one period, live in it, and sell it in the next. Even with transaction costs, it is reasonable to ask whether these costs are high enough to motivate marriage: cohabiting couples, after all, do own houses.

A child is different: parents tend to be extremely attached to their "own" children, whether defined by birth or adoption, and child well-being is enhanced by stability and consistency in parenting. We argue that a principal role of marriage is as a social institution that enables parents to commit themselves and their partners to intense and long-term investments in their children. Hence, we expect differences in marriage patterns across education and income groups and, particularly, differences in the timing of marriage and childbearing to be associated with differences in parental investment strategies.

7.4   Marriage and Investments in Children

> Middle-class parents tend to adopt a cultural logic of child rearing that stresses the concerted cultivation of children. Working-class and poor parents, by contrast, tend to undertake the accomplishment of natural growth.
> —Lareau, *Unequal Childhoods: Class, Race, and Family Life* (2003, 3)

Patterns of marriage, childbearing, and child rearing across education and income groups are consistent with the existence of a close connection between the decision to marry and child-rearing practices. Within each

---

21. The weasel word "seem" is deliberate. The findings of Buckles, Guldi, and Price (2011) on the effect of state blood test requirements for marriage imply that modest increases in the cost of marriage can deter couples near the margin between marriage and nonmarriage.

Table 7.2   Nonmarital births as a proportion of all births by mother's education, 2010

	Non-Hispanic white	Black	Hispanic
High school or Less	53.6	83.5	59.6
Some college	31.0	68.7	45.3
College graduate or more	5.9	32.0	17.4

Sources: Centers for Disease Control and Prevention, National Center for Health Statistics, and VitalStats, http://www.cdc.gov/nchs/vitalstats.htm.

race/ethnic group, the rate of nonmarital childbearing declines sharply as mothers' educational attainment increases. Single or cohabiting motherhood remains uncommon among non-Hispanic white college graduates, the women who are most likely to have the earnings and benefits that would enable them to support a child alone (table 7.2).[22]

As Bailey, Guldi, and Hershbein (this volume, chapter 8) show, most women in all education groups eventually marry—the proportions of women in the upper- and lower-education quartile who are currently married or have been married by age thirty-five are close to 80 percent for recent cohorts. However, they also show that the age at first birth has risen along with the age at first marriage for high-education women, while the age at first birth for women in the lowest education group has remained essentially constant for decades. The decoupling of marriage and childbearing has simply not occurred for the most advantaged women.

Direct evidence on parental investments in children also shows pronounced and increasing inequality. Time use and expenditure data indicate that parents with more education spend more time with children and that parents with more income spend more money on children. Sorting out the relative importance of time and money investments in determining child outcomes is difficult, but the increasing divergence in child inputs across income and education groups is striking.

Parental time with children has been increasing in recent decades despite rising rates of maternal employment (Bianchi 2000; Bianchi, Robinson, and Milkie 2006; Aguiar and Hurst 2007). Guryan, Hurst, and Kearney (2008) show that there is a positive relationship between parental education and time with children: despite their higher rates of employment, mothers with a college education spend about 4.5 more hours per week with children than mothers with a high school degree or less. This pattern holds for both working and nonworking mothers, and also for working fathers, and can be documented not only in the United States, but across a sample of thirteen

22. A closer look at the vital statistics data reveals additional evidence that high-education women wait for marriage until the biological clock has almost run out—for college-educated women in their early forties, the rate of nonmarital childbearing rises to 10 percent.

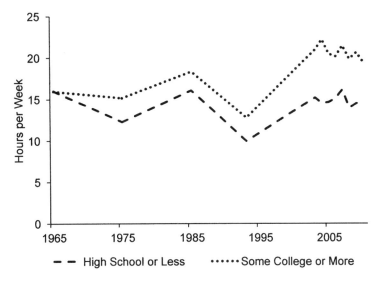

Fig. 7.6   Child-care time of mothers with children under five (under four in 1965)
Sources: 1965–1966 America's Use of Time; 1975–1976 Time Use in Economics and Social Accounts; 1985 Americans' Use of Time; 1992–1994 National Human Activity Pattern Survey; and the 2003–2010 waves of the American Time Use Survey.

other countries. Ramey and Ramey (2010) examine the trends in US child-care time separately by parental education, and find that the increase in child-care time that began in the mid-1990s was particularly pronounced for college-educated parents. They attribute this change to increased competition for admission to selective colleges. Figures 7.6 and 7.7 show a widening gap between the child-care time of parents of younger children (i.e., whose youngest child is under five), a divergence that is particularly pronounced for fathers.[23]

Real expenditures on children have increased over time and these increases have been especially pronounced for high-income households. Kornrich and Furstenberg (2013) find that expenditures on children increase with income, and that both parental spending and the inequality of this spending has risen from the early 1970s through the first decade of the twenty-first century (figure 7.8). To a large extent, this increase in spending inequality across income deciles has been driven by the increase in income inequality during this period. But expenditures on children as a percentage of income have also been rising overall (particularly in the 1990s), especially for the top two income deciles. Kornrich and Furstenberg note that increased parental

23. The fathers included are only those who live in the same household as their children. In figures 7.6 and 7.7 parents with some college and college graduates are combined for the high-education group to avoid very small sample sizes for some years.

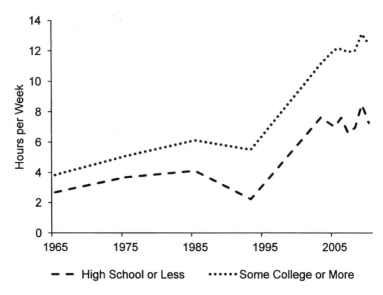

Fig. 7.7 Child-care time of fathers with children under five (under four in 1965)
Sources: See figure 7.6.

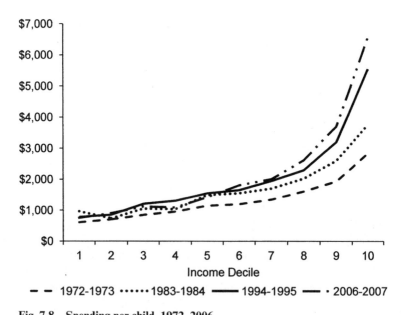

Fig. 7.8 Spending per child, 1972–2006
Source: Kornrich and Furstenberg (2013), from the Consumer Expenditure Survey.
Note: Dollar figures adjusted to year 2008 dollars using the CPI-U-RS.

spending "may reflect growing pressures to invest in children," particularly for middle- and upper-class parents. Kaushal, Magnuson, and Waldfogel (2011) document rising expenditures on child "enrichment items" by income quintile. In both cross-sectional and longitudinal analyses, they find that parental expenditures on items such as education and child care, trips and recreation, and books and computers rise with total expenditure, and that many expenditure elasticities exceed one, particularly for older children.[24] The significance of income-driven changes in child expenditures for child outcomes is unclear. Recent studies using natural experiments or policy-driven changes in family income find significant effects of increases in income on test scores and school achievement, but principally for young children from low-income families (Akee et al. 2010; Dahl and Lochner 2012; Duncan, Morris, and Rodrigues 2011; Løken, Mogstad, and Wiswall 2012).[25]

The differences in time and money inputs to child rearing are reflected in parenting practices and attitudes. In her ethnographic research, the sociologist Annette Lareau (2003) has documented pronounced class differences in child-rearing practices.[26] What Lareau terms "concerted cultivation" of middle-class children includes parental involvement in recreational and leisure activities as well as school and schoolwork, and is one source of the large gaps in skills and behavior that are present when children enter school (Duncan and Magnuson 2011). In Lareau's analysis, these child-rearing practices reflect parents' class-determined "cultural repertoires" for child rearing. Concerted cultivation is the child-rearing script consistent with the advice of "experts" and is designed to foster children's cognitive and social skills.[27] Working-class and poor families consider the consistent provision of food, shelter, and other basic support to constitute successful parenting. Given their time and resource constraints, few low-income parents attempt concerted cultivation.[28] Sociologists Kathryn Edin and Maria Kefalas (2005), in their ethnographic study of low-income single mothers, conclude that in the face of economic hardship poor mothers "adopt an approach to childrearing that values survival, not achievement" (166).

24. The longitudinal expenditure elasticities tend to be about two-thirds of the cross-sectional elasticities, indicating some unobserved heterogeneity between high- and low-income families in the propensity to spend on child enrichment.

25. The causal effect of family income on child outcomes was hotly contested in the 1990s. Duncan and Brooks-Gunn (1996) argued for the causal effect of income on child achievement. Mayer (1997) argued that the correlation between income and child achievement reflected parental education and unobserved heterogeneity. Blau (1999) summaries the debate. Also, see Gennetian, Castells, and Morris (2010).

26. Lareau's analysis is based on intensive observation of twelve families in a "large northeastern city" and its suburbs.

27. Hulbert (2003) traces the history of expert child-rearing advice in the United States in the twentieth century.

28. Lareau raises the question of whether concerted cultivation requires a two-parent family but cannot, with her small sample, attempt an answer.

Culturally determined child-rearing scripts leave little room for deliberate choice. Easterlin, Pollak, and Wachter (1980) use the phrase "unperceived jointness" to describe situations in which individuals do not recognize the relationship between their actions and outcomes.[29] To restate Lareau's analysis in these terms, suppose parents do not realize that talking with or reading to their children would increase their children's vocabularies. Then the class gradient in children's vocabularies would be an unintended by-product of following different class-specific cultural scripts, not the result of parents choosing different investment strategies. If differences in child outcomes arise because of unperceived jointness, teaching parents about the effects of alternative parenting practices could affect their behavior and, hence, outcomes for children. But if differences arise because informed parents with different preferences and opportunities choose different investment strategies, providing information to parents will not affect their parenting practices or outcomes for their children.

In a rational-choice (i.e., maximizing) framework, parents choose different child investment strategies because their preferences or their perceived opportunities differ. To the extent that preferences over outcomes for children or activities with children vary systematically by income or education, the rational-choice framework intersects with the cultural scripts story of divergent parenting practices.[30] First, prospective parents may differ in the kind of children that they want to produce. If all parents love and are attached to their children, then they will want their children to be happy and economically successful, but also to remain emotionally close (and possibly physically close) and to share their social and cultural values. For high-education and high-income parents, these objectives are more or less consistent; economically successful children are likely to accept their family's culture and values. For low-education and low-income parents, these objectives may conflict: children who are economically successful may reject their family's culture and values and, for this reason, these parents may be ambivalent about what they want for their children.[31] Thus, faced with the same opportunity set, parents with different levels of education and income might rationally choose different child-rearing practices.

29. Easterlin, Pollak, and Wachter focused on breastfeeding, practiced because it nourished the child; the reduction in fertility was an unintended effect.
30. The dichotomy between culture and choice is perhaps overdrawn. The sociologist Andrew Cherlin (2009, 9) writes, "Social scientists who think about culture these days claim that people often learn more than one cultural model of the social world and actively choose which one to apply." For surveys on the use of cultural differences in empirical economics, see Guiso, Sapienza, and Zingales (2006) and Fernández (2008). In economic theory, the threshold question is whether culture operates through preferences alone or through both preferences and beliefs; for differing interpretations, see Becker (1996) and Pollak and Watkins (1993).
31. The children may also be ambivalent, but economists generally assume that the parents are the decision makers and children are passive.

Second, parents may have direct preferences regarding the nature of their interactions with children, and therefore in the investments they make in them. "Process preferences" (i.e., direct preferences for engaging in some household production activities rather than others) may also contribute to the class gradient in outcomes for children.[32] The usual assumption that individuals have preferences for the outputs of activities (e.g., home-cooked meals, clean houses) but not direct preferences for engaging in particular activities rules out process preferences (see Pollak 2013). Parents who enjoy reading to, or verbally interacting with, children (an assumption about process preferences) are more likely to do so than parents who do not enjoy these activities. Divergent preferences over parenting practices, which may in turn stem from the parents' own upbringing, are one possible route, among many, to the class-divergent parenting practices observed by Lareau and others.[33]

Even if parents at different education and income levels have identical goals for their children and identical process preferences, however, differences in parental resources and the productivity of parental time, combined with complementarities between early and later investments, can produce a parenting strategy divide across education and income groups. Rising returns to skill in the labor market and growing income inequality may have accentuated the class divide in child investments through diverging parental resources. Greater nonlabor income or greater wealth leads to better outcomes for children provided investment in children is not an inferior good. But the effect of higher parental wages on time allocated to children is theoretically indeterminant because income and substitution effects work in opposite directions. On the one hand, the opportunity cost of time allocated to children is higher, which would tend to reduce time allocated to children. On the other hand, higher wages imply higher "real income," which would tend to imply greater expenditure on children and better outcomes for children, although not necessarily more time allocated to children. The productivity of parental time with children may also increase with parents' education—at least for outcomes such as school and occupational success. Higher productivity of parental time with children implies better outcomes

32. This paragraph elaborates a comment by Betsey Stevenson about "accidental" investments in children.

33. Cherlin (1996) summarizes the classic literature on socialization and social class and provides references to the literature. Fernald, Marchman, and Weisleder (2013) provide references to the recent literature in psychology.

Psychologists Betty Hart and Todd Risley (1995), who conducted a two-year longitudinal study of children's exposure to language and use of language in their homes, also emphasize class differences. In their study, researchers spent one hour a month with each of forty-two children, following the children from age one until age three and measuring, inter alia, the parents' and the children's vocabularies. Fernald, Marchman, and Weisleder (2013) "found significant differences in both vocabulary learning and language processing" at eighteen months "with a six-month gap emerging between higher- and lower-SES toddlers by twenty-four months."

for children, at least in the simplest case in which the marginal productivity of parental time is constant (i.e., independent of the level of time and money inputs).[34] Even in this simplest case, however, whether higher productivity implies more time with children or less time with children is theoretically indeterminant.[35]

Recent work in economics has modeled and estimated dynamic production functions for children's human capital or "capabilities" in which child development is treated as a cumulative process that depends on the full history of parental and school-based investments (Heckman 2000; Todd and Wolpin 2003, 2007). A key feature of these models is complementarity between the child's stocks of human capital and the productivity of subsequent investments. Cunha and Heckman (2007) construct a multiperiod model in which parental investments in different periods are complements in the production of human capital, and Aizer and Cunha (2012) find evidence of dynamic complementarities in the effects of preschool on children with different stocks of early human capital. These complementarities suggest that parental investments (and also formal schooling) will be more productive for children who have early cognitive and health advantages, whether these are due to genetic endowments, prenatal environment (Currie 2011), or early postnatal investments. The increasing evidence that "skill begets skill" (Heckman 2000) implies that even if the time inputs of high-education parents are not inherently more productive, payoffs to parental investments, and especially to paternal investments, are highest for the most-advantaged children.

The observed divide in parenting strategy between parents at different education and income levels can be rationalized by differences in preferences, perhaps reflective of divergent cultural scripts for parenting, or by differences in parental resources and the productivity of parental time, combined with complementarities between early and later investments. If parents differ in their motivation to make intense investments in their children's human capital, they may also differ in their desire to enter into the long-term, cooperative joint parenting arrangement that marriage facilitates. If marriage is a mechanism by which parents support a mutual commitment to continue to invest in their children's human capital, then for parents following a relatively low-investment strategy for their children, the benefits of marriage before child rearing will be substantially lower than for high-investment parents.

---

34. Becker and Murphy (2007) suggest that the time that high-education parents spend with their children is likely to be more productive in enhancing children's skills. A productivity effect may occur because parents possess a higher level of the skills they wish to impart, or because they have better information about how children learn: parents with higher levels of education may be better able to read with a younger child or help an older child with homework.

35. Guryan, Hurst, and Kearney (2008) point out that both the wage effect and the productivity effect on time allocated to children are theoretically indeterminate.

7.5 Marriage Trends and Class Divergence

Couples rarely referred to their children when discussing marriage, and none believed that having a child was a sufficient motivation for marriage. Furthermore, no parent talked about marriage enhancing the life chances of their child.

—Gibson-Davis, Edin, and McLanahan, "High Hopes but Even Higher Expectations: The Retreat from Marriage among Low-Income Couples" (2005)

One of the most striking aspects of the trends in marriage behavior documented in section 7.2 is the relative stability of traditional patterns of marriage and childbearing among the highly educated, compared with the pronounced retreat from marriage and marital childbearing among men and women with a high school diploma or less and, to a lesser extent, among those with some college. Although college-educated couples are much less likely than in the past to require marital commitment to support a sharply gender-specialized division of labor, marriage has persisted as the standard context for child rearing. High-education couples choose marriage because it entails a greater degree of commitment, a choice that is consistent with decreased returns to gender specialization that are offset by increased returns to joint investments in children. Intensive investment is a characteristic parenting pattern among the well educated and well off, and these investments are increasing in absolute terms and relative to the investments made by those with less education and fewer resources. These increases are probably due to some combination of rising returns to human capital as income inequality rises, increasing real incomes at the top of the distribution, and improved information about the payoffs to early child enrichment activities—perhaps reinforced by evolving class-specific social norms.

Couples with low levels of education are more likely to choose cohabitation or lone parenthood, suggesting that for many of them the decreased returns to specialization are not offset by increased returns to joint investments in children. For these couples, a child's limited prospects for upward mobility combined with falling real resources, particularly those of fathers with little education, precludes an intensive investment strategy for parents and limits the value of marriage and the commitment it implies.[36] Kearney and Levine (2012) offer a related explanation for the very high rate of teenage childbearing in the United States, attributing it to a limited expectation of economic success caused by high inequality and low mobility, and leading

---

36. Autor and Wasserman (2013) provide a compelling summary of the declining economic fortunes of men with high school education or less. To explain the gender difference in outcomes for boys and girls from disadvantaged backgrounds, they emphasize the role of family structure. More specifically, they argue that female-headed families are particularly damaging for boys and speculate that this may be because it is important for children to have a same-sex parent as a role model. Bertrand and Pan (2011) focus on boys' disruptive behavior. They suggest that boys may be more sensitive than girls to parental time inputs and find that mothers in female-headed families spend less time with sons than with daughters.

to "choices that favor short-term satisfaction—in this case, the decision to have a baby when young and unmarried." Their analysis focuses on the young mother's own prospects for upward mobility while we focus on the child's limited prospects for economic success and low expected returns to parental investment.

The social science literature generally treats differences in investments in children as a by-product of changing patterns in marriage, cohabitation, and lone parenting and identifies three other factors as contributing to or causing the uneven retreat from marriage: the decline in the marriageability of men with low levels of education; the incentives created by government policies (e.g., welfare benefits and the Earned Income Tax Credit); and the increasing cultural significance of marriage to women in low-income communities. To some extent, we view these as complements to our emphasis on marriage as a commitment to invest in children.

The marriageability explanation attributes the decline in marriage to the decline in the employability of men with low levels of education and the fall in their wages. The marriageability explanation is related to the wage ratio explanation that we have already discussed (i.e., the fall in the ratio of men's wages to women's wages drastically reduced the gains to the traditional pattern of gender specialization) but, unlike the wage ratio explanation, it applies only to the experiences of men at the bottom of the wage/earnings distribution. Wilson (1987) points to the decline in industrial jobs in inner-city neighborhoods as the cause of a shortage of marriageable men and, since then, this shortage has been exacerbated in black marriage markets by the rise in incarceration (Charles and Luoh 2010). Ethnographic research by sociologists Kathryn Edin and Timothy Nelson (2013) suggests that many men living in inner cities earn so little that they are likely to be net drains on household resources. The decline in wages and employability reduced the ability of these men to contribute to a joint household and, hence, reduced their attractiveness as cohabiting partners or husbands. This analysis is consistent with our emphasis on investments in children as a principal motive for marriage, since men who can contribute neither income nor quality child-care time to this joint household investment are poor candidates for a coparenting contract. It is worth noting, however, that marriage to or cohabitation with less-employable men may carry additional costs if they also represent commitments to partners who are likely to be incarcerated or prone to substance abuse or violence.[37]

In two books published almost three decades apart, Charles Murray

---

37. In apparent contrast to the marriageability claim, Thomas and Sawhill (2002, 2005) argue for "marriage as an antipoverty strategy." They show that if the unmarried mothers were to marry men similar to the unmarried fathers of their children, the couples and their child(ren) would often be above rather than below the poverty line. This analysis, however, is not restricted to the extremely disadvantaged subpopulation that Edin-Nelson focus on, and does not consider the possible ancillary costs of these relationships.

argues that government welfare benefits and welfare policy caused the retreat from marriage. Murray (1984) argued that both the value of welfare benefits and conditioning eligibility for benefits on not having a man in the house caused poor women to substitute away from marriage and toward welfare dependency in order to provide for their children. In his more recent book, Murray (2012) argues that the availability of welfare benefits sapped the moral fiber of the working poor and triggered a cascade of bad behaviors. Neal (2004) also treats the provision of government aid as a necessary condition for widespread lone motherhood, reinforced by the declining economic prospects of less-educated men.

Most studies of the effect of government tax and transfer programs on marriage, cohabitation, and lone parenthood focus on the incentives created by a particular means-tested program (e.g., EITC, food stamps, TANF) and the behavioral responses of individuals and couples to these incentives. Most empirical studies find that these programs have had little or no effect on these outcomes (Ben-Shalom, Moffitt, and Scholz 2011; Lopoo and Raissian 2013). A study of the full effect of means-tested programs on family structure and incentives to marry and cohabit would need to take into account state-specific rules and the complex interactions among the various programs (Primus and Beeson 2001). Few papers investigate the effect of the marriage penalties and bonuses in the tax system on marriage and cohabitation in the general (i.e., nonwelfare) population. An exception is Alm and Whittington (2003), who find that cohabiting couples are significantly more likely to transition to marriage when faced with positive tax incentives, but that the effect size is small.

Based on their ethnographic work, Edin and Kefalas (2005) offer a cultural explanation of the decline in marriage among women in low-income communities, arguing that these women have unrealistically high aspirations for marriage. In these communities marriage is no longer closely connected to parenting, but is about "the white picket fence dream": good stable jobs and maturity are prerequisites. In a similar vein, Cherlin (2004) asserts that, as the "practical significance" of marriage has diminished, its "cultural significance" has grown. The practical significance of marriage as a contract that supports the traditional gendered division of labor has certainly decreased: our argument is that, for college-educated men and women, marriage retains its practical significance as a commitment device that supports high levels of parental investment in children.

Cultural explanations are more useful in understanding persistent similarities or differences in behavior across groups than in understanding change. We view the rapid changes in cohabitation, marriage, and nonmarital fertility since 1960 as responses to changing incentives, not as responses to exogenous changes in the cultural significance of marriage. One could argue that the continuity in family life among white college-educated women reflects their commitment to traditional cultural values, but this argument assumes that college-educated women are more committed to traditional cultural values than less-educated women. We think it is more likely that the limited change in marriage among college-educated women is the result of offsetting changes in incentives—the decrease in the returns to traditional patterns of gender specialization and the increase in the returns to investment in children's human capital, perhaps reinforced by a cultural script that emphasizes concerted cultivation.

7.6   Conclusion

Since 1950 the sources of the gains from marriage have changed radically. As the educational attainment of women overtook and surpassed that of men and the ratio of men's to women's wage rates fell, the traditional pattern of gender specialization and division of labor within the household weakened. The primary source of the gains to marriage shifted from the production of household services and commodities to investment in children. As a result, the gains from marriage fell sharply for some groups and may have risen for others.

For some, the decline in the male-female wage ratio and the erosion of traditional patterns of gender specialization meant that marriage was no longer worth the costs of limited independence and potential mismatch. Cohabitation became a socially and legally acceptable living arrangement for all groups, but cohabitation serves different functions among the poor and less educated than among the affluent and highly educated. The poor and less educated are much more likely to have and rear children in cohabitating relationships, although the extent of this decoupling of marriage and parenthood is often exaggerated. Among the college educated, marriage and parenthood remain tightly linked. College-educated men and women have delayed marriage and typically cohabit before marriage, but they marry before conceiving children and their marriages are relatively stable.[38]

This class divergence in patterns of marriage and parenthood is associated with class differences in child rearing. Lareau characterizes the child-rearing practices of poor and working-class parents as one of "natural growth," which she contrasts with middle-class practices of "concerted cultivation." Time-use data are consistent with Lareau's ethnographic findings: college-graduate mothers and fathers spend considerably more time interacting with their children than mothers and fathers with less education.

How do we understand these class differences (and divergence) in mar-

---

38. We have focused on non-Hispanic whites in discussing differences by education but, as table 7.2 shows, both Hispanic and black marriage and cohabitation patterns also exhibit strong education gradients. Black marriage and childbearing patterns are substantially different from those of both non-Hispanic whites and Hispanics, and these differences are the subject of an enormous literature; Banks (2011) is a recent example and provides extensive references to the literature.

riage, parenthood, and child rearing? We have suggested that different patterns of child rearing are the key to understanding class differences in marriage and parenthood, not an accidental or unintended by-product of it. Rising returns to human capital, dynamic complementarities in human capital production, and diverging parental resources across the education and income distribution have increased the returns to joint investments in children especially by high-education, high-income parents. We view marriage as the commitment mechanism for this joint project and, hence, marriage is more valuable for parents adopting a high-investment strategy for their children.

References

Abma, Joyce C., and Gladys M. Martinez. 2006. "Childlessness among Older Women in the United States: Trends and Profiles." *Journal of Marriage and Family* 68 (4): 1045–56.

Aguiar, Mark, and Erik Hurst. 2007. "Measuring Trends in Leisure: The Allocation of Time over Five Decades." *Quarterly Journal of Economics* 122 (3): 969–1006.

Aizer, Anna, and Flávio Cunha. 2012. "The Production of Human Capital: Endowments, Investments and Fertility." NBER Working Paper no. 18429, Cambridge, MA.

Akee, Randall K. Q., William E. Copeland, Gordan Keeler, Adrian Angold, and E. Jane Costello. 2010. "Parents' Incomes and Children's Outcomes: A Quasi-Experiment Using Transfer Payments from Casino Profits." *American Economic Journal: Applied Economics* 2 (1): 86–115.

Akerlof, George A., Janet L. Yellen, and Michael L. Katz. 1996. "An Analysis of Out-of-Wedlock Childbearing in the United States." *Quarterly Journal of Economics* 111 (2): 277–317.

Alm, James, and Leslie Whittington. 2003. "Shacking Up of Shelling Out: Income Taxes, Marriage, and Cohabitation." *Review of Economics of the Household* 1 (3): 169–86.

Arroyo, Julia, Krista K. Payne, Susan L. Brown, and Wendy D. Manning. 2012. "Crossover in Median Age at First Marriage and First Birth: Thirty Years of Change." National Center for Family & Marriage Research. http://ncfmr.bgsu.edu/pdf/family_profiles/file107893.pdf.

Autor, David, and Melanie Wasserman. 2013. "Wayward Sons: The Emerging Gender Gap in Labor Markets and Education." Third Way Report. www.thirdway.org/publications/662.

Banks, Ralph Richard. 2011. *Is Marriage for White People? How the African American Marriage Decline Affects Everyone.* New York: Dutton.

Becker, Gary S. (1981) 1991. *A Treatise on the Family.* Cambridge, MA: Harvard University Press.

———. 1996. *Accounting for Tastes.* Cambridge, MA: Harvard University Press.

Becker, Gary S., and Kevin M. Murphy. 2007. "Education and Consumption: The Effects of Education in the Household Compared to the Marketplace." *Journal of Human Capital* 1 (1): 9–35.

Ben-Shalom, Yonatan, Robert A. Moffitt, and John Karl Scholz. 2011. "An Assessment of the Effectiveness of Anti-Poverty Programs in the United States." NBER Working Paper no. 17042, Cambridge, MA.

Bertrand, Marianne, and Jessica Pan. 2011. "The Trouble with Boys: Social Influences and the Gender Gap in Disruptive Behavior." NBER Working Paper no. 17541, Cambridge, MA.

Bianchi, Suzanne M. 2000. "Maternal Employment and Time with Children: Dramatic Change or Surprising Continuity?" *Demography* 37 (4): 139–54.

Bianchi, Suzanne M., John P. Robinson, and Melissa A. Milkie. 2006. *Changing Rhythms of American Family Life.* New York: Russell Sage Foundation.

Blau, David M. 1999. "The Effect of Income on Child Development." *Review of Economics and Statistics* 81 (2): 261–76.

Borenstein, Severin, and Paul N. Courant. 1989. "How to Carve a Medical Degree: Human Capital Assets in Divorce Settlements." *American Economic Review* 79 (5): 992–1009.

Buckles, Kasey, Melanie Guldi, and Joseph Price. 2011. "Changing the Price of Marriage: Evidence from Blood Test Requirements." *Journal of Human Resources* 46 (3): 539–67.

Charles, Kerwin Kofi, and Ming Ching Luoh. 2010. "Male Incarceration, the Marriage Market, and Female Outcomes." *Review of Economics and Statistics* 92 (3): 614–27.

Cherlin, Andrew J. 1996. *Public and Private Families: An Introduction.* New York: McGraw-Hill.

———. 2004. "The Deinstitutionalization of American Marriage." *Journal of Marriage and Family* 66:848–61.

———. 2009. *The Marriage-Go-Round: The State of Marriage and the Family in America Today.* New York: Alfred A. Knopf.

Cigno, Alessandro. 2012. "Marriage as a Commitment Device." *Review of Economics of the Household* 10 (2): 193–213.

Copen, Casey E., Kimberly Daniels, Jonathan Vespa, and William D. Mosher. 2012. "First Marriages in the United States: Data from the 2006–2010 National Survey of Family Growth." *National Health Statistics Reports* 49:1–22.

Cunha, Flavio, and James Heckman. 2007. "The Technology of Skill Formation." *American Economic Review* 97 (2): 31–47.

Currie, Janet. 2011. "Inequality at Birth: Some Causes and Consequences." *American Economic Review* 101 (3): 1–22.

Dahl, Gordon B., and Lance Lochner. 2012. "The Impact of Family Income on Child Achievement: Evidence from the Earned Income Tax Credit." *American Economic Review* 102 (5): 1927–56.

Duncan, Greg J., and Jeanne Brooks-Gunn, eds. 1996. *Consequences of Growing Up Poor.* New York: Russell Sage Foundation.

Duncan, Greg J., and Katherine Magnuson. 2011. "The Nature and Impact of Early Achievement Skills, Attention Skills, and Behavior Problems." In *Whither Opportunity? Rising Inequality, Schools, and Children's Life Chances*, edited by Greg J. Duncan and Richard J. Murnane, 47–69. New York: Russell Sage Foundation.

Duncan, Greg J., Pamela A. Morris, and Chris Rodrigues. 2011. "Does Money Really Matter? Estimating Impacts of Family Income in Young Children's Achievement with Data from Random-Assignment Experiments." *Developmental Psychology* 47 (5): 1263–79.

Easterlin, Richard A., Robert A. Pollak, and Michael L. Wachter. 1980. "Towards a More General Model of Fertility Determination: Endogenous Preferences and Natural Fertility." In *Population and Economic Change in Less Developed Coun-*

tries, edited by Richard A. Easterlin, 81–135. Chicago: University of Chicago Press.

Edin, Kathryn, and Maria Kefalas. 2005. *Promises I Can Keep: Why Poor Women Put Motherhood before Marriage.* Berkeley, CA: University of California Press.

Edin, Kathryn, and Timothy J. Nelson. 2013. *Doing the Best I Can: Fatherhood in the City.* Berkeley, CA: University of California Press.

England, Paula, Lawrence L. Wu, and Emily Fitzgibbons Shafer. 2013. "Cohort Trends in Premarital First Births: What Role for the Retreat from Marriage?" *Demography* 50 (6): 2075–104.

Fernald, Anne, Virginia A. Marchman and Adriana Weisleder. 2013. "SES Differences in Language Processing Skill and Vocabulary Are Evident at 18 Months." *Developmental Science* 16 (2): 234–48.

Fernández, Raquel. 2008. "Culture and Economics." In *The New Palgrave Dictionary of Economics*, 2nd ed., edited by Steven N. Durlauf and Lawrence E. Blume. Palgrave Macmillan. http://www.dictionaryofeconomics.com/dictionary.

Gennetian, Lisa. 2005. "One or Two Parents? Half or Step Siblings? The Effect of Family Structure on Young Children's Achievement." *Journal of Population Economics* 18 (3): 415–36.

Gennetian, Lisa A., Nina Castells, and Pamela Morris. 2010. "Meeting the Basic Needs of Children: Does Income Matter?" *Children and Youth Service Review* 32 (9): 1138–48.

Gibson-Davis, Christina M., Kathryn Edin, and Sara McLanahan. 2005. "High Hopes but Even Higher Expectations: The Retreat from Marriage among Low-Income Couples." *Journal of Marriage and Family* 67 (5): 1301–12.

Ginther, Donna K., and Robert A. Pollak. 2004. "Family Structure and Children's Educational Outcomes: Blended Families, Stylized Facts, and Descriptive Regressions." *Demography* 41 (4): 671–96.

Goldin, Claudia. 2006. "The Quiet Revolution that Transformed Women's Employment, Education, and Family." *American Economic Review* 96 (2): 1–21.

Goldin, Claudia, and Lawrence F. Katz. 2002. "The Power of the Pill: Oral Contraceptives and Women's Career and Marriage Decisions." *Journal of Political Economy* 110 (4): 730–70.

Greenwood, Jeremy, Ananth Seshadri, and Mehmet Yorukoglu. 2005. "Engines of Liberation." *Review of Economic Studies* 72 (1): 109–33.

Grossman, Joanna L., and Lawrence M. Friedman. 2011. *Inside the Castle: Law and Family in 20th Century America.* Princeton, NJ: Princeton University Press.

Guiso, Luigi, Paola Sapienza, and Luigi Zingales. 2006. "Does Culture Affect Economic Outcomes?" *Journal of Economic Perspectives* 20 (2): 23–48.

Guryan, Jonathan, Erik Hurst, and Melissa Kearney. 2008. "Parental Education and Parental Time with Children." *Journal of Economic Perspectives* 22 (3): 23–46.

Hart, Betty, and Todd R. Risley. 1995. *Meaningful Differences in the Everyday Experience of Young American Children.* Baltimore: Paul H. Brookes Publishing.

Heckman, James J. 2000. "Policies to Foster Human Capital." *Research in Economics* 54 (1): 3–56.

Hulbert, Ann. 2003. *Raising America: Experts, Parents, and a Century of Advice about Children.* New York: Random House.

Isen, Adam, and Betsey Stevenson. 2011. "Women's Education and Family Behavior: Trends in Marriage, Divorce, and Fertility." In *Demography and the Economy*, edited by John B. Shoven, 107–40. Chicago: University of Chicago Press.

Kaushal, Neeraj, Katherine Magnuson, and Jane Waldfogel. 2011. "How Is Family Income Related to Investments in Children's Learning?" In *Whither Opportunity?*

Rising Inequality, Schools, and Children's Life Chances, edited by Greg J. Duncan and Richard J. Murnane, 187–205. New York: Russell Sage Foundation.

Kearney, Melissa S., and Phillip B. Levine. 2012. "Why Is the Teen Birth Rate in the United States So High and Why Does It Matter?" *Journal of Economic Perspectives* 26 (2): 141–63.

Kennedy, Sheela, and Larry Bumpass. 2008. "Cohabitation and Children's Living Arrangements: New Estimates from the United States." *Demographic Research* 19 (47): 1663–92.

Klüsener, Sebastian, Brienna Perelli-Harris, and Nora Sánchez Gassen. 2013. "Spatial Aspects of the Rise of Nonmarital Fertility across Europe Since 1960: The Role of States and Regions in Shaping Patterns of Change." *European Journal of Population* 29 (2): 137–65.

Kornrich, Sabino, and Frank Furstenberg. 2013. "Investing in Children: Changes in Parental Spending on Children, 1972–2007." *Demography* 50 (1): 1–23.

Lam, David. 1988. "Marriage Markets and Assortative Mating with Household Public Goods: Theoretical Results and Empirical Implications." *Journal of Human Resources* 23 (4): 462–87.

Lareau, Annette. 2003. *Unequal Childhoods: Class, Race, and Family Life*. Berkeley, CA: University of California Press.

Lichter, Daniel T. 2012. "Childbearing among Cohabiting Women: Race, Pregnancy, and Union Transitions." In *Early Adulthood in a Family Context*, edited by A. Booth, S. L. Brown, N. S. Landale, W. D. Manning, and S. M. McHale, 209–19. New York: Springer.

Lichter, Daniel T., and Zhenchao Qian. 2008. "Serial Cohabitation and the Marital Life Course." *Journal of Marriage and Family* 70:861–78.

Lichter, Daniel T., Richard N. Turner, and Sharon Sassler. 2010. "National Estimates of the Rise in Serial Cohabitation." *Social Science Research* 39:754–65.

Løken, Katrine V., Magne Mogstad, and Matthew Wiswall. 2012. "What Linear Estimators Miss: The Effect of Family Income on Child Outcomes." *American Economic Journal: Applied Economics* 4 (2): 1–35.

Lopoo, Leonard M., and Kerri M. Raissian. 2013. "US Social Policy and Family Complexity." Prepared for the IRP Family Complexity, Poverty, and Public Policy conference, Madison, Wisconsin, July 11–12.

Lundberg, Shelly. 2008. "Gender and Household Decision Making." In *Frontiers in Gender Economics*, edited by Francesca Bettio. New York: Routledge.

Lundberg, Shelly, and Robert A. Pollak. 2007. "American Family and Family Economics." *Journal of Economic Perspectives* 21 (2): 3–26.

Manlove, Jennifer, Suzanne Ryan, Elizabeth Wildsmith, and Kerry Franzetta. 2010. "The Relationship Context of Nonmarital Childbearing in the US." *Demographic Research* 23 (22): 615–54.

Manning, Wendy D., and Pamela J. Smock. 2005. "Measuring and Modeling Cohabitation: New Perspectives from Qualitative Data." *Journal of Marriage and the Family* 67 (4): 989–1002.

Matouschek, Niko, and Imran Rasul. 2008. "The Economics of the Marriage Contract: Theories and Evidence." *Journal of Law and Economics* 51 (1): 59–110.

Mayer, Susan E. 1997. *What Money Can't Buy: Family Income and Children's Life Chances*. Cambridge, MA: Harvard University Press.

McLanahan, Sara. 2004. "Diverging Destinies: How Children Are Faring under the Second Demographic Transition." *Demography* 41 (4): 607–27.

Murray, Charles. 1984. *Losing Ground: American Social Policy, 1950–1980*. New York: Basic Books.

———. 2012. *Coming Apart: The State of White America, 1960–2010.* New York: Crown Forum.
Neal, Derek A. 2004. "The Relationship between Marriage Market Prospects and Never-Married Motherhood." *Journal of Human Resources* 39 (4): 938–57.
Perelli-Harris, Brienna, Wendy Sigle-Rushton, Trude Lappegard, Renske Keizer, Michaela Kreyenfeld, and Caroline Berghammer. 2010. "The Educational Gradient of Childbearing within Cohabitation in Europe." *Population and Development Review* 36 (4): 775–801.
Pollak, Robert A. 2012. "Allocating Time: Individuals' Technologies, Household Technology, Perfect Substitutes, and Specialization." *Annals of Economics and Statistics. (Annales d'Economie et Statistique).* 105–106:75–97.
———. 2013. "Allocating Household Time: When Does Efficiency Imply Specialization?" NBER Working Paper no. 19178, Cambridge, MA.
Pollak, Robert A., and Susan Cotts Watkins. 1993. "Cultural and Economic Approaches to Fertility: Proper Marriage or Mésalliance?" *Population and Development Review* 19 (3): 467–96.
Primus, Wendell E., and Jennifer Beeson. 2001. "Safety Net Programs, Marriage, and Cohabitation." In *Just Living Together: Implications of Cohabitation on Children, Families and Social Policy,* edited by Alan Booth and Ann C. Crouter. Mahwah, NJ: Lawrence Erlbaum Associates.
Ramey, Garey, and Valerie A. Ramey. 2010. "The Rug Rat Race." *Brookings Papers on Economic Activity* Spring:129–76.
Rossin-Slater, Maya. 2012. "Engaging Absent Fathers: Lessons from Paternity Establishment Programs." Department of Economics, Columbia University. http://www4.gsb.columbia.edu/filemgr?&file_id=7221308.
Rotz, Dana. 2011. "Why Have Divorce Rates Fallen? The Role of Women's Age at Marriage." Mathematica Policy Research Reports, Mathematica Policy Research, http://EconPapers.repec.org/RePEc:mpr:mprres:7714.
Stevenson, Betsey. 2007. "The Impact of Divorce Laws on Marriage-Specific Capital." *Journal of Labor Economics* 25 (1): 75–94.
Stevenson, Betsey, and Justin Wolfers. 2007. "Marriage and Divorce: Changes and their Driving Forces." *Journal of Economic Perspectives* 21 (2): 27–52.
———. 2008. "Marriage and the Market." *Cato Unbound.* http://www.cato-unbound.org/2008/01/18/betsey-stevenson-and-justin-wolfers/marriage-and-the-market/.
Thomas, Adam, and Isabel Sawhill. 2002. "For Richer or for Poorer: Marriage as an Antipoverty Strategy." *Journal of Policy Analysis and Management* 21 (4): 587–99.
———. 2005. "For Love and Money? The Impact of Family Structure on Family Income." *The Future of Children* 15 (2): 57–74.
Thornton, Arland, and Linda Young-DeMarco. 2001. "Four Decades of Trends in Attitudes Toward Family Issues in the United States: The 1960s through the 1990s." *Journal of Marriage and Family* 63 (4): 1009–37.
Todd, Petra E., and Kenneth I. Wolpin. 2003. "On the Specification and Estimation of the Production Function for Cognitive Achievement." *Economic Journal* 113 (485): F3–F33.
———. 2007. "The Production of Cognitive Achievement in Children: Home, School, and Racial Test Score Gaps." *Journal of Human Capital* 1 (1): 91–136.
Weiss, Yoram. 1997. "The Formation and Dissolution of Families: Why Marry? Who Marries Whom? And What Happens Upon Divorce." In *Handbook of Population and Family Economics 1,* edited by Mark R. Rosenzweig and Oded Stark, 81–123. Amsterdam: Elsevier.

————. 2008. "Marriage and Divorce." In *The New Palgrave Dictionary of Economics*, edited by Lawrence Blume and Steven N. Durlauf. New York: Palgrave Macmillan.

Weiss, Yoram, and Robert J. Willis. 1985. "Children as Collective Goods and Divorce Settlements." *Journal of Labor Economics* 3 (3): 268–92.

Willis, Robert J. 1999. "A Theory of Out-of-Wedlock Childbearing." *Journal of Political Economy* 107 (S6): S33–S64.

Wilson, William J. 1987. *The Truly Disadvantaged: The Inner City, the Underclass, and Public Policy.* Chicago: University of Chicago Press.

8

Is There a Case for a "Second Demographic Transition"?
Three Distinctive Features of the Post-1960 US Fertility Decline

Martha J. Bailey, Melanie Guldi, and Brad J. Hershbein

Over the course of the last 100 years, American childbearing has changed dramatically. American women reaching childbearing age around 1890 averaged 4.2 live births during their reproductive years. For women reaching childbearing age a century later, this number had fallen to a stable 2, just below replacement levels.[1] The US baby boom temporarily reversed this trend. Between 1940 and 1960, the general and total fertility rates rose by 60 percent and cohort measures of completed fertility rates rose by 45 percent.

The causes of these dramatic fertility swings have been the subject of large literatures in economics and demography. The economics literature

Martha J. Bailey is associate professor of economics at the University of Michigan and a research associate of the National Bureau of Economic Research. Melanie Guldi is assistant professor of economics at the University of Central Florida. Brad J. Hershbein is an economist at the W. E. Upjohn Institute for Employment Research.

We thank George Alter, John Bound, John DiNardo, Richard Easterlin, Melissa Kearney, Lisa Neidert, Paul Rhode, and Elyce Rotella as well as the conference organizers, Leah Boustan, Carola Frydman, and Robert A. Margo. We also thank all participants for their helpful comments and suggestions. We are also grateful to two anonymous reviewers. The authors gratefully acknowledge use of the services and facilities of the Population Studies Center at the University of Michigan, funded by NICHD Center Grant R24 HD041028. Financial assistance was provided by the University of Michigan's Population Studies Center Eva Mueller Fund, the University of Michigan's Institute of Social Research's Graduate Student Research Assistant Tuition Support Grant, the University of Michigan Rackham Research Grant, and an NICHD Population Studies Center Trainee Grant (T32 HD0007339). Anna Erickson, Sayeh Nikpay, and Johannes Norling provided outstanding research assistance. For acknowledgments, sources of research support, and disclosure of the authors' material financial relationships, if any, please see http://www.nber.org/chapters/c12894.ack.

1. These statistics use completed childbearing from the US Census (for 1890) and the June Current Population Survey (for 1990) and are close to calculations of the US total fertility rate (TFR). In 1890, the TFR was approximately 3.9 (Haines 1989) and had fallen in half to 1.9 by 2010—just below replacement levels (Martin et al. 2012).

has largely focused on demand-side explanations—changes in preferences, income, and the shadow price of children that affect how many children couples choose to have.[2] This literature generally assumes that fertility decline was driven by the same forces before and after the baby boom. The demographic literature has modeled the fertility decline as part of a larger "demographic transition" (Kirk 1996). More recently, Lesthaeghe and van de Kaa (1986) argue that the diffusion of "the Pill" and the women's rights revolution beginning in the 1960s sparked a "Second Demographic Transition," or SDT. This argument builds on Ryder and Westoff's (1971) claim that the "contraceptive revolution" had a large effect on women's childbearing, so large that Westoff's (1975, 579) presidential address to the Population Association of America asserted that, "the *entire* [emphasis added] decline in births within marriage across the decade of the 'sixties' can be attributed to the improvement in the control of fertility."[3]

An obvious counterargument to these claims is that the period looks more like mean reversion rather than a distinct transition in its own right. Becker's *Treatise on the Family* (1981) challenges Ryder and Westoff's claim of post-1960s exceptionalism, noting that the decline in childbearing in the 1920s—before the availability of the Pill—was almost as rapid. In an often-cited response to Lesthaeghe and van de Kaa, Cliquet (1991) argues that the trends they emphasize "already existed before the sixties [for Council of Europe member states]; in fact, most of them emerged with the . . . demographic transition around the turn of the century" (72). In another prominent article, Coleman (2004, 14) criticizes the SDT literature as ahistorical: "A graph truncated at [the 1950s and 1960s] gives a false impression of an inexorable downward slide coinciding with the onset of the [second demographic transition], while in fact in most countries the real decline was forty years earlier. The 1950s and the 1960s are a deceptive aberration in fertility history" (18).

An important open question is whether the case for a SDT remains after comparing the post-1960 period with changes in childbearing during the early twentieth century. Our chapter investigates this question for the United States, and we compare features of the post-1960 fertility decline (roughly 1960 to 1990) with features of the early twentieth-century fertility decline

2. Economists generally model the decline in childbearing as a by-product of rising wages, which increase the opportunity cost of children, or of rising incomes, which induce substitution away from the quantity of children toward child quality (Becker and Lewis 1973). Economic models treat the baby boom as a price shock (Barro and Becker 1989; Greenwood, Seshandri, and Vandenbroucke 2005; Albanesi and Olivetti 2009; Doepke, Hazan, and Maoz 2008) or income shock (Easterlin 1966, 1971, 1980).

3. Economists have also noted the potential importance of the supply side (Easterlin 1975; Michael and Willis 1976; Easterlin, Pollak, and Wachter 1980; Easterlin and Crimmins 1985; Hotz and Miller 1988). For empirical papers on the role of greater access to reliable medical contraceptives, see Goldin and Katz (2002); Bailey (2006); Guldi (2008); Kearney and Levine (2009); Bailey (2010); Bailey, Hershbein, and Miller (2012); and Bailey (2012).

(roughly 1900 to 1930), rather than the baby boom era. To this end, our analysis compiles evidence from many data sets including the decennial censuses, the June Current Population Surveys (CPS), Vital Statistics, and the National Surveys of Family Growth (NSFG).

Our findings affirm many critiques of the SDT literature. Both the early and later periods experienced similar declines in fertility rates, and the affected cohorts averaged the same number of live births over their lifetimes. In contrast to conventional wisdom, the mean ages of household formation (by marriage or nonmarital cohabitation) and first birth for women today are nearly identical to those of women reaching childbearing age in the 1920s and 1930s. Yet three distinct features of the post-1960 period stand out.

Feature 1. The emergence of a two-child norm and *reduction* in childlessness. Among cohorts reaching childbearing age after 1960, the two-child family became more universal and the variance in the number of children born fell significantly from its level in the early twentieth century. Recent cohorts were also significantly *less* likely to be childless. These empirical patterns are consistent with the predictions of a simple economic framework that includes a supply side characterized by changes in contraceptive technology. One key prediction within this framework is that the greater availability of reliable and lower marginal cost contraception should reduce the *dispersion* in childbearing outcomes by reducing both precautionary undershooting and unintended pregnancy.

Feature 2. The decoupling of marriage and motherhood. Age at first union (historically through marriage, more recently through cohabitation) and age at first birth had a strong positive association in the early twentieth century, but this interrelationship broke down among women after 1960. Recent cohorts formed their first households at similar ages to cohorts born earlier in the century but more often cohabited before marriage. Age at first union and age at first intercourse have become less predictive of motherhood timing, as many women give birth outside of marriage. Among women marrying before having children, the interval between first marriage and motherhood has increased.

Feature 3. A transformation in the relationship between mothers' education and childbearing. When comparing highly and less educated women, completed childbearing, childlessness, and the likelihood of marriage are much *more similar* today than in the early twentieth century. Despite these similarities, age at first household formation, age at first birth, and nonmarital childbearing diverged after 1960 by mothers' education, with more educated mothers more likely to delay household formation, motherhood, and childbearing within marriage.

It is unclear whether these changes are significant enough to constitute a SDT or are simply the most recent stage in the ongoing *first* demographic transition (Lee and Reher 2011). Continued shifts in the demand for children due to, for instance, rising wages (Becker 1965) and incomes (Easterlin 1966,

1971, 1980; Becker and Lewis 1973; Willis 1973) are key to understanding the longer-term narrative of US fertility decline. In the absence of important shifts in the demand for children, the contraceptive revolution may have mattered little.

This analysis describes three distinctive features of the post-1960 period that are consistent with the contraceptive revolution playing an important role in fertility decline—a role that complements (but does not supplant) shifts in the demand for children. This suggestive evidence extends a growing empirical literature on the Pill that likely understates its broader significance (Goldin and Katz 2002; Bailey 2006; Guldi 2008; Bailey 2010; Bailey, Hershbein, and Miller 2012; Bailey 2012) by virtue of the fact that the research designs may difference out spillover and general equilibrium effects.

Of particular importance is that these features suggest that the contraceptive revolution has exacerbated economic inequality among children. The decoupling of marriage and motherhood and the changing relationship of women's education with childbearing is consistent with class-based polarization in children's resources (McLanahan 2004). The fact that trends in nonmarital childbearing and age at first birth have not stabilized suggests a continued, if not increasing, polarization in these resources in years to come. The late twentieth-century fertility decline, therefore, has implications for the evolution of children's opportunities, their educational achievement, and the widening inequality in US labor markets.

8.1 The Twentieth-Century US Fertility Transition

"Fertility transitions" are generally defined by population scientists as "long-term declines in the number of children from four or more per woman to two or fewer" (Mason 1997). Until recently, US (marital) fertility decline was believed to have begun in the late eighteenth century, almost seventy-five years before marital fertility rates began to decline in most other nations (France excepted; Haines 2000; Binion 2001). Using new estimates of nineteenth-century mortality and newly available census microdata, Hacker (2003) shows that it is likely that the longer-term decline in US fertility began closer to the mid-nineteenth century. Furthermore, among white women, his estimates suggest that the decline in marital fertility did not begin until after the Civil War. Although the features and timing of demographic transitions vary considerably across places (Guinnane 2011; Lee and Reher 2011), the longer-term demographic transition in the United States was characterized by declines in infant and child mortality, the disappearance of the Malthusian pattern of late marriage, and the emergence of birth-order specific fertility control.

The American fertility transition presents a fascinating challenge to scholars—particularly among those who desire an integrated model of demographic change. The early fertility decline took place in the absence of modern contraception and is believed to have been driven by changes in the demand for children. The baby boom took place in the context of increasing income, urbanization, educational attainment, and women's labor force participation—all trends that are associated with declining fertility in the early twentieth century. Adding to the puzzle is that the post-1960 period saw falling fertility rates even as incomes, urbanization, educational attainment, and women's labor force participation continued to rise.

8.1.1   Models of Fertility Decline in Economics and Demography

The challenge of explaining US fertility transition has led to the development of two main schools of thought in economics. One cornerstone of the literature has been Richard Easterlin's "relative income hypothesis" (1966, 1971, 1980). Easterlin argues that the importance of a cohort's perceived "earnings potential" relative to its "material aspirations" is critical in the formation of adult preferences for material goods and children. In this view, children who grew up in the Great Depression during the 1930s formed modest material aspirations that were surpassed by their actual experience as young adults in the 1940s and 1950s. When these children of the Depression found that they could afford more of everything, they consumed more and had more children. Children growing up in the more affluent 1940s and 1950s had the reverse experience and, consequently, had fewer children. This led to subsequent fertility declines. Problematic for this theory is that fertility rates have not cycled since the baby boom.

Another cornerstone of the literature has been Gary Becker's neoclassical theory (1960, 1965; Becker and Lewis 1973). This school of thought pushes Easterlin's endogenous preference formation into the background and emphasizes the importance of prices and absolute incomes. Becker explains the negative association between childbearing and income as reflecting the difference in the opportunity cost of childbearing (higher wage rates for higher income individuals) as well as the greater income elasticity of child quality (compared to the quantity of children). Becker, in collaboration with Robert Barro, has extended the reach of the neoclassical school to macroeconomics with two joint articles (Becker and Barro 1988; Barro and Becker 1989). These articles reformulated Becker's initially static theory of fertility to extend across generations. This reformulation models decision makers as altruistic parents who care about the utility of their children and, therefore, incorporate their children's utility into their own utility function. The Barro-Becker framework has led to the development of a new subfield in economics called "family macro," which has created several alternative theories of the baby boom (see Greenwood, Seshadri, and Vandenbroucke 2005; Doepke, Hazan, and Maoz 2008; Albanesi and Olivetti 2009). With slightly different formulations of the problem, each of these models examines a different potential price change (as suggested in Barro and Becker's articles) that could have produced the baby boom. In the spirit of Becker

(1965), these models rely upon the increasing *opportunity* cost of child rearing (primarily due to the growth in women's wages) to generate the longer-term decline in US childbearing. Problematic for these models is that when calibrated to match the baby boom, they have difficulty generating the speed of the post-1960 US fertility decline.

Much of the demographic literature has maintained a different focus in explaining the post-1960 fertility decline. Citing newly collected national surveys documenting increased use of the Pill, Ryder and Westoff (1971) heralded the 1960s as a period of "contraceptive revolution." Building on this claim, Lesthaeghe and van de Kaa (1986) hypothesize that the arrival of the contraceptive, sexual, and women's rights revolutions of the 1960s engendered a *distinct* demographic transition—a period *exceptional* enough to be called the "Second Demographic Transition" (SDT). Their initial work focuses on Europe, but recent work by Lesthaeghe and Neidert (2006) argues that a SDT is underway in the United States as well. The distinctive characteristics of the SDT, they argue, are persistently low fertility rates, substantially delayed marriage and childbearing, increases in nonmarital cohabitation and childbearing, and high divorce rates.[4] Even as demographers have stressed these changes, the demand-side formulations of both the Easterlin and Becker schools of thought have continued to shape the theoretical and empirical literature on childbearing in economics.

8.1.2   Integrating the Neoclassical Model with a Supply Side

Augmenting demand-based economic models of childbearing with a "supply side" is one way to operationalize the hypotheses of Ryder and Westoff (1971) and Lesthaeghe and van de Kaa (1986). To this end, the pioneering work of Michael and Willis (1976) provides a useful bridge between the neoclassical demand for children (Becker 1960, 1965; Willis 1973; Becker and Lewis 1973) and the supply side stressed elsewhere (Coale 1973; Sheps 1964; Sheps and Perrin 1964; Westoff 1975; Easterlin, Pollak, and Wachter 1980). Their framework relaxes two assumptions in neoclassical models: (1) that childbearing is deliberately determined and (2) that regulating fertility is costless. In their model, the number of children is a random variable, and couples choose a contraceptive strategy to reduce the monthly probability of conception. In addition, fertility regulation has a price. Each contraceptive strategy—the adoption of behaviors or use of contraceptives—is associated with a fixed and marginal cost and yields an expected number of children. Couples maximize utility by weighing the marginal costs of averting births against the marginal benefit of attaining an ex ante distribution

---

4. In some formulations, the rise in women's labor force participation is also attributed to the SDT. We omit discussion of women's labor force participation rates here because this is covered in Olivetti's chapter (chapter 5, this volume).

of childbearing. That is, couples optimize by choosing a distribution of possible childbearing with mean, μ^*, to maximize utility net of the costs of fertility regulation, or max $U(\mu) - C(\mu)$.

Within this framework, Ryder and Westoff's "contraceptive revolution" is simply the claim that shifts in $C(\mu)$ became much more important in the determination of childbearing outcomes in the post-1960 period. Lesthaeghe and van de Kaa's (1986) distinction between the first and second demographic transitions is summarized by saying that the first transition was driven by shifts in $U(\mu)$, whereas the SDT was driven by changes in $C(\mu)$. This framework also provides a starting point for conceptualizing why standard demand-side models in economics may fail to capture important features of the post-1960 fertility decline.

Effects on the Mean Number of Children Born

The framework of Michael and Willis provides testable predictions regarding how the introduction of modern contraceptives like the Pill could have changed the distribution of children ever born. The model's insight about the effect of modern contraception on the *mean* number of children ever born is straightforward. Michael and Willis consider a simple division of costs of attaining a fertility distribution, μ, using contraceptive strategy, j, into a fixed cost, α_j, and a marginal cost, β_j. The cost of using strategy j to attain an ex ante birth distribution, μ, is given by $c_j = \alpha_j + \beta_j(\mu_N - \mu)$, where μ_N indexes the expected distribution of children born in the absence of any contraceptive method. The term $\mu_N - \mu$ is, therefore, the expected number of births averted. The (constant) marginal cost of averting a birth, β_j, might be a behavioral cost (abstinence or withdrawal), the inconvenience or discomfort of birth control use (barrier methods), or the necessity of purchasing supplies (as with condoms or the birth control pill). Fixed costs include the price of searching for a supplier, learning about a method, and perhaps side effects as well. The total cost function includes only the lowest cost option for achieving an expected number of births, or $C(\mu) = \min_j\{\alpha_j + \beta_j(\mu_N - \mu)\}$.

Modern contraceptive methods (such as the Pill or IUD) can be modeled as reducing the marginal costs of preventing births, because no interruption, effort, or discomfort at the time of intimacy is required. Thus, modern methods would reduce β for some range of births averted. Holding the demand for births constant, reducing the marginal costs of preventing births would normally lead to a reduction in the number of children born per woman. But because the effectiveness of these methods also reduced the uncertainty surrounding childbearing outcomes, there is potential for offsetting theoretical effects. Michael and Willis point out that more reliable contraception may, somewhat counter to intuition, increase the number of children born by eliminating precautionary undershooting. This effect may be small but it makes the theoretical impact of modern contraception ambiguous.

Effects on the Distribution of Children Born

The Michael and Willis model also provides straightforward predictions of how different contraceptive methods affect the distribution of children ever born. Michael and Willis present figures that show how the expected number of children and variance in the number of children change with contraceptive technique (1976, table 2). Techniques with lower contraceptive efficiency (for example, the rhythm method) tend to have higher mean and variance (5.11, 2.15) than do techniques with higher contraceptive efficacy (for example, condoms, 2.33 and 1.64; or the Pill, 0.19 and 0.18), but this relationship is not monotonic. In particular, the use of no method at all (or reduced frequency of sex) produces a high number of children in expectation but small variance. The intuition for this is that most women achieve near their natural biological fertility without using any method, and that this varies relatively little across women. Less effective methods, while reducing the mean, still fail frequently enough that many women have more children than intended, *increasing the variance*.[5] Thus, for women in the early twentieth century, the methods of fertility control readily available to them would be expected to reduce the mean without reducing the variance, which might *rise* with the use of such methods. In contrast, as women in the latter half of the twentieth century began to use more effective methods in greater proportion, both the mean number of children and the variance should fall, assuming the distribution of preferences, prices, and income remained constant.

Thus, the Michael and Willis framework of fertility choice provides a simple, mathematically tractable bridge between economic and sociodemographic models. It explicitly models the importance of the "supply side" as technologies affecting the marginal costs of averting births in the spirit of Easterlin (1975) and Easterlin, Pollak, and Wachter (1980): the model's birth production function separates natural fertility, μ_N, from targeted childbearing, μ^*, in a stochastic framework with costs of fertility control. Finally, it formalizes Coale's (1973) conceptual framework: "ready" is captured by the formal calculus; "willing" is captured by the utility function, prices, and income; and "able" enters as the technology and cost of contraception based upon the mathematical demography of Sheps (1964) and Sheps and Perrin (1964).

For our purposes (and those of other empirical researchers wishing to examine the appropriateness of different theories), another valuable feature of the Michael and Willis (1976) model is that it provides a richer set of testable predictions than does theory based solely on changes in the number of children. Although Michael and Willis's insights about changes in the

---

5. The nonmonotonic relationship between the mean and the variance in the Michael-Willis model rests—in part—on their assumption that childbirth is a Markov renewal process, or that intervals between childbearing can be assumed to be independent and identically distributed.

dispersion of outcomes do not cover other features of Ryder and Westoff's (1971) contraceptive revolution or Lesthaeghe and van de Kaa's (1986) SDT, they provide an additional moment of the distribution (the variance) that can be used to test claims of post-1960 exceptionalism.

8.2   How Different Is the Post-1960 Period?

The case for the exceptionalism of the post-1960 fertility decline rests on the claim that there are meaningful differences from the pre–baby boom fertility decline. The implicit hypothesis is that the longer-term forces leading fertility rates to decline in the early twentieth century are the same forces (e.g., the opportunity cost of childbearing or substitution toward child quality) that contributed to fertility decline in the post-1960 period. To examine the similarities across periods, our analysis compares outcomes across birth cohorts. For the early twentieth-century transition, we focus on women born from 1880 to 1910 who reached the age of twenty from 1900 to 1930. We often refer to the cohorts born between 1900 and 1910 as the early twentieth-century or (following the demographic literature) the "low-fertility" cohorts. For the later twentieth-century transition, we focus on the 1940 to 1970 cohorts, who reached the age of twenty from 1960 to 1990. We often refer to these cohorts as the later or mid-twentieth-century cohorts.

8.2.1   Similarities in Early and Later Twentieth-Century Period Fertility Rates

Figure 8.1 presents the general fertility rate (GFR) by year and cohort-based measures of mean "children ever born" (live births excluding miscarriages and still births) to women age forty-one to seventy from the decennial census and the June Current Population Survey (CPS).[6] For the mean number of children born, we have advanced the series twenty-five years (approximating the period when the birth cohort was having children) to correspond to the GFR. The pattern of the cohort-based measure corresponds closely to the period measures. Women born in 1875 (linked to 1900 in figure 8.1) averaged 3.3 births over their lifetimes, whereas women in the early twentieth-century cohorts averaged 2.3 births over their lifetimes. This number rose sharply to over three children for the cohorts reaching childbearing age during the baby boom (born between 1915 and 1935), and then fell to around two births for the 1945 to 1970 cohorts.[7] A second series

6. Because the census stopped asking about children ever born after 1990, we use the June Current Population Survey (CPS) to extend these figures to 2010 (birth cohort of 1969). Changes in age restrictions and regression-based age-at-observation adjustments alter these figures very little.

7. Child survival rates to age ten were historically much lower than today, so—while holding constant the demand for surviving children—increases in survival provide one reason for the reduction in children ever born over the last 100 years. Unfortunately, because the census after

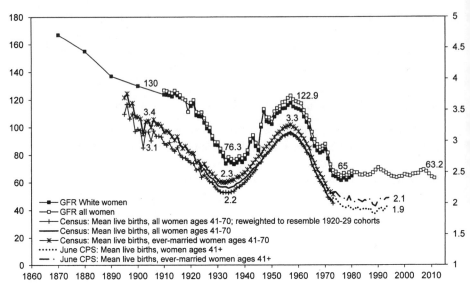

Fig. 8.1   US general fertility rate (GFR) and completed childbearing, 1895–1995

Sources: Fertility rates are from historical statistics, http://www.cdc.gov/nchs/data/statab/t001x01.pdf. Mean live births are computed using the 1940–1990 decennial census IPUMS samples (Ruggles et al. 2010) and the 1995–2010 June CPS.

Notes: The general fertility rate (GFR) (right vertical axis) is the number of births per 1,000 women (all or white women only) age fifteen to forty-four in the population from Vital Statistics. Mean live births (left vertical axis) is the mean self-reported number of children ever born for each birth cohort as measured between the age of forty-one and seventy (indexed to year by adding twenty-five years to mother's year of birth; e.g., mean children ever born to the birth cohort of 1870 corresponds to the year 1895 on the graph's horizontal axis). In addition, we include rates for never-married women as measured in the 1970–1990 censuses. Computations use population weights.

shows that the addition of never-married women (first asked about their childbearing in 1970) alters the overall pattern very little except to reduce the levels of childbearing. Consistent with the literature, figure 8.1 shows that the decline in the mean number of live births was almost identical for the early and late twentieth-century cohorts.[8]

Two kinds of survival bias may influence these estimates. First, income is positively associated with life expectancy, so lower-income women—who also tend to have more children—may be less likely to survive to answer cen-

---

1910 did not ask about children surviving, we cannot use these data to investigate the role of child survival on completed fertility. That said, because infant and child mortality rates were higher for the early fertility cohorts, differences in surviving children would tend to make the early and later cohorts look even more similar.

8. The decline is slightly faster for the late cohorts at 0.04 versus 0.036 births per year for the early twentieth-century cohorts. The average annual rate of decline in the general fertility rate (GFR) in the 1960s was 2.2 births per 1,000 women of childbearing age per year, only slightly faster than that in the 1920s (approximately two births per 1,000 women of childbearing age per year).

sus questions about their childbearing. Because we observe earlier cohorts at older ages, this differential mortality would be more pronounced for the earlier cohorts. Second, women having more children face greater risk of death from childbirth and are, therefore, less likely to be enumerated later. Both of these sources of survival bias should lead live births to be understated for the older cohorts. As a result, the speed of fertility decline in the early twentieth century will be understated.

To gauge the importance of the first factor, we limit our sample to women age forty-one to fifty, but this has a negligible effect on our estimates. This implies that the mean number of children ever born to women surviving to age forty-one to fifty versus those who survive to age fifty-one to seventy are not appreciably different. Assessing the importance of differential maternal mortality is more difficult, and we can provide only a crude adjustment. Extrapolating average annual maternal mortality rates from Albanesi and Olivetti (2009, figure 1), we determine that approximately 1 in 100 live births resulted in the mother's death. If we assume that mortality risk is equally probable across birth parity and maternal cohorts (which, admittedly, is a big simplification), the probability that a woman survives giving birth to n children is $p = 0.99^n$. Dividing by this factor across the entire distribution of children born to pre-1900 maternal cohorts leads the mean number of children born to be approximately 0.1 higher for women born in 1870. Correcting for these sources of bias tends to increase the rate of fertility decline among the early cohorts and, thus, tends to make the fertility declines for earlier and later cohorts more similar. Neither adjustment, however, alters the broad conclusion that the decline in the mean number of live births was similar in magnitude during the early twentieth century and after 1960.

Compositional changes in the US population, especially those due to urbanization and immigration, may also influence our findings. Potentially important for our conclusions about the speed of the early fertility decline is that the representation of these groups in the US population shifted during the twentieth century. As shown in figure 8.2 (and noted in Easterlin 1961), both the levels and changes in completed childbearing differed across native and foreign-born women as well as women residing in urban and rural areas. Racial differences were also large. To account for these compositional changes, we reweight the individuals within each birth cohort using inverse propensity score weighting (DiNardo, Fortin, and Lemieux 1996). This procedure adjusts the distribution of each cohort's characteristics—the share of the population in urban areas, share of immigrants from different source countries, race and ethnicity, and age composition—to resemble the distribution of characteristics among the cohorts of 1920 to 1929.[9] Figure 8.1 also

---

9. The specific covariates used to construct the propensity weights include a dummy for whether the woman lives in an urban area, a set of eleven dummies for region of the world (country groups) of birth, a dummy for whether the woman is white, a dummy for whether she is Hispanic, and a set of five dummies for her five-year age group at time of observation.

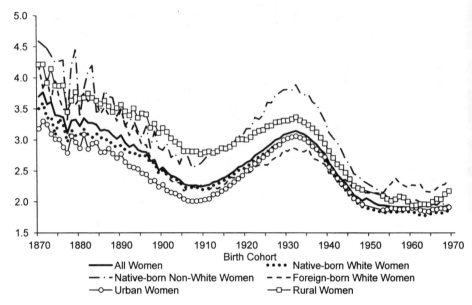

Fig. 8.2   Completed childbearing, by group and birth cohort, 1870–1970

Sources: See figure 8.1.

Notes: The figure plots the mean number of live births among women age forty-one to seventy, by birth cohort, for the census (1870 through 1948 cohorts) and the same statistic for women age forty-one to forty-four in the June CPS (1949 through 1969 cohorts). The native born include women who were born in the fifty US states (including the time in which they were territories) and the District of Columbia. Nonwhites include all races other than white. Urban/rural is based on the "urban" variable for 1960, 1970, and 1990 censuses and on the "metro" variable for the 1940, 1950, and 1980 censuses, as well as the June CPS (urban if in a metro area, rural if outside a metro area). All computations use the recommended population weights and the CPS series are three-cohort moving averages.

plots this reweighted series (the cohorts of 1920 to 1929 corresponds to the years 1945 to 1954). This reweighting has a negligible impact for more recent cohorts and a small (but more noticeable) impact on the early twentieth-century cohorts. After reweighting, mean completed childbearing declined by 0.9 births between cohorts born in 1875 and 1910. Without reweighting, the decline is roughly similar. This also underscores the argument that—in both the early twentieth century and post-1960 period—fertility decline was driven by *within-group* (behavioral) changes rather than changes in population composition.

8.2.2   Similarities in Mean Age at First Union and Birth in the Early and Later Twentieth Century

According to Lesthaeghe and van de Kaa (1986), two further hallmarks of the SDT are delayed marriage and childbearing. This section assesses this claim in historical perspective by comparing outcomes for the cohorts reaching childbearing ages during each period: the low-fertility cohorts (cohorts born from 1900 to 1910 who reached childbearing age in the 1920s and 1930s) and the cohorts born from 1940 to 1950 (who reached childbearing age in the 1960s and 1970s).

Figure 8.3 shows a remarkable correspondence in the age at first union (either through marriage or cohabitation) for the low-fertility cohorts and cohorts reaching childbearing age in the 1960s and 1970s. During the early twentieth-century fertility decline, average age at marriage remained very stable. Even as completed childbearing fell fairly linearly from 3.4 for the birth cohort of 1875 to 2.3 for the birth cohort of 1915, mean age at first marriage hovered around twenty-two and nudged upward only slightly for the low-fertility cohorts. It is unlikely that the stability in marriage age reflects selection into marriage. Figure 8.3 also shows that the share of women ever marrying for these cohorts stayed relatively constant at around 90 percent.

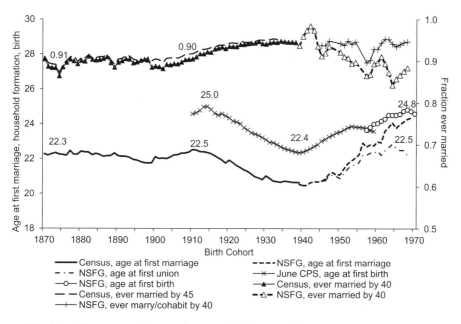

Fig. 8.3   Mean age at first marriage/cohabitation and first birth and share ever marrying, by birth cohort

Sources: 1940–1980 decennial census IPUMS samples (Ruggles et al. 2010); 1979–1995 June CPS; 1982–2010 NSFG.

Notes: The figure plots the mean age at first marriage (conditional on ever married by age thirty-nine), first household formation or union (the younger of first marriage or first non-marital cohabitation), first birth (left vertical axis), and share ever married (right vertical axis) against single year-of-birth cohort. The NSFG and CPS trends are based on three-year cohort moving averages.

The baby boom disrupted these patterns. The share of women ever marrying increased from around 90 percent to 95 percent, and the mean age at first marriage for the 1935 cohort fell by almost two years to 20.7 (figure 8.3). Increases in childbearing during the baby boom were accompanied by earlier, more universal marriage and childbearing. The share of women with their own child in the household rose sharply for cohorts born in the 1930s.

Women reaching childbearing age after 1960 did not delay marriage or shy away from it altogether. The mean age at first marriage remained *stable* for the 1935 to 1945 birth cohorts and began to rise for women born after 1945. Similarly, the share who ever married did not begin to fall until after the 1945 cohort. The mean age at first marriage for the cohort of 1910 (conditional upon being married before age 35) was 22.5. During the baby boom, when completed childbearing was at its fifty-year peak and very few women never married, the mean age at first marriage was lower and more concentrated around age twenty-one. Yet, as the baby boom ended and completed fertility rates fell for cohorts born in the 1940s, early marriage persisted. The mean age at first marriage remained low at 20.6 for the cohort of 1940 and 21.3 for the cohort of 1950.

Age at first marriage rose rapidly for cohorts born after 1950 and surpassed the mean of the low-fertility cohorts. The rise in nonmarital cohabitation, however, makes these trends misleading statistics for the age at first household formation—what we will call "age at first union." For instance, if women born in the 1950s who would have married at younger ages in the past began substituting toward nonmarital cohabitation, the rise in mean age at first marriage may overstate the actual rise in the age at household formation. It also implies that differential selection into marriage by age thirty-five in the lower fertility and later cohorts could bias these comparisons. Figure 8.4 shows that only 78 percent had married by age thirty-five for the most recent cohort we can measure versus 87 percent for the low-fertility cohorts.

Information from the 1988 to 2010 NSFG allows us to investigate how much of the trend toward later marriage has been due to premarital cohabitation—a change in the "label" and definition of a long-term relationship rather than household formation. Assuming that nonmarital cohabitation rates were historically low (or were reported as "marriages" in the census), figure 8.3 shows that—after accounting for nonmarital cohabitation—the current mean age at first union is identical to the mean in the early twentieth century (22.5) and that the post–baby boom increase in age at first household formation is much more gradual. It also shows that the decline in the fraction ever married is completely offset by rising nonmarital cohabitation. Figure 8.4 shows the evolving distribution in age at first union and underscores the similarity in the distribution today with the distribution earlier in the century. Only 20 percent of women born in 1970 had married by age twenty, but 35 percent had cohabited. By age twenty-five, 55 percent of the same cohort

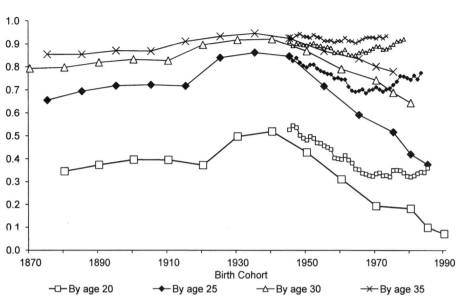

Fig. 8.4   Share of women ever married or cohabiting, by age and birth cohort

Sources: 1900–2000 decennial census IPUMS samples and 2006–2010 ACS (Ruggles et al. 2010); 1988–2010 NSFG.

Notes: The series with larger markers represent the share of women ever married by the indicated age and is based on current marital status being any category other than never married in the census. The smaller markers represent the share of women ever married or cohabiting by the indicated age from the NSFG and are smoothed using three-cohort moving averages.

had married, but over 70 percent had cohabited.[10] Marriage plus cohabitation trends seem to have stabilized around the historical level of age at first union for cohorts born after 1960, and women in their thirties may even be slightly more likely to have married or cohabited than women of the past.

Presuming nonmarital cohabitation was rare in the early twentieth century, combining these nonmarital cohabitation and marriage rates suggests a surprising similarity in the age at first union in the early and later twentieth century. The apparent "delay in marriage" is an artifact of the rise in nonmarital cohabitation, and the share of women married or cohabiting by age thirty-five is higher today than it was earlier in the twentieth century (the share was around 87 percent before the 1915 birth cohort and rose to around 95 percent for cohorts born in the 1930s, where it has remained).

---

10. Appendix figure 8A.1, panel A, shows the distribution of age at first marriage for select birth cohorts. Appendix figure 8A.1, panel B, shows the effect of including nonmarital cohabitation to this distribution for two recent cohorts. Whereas cohabitation alters the distribution for the birth cohort of 1950 negligibly, it significantly revises the distribution for women born in 1970 to look more like the 1950 distribution.

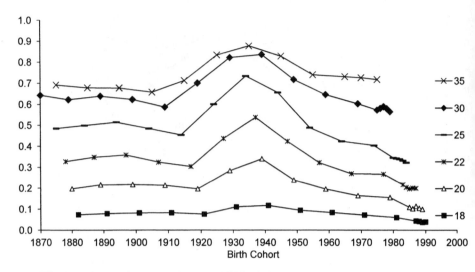

Fig. 8.5   Share of women with own child in their household, by age and cohort

Sources: 1900–2000 decennial census IPUMS samples and 2006–2010 ACS (Ruggles et al. 2010).

Note: The series show the share of all women with at least one own (but not necessarily biological) child in their household at the indicated age.

Changes in the mean age at first birth today are also similar to their early twentieth-century mean. Although the June CPS does not provide information on older cohorts' ages at first birth (so they cannot be included in figure 8.3), figure 8.5 uses census data to track the share of women with their own child in the household for the birth cohorts of 1875 to 1990 across several ages.[11] Consistent with age at first birth rising and birth spacing increasing, the low-fertility cohorts experienced modest reductions in the share of women with children at home by age twenty (2 percentage points), age twenty-two (6 percentage points), age twenty-five (5 percentage points), and age thirty (6 percentage points) and a 6 percentage point *increase* in the share at age thirty-five.

Unlike the low-fertility cohorts, the timing of marriage and age at first birth diverged sharply for cohorts reaching childbearing age after 1960. Figure 8.3 shows that the mean age at first birth was approximately 25 for the low-fertility cohorts, whereas it was 22.4 for the birth cohort of 1940 and about one year older at 23.5 for the cohort of 1950. Although their age at first marriage and age at first birth were both *lower* than the low-fertility cohorts, most of the women born in or after the late 1940s would go on to

11. The census allows us to identify that a child belongs to a particular mother in the household, but we cannot identify whether that child was born to the woman, adopted by her, or is a stepchild.

have just two or fewer children in their lifetimes—fewer than the low-fertility cohorts. For instance, 42 percent of the 1947 birth cohort had a child by age 22, whereas only 32 percent of the 1907 cohort did so (figure 8.5). For the low-fertility cohorts, motherhood delay was not just at very early ages but continued into older ages. By age thirty, 72 percent of the 1949 birth cohort had a child whereas only 59 percent of the 1909 birth cohort did.[12] In fact, in terms of levels, motherhood timing among women born in the 1940s looks more similar to that of baby boom mothers than to that of the low-fertility cohorts. Only recently has motherhood delay reached and then surpassed levels observed in the early twentieth century.[13] The cohorts born in the *late* 1970s were just as likely to be mothers at age thirty as women born seventy years earlier.

In summary, our analysis of completed childbearing, age at first marriage, and age at first birth affirms the findings of other studies. The early and later twentieth-century cohorts both achieved low mean levels of completed childbearing (2.3 and 1.9, respectively), and the speed of fertility decline was comparable for period and cohort-based measures. Lesthaeghe and van de Kaa (1986) argue that today's low rates of childbearing are a hallmark of the SDT, but US fertility rates in the post-1960 period do not appear exceptional relative to the early twentieth century. In addition, comparing today's cohorts to the low-fertility cohorts shows small differences in the mean age at first union after accounting for increases in nonmarital cohabitation. They are also similar in terms of the mean age at first birth. Based on means alone, one might agree with Cliquet (1991), who argues that the hallmarks of the SDT existed before the baby boom and emerged around the turn of the century (72). These similarities also motivate Becker's argument that "the 'contraceptive revolution' . . . ushered in by the pill has probably not been a major cause of the sharp drop in fertility in recent decades . . . [W]omen in the United States born between 1900 and 1910 had quite small families without the pill by using other contraceptives, abstinence, and induced abortions" (1981, 101–102).

As the next sections will show, these similarities in means mask important changes in the underlying distribution of children ever born (feature 1), the distributions of age at first marriage and age at first birth, and the

12. This can also be seen in appendix figure 8A.2, which plots the distribution of age at first birth for these cohorts using data from the June CPS and NSFG.

13. See appendix figure 8A.3. During the early twentieth century, women in their early twenties had the highest birth rates, followed by women in their late twenties, early thirties, late thirties, and then by teens and older women. Consistent with substantial delays in motherhood today, women in their late twenties now have the highest birth rates. In 2010, birth rates to women in their early thirties exceeded those among women in their early twenties for the first time in ninety years (Linder and Grove 1947; Grove and Hetzel 1968; Martin et al. 2012). Age-specific birth rates also show that the levels of teen birth rates today are closer to those of the early twentieth century than they have been since the 1930s. Given frequently cited concerns about high rates of teen childbearing in the United States, only in the last few years have teen birth rates dipped to ninety-year lows (i.e., lower than rates recorded in 1918).

interrelationship between marriage and childbearing (feature 2). They also mask the transformation in the relationship between women's education and childbearing outcomes (feature 3).

8.3   The Emergence of the Two-Child Family and Falling Childlessness

An important part of our story is that the earlier and later cohorts reduced their fertility in strikingly different ways. For instance, the distribution of live births for the 1850 birth cohort looks almost uniform between 0 and 6 live births, as roughly 8 to 10 percent of women each achieved exactly one of those numbers (figure 8.6). For the 1850 cohort, the share having each of 7 to 11 children ranges from 7 to 3 percent, respectively.

Becker (1981, 100) shows that the number of children one could expect to have, n, can be written as $n = E/(C + S)$, where E is the number of months one is at risk of becoming pregnant (the interval from first coitus to when one is no longer fecund), and $C + S$ represents the average number of months between births, often called spacing. He argues that fertility rates could be

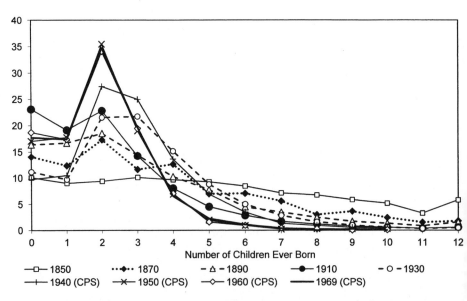

Fig. 8.6   Distribution of completed childbearing, by birth cohort, 1850–1969

Sources: 1850 to 1930 cohorts use the 1900, 1910, and 1940–1990 decennial census IPUMS samples (Ruggles et al. 2010); 1940 to 1969 cohorts use the 1981 through 2010 June CPS.

Notes: The figure plots the percentage of women age forty-one to seventy who report having each number of children. We include never-married women in the 1970 to 1990 censuses and June CPS when available so that figures include the recent rise in nonmarital childbearing. Children ever born is top-coded at twelve in the census and ten in the CPS. Differences between the CPS and census in overlapping cohorts were trivial (see figure 8.1), so seaming issues between surveys should be minimal.

reduced by almost 25 percent by delaying marriage (and thus reducing E) but that they could also be reduced by greater spacing (increasing $C + S$). The reduction in childbearing between the cohorts of 1850 and 1910 is consistent with using these types of strategies to reduce completed childbearing. During the late-nineteenth- to early-twentieth-century period of fertility decline, each generation of women substituted toward fewer children. As we subsequently show, changes in the age at first marriage seem much less important than spacing and stopping in this period of US history. Two-thirds of women in the cohort of 1910 achieved two or fewer children. A striking 23 percent of this birth cohort were childless at ages forty-one to seventy, another 20 percent had only one child, and 23 percent had exactly two children—thus, the commonly used label, the "low-fertility cohorts."

A similar share of women born from 1940 to 1970 had two or fewer children, yet these cohorts are different in two (related) ways. First, the post-1960 cohorts realized the "two-child norm." Figure 8.6 shows this as a collapse of the childbearing distribution about the two-child mode. Furthermore, a substantially larger share of the later cohorts achieved *exactly* two children. In contrast to the fairly equal division of mass between zero, one, and two children for the cohort of 1910, 17 percent of the 1950 cohort had no children at age forty-one to seventy. Another 17 percent had one child, and over 35 percent had exactly two children. Moreover, a significantly greater share of the later cohort had three children (19 percent versus 14 percent in the cohort of 1910), though fewer had four or more children. The distributions for the 1960 and 1969 cohorts from the June CPS are almost identical to the 1950 distribution; they are difficult to make out in figure 8.6 because they lie almost exactly on top of one another. The only discernible difference is a very small rise in the share of women remaining childless: from 17 percent for the cohort of 1950 to 18 percent for the cohort of 1969. In contrast to the fairly large changes every twenty years since the 1850s, the distribution of children ever born has been remarkably stable among women completing their childbearing in the last twenty years.

Second, the post-1960 cohorts experienced dramatic declines in within-cohort dispersion, in terms of both standard deviation (and range), and the coefficient of variation, which normalizes the standard deviation by the falling mean.[14] For the birth cohorts of 1880 through 1910, the coefficient of variation suggests that within-cohort dispersion *grew* during the early twentieth-century fertility decline, as certain groups (such as foreign-born white women) decreased their childbearing to native levels while the childbearing of other groups (such as rural women and nonwhite native women) remained much higher (figure 8.2). The within-cohort dispersion

14. The coefficient of variation (the ratio of the standard deviation to the mean) provides a succinct, scale-invariant summary of within-cohort differences. Scale invariance is desirable in this context because the mean number of children born falls so dramatically across cohorts, mechanically reducing the variance and standard deviation.

in live births was highest for women born from 1900 to 1910—the cohorts experiencing the lowest pre–baby boom levels of completed childbearing.

During the baby boom, however, dispersion in childbearing fell, as groups with previously falling fertility rates changed course to have more children. This reversal reduced within-cohort differences in childbearing, and the coefficient of variation reached a one hundred-year nadir for cohorts born in the mid-1930s—those giving birth to the largest number of children during the baby boom. For cohorts reaching childbearing age after 1960, the strong negative relationship between the mean and dispersion in childbearing disappeared. As completed childbearing fell to 1.9 for the later cohorts and the two-child family became far more universal, the coefficient of variation grew only slightly, from 0.66 to 0.73.

These two findings challenge the conventional wisdom about the recent period as well as assertions of exceptional and increasing rates of childlessness. It is true that childlessness rates for the most recent cohort we can measure (born 1969) are 6 to 7 percentage points higher than those for cohorts thirty to forty years older (born 1930 to 1940), but they are 6 percentage points *lower* (17 versus 23 percent) than the low-fertility cohorts. Similarly, a *smaller* share of recent cohorts had exactly one child relative to the low-fertility cohorts. Consistent with Michael and Willis's model that better contraception reduces precautionary undershooting, more recent cohorts are less likely to have fewer than two children. This finding may be surprising given qualitative evidence and media accounts of women having overestimated their ability to get pregnant at older ages. Taking these accounts at face value, however, suggests that childlessness rates may fall even further if younger cohorts of women adapt their behavior to minimize the risk of subfecundity or if medical technology increasingly facilitates births to older women. The two-child mode, decreasing childlessness, and reduced variance in number of children suggest that women have been better able to reach their desired number of children since 1960 than in the 1920s and 1930s.[15]

Both patterns in marriage and childbearing suggest that spacing between births and perhaps stopping at the desired number of children *within* marriage played major roles in the fertility decline of the early twentieth century. During this period, a large market developed for devices and nostrums to limit childbearing, and knowledge—some factual and some quackery—diffused quickly in the late nineteenth century (Tone 2001). Many of the advertised "contraceptives" were highly ineffective, and couples largely relied on natural methods like rhythm and abstinence to achieve their desired numbers (Brodie 1997).

The low-fertility cohorts were not limiting childbearing by delaying

---

15. Using data on the "ideal" (or desired) number of children for each woman in the NSFG, we have verified that the distribution of actual children born changed substantially more than did the distribution of ideal children between the earlier and later cohorts. This can be seen in appendix figures 8A.4, panel A and 8A.4, panel B.

intercourse and marriage (shortening the period of exposure to the risk of pregnancy) but were limiting childbearing within marriage (David and Sanderson 1987). The shift in figure 8.6 from a more diffuse distribution of children ever born for the birth cohort of 1870 to a distribution with a high concentration of two or fewer births for the birth cohort of 1910 was achieved *within* marriage. Women achieved much smaller families in the early twentieth century by spacing children as in figure 8.5, or by increasing the denominator in $n = E/(C + S)$.

One fascinating pattern of the later twentieth-century fertility decline is that it occurred *despite* a younger (and stable) age at first union and, initially, a younger age at first birth. As with the low-fertility cohorts, women reaching childbearing age after 1960 achieved low completed childbearing without delaying marriage. Yet, completed fertility ended up being lower for women born after 1945 than for the low-fertility cohorts *despite* considerably earlier and more universal marriage. In addition, the mean age at first birth for women born in 1945 was lower than that of many of the baby boom mothers. This pattern, together with the sharp reduction in the variance of childbearing, hints that women were able to stop much more easily at their desired number of children.

8.4 The Decoupling of Marriage and Motherhood

Historically, decisions about whether and when to marry were strongly related to the age at first birth and completed childbearing. They were also tightly connected through their relationships to age at first intercourse. The shift to nonmarital cohabitation, however, foreshadows one of the most distinctive shifts in childbearing since 1960: its disassociation with marriage. The relationship between age at first marriage, sex, and motherhood changed dramatically over the twentieth century and became much weaker during the second half.

Figure 8.3 shows that the mean age at first marriage and the mean age at first birth have become increasingly similar—separated by less than one year for cohorts born in 1970. This convergence could mean that marriage increasingly signals that couples are ready to have children, but in reality the reverse is the case. Marriage and childbearing have become less—not more—interrelated in recent years.

The overall narrowing in the mean age at first birth and the mean age at first marriage is closely related to changes in the interval between first marriage and first birth. Among those who married and gave birth by age thirty-five (but not in a particular order), 57 percent of the 1910 cohort first gave birth within two years after marriage, 45 percent of the 1950 and 1960 cohorts did so, and only 35 percent of the 1970 cohort did so. The mean length of the interval between marriage and motherhood fell from 2.2 years for the cohort of 1910 to 1.5 years for the cohort of 1940 before rising back to 2.0 years for the 1950 cohort. For younger cohorts, the interval between marriage and motherhood fell *again*, to 1.7 for the 1960 cohort and to 0.9 for the 1970 cohort. This pattern conflates two opposing trends. Among women who married *before* giving birth, the interval from first marriage to first birth *increased* from 2.8 years for the 1950 cohort to 3.2 for the 1970 cohort. Aggregate declines in the interval are driven by an increasing number of women marrying *after* the birth of their first child—a negative interval between first marriage and first birth.

Figure 8.7 quantifies what many have referred to as the "sexual revolution." The share of women who first had intercourse in their teens increased sharply for cohorts born in the late 1940s. Although the distribution of age at first intercourse appears relatively stable from the calendar years 1955 to 1965 (calendar year series suppressed for brevity; figure 8.7 shows statistics by cohort), the mean age at first intercourse began to fall rapidly starting in the late 1960s. This strong period effect, less evident in our cohort figure, is consistent with cohorts being affected at different ages. The birth cohort of 1948 was eighteen in 1966, and the share having intercourse by eighteen rose for subsequent cohorts. Similarly, the birth cohort of 1950 was sixteen in 1966, and the share having intercourse by age sixteen rose rapidly for subsequent cohorts. We cannot construct similar statistics for the early cohorts,

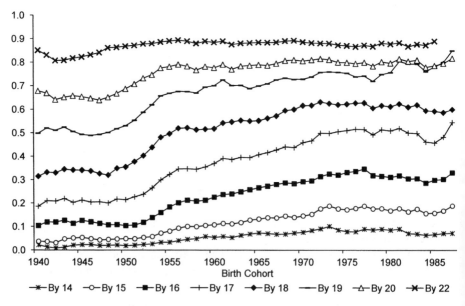

Fig. 8.7   Fraction of women having first sex, by age and birth cohort
Source: 1982–2010 NSFG.
Note: The series show the fraction of women having had vaginal intercourse with a man by the specified ages across birth cohorts. Trends are smoothed using three-cohort moving averages.

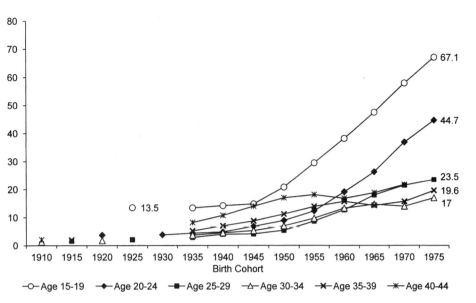

−○−Age 15-19   −◆−Age 20-24   −■−Age 25-29   −△−Age 30-34   −✱−Age 35-39   −※−Age 40-44

Fig. 8.8   Percentage of births to unmarried women, by birth cohort
Source: National Vital Statistics Reports (Ventura and Bachrach 2000; Martin et al. 2007, 2012).
Notes: The series are the percentage of births to unmarried women for the indicated age groups for each cohort (x-axis). The births are reported for five-year age groups, and we assume the start of the age group for the five-year band. For example, 13.5 percent of births to women born between 1921 and 1925 between the ages of fifteen and nineteen were born to unmarried women.

but all of our analysis thus far suggests that the baby boom period should have led to *earlier* first intercourse (along with earlier first marriage and birth) relative to the low-fertility cohorts.[16] In short, age at first intercourse fell during the 1960s and 1970s as *both* age at first marriage and age at first birth rose.

The post-1960 period has also witnessed a rise in births to unmarried women (figure 8.8). As premarital sex increased, so did the proportion of births that were nonmarital—especially among teens.[17] For cohorts born between 1940 and 1960, nonmarital teen births rose from approximately 14 percent to almost 40 percent of all births. Similarly, the same cohorts experienced a noticeable rise in nonmarital births during their early twenties. As completed fertility for the youngest cohorts has stabilized, the nonmari-

16. We expect that data on age at first intercourse for these earlier cohorts of women would show that even fewer had sex as teens (rather than more). Using the baby boom cohorts as our starting point, therefore, should lead us to understate the increase in sexual activity among younger teens.
17. We do not intend to convey a causal direction with the ordering of this statement. Nonmarital sex may have increased because more women desired children but not husbands.

tal share of births has risen dramatically. Older women have also seen rising nonmarital birth rates, although the increase is more muted. In 2011, over 40 percent of all births were to unmarried women.

These numbers do not imply that premarital sex or premarital *pregnancies* were uncommon in the United States before 1960. Smith and Hindus (1975) argue that in the late 1800s and early 1900s as many as 10 to 15 percent of brides gave birth within six to eight months of marriage. In the past, however, nonmarital *births* occurred far less frequently because nonmarital conceptions more often resulted in "shotgun" marriages.[18] A distinctive feature of the post-1960 period fertility decline is that marriage and motherhood became decoupled—motherhood more frequently occurred before marriage and many married couples increasingly delayed childbearing until later ages in marriage.

8.5 The Changing Relationship between Mothers' Education and Childbearing

A third distinctive feature of the post-1960 period is the changing predictive importance of mothers' education. On the one hand, more and less educated women have converged in terms of the likelihood of marriage and childlessness as well as the number of children they have. On the other, they have diverged, often sharply, in terms of their age at first union, their age at first birth, and nonmarital childbearing.

This section presents trends in women's childbearing outcomes by relative educational attainment because education serves as a consistent proxy for socioeconomic status over the twentieth century. It is related to a woman's family earnings (own and spouse's) and her husband's education. Moreover, each woman's education is observed in the census even when we do not observe her earnings, occupation, or her spouse's earnings. Our analysis uses a *relative* measure of education because the share of women with a given absolute level of education has changed dramatically over the twentieth century.[19] Women whose educational attainment is below the 25th percentile for their cohort are grouped with the "lower quartile" and those above the 75th percentile are grouped with the "higher quartile."

Our analysis summarizes trends across birth cohorts in six outcomes

---

18. Akerlof, Yellen, and Katz (1996) provide an economic bargaining model that relates availability of abortion and modern contraception to the decline in "shotgun" marriages.

19. We employ a quantile regression of an individual woman's years of schooling on birth year dummies and a quartic in age interacted with dummies for twenty-year birth cohort intervals (1880–1899, 1900–1919, etc.). Predicted values from the quantile regression (either at the 25th or 75th percentiles) are then compared with actual values for each woman. Because there is significant heaping in the education distribution (particularly at twelve and sixteen years), we first "smooth" actual education values by adding a stochastic noise term drawn from a uniform distribution of width 1, centered at 0. This procedure preserves the cohort quantiles while alleviating composition changes due to heaping in the education distribution.

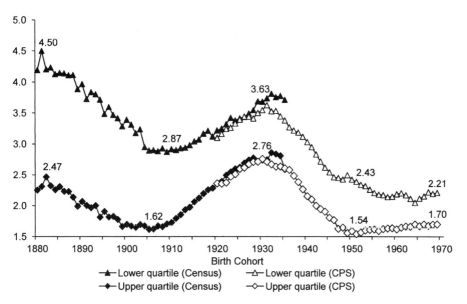

Fig. 8.9   Children ever born, by education quantile and birth cohort

Sources: 1940–1990 decennial census IPUMS samples (Ruggles et al. 2010) and 1979–2010 June CPS.

Notes: The figure plots the mean number of live births among women ages forty-one and older, by birth cohort, for the census (1880 through 1935 cohorts) and the same statistic for women in the June CPS (1920 through 1969 cohorts). See text for education group definitions. All computations use the recommended population weights, and the CPS series are three-cohort moving averages.

associated with the distinctive features of the post-1960 period: (1) mean children ever born, (2) childlessness (the share of women who have not given birth), (3) the share of women ever married or cohabiting by age thirty-five, (4) age at first marriage, (5) age at first birth, and (6) the share of women whose first birth was nonmarital. In the first two cases, we restrict the sample to women at least forty-one years of age for comparison with the trends in figures 8.1 and 8.2. For the other four, we use women at least thirty-six years of age in order to balance the need to preserve sample size (the analysis relies on the smaller samples of the NSFG for the more recent cohorts) and consistency across cohorts.[20]

Figure 8.9 documents changes in childbearing for women in the upper and lower quantiles of the education distribution. It is well known that women with less education have tended to have more children than women with more education. Less well known is that the most educated women in the low-fertility cohorts were having approximately 1.6 children over their

20. We have calculated the trends for outcomes (3) through (6) using women at least forty-one years of age. Although noisy, they are qualitatively similar to the figures we present.

lifetimes—fewer, on average, than today. After reaching a nadir at a mean of 1.5 children for the 1950 cohort, the more educated women increased the number of children they had to approximately 1.7 for the cohort of 1970. In contrast, the less educated women have far fewer children today than did the low-fertility cohorts, reaching a ninety-year low of 2.2 for the 1970 cohort. The result is that inequality in completed childbearing between these two groups of mothers is also at a ninety-year low. The overall narrowing in the education gap in childbearing has been driven not just by falling completed fertility among the less educated but also by an increase in childbearing among the more educated women.

Similarly, childlessness is much lower among the more educated women today than it was for the low-fertility cohorts and cohorts born in the 1950s. Figure 8.10 shows that childlessness rates have tended to be higher among the more educated women (a relationship that almost disappeared during the baby boom). The more educated women in cohorts reaching childbearing age in the 1970s had roughly the same rates of childlessness as the early twentieth-century cohorts (around 29 percent) but, in more recent cohorts, childlessness has *fallen*. Only 21 percent of the more educated women born in 1969 were childless by age forty-one. Similarly, childlessness rates among the less educated are lower for recent cohorts compared to the early twentieth-century cohorts.

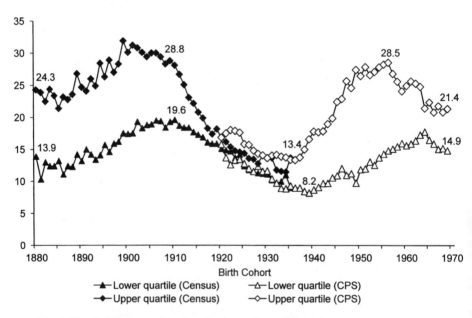

Fig. 8.10   Childlessness, by education quantile and birth cohort
Sources: See figure 8.12.
Notes: The figure plots the percentage of women age forty-one and older who have not had a live birth, by birth cohort, for the census (1880 through 1935 cohorts) and the same statistic for women in the June CPS (1920 through 1969 cohorts). See notes for figure 8.12.

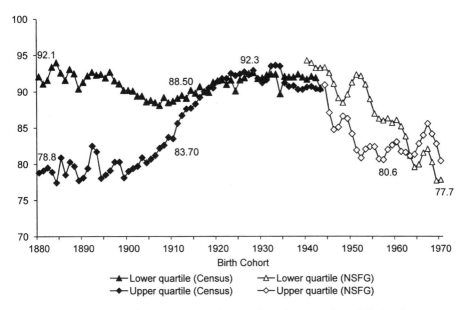

Fig. 8.11   Ever married by age thirty-five, by education quantile and birth cohort

Sources: 1940–1980 decennial census IPUMS samples (Ruggles et al. 2010) and 1982–2010 NSFG.

Notes: The figure plots the percentage of women ever married by age thirty-five among women age thirty-six and older, by birth cohort, for the census (1880 through 1943 cohorts) and the same statistic for women in the NSFG (1940 through 1970 cohorts). See text for education group definitions. All computations use the recommended population weights and the NSFG series are five-cohort moving averages.

Marital decisions have changed differentially by education group as well. Figure 8.11 shows that among women born at the turn of the twentieth century, the less educated were 10 to 15 percentage points *more* likely to have married by age thirty-five. Unlike the other series we present, the education gap began disappearing for women in the low-fertility cohorts—before the baby boom began. Between the cohorts of 1900 and 1920, the likelihood of ever marrying trended upward among the more educated women. For women born over the next twenty years (the mothers of the baby boom), the likelihood of marriage reached parity for both education groups. The education gap reemerged for the 1940s and 1950s birth cohorts, but has since reversed. Today, the more educated women appear slightly *more likely* to marry than do the less educated women, although the NSFG data are too noisy to conclude this definitively.[21]

For these first three series (mean completed childbearing, childlessness, and the likelihood of marriage or cohabitation by age thirty-five), the more educated women today appear more similar to their less educated counterparts than do women in the low-fertility cohorts. That is, women's education

---

21. This conclusion is unaltered if we restrict the sample to women at least age forty-one.

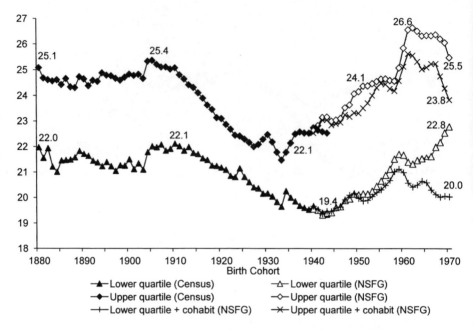

Fig. 8.12   Age at first marriage and cohabitation, by education quantile and birth cohort

Sources: 1940–1980 decennial census IPUMS samples (Ruggles et al. 2010) and 1982–2010 NSFG.

Notes: The figure plots age at first marriage among ever-married women age thirty-six and older by birth cohort using the census (1880 through 1943 cohorts) and the NSFG (1940 through 1970 cohorts). For the NSFG cohorts, there are also series plotted for the younger of age at first marriage or age at first cohabitation (conditional on one of these events occurring by age thirty-five). See text for education group definitions. All computations use the recommended population weights and the NSFG series are five-cohort moving averages.

has become a less important predictor of these outcomes. The reverse is true for age at first union, age at first birth, and nonmarital childbearing.

Age at first union (either through marriage or cohabitation, figure 8.12) for the less educated women is lower today than it was for women born at the beginning of the twentieth century and higher than it was during the baby boom. Excluding cohabitation, on the other hand, age at first marriage is higher than that of the low-fertility cohorts and 3.5 years higher than during the baby boom. The pattern for more educated women is qualitatively similar although the swings have been somewhat larger. As a result, the education gap in age at first union is about one year larger today than it was for the low-fertility cohorts.[22]

---

22. The education gap is about half a year smaller if one looks strictly at marriage. This smaller gap, however, emerged only for cohorts born in the late 1960s. The education gap in marriage age was larger than that for the low-fertility cohorts as recently as the 1968 cohort.

Age at first birth (figure 8.13) and nonmarital childbearing (figure 8.14) have shown the most dramatic changes by education since 1960. In the early twentieth century, the gap in age at first birth between more and less educated women was around 3.5 years. After falling by about 0.5 years during the baby boom, as mean age at first marriage fell faster for the more educated women, the gap has expanded to almost seven years in the post-1960 period—roughly *twice* the size of the education gap for the 1910 cohort. The more educated women born around 1970 waited two years longer to first give birth than did their counterparts fifty-five years earlier, whereas the less educated gave birth 1 to 1.5 years *earlier* than they did historically—leading to an overall mean that is nearly identical for the 1910 and 1970 cohorts. Interestingly, the mean age at first birth for the less educated has remained essentially the same since the baby boom.

As the age at first birth of the less educated mothers remained at sixty-year lows, their rate of nonmarital childbearing grew rapidly. Following a period of stability during the baby boom, at around 11 to 13 percent for the less educated mothers and 4 to 6 percent for the more educated mothers, the gap in nonmarital births exploded for cohorts born after 1950. Nonmarital

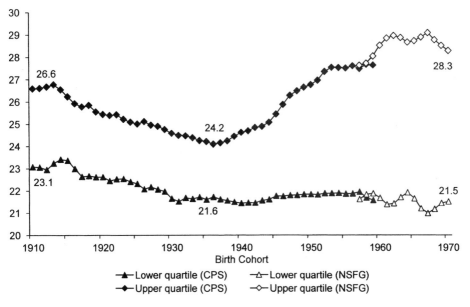

Fig. 8.13 Age at first birth, by education quantile and birth cohort

Sources: 1979–1995 June CPS and 1995–2010 NSFG.

Notes: The figure plots age at first birth among women age thirty-six and older, by birth cohort, for the June CPS (1910 through 1959 cohorts) and the same statistic for women in the NSFG (1957 through 1970 cohorts). See text for education group definitions. All computations use the recommended population weights. The June CPS series use three-cohort moving averages, and NSFG series are five-cohort moving averages.

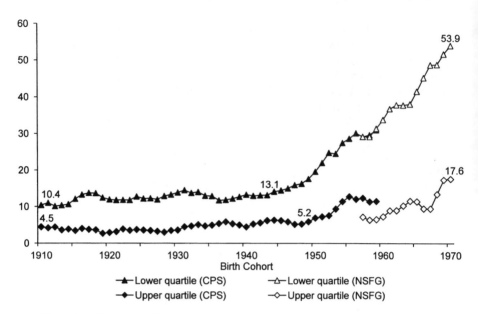

Fig. 8.14   Nonmarital first childbirth, by education quantile and birth cohort
Sources: 1979–1995 June CPS and 1995–2010 NSFG.
Notes: The figure plots the percentage of first births that are nonmarital among women age thirty-six and older, by birth cohort, for the June CPS (1910 through 1959 cohorts) and the same statistic for women in the NSFG (1957 through 1970 cohorts). See text for education group definitions. All computations use the recommended population weights. The June CPS series use three-cohort moving averages and NSFG series are five-cohort moving averages.

childbearing grew across the education distribution, but relatively slowly for the top quartile. Among women born in the late 1960s, the share of nonmarital childbearing reached three times the historic average for more educated women and over four times the historically higher average among less educated women. For the most recent cohorts, 54 percent of first births among the less educated are nonmarital.

This growing divergence indicates that the second distinctive feature of the post-1960 period—the decoupling of marriage and motherhood—has taken place along class lines. Whereas trends in children ever born, childlessness, marriage age and rates, nonmarital childbearing, and age at first birth moved in tandem across the educational distribution during the early twentieth-century fertility decline, the latter three outcomes diverged for more and less educated women after 1960.

8.6   Conclusions and Implications for Human Capital

At first glance, the US fertility decline in the post-1960 period does not appear to be a significant departure from the one in the early twentieth century. Aggregate fertility fell at similar rates in both periods and this similarity reinforces just *how different* the 1940s and 1950s were. In each series presented, the 1940 to 1960 period (or the 1915 to 1935 cohorts) exhibits a substantial departure from earlier and later trends. Changes in sexual behavior within marriage—a *behavioral* revolution before the contraceptive revolution—may in part explain the decoupling of marriage from birth rates in the early twentieth century. The low-fertility cohorts in the United States were successful in limiting childbearing through increased spacing and stopping—especially given the relatively stable age at first marriage during the period. Thus, our analysis presents evidence that Coleman's (2004) argument holds in the United States: many trends in reproductive and relational behavior "already existed before the sixties; in fact, most of them emerged with the . . . demographic transition around the turn of the century" (72).

Yet distinctive features of the post-1960 US fertility decline should give pause to scholars who wish to argue that the two twentieth-century fertility declines are identical. After 1960, women were significantly more likely to have exactly two children and were *less likely* to remain childless. Although women reaching childbearing age in the 1930s and 1970s had similar numbers of children on average, these cohorts achieved these means in very different ways. Most economic models simplify childbearing decisions to the number of children and proxy for this theoretical concept in empirical work by using the mean number of live births (or a measure of period fertility). Our analysis shows that this single moment of the childbearing distribution misses empirical regularities that enhance our understanding of the motivations and constraints individuals faced over the twentieth century—regularities that could help distinguish between theories of childbearing.

After 1960, marriage and motherhood became increasingly disassociated as more children were born outside of marriage. Consistent with Goldin's (2004) claim that recent cohorts are more likely to "have it all" (i.e., achieve career and motherhood), completed childbearing, childlessness, and the likelihood of eventual marriage are *more* similar across educational groups of mothers today than in the early twentieth century. On the other hand, age at first union, age at first birth, and nonmarital childbearing have diverged sharply across educational groups. The decoupling of marriage and childbearing and the changing predictive importance of mothers' education hint that a larger demographic and economic transition is underway. The fact that these patterns have not stabilized suggests that the current fertility transition, perhaps part of a larger gender (Goldscheider 2012) and cultural revolution, is still ongoing.

It is unclear whether these changes are large enough to constitute a "Second Demographic Transition." A different way to think about this debate is in terms of which forces drove fertility decline in the early and later twentieth century—specifically, the relative importance of shifts in the demand or supply (the reliability and cost of preventing pregnancy) for children in both periods. Our argument is not that *either* supply *or* demand mattered, but that both matter and have mattered differently at different points in time. The reduction in childbearing during the early twentieth century surely reflected large shifts in the demand for children. And reduced childbearing was realized at great cost, as individuals reduced the frequency of intercourse with their partners, used dangerous or debilitating contraceptive techniques,[23] attempted often lethal abortions, and missed their targeted number of children due to precautionary undershooting.[24] Shifts in the demand for children certainly played a role during the baby boom as well as in the post-1960 period.

Yet it is hard to ignore the contraceptive revolution (the supply side) of the 1960s, especially as a growing literature in economics—started by Goldin and Katz (2002)—has built an empirical case for its importance. Goldin and Katz (2002) argue that availability of modern and effective contraception (such as the birth control pill) to younger, unmarried women relaxed the constraints on their marital and human capital investment decisions. Bailey (2010) shows that faster diffusion of the Pill in states without preexisting Comstock bans on the sales of contraceptives led to a more rapid decline in fertility rates. The consequence was that younger women delayed their marriages, increased their educational attainment, and pursued previously male-dominated careers (Goldin and Katz 2002; Hock 2008). Modern birth control also increased women's labor force attachment and wages (Bailey 2006; Bailey, Hershbein, and Miller 2012).

Christensen (2011) also suggests that early access to the Pill affected decisions to cohabit before marriage, which in turn may have directly and indirectly altered women's incentives to specialize in household production. Greater cohabitation rates imply important changes in matching between men and women as well as changes in women's bargaining power within marriage. The greater rise in age at first marriage among more educated women means that they have more time to search for a mate, increasing both the quality of their matches and, potentially, the earnings of their households. The rise in cohabitation may also imply substantial changes in matching between men and women as well as in traditional gendered forms of household/labor force specialization. It also implies a shift in the meaning and/or implications of "marriage." For instance, marriage may have increasingly become a status symbol (McLanahan and Watson 2011) or motivated

23. One letter to Margaret Sanger read, "I am the mother of two lovely little girls. I have been married fifteen years. I married at the age of fifteen to escape a home that was overcrowded with unloved and unwanted children, where there was never clothing or food enough to divide among the eight of us . . . I have been pregnant 15 times, most of the time doing things myself to get out of it and no one knows how I have suffered from the effect of it, but I would rather die than bring as many children into the world as my mother did and have nothing to offer them" (Sanger 1923, 181–82).

24. In the Low Fertility Cohorts Study (Ridley 1978), for instance, 14 percent of women indicated that they desired fewer than two children, but 39 percent had fewer than two.

by consumption (rather than production) complementarities (Stevenson and Wolfers 2007).

The distinctive features of the post-1960 period suggest that the contraceptive revolution may have had broader effects on the US economy and may signal longer-term changes. Standard economic models predict that increases in women's human capital, their wages (an important component of the opportunity cost of childbearing), their ages at marriage, and their incomes would tend to increase investments in each child. Modern contraception may also directly reduce the relative price of child "quality" and thereby increase investments in the average child ceteris paribus (Becker and Lewis 1973). These hypothesized effects are consistent with recent evidence by Ananat and Hungerman (2012) and Bailey, Malkova, and McLaren (2013) showing that increased access to contraception increases the economic resources of children. Bailey (2013) also provides evidence that these investments may have affected the economic resources of these children thirty to forty years later.

The decoupling of marriage and motherhood and the changing role of women's education may have distributional implications as well. The recently *growing* educational gap in age at first birth and nonmarital childbearing anticipates a growing divergence in the resources available to children in households of lower and higher socioeconomic status. Consistent with this recent trend, the distribution of resources to children is becoming increasingly polarized—the destinies of higher and lower socioeconomic status children are diverging. McLanahan (2004), for instance, summarizes the empirical support for the idea that a child's environment has become more closely determined by socioeconomic factors. Mothers with higher relative education are more likely to be married, are more likely to work, give birth at older ages, and live in higher income households. Children who have a college-educated father spend more time with him than children who do not. Similarly, studies using data from the American Time Use Surveys have found that more educated mothers not only spend more time on all forms of child care than do less educated mothers (Guryan, Hurst, and Kearney 2008), but that they are also more likely to change the type of child care based on children's developmental needs (Kalil, Ryan, and Corey 2012). Ramey and Ramey (2010) argue that the objective of more educated parents to get their children into competitive colleges has further exacerbated gaps in parental investments.[25] Future research should consider how characteristics of the later twentieth century fertility transition relate to children's opportunities, educational achievement, and widening inequality in US labor markets.

---

25. To the extent that some of this behavior may be status-seeking signaling rather than productivity-enhancing investment, it may not affect outcomes much among the children of the more educated if the behavior is near universal among them.

Appendix

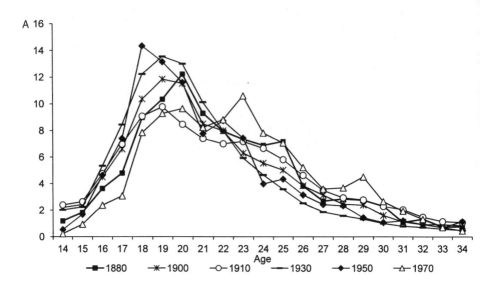

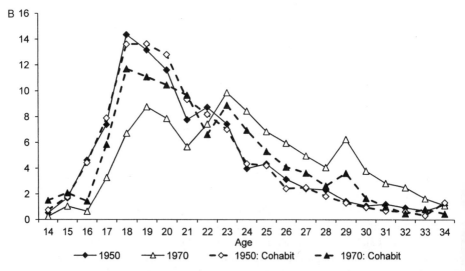

Fig. 8A.1   Percentage of women first marrying or cohabiting at each age, by birth cohort: *A*, distribution of age at first marriage; *B*, distribution of age at first marriage or first cohabitation

Sources: 1900 through 1940 cohorts use the 1940–1980 decennial census IPUMS samples (Ruggles et al. 2010), and 1950 and 1970 cohorts use the 1988–2010 NSFG.

Notes: The figure shows the percentage of women in the indicated single-year-of-birth cohort who had married (panel A), or who had married or cohabited (panel B), by the age on the horizontal axis among those who had married or cohabited by age thirty-four. Distributions for 1950 to 1970 are from the NSFG and are based on three-cohort moving averages. For example, the 1950 birth cohort is an average of the 1949, 1950, and 1951 cohorts.

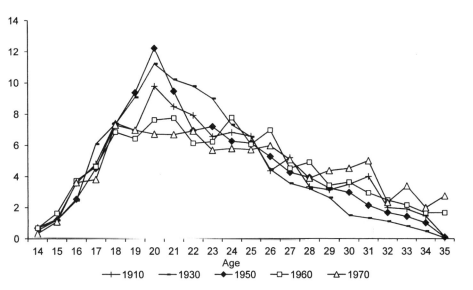

Fig. 8A.2   Percentage of women first giving birth at each age, by birth cohort

Sources: 1979 to 1995 June CPS (1910 through 1950 cohorts); 1995 through 2010 NSFG (1960 and 1970 cohorts).

Notes: The series show the percentage of women having their first birth at the indicated age (x-axis) conditional upon giving birth by age thirty-five and being at least age thirty-six at time of observation. Distributions from the NSFG are based on three-cohort moving averages; thus, the 1960 birth cohort is an average of the 1959, 1960, and 1961 cohorts.

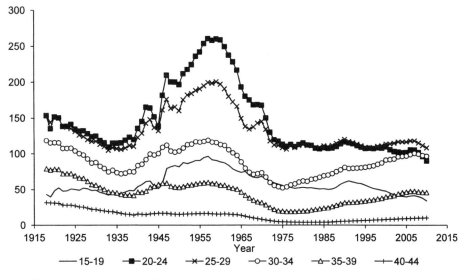

Fig. 8A.3   Age-specific birth rates, by year

Sources: National Vital Statistics Reports (Linder and Grove 1947; Grove and Hetzel 1968; Martin et al. 2012).

Notes: The series plot the number of births per 1,000 women in a given age group by the year that the births occurred (not mother's birth cohort).

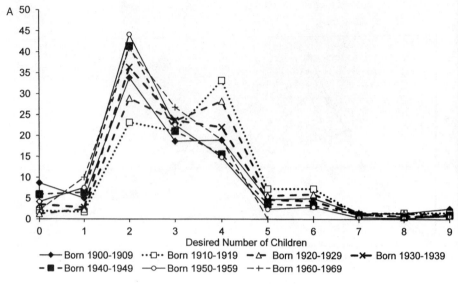

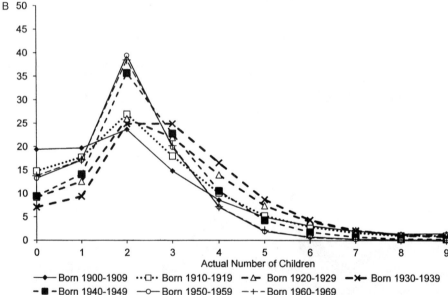

Fig. 8A.4 Percentage of women with desired and actual children born, by decadal birth cohort: *A*, distribution of desired childbearing, women ages 35+; *B*, distribution of actual childbearing, women ages 41–70

Sources: For panel A, 1900–1909 cohorts use the Low-Fertility Cohort Study (Ridley 1978); the remaining cohorts use the Integrated Fertility Survey Series (Smock et al. 1955–2002). For panel B, see sources in figure 8.6.

Notes: The figure shows the percentage of women in the indicated decadal birth cohort who desired the number of children (panel A), or who had given birth to the number of children (panel B), specified on the horizontal axis. Both series are top-coded at nine children. The desired number of children is taken from questions asking about the ideal number of children for the respondent specifically.

References

Akerlof, George A., Janet L. Yellen, and Michael L. Katz. 1996. "An Analysis of Out-of-Wedlock Childbearing in the United States." *Quarterly Journal of Economics* 111 (2): 277–317.

Albanesi, Stefania, and Claudia Olivetti. 2009. "Medical Progress, Fertility and Women's Work in the Twentieth Century." Working Paper, Boston University Department of Economics.

Ananat, Elizabeth, and Daniel Hungerman. 2012. "The Power of the Pill for the Next Generation: Oral Contraception's Effects on Fertility, Abortion, and Maternal and Child Characteristics." *Review of Economics and Statistics* 94 (1): 37–51.

Bailey, Martha J. 2006. "More Power to the Pill: The Impact of Contraceptive Freedom on Women's Lifecycle Labor Supply." *Quarterly Journal of Economics* 121 (1): 289–320.

———. 2010. "Momma's Got the Pill: How Anthony Comstock and *Griswold v. Connecticut* Shaped US Childbearing." *American Economic Review* 100 (1): 98–129.

———. 2012. "Reexamining the Impact of US Family Planning Programs on Fertility: Evidence from the War on Poverty and the Early Years of Title X." *American Economic Journal-Applied Economics* 4 (2): 62–97.

———. 2013. "Fifty Years of US Family Planning: Evidence on the Long-Run Effects of Increasing Access to Contraception." *Brookings Papers on Economic Activity*. Spring: 341–409.

Bailey, Martha J., Brad J. Hershbein, and Amalia R. Miller. 2012. "The Opt-In Revolution? Contraception and the Gender Gap in Wages." *American Economic Journal: Applied Economics* 4 (3): 225–54.

Bailey, Martha J., Olga Malkova, and Zoe McLaren. 2013. "The Long-Term Effects of Family Planning Programs on Children's Resources." Working Paper, University of Michigan.

Barro, Robert J., and Gary S. Becker. 1989. "Fertility Choice in a Model of Economic Growth." *Econometrica* 57 (2): 481–501.

Becker, Gary. 1960. "An Economic Analysis of Fertility." In *Demographic and Economic Change in Developed Countries*, Conference of the Universities-National Bureau Committee for Economic Research, a Report of the National Bureau of Economic Research, 209–40. Princeton, NJ: Princeton University Press.

———. 1965. "A Theory of the Allocation of Time." *Economic Journal* 75 (299): 493–517.

———. 1981. *A Treatise on the Family*, enlarged edition. Cambridge, MA: Harvard University Press.

Becker, Gary, and Robert J. Barro. 1988. "A Reformulation of the Economic Theory of Fertility." *Quarterly Journal of Economics* 103 (1): 1–25.

Becker, Gary, and H. Gregg Lewis. 1973. "On the Interaction between the Quantity and Quality of Children." *Journal of Political Economy* 81 (2): S279–S288.

Binion, R. 2001. "Marianne in the Home: Political Revolution and Fertility Transition in France and the United States." *Population: An English Selection* 13 (2): 165–88.

Brodie, Janet Farrell. 1997. *Contraception and Abortion in Nineteenth-Century America.* Ithaca, NY: Cornell University Press.

Christensen, Finn. 2011. "The Pill and Partnerships: The Impact of the Birth Control Pill on Cohabitation." *Journal of Populations Economics* 25 (1): 29–52.

Cliquet, Robert L. 1991. *The Second Demographic Transition: Fact or Fiction?* Population Studies 23. Strasbourg, France: Council of Europe.

Coale, Ansley J. 1973. "The Demographic Transition Reconsidered." International

Population Conference (International Union for the Scientific Study of Population, Liege): 53–72.

Coleman, David. 2004. "Why We Don't Have to Believe without Doubting in the 'Second Demographic Transition'—Some Agnostic Comments." *Vienna Yearbook of Population Research* 2:11–24.

David, Paul A., and Warren C. Sanderson. 1987. "The Emergence of a Two-Child Norm among American Birth Controllers." *Population and Development Review* 13 (1): 1–41.

DiNardo, John, Nicole M. Fortin, and Thomas Lemieux. 1996. "Labor Market Institutions and the Distribution of Wages, 1973–1992: A Semiparametric Analysis." *Econometrica* 64 (5): 1001–44.

Doepke, Matthias, Moshe Hazan, and Yishay Maoz. 2008. "The Baby Boom and World War II: A Macroeconomic Analysis." CEPR Discussion Paper no. 6628, Centre for Economic Policy Research.

Easterlin, Richard A. 1961. "The American Baby Boom in Historical Perspective." *American Economic Review* 51 (5): 869–911.

———. 1966. "Economic-Demographic Interactions and Long Swings in Economic Growth." *American Economic Review* 56 (5): 1063–104.

———. 1971. "Does Human Fertility Adjust to the Environment?" *American Economic Review* 61 (2): 399–407.

———. 1975. "An Economic Framework for Fertility Analysis." *Studies in Family Planning* 6 (3): 54–63.

———. 1980. *Birth and Fortune.* Chicago: Basic Books.

Easterlin, Richard A., and Eileen M. Crimmins. 1985. *The Fertility Revolution: A Supply-Demand Analysis.* Chicago: University of Chicago Press.

Easterlin, Richard A., Robert Pollak, and Michael Wachter. 1980. "Toward a More General Economic Model of Fertility Determination: Endogenous Preferences and Natural Fertility." In *Population and Economic Change in Developing Countries*, edited by R. A. Easterlin, 81–149. Chicago: University of Chicago Press.

Goldin, Claudia. 2004. "The Long Road to the Fast Track: Career and Family." *Annals of the American Academy of Political and Social Science* 596 (1): 20–35.

Goldin, Claudia A., and Lawrence Katz. 2002. "The Power of the Pill: Oral Contraceptives and Women's Career and Marriage Decisions." *Journal of Political Economy* 110 (4): 730–70.

Goldscheider, Frances. 2012. "The Gender Revolution and the Second Demographic Transition: Understanding Recent Family Trends in Industrialized Societies." Keynote Address for the 2012 European Population Conference, Stockhold, Sweden, June 13.

Greenwood, Jeremy, Ananth Seshadri, and Guillaume Vandenbroucke. 2005. "The Baby Boom and Baby Bust." *American Economic Review* 95 (1): 183–207.

Grove, Robert D., and Alice M. Hetzel. 1968. *Vital Statistics Rates in the United States 1940–1960.* Washington, DC: US National Center for Health Statistics.

Guinnane, Timothy W. 2011. "The Historical Fertility Transition: A Guide for Economists." *Journal of Economic Literature* 49 (3): 589–614.

Guldi, Melanie. 2008. "Fertility Effects of Abortion and Pill Access for Minors." *Demography* 45 (4): 817–27.

Guryan, Jonathan, Erik Hurst, and Melissa S. Kearney. 2008. "Parental Education and Parental Time with Children." *Journal of Economic Perspectives* 22 (3): 23–46.

Hacker, J. David. 2003. "Rethinking the 'Early' Decline of Marital Fertility in the United States." *Demography* 40 (4): 605–20.

Haines, Michael R. 1989. "American Fertility in Transition: New Estimates of Birth Rates in the United States, 1900–1910." *Demography* 26 (1): 137–48.

————. 2000. "The White Population of the United States, 1790–1920." In *A Population History of North America*, edited by M. R. Haines and R. H. Steckel, 305–69. New York: Cambridge University Press.

Hock, Heinrich. 2008. "The Pill and the College Attainment of American Women and Men." Working Paper, Florida State University.

Hotz, V. Joseph, and Robert A. Miller. 1988. "An Empirical Analysis of Life Cycle Fertility and Female Labor Supply." *Econometrica* 56 (1): 91–118.

June Current Population Surveys. 1995–2010. National Bureau of Economic Research. Available at: http://www.nber.org/data/current-population-survey-data.html.

Kalil, Ariel, Rebecca Ryan, and Michael Corey. 2012. "Diverging Destinies: Maternal Education and the Developmental Gradient in Time With Children." *Demography* 49 (4): 1361–83.

Kearney, Melissa S., and Phillip B. Levine. 2009. "Subsidized Contraception, Fertility, and Sexual Behavior." *Review of Economics and Statistics* 91 (1): 137–51.

Kirk, Dudley. 1996. "Demographic Transition Theory." *Population Studies* 50 (3): 361–87.

Lee, Ronald D., and David S. Reher. 2011. "Introduction: The Landscape of Demographic Transition and Its Aftermath." *Population and Development Review* 37 (1): 1–7.

Lesthaeghe, Ron J., and Lisa Neidert. 2006. "The Second Demographic Transition in the United States: Exception or Textbook Example?" *Population and Development Review* 32 (4): 669–98.

Lesthaeghe, Ron J., and D. J. van de Kaa. 1986. "Twee Demografische Transities." In *Bevolking, Groei en Krimp*, edited by R. J. Lesthaeghe and D. J. van de Kaa, 19–68. Deventer, Netherlands: Van Loghum Slaterus.

Linder, Forrest E., and Robert D. Grove. 1947. *Vital Statistics Rates in the United States 1900–1940*. Washington, DC: US Government Printing Office.

Martin, Joyce A., Brady E. Hamilton, Paul D. Sutton, Stephanie J. Ventura, Fay Menacker, Sharon Kirmeyer, and Martha L. Munson. 2007. "Births: Final Data for 2005." *National Vital Statistics Reports* 56 (6): 1–103.

Martin, Joyce A., Brady E. Hamilton, Stephanie J. Ventura, Michelle J. K. Osterman, Elizabeth C. Wilson, and T. J. Mathews. 2012. "Births: Final Data for 2010." *National Vital Statistics Reports* 61 (1): 1–72.

Mason, Karen Oppenheim. 1997. "Explaining Fertility Transitions." *Demography* 34 (4): 443–54.

McLanahan, Sara. 2004. "Diverging Destinies: How Children Are Faring under the Second Demographic Transition." *Demography* 41 (4): 607–27.

McLanahan, Sara, and Tara Watson. 2011. "Marriage Meets the Joneses: Relative Income, Identity, and Marital Status." *Journal of Human Resources* 46 (3): 482–517.

Michael, Robert T., and Robert J. Willis. 1976. "Contraception and Fertility: Household Production under Uncertainty." In *Household Production and Consumption*, edited by Nestor E. Terleckyj, 25–98. New York: National Bureau of Economic Research.

Ramey, Garey, and Valerie A. Ramey. 2010. "The Rug Rat Race: Comments and Discussion." *Brookings Papers on Economic Activity* Spring:129–76.

Ridley, Jeanne C. 1978. Low-Fertility Cohorts Study: A Survey of White, Ever-Married Women Belonging to the 1901–1910 United States Birth Cohorts. ICPSR04698-v1. Ann Arbor, MI: Inter-university Consortium for Political and Social Research [distributor], 2007-08-13.

Ruggles, Steven, J. Trent Alexander, Katie Genadek, Ronald Goeken, Matthew B.

Schroeder, and Matthew Sobek. 2010. Integrated Public Use Microdata Series: Version 5.0 [Machine-readable database]. Minneapolis: University of Minnesota.

Ryder, Norman, and Charles F. Westoff. 1971. *The Contraceptive Revolution.* Princeton, NJ: Princeton University Press.

Sanger, Margaret. 1923. "Prevention or Abortion—Which? Letters Showing the Dilemma Faced by Many Mothers." *Birth Control Review* 7 (7): 181–2.

Sheps, Mindel C. 1964. "On the Time Required for Conception." *Population Studies* 19 (3): 85–97.

Sheps, Mindel C., and Edward B. Perrin. 1964. "The Distribution of Birth Intervals under a Class of Stochastic Fertility Models." *Population Studies* 17 (3): 321–31.

Smith, Daniel S., and Michael S. Hindus. 1975. "Premarital Pregnancy in America, 1640–1971: An Overview and Interpretation." *Journal of Interdisciplinary History* 5 (4): 537–70.

Smock, Pamela J., Peter Granda, and Lynette Hoelter. 1955–2002. Integrated Fertility Survey Series [Machine-readable database]. Ann Arbor: University of Michigan.

Stevenson, Betsey, and Justin Wolfers. 2007. "Marriage and Divorce: Changes and their Driving Forces." *Journal of Economic Perspectives* 21 (2): 27–52.

Tone, Andrea. 2001. *Devices and Desires: A History of Contraceptives in America.* New York: Hill and Wang.

Ventura, Stephanie J., and Christine A. Bachrach. 2000. "Nonmarital Childbearing in the United States, 1940–99." *National Vital Statistics Reports* 48 (16): 1–40.

Westoff, Charles F. 1975. "The Yield of the Imperfect: The 1970 National Fertility Study." *Demography* 12 (4): 573–80.

Willis, Robert J. 1973. "A New Approach to the Economic Theory of Fertility Behavior." *Journal of Political Economy* 81 (2): S14–S64.

9

A Pollution Theory
of Discrimination
Male and Female Differences
in Occupations and Earnings

Claudia Goldin

> It is not difficult to see how pollution beliefs can be used in a
> dialogue of claims and counter-claims to status.
> —Mary Douglas, *Purity and Danger* (1966,3)

Women work in occupations that are different from those of men and get paid less for apparently the same personal and job characteristics.[1] These differences have, in part, been attributed to economic discrimination that some have ascribed to "tastes." The most cited treatise on the subject posits that some individuals desire to work and live apart from others and would require a premium to interact with them.[2]

Claudia Goldin is the Henry Lee Professor of Economics at Harvard University and a research associate and director of the Development of the American Economy Program at the National Bureau of Economic Research.

Presented at the NBER-Spencer conference, "Human Capital in History: The American Record," December 7 and 8, 2012. At its inception, about two decades ago, this chapter benefited from the comments of seminar participants at Columbia University, Indiana University, University of Michigan, and Princeton University, and from suggestions made by Becky Blank, Nancy Folbre, Alan Krueger, Peter Kuhn, and Gavin Wright. In its 2002 incarnation, it profited from comments by Francine Blau and Larry Katz and was an integral part of my Marshall Lectures, University of Cambridge, April 30 and May 1, 2002. The current version has been greatly improved through the able research assistance of Chenzi Xu, a careful reading by Stephanie Hurder, and the comments of my discussant, Cecilia Rouse, and two referees. For acknowledgments, sources of research support, and disclosure of the author's material financial relationships, if any, please see http://www.nber.org/chapters/c12904.ack.

1. The ratio of the (full-time, year-round) weekly earnings of white women to white men increased from 0.631 to 0.792 between 1980 and 2010, and that for all twenty-five-to-thirty-four-year-olds with four years of college increased from 0.736 to 0.832 between 1980 and 2010 (Current Population Survey, Outgoing Rotation Groups). A standard measure of occupational segregation (the dissimilarity index) decreased from 64.5 in 1970 to 51.0 in 2009 using year 2000 codes and from 68.7 in 1970 to 50.7 in 2009 using year 1990 codes (Blau, Brummund, and Liu 2012). See also Jacobsen (1994). Despite these gains, most studies of wage and occupational differences find a substantial unexplained gap, although the unexplained portion has decreased over time. See the literature reviews in Altonji and Blank (1999) and Bertrand (2011); see Goldin (1990) for long-term trends. Bertrand, Goldin, and Katz (2010), however, demonstrate for a group of MBAs that when using detailed data even large raw differences in female-to-male earnings can be "explained" by hours, job experience, and pre-job characteristics such as education.

2. The earliest treatment, as well as the most cited, is Becker (1957).

Yet men and women seem to get along under a wide variety of circumstances. Men often have wives, sometimes daughters and sisters, and by necessity mothers. One cannot attribute to most men a desire for distance from women the same way one might interpret current or past discrimination between other groups, such as blacks and whites, Catholics and Protestants, Arabs and Israelis, and Hindus and Muslims. One might, however, attribute to men a desire for distance from women to protect their status as members of an occupational group.

The model developed here treats discrimination as the consequence of a desire by men to maintain their occupational status or prestige, distinct from the desire to maintain their earnings. (The reason for focusing on prestige rather than wages is later defended.) Prestige, in this setting, is conferred by some portion of "society," the bounds of which will be discussed, and is based on the level of a productivity-related characteristic (e.g., strength, skill, education, ability) that originally defines the minimum needed to enter a particular occupation. But prestige can be "polluted" by the entry of an individual who belongs to a group whose members are judged on the basis of the group's average and not by their individual merits.[3] Men in an all-male occupation might be hostile to allowing a woman to enter their occupation even if the woman meets the qualifications for entry. The reason is that those in the wider society will not know that the woman was qualified and might, instead, view her entry as signaling that the occupation had been altered. She will be seen as "polluting" the occupation.[4]

A woman's entry to an occupation might be a signal of change in the standards for admission because the economy is dynamic. Technological change can reduce the minimum level of the characteristic required for entry. For example, firefighters once had to be strong enough to carry heavy and unwieldy equipment. The advent of lighter hoses diminished the actual physical strength required (although it remains far higher than that for most jobs). Similarly, in certain bookkeeping trades, the ability to add up long columns of numbers in one's head was a skill that comptometers and calculators later replaced and made less valuable.

Society has imperfect information regarding changes in technology and infers change from certain observables. One of these observables is the sex (or any group descriptor, such as race) of new entrants. Thus men might want women barred from their occupation to protect their status even if *no* skill-reducing technological change affected their occupation. Whether or not men in a previously all-male occupation will want to bar the entry of women will depend on the distribution of the productivity-enhancing char-

3. The term "pollution," in this context, is from the anthropological literature and originates in the works of Mary Douglas (Douglas 1966). Women, across many cultures, are separated from men during menstruation, and sexual intercourse is thought to pollute men. These beliefs enforce, and perhaps reinforce, the separation of the sexes in production and consumption.
4. See Akerlof and Kranton (2000) for a related model on the protection of identity.

acteristic in the male and female populations and the minimum level of the characteristic initially required for the occupation in question. Asymmetric information is a key feature of the model.[5]

The model contains predictions about the relationship between occupational segregation by sex and earnings (or the level of the characteristic). The prediction is that sex segregation for men and women will be greater for occupations requiring a level of the characteristic above the female median and that segregation, perhaps surprisingly, will be nonmonotonic with respect to the characteristic.[6] Occupations are more likely to be segregated at the tails of the female characteristic distribution but integrated somewhere toward the middle, generally just below the median of the female characteristic distribution. Occupations requiring a high level of the characteristic will not be integrated unless society has verifiable information regarding qualifications.

The model also suggests how discrimination and earnings respond to changes in the distributions of the characteristic and why knowledge of past distributions helps explain current gender distinctions in the labor market. Evidence consistent with these predictions is presented for various time periods. The model is inherently historical: the past affects the present.

Similar models have been proposed elsewhere. In hierarchical models men require a premium to work with women who have higher occupational status or authority. Other frameworks posit that interactions between men and women reduce productivity because of communication obstacles or the precise opposite—flirting, jealous spouses, and sexual tension—may decrease output or profits.[7] Several versions of the statistical theory of discrimination exist in which men and women as groups differ in some actual or perceived characteristic.[8] Discrimination can reinforce these skill disparities or result in differences in promotion if certain workers are more visible than others.[9]

The pollution theory of discrimination is complementary to other models of discrimination and can be viewed as a hybrid of Becker's original "taste" model with that of statistical discrimination. Rather than assuming taste-

---

5. The type of "asymmetric information" in this model differs from that in most others in which managers have incomplete information about worker ability. In this model, the asymmetry comes from incomplete information by those who confer "prestige" on workers and the group who confers prestige is "society."

6. The median of the characteristic, not its mean, is the key factor because individuals often judge the ability of a group of people by the skills of a random individual drawn from that group.

7. See Lang (1986) on communication. Humphries (1987) considers the explicit problem of sex in the workplace. On the latter, Sophonisba Breckinridge (1906) noted: "It is well known that the unregulated mingling of men and women under conditions of darkness, fatigue, or the excitement due to the constant apprehension of danger may give rise to immoral intercourse. On this account we find women generally prohibited from working in mines, and . . . other forms of employment at night" (107).

8. On statistical discrimination see Arrow (1973) and Phelps (1972), and the interpretation given by Aigner and Cain (1977).

9. See Lundberg and Startz (1983) on discrimination and incentives to acquire skill, and Milgrom and Oster (1987) on visibility.

based discrimination, it seeks the reasons for it. It posits that male employees discriminate against prospective female employees as a way of protecting their prestige in an asymmetric information context. The pollution theory model contains various predictions that are not contained in other models and serves to explain historical features of the labor market that others cannot. A more formal version of the model will make the assumptions and implications clearer.

9.1   A Pollution Theory of Discrimination

9.1.1   Model Setup

Assume there is a productivity related, single-valued characteristic (C), such as ability, strength, skill, education, or determination. The attribute need not be inherent. It can be acquired and can be altered by complementary factors such as machinery.[10] The characteristic is continuously distributed, perhaps differentially, among men and women. The entire distribution of C for males and the median of the female distribution are known by all workers as well as all others in society.[11]

The model contains two periods. In period 1 only men have labor market jobs, known as "occupations," and women are in the home. Men remain in the *same* occupation in period 2 and women enter the labor force in period 2.[12]

Every occupation, i, requires a minimum level of the characteristic, C_i, and no one with a C below that level can produce at all in occupation i. In addition, productivity in occupation i does not rise with C above the minimum required in each occupation. For example, suppose the firefighting occupation requires a C of 100. An individual with a 90 cannot produce at all in that occupation and one with a 110 will be overqualified.

Workers are paid according to their productivity (that is their level of C) in each occupation and will therefore sort into occupations. In equilibrium,

10. The characteristic can be thought of as one's strength rating on a particular machine. Refinements to the machine can lead weaker individuals to be measured as stronger. The characteristic can also be a skill or an education level that can be augmented over time.

11. Knowledge of the full distribution for males and females might allow individuals to figure out the "correct" number or proportion of women who ought to be in each occupation, given that no occupations above it in the skill distribution are "discriminating." To get around that problem, individuals here have knowledge only of the female median. In the case of the symmetric form of the model, given below, in which both men and women enter in period 2 knowledge of each distribution is assumed.

12. I do not directly consider why women enter the labor market in period 2. One possibility is that the characteristic distribution for women shifts to the right because of an increase in education or more of a complementary physical capital. The justification for why men remain in their period 1 occupations in period 2 might be that specific skills are accumulated or that there are sufficiently large moving costs.

therefore, each value of C_i in period 1 defines one and only one occupation for men.[13]

Men receive utility from their income, (Y_i), and the prestige of their occupation, (C_i^*), where prestige is the minimum level of C required for the occupation as perceived by society.[14] Women receive utility from the income of their occupation in period 2 and the value of their home production in period 1, although that will be ignored here.

It is convenient to assume that the demand for all goods is perfectly elastic and that the production technology is characterized by constant returns to scale. The "small country" and production technology assumptions ensure that the wage does not depend on the number of individuals in the occupation and, consequently, that there can be no wage effects or "crowding."[15] These assumptions are relaxed below. They ensure that a simple version of employee discrimination—the protection of income—is not confused with the protection of prestige in the pollution theory setup.

But—and this is crucial—because the world is dynamic, an occupation may not require the same level of C in period 2. *Technology shocks, $\Omega = 1$*, that reduce skill requirements occur between periods 1 and 2. A value of Ω that is either 0 or 1 is randomly drawn for each occupation and if $\Omega = 1$ the shock lowers the minimum level of C required for an occupation. The realized value of Ω for occupation i is known only to those in occupation i in period 1. Women enter the labor market in period 2 and apply to the various occupations.

Thus the utility received by men in period 1 is $U^{M,1} = U^M(Y_i^1, C_i^{*,1})$, where $C_i^{*,1}$ is the prestige received by occupation i in period 1. The first period utility is equivalent to $U^M(C_i^1, C_i^{*,1})$ since income in period 1 is a function of the person's level of C and also the minimum needed for the occupation in period 1. In period 2, however, utility received by men is $U^{M,2} = U^M(Y_i^2, C_i^{*,2})$, which may not be equivalent to $U^M(C_i^1, C_i^{*,1})$ if $\Omega = 1$.

Whatever the value of Ω, men will want to maintain their level of prestige. Prestige, C_i^*, arises from how *society* views the C level of an individual's occupation. The level of C associated with an occupation in period 1 is known to everyone. But only those in the occupation know whether $\Omega = 1$. Because male workers remain in their period 1 occupation during period 2,

---

13. In this simple setup there is no capital, and the workers are "hired" by an entrepreneur who is the first entrant in the occupation.

14. Prestige is different from income or from one's position in the income distribution. But prestige might also be a signal of one's income-earning ability, as in the case of a man who is turned down for a loan because the loan officer thinks the man's occupation has undergone a loss in income-generating ability.

15. Assume the production function takes the form $Q = \lambda \cdot L \cdot C_i$, where L is the number of employees, and C_i is the minimum characteristic level of the occupation, and that each unit of Q sells at the exogenous price P. Therefore the value of the marginal product, and thus the wage, is a function only of C_i and λ.

if there was a technology shock ($\Omega = 1$), their income will decrease. Their characteristic is not being fully utilized and they are misallocated and over-qualified for the job. But even if their income decreases, their prestige can remain just as it was in period 1. Though they are financially less well-off they can maintain equal status.

It is useful to review the informational asymmetries in the setup: what is known to all, to each individual, and to those in an occupation in each of the two periods. The variables known to all, that is, those that are common knowledge are: the distribution of C for men, the median of C for women, and the minimum value of C required for all occupations in period 1, that is C_i^1. Everyone knows his or her own C, but only those in occupation i in period 1 know the value of Ω, that is only they know C_i^2, the value of C required by that occupation in period 2.

Because of the informational asymmetry concerning Ω, the prestige or status associated with being a weaver, printer, doctor, bookkeeper, or widget maker depends on the identity of new workers even if there has been no actual "de-skilling" (even if $\Omega = 0$). The entry of an individual who comes from a group known to have a lower *average* (median) level of skill than that required in the occupation may signal the de-skilling of an occupation even if nothing has changed. Individuals outside the occupation do not know whether the "test" or criterion for entry has changed, and it is costly for them to obtain such information (e.g., trying out for the occupation). Society is the arbiter of prestige and updates its information about the C level required for the occupation by observing the median characteristic of a new entrant.

The C level of a woman is known only to her and can be discerned only by administering a test. Thus the employer for an occupation can determine whether a woman meets the minimum requirements and, once on the job, her fellow colleagues (all men) can also see that she is qualified. But society does not know her qualifications. Had no technology shock occurred between periods 1 and 2, society would know that the female applicant had precisely the same C level as the men already in the occupation. But society does not know the value of Ω. Technology shocks add uncertainty. The question, therefore, is whether male workers in occupation i will resist the introduction of a woman or whether they will be pleased to have her.

9.1.2 Model Equilibrium and Implications: Identical Characteristic Distributions

The characteristic or C distributions for men and women can be identical or can differ, as would be the case if strength were an important part of productivity. It is likely that these distributions changed over time, for example, with the introduction of machinery, the substitution of "brain" power for "brawn" power, and changes in educational attainment.

The C probability distribution for women is given by $g(C^F)$ and that for men is given by $h(C^M)$. Assume, for the moment, the gender-neutral case in

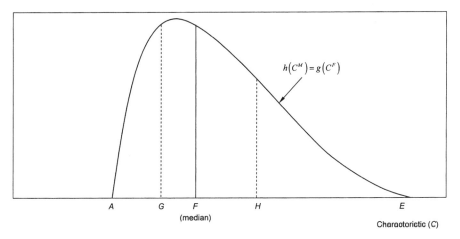

$$h(C^M) = g(C^F)$$

A   G   F   H   E
(median)

Charaotoristio (C)

Fig. 9.1   The model with identical distributions of C for men and women

which the C distributions are identical for men and women, thus $g(C^F) = h(C^M)$, as in figure 9.1, where the median C level is given by F. Recall that only men are employed in occupations in period 1 and that each value of C_i defines an occupation and a wage in equilibrium. Because the characteristic distributions are identical for men and women, women can produce at the minimum required in each occupation. The question is whether men will allow women into their occupation in period 2.

Consider a male employee with a characteristic value somewhere in region FE, for example at H. What is his response to hiring a woman into his occupation? Recall that everyone knows that an H-level of the characteristic is required for the occupation in period 1, and the worker's status is related to society's perception of his characteristic value. Thus in period 1 his utility is given by $U_H^{M,1} = U_H^M(Y_H^1, C_H^{*,1})$.

The world is dynamic and an occupation's level of C can be altered by a technological shock that reduces skill requirements. Handloom weavers required considerably more skill than did factory weavers; cobblers were more skilled than workers assembling shoes after the introduction of the sewing machine; hand bookkeepers probably used more skill than their successors did after the introduction of calculators. One's status can actually be reduced in a dynamic world. But it can also be polluted in a manner that is more apparent than real—by the hiring of workers whose median level of the characteristic is lower than that currently required in the occupation. The introduction of such workers is a signal that the occupation probably underwent change in its skill requirement, even when it did not.[16]

16. This notion of pollution is similar to "tipping" in housing segregation models. See Pan (2011) on tipping models in occupational segregation by sex.

Returning to whether the worker at H would oppose a woman in his occupation, consider the type of signal that hiring a woman would provide and recall that the C level of a particular woman is private information. Assume that society picks a decision rule such that probabilities below 0.5 signal a technology shock for that occupation, that is they signal $\Omega = 1$, and that those above do not, that is they signal $\Omega = 0$. If a female applicant is accepted into the H occupation, society infers whether the occupation underwent change, between periods 1 and 2, by calculating whether:

(1) $$\int_{i=H}^{E} g(C^F)\,dC_i \lessgtr 0.5.$$

Society calculates whether H is above or below the C value of the median woman; that is, the probability a female applicant has a C value above or below H.

In the case under consideration, occupation H requires a C level above the median. Thus if a woman is hired into this occupation society will infer that the occupation has drawn a value of 1 for Ω, and all men in the occupation will suffer a loss in prestige if a woman enters the occupation. Even if Ω were actually 0, women will be barred from entering occupations above the female median to protect that status of existing male workers. Thus male workers above the median of the female distribution will oppose the entry of women in their occupation and those below the median will not oppose their entry.

As in the classic Becker model of discrimination, men in the range FE will demand a premium to fully compensate them for their loss in prestige if women are hired. The premium would increase with the distance from F if the reduction in prestige was always to the value at the female median, thus independent of the initial C_i. The fewer the number of men in the occupation the less costly would be the total compensation.[17]

Rather than fully compensate the men in the occupation for their loss of prestige, it may be less costly to create another occupation for women (at the same level of C). Two occupations having the same minimum level of C can exist within a firm, one for men and another for women (e.g., waiter and waitress, seamstress and tailor, doctor and nurse practitioner, stenographer and accounting clerk). But there may be a cost advantage within each firm of having only one occupation for each level of C. Alternatively, one firm can have only men do a job and another firm can have only women do the same job.

In a competitive equilibrium women will be paid the same as men hav-

---

17. The wage premium demanded can be modeled as a function of the probability that the randomly drawn woman is less qualified, with lower probabilities demanding less compensation. The occupation could be defined by place, firm, or industry. If male machinists, for example, perceive their prestige to depend on the existence of female machinists in *any* firm, an externality could be imposed by one firm on the workers in another. Occupations that are rare across firms will be less likely to be segregated than those that are numerous within firms, since total compensation will be greater the more workers to compensate. In the model, however, the firm cannot provide additional compensation since goods prices are given.

ing equal characteristics, but they will be in a different firm or in a different occupation. Two occupations, or two firm-occupations, will exist that use the same level of skill. They will be found at levels of C above F. But the creation of these all-female occupations could take considerable time. In the meantime, women will be "crowded" into occupations for which they are "overqualified," and these overqualified women will have C levels above the median of the female distribution.

Consider, instead, a male worker at point G. That worker will not perceive his status or prestige polluted if a woman is hired into his occupation. Using the rule set down in equation (1), the probability that the new (female) worker has an attribute value exceeding that of the initial workers is greater than 0.5. Men in occupations below the median of the female distribution will find that women do not pollute their status and these occupations will be integrated. The model predicts that occupations will be segregated in range FE and integrated in range AF.

9.1.3 Model Equilibrium and Implications: Dissimilar Characteristic Distributions

The characteristic distributions may not be identical for men and women or may have been dissimilar in the past and then became equal. An extension of the basic model allows the distributions to be different at the start, but less so with time. The implications are similar yet more revealing about the historical process of sex segregation.[18]

At some distant time men and women may have had characteristic distributions that were so divergent as to be nonoverlapping. The ratio of female to male wages in New England farm communities around 1800, for example, was extremely low, probably below 0.30, and men and women were rarely employed at the same tasks.[19] Given the technology, crop, inherent differences between the sexes, and possibly social custom, women had considerably lower relative productivity in the work force.[20] The industrial revolution in America, beginning around the 1820s, may have shifted the female characteristic distribution to the right and possibly widened both distributions through the differentiation of tasks. A further shift can be associated historically with the increase in education in the first decades of this century and the

18. Various extensions of the basic form of the model are given in the model appendix. These extensions include a symmetric form of the model in which both males and females can pollute, but males are in the occupations earlier.

19. In places that used the plough, women had far lower relative productivity. See Alesina, Giuliano, and Nunn (2011); Bidwell and Falconer (1925); and Goldin and Sokoloff (1982, 1984).

20. Another way of justifying why the female distribution of the characteristic may be to the left of that of men is that until the 1940s both married and single women in the paid labor force (outside the home) were drawn from the less educated portion of the female population. Thus, even though the male and female populations had nearly identical levels of education, the two working populations did not.

evolution of occupations, such as those in the clerical, sales, managerial, and professional sectors, that had higher returns for schooling than did those in manufacturing. As brain power replaced brawn power, the two distributions may have become more similar, if not identical.

In this version of the model, given in figure 9.2, the two characteristic distributions are overlapping but not identical. Similar to the setup before, men are hired into jobs in period 1, say in the manufacturing sector, and they receive occupations depending on their level of C. Women try to enter occupations in period 2 and men respond.

Two regions in figure 9.2 are of interest and two are not. Only women will be employed in AD and only men in BE. Just DF and FB (where $F =$ the female median) offer the possibility of integration. The model predicts that occupations will be segregated by necessity in range AD, integrated in range DF, segregated by design in FB, and by necessity in BE. Only in range FB will there be both male and female occupations, which can be segregated within a firm or firms, that can hire either men or women to perform the same occupation.

Now consider a shift of $g(C^F)$ to the right, resulting in $g'(C^F)$ in figure 9.3, as may have occurred with the increase in education during the first decades of the twentieth century. What is the response? At some point the result must be identical to that outlined above in section 9.1.2. Segregation will exist from the new female median at F' to E and the range of integration will be larger by FF'. Certain occupations, those in range AA', will disappear and others, those in range BB', might be added. But there are several reasons why this transition may take considerable time and why the path to it may be of great interest.

The areas of greatest change will be FF', the new integration range, and

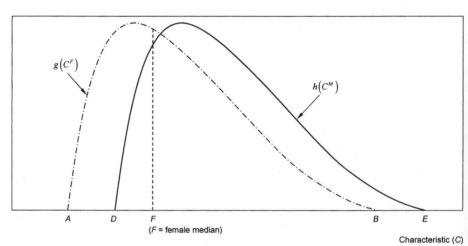

Fig. 9.2   The model with different distributions of C for men and women

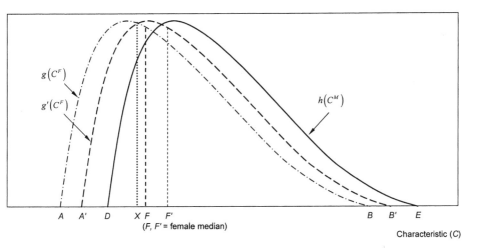

Fig. 9.3   The model with different distributions of *C* for men and women and a change in the *C* distribution for women

BB', the new occupation range. Male workers in range *FF'* might resist integration with prospective female employees if they do not know that the median of the female characteristic distribution has increased, or if they believe that others do not yet know. Once everyone knows the median of the new female characteristic distribution, men in range *FF'* will not be polluted by the presence of women colleagues and will let them enter. In the interim, women in range *FF'* will remain in preexisting "female-only" occupations, should those occupations have been set up.

Women in the range *BB'* will not be able to enter the male occupations for which they are qualified and will have to enter newly created female-only occupations. If the creation of these occupations takes time, they will be "crowded" into the next best alternative in the interim—the occupation at point *B*. Under the "small country" and constant returns assumptions, wages will not change in those crowded occupations. But some female workers will be earning too little given their characteristics. Econometric studies of earnings differences by gender will reveal "wage discrimination" because women will be overqualified, but jobs will receive the correct remuneration given the requirements for the occupation.[21]

9.1.4   Feedback and Wage Effects

The absence of women from the upper tail of the occupational distribution, range *BB'*, even during an interim period may have a lasting impact

---

21. Under these circumstances, a comparable worth policy will not eradicate discrimination but an affirmative action policy might; however, see Coate and Loury (1993) on the potential for such a policy to backfire even when the two groups are identical.

on the perceptions of all workers about the characteristic distribution of women and about occupations that are "appropriate" for young women. If, for example, the characteristic is education and B is "teacher," then women with education levels in BB' will all be teachers rather than principals, lawyers, and doctors. Young women will not have an incentive to attain higher levels of education. The nurse in range FB may have been appropriately placed initially, albeit in a sex-segregated occupation. But at a subsequent date women with a higher level of the characteristic may be inappropriately trained to be nurses due to an absence of opportunities in range BB' or to perceptions of an appropriate career for women. Occupational segregation by sex may produce appropriate financial rewards at one date, but may lead to unfair rewards and incorrect expectations at a later date.

Occupations in range FB (and later in $F'B'$) may become "protected," either through actual barriers to entry or through rhetoric that creates an "aura of gender." Firms may be able to attract men into an occupation only if they can promise that the occupation will remain male only. Once in an occupation, men in range FB have an incentive to use rhetoric and construct a set of norms that inform prospective entrants (and employers) of the occupation's gender, even if the occupation can be performed by either sex. At times this involves the creation of, what may be called, "secondary sex characteristics."[22]

One of Becker's keenest insights in his classic discrimination model is that the economic marketplace has an ameliorative impact on prejudice and that occupational segregation can substitute for the wage effects of discrimination. But occupational segregation may not be a benign consequence if the past affects the present through the formation of expectations, through the appearance of "holes" in the occupational spectrum, and through the institutionalization of barriers. If men infer the median of the female characteristic, rather than knowing it, from the distribution of occupations containing women, adjustment lags—caused by preexisting norms, barriers, and slow informational flows—will lead to an underestimate of the new median for women. This underestimate will lead a greater proportion of men to be hostile to female entrants. Programs and policies that make highly educated and successful women, of the present and past, more visible, serve to counteract the effect.[23]

Dropping either the assumption of exogenous prices or that of constant returns to scale produces wage effects. Integrated and female-only occupations will have changed wages as the relative supply of workers is altered across the attribute spectrum. The number of workers will increase to the right of point X, the crossing point of the previous and new female distribu-

---

22. See Goldin (1990).
23. See, for example, Beaman et al. (2009) on the impact of exposure to female Indian village council chiefs on perceptions of women leader effectiveness.

tions in figure 9.3, and a decrease to the left. The increase and the decrease, as a percentage of previous workers, are greatest at the tails (A' and B') and diminish moving in from both to X. If the change in the wage depends on the percentage increase in workers, the wage will rise most at A' with diminishing impact as one moves toward X. Similarly, the wage will fall from X to B' in an increasing fashion. Male workers to the right of point X have the most to fear from the introduction of female workers and their fear should increase moving toward point B'. Note as well that if workers with similar skills produce goods that are close substitutes, even workers in range $B'E$ will face changed wages with a shift in the skill distribution.

There will be additional wage effects around point B if the female-only occupations in range BB' take time to emerge. Individuals in jobs located between F' and B and all female workers in range BB' will be paid too little given job requirements and individual attributes.

In sum, the implications of the model are that occupations above the median of the female distribution will be segregated and that occupations may be segregated in a nonmonotonic fashion with regard to the attribute and the wage. For some distributions of the attribute, occupations will be segregated in the tails and integrated in the middle of the female distribution. For other distributions, in which the male and female distributions fully overlap at the bottom of the characteristic range, there will be integration at the lower end and segregation at the upper end. And in the upper range, male-only occupations will develop barriers against female entrants and female-only occupations may be created in that range to use women's talents.

9.2   Taking the Model into the Real World

Exactly how one takes the model to the real world depends on the spatial boundaries of human association.[24] Male firefighters or police officers, to take two examples, may perceive their status to depend on the sex composition of their own police station or firehouse. Some, however, may believe that their stake encompasses a wider geographic area, such as the municipality or the state. Thus, if employees in an occupation are scarce within firms (e.g., bookkeepers in small offices, teachers in rural areas), there can be wide differences in the gender of an occupation across space. Much will depend on whether employees have knowledge of their counterparts in other firms and view them as equals, as well as whether their status is conferred by the same societal group.

Certain assumptions can be amended in application, in particular that a specific female entrant's C level is unknown to society. The degree to which her admission into the occupation will pollute the status of existing male workers is dependent on the assumption that she is viewed as a random draw

---

24. Frank (1985) would call these "frog ponds."

from the female distribution. Credentialization of occupations (e.g., degrees, licenses, admission tests) in the upper end of the characteristic distribution could eliminate the negative signal provided by hiring a woman particularly if the credential were well known and verifiable. The absence of occupations that fully use women's talents, resulting in "overqualified" women workers, can result in low wages ("wage discrimination") given characteristics and can reinforce discrimination. Credentialization could eliminate these effects.[25]

The model developed here explains why men object to women's entering their occupations apart from their desire to maintain wages. Several reasons have motivated the construction of the model in this fashion. For one, it is too obvious that individuals and groups object to having their earnings depressed and their jobs endangered. Union members erect barriers to entry even when the prospective hires are of the same sex, race, and ethnicity. Nationals want to restrict immigration to protect their earnings and jobs.

Men have objected to having women in their occupation even when earnings could not have depressed their entry and in cases even after earnings were eroded by changes in either supply or technology. Men objected to female manufacturing workers during World War II even though men were promised "equal pay for equal work."[26] In other cases the number of women attempting to enter the contested occupation was far too small to have depressed wages by more than a trivial amount. And there are examples of all-male occupations in which relative wages for the occupation decreased long before women were allowed to enter. Women were first employed as bank tellers as an emergency measure during World War II even though the relative wages of male bank tellers had already decreased a decade or more earlier.[27]

To demonstrate the potential importance of the pollution theory, I explore the historical record to find evidence concerning the empirical implications derived from the model. The implications are related to occupational segregation and its change over time, the relationship between occupational segregation and the characteristic (or earnings) distribution, the degree of and emergence of "wage discrimination," and the role of credentialization and incentive pay in integrating occupations by sex.

9.2.1 Occupational Segregation: Origins and Maintenance

Historically, occupations have been highly segregated by sex. A national index of dissimilarity by sex across all occupations remained fairly constant

---

25. Licensing, by restricting entry, could disadvantage women (see, for example, the literature review in Law and Marks [2009]). Kleiner and Krueger (2013), using recent data, conclude that licensing may restrict entry but does not appear to differentially impact women. Law and Marks (2009), using historical data, find that some licensed occupations (e.g., teaching) had reduced female representation but others (e.g., engineers, pharmacists) saw increased numbers.

26. See the discussion in Milkman (1987).

27. Strober and Arnold (1987) discuss the switch from male to female tellers in the 1940s.

at about 0.66 from 1900 to 1950 although that for the nonfarm labor force fell from 0.75 to 0.67. Since 1950 the index has steadily declined, especially in the decades of the 1970s and 1980s. It is now between a quarter and a third lower than it was a half century ago.[28]

Although some occupations have changed sex over time (e.g., librarians, bank tellers, teachers, telephone operators, sales positions), new occupations and new industries (e.g., clerical positions in the 1910s, electrical machinery operatives in the 1920s) as well as those experiencing substantial growth in demand (e.g., teachers in the nineteenth century, stenographers) are most likely to become "feminized."[29] Several occupations that were integrated by necessity during wartime were quickly feminized thereafter (e.g., bank tellers) whereas others returned to being male dominated (e.g., craft jobs in manufacturing). Some occupations were feminized slowly and incompletely (e.g., sales, teaching), whereas the process was swift and complete in others (e.g., telephone operators, typists, secretaries).

Most occupations are not inherently male or female. Instead, they often gain what I have termed an aura of gender through a rhetoric that surrounds the labor market, by the evolution of certain norms, and the use of particular forms of physical capital. The origin of these differences can often be found in factor endowments, as well as other factors.

Dairying in the early nineteenth century, for example, was considered men's work in the East but women's work in the Midwest, where a male milker was thought to be doing "women's work." Farmers in the East had smaller farms and less fertile land than in the Midwest. Thus male agriculturalists in the East had little else to do than milk cows and run the dairy. Factor endowments influenced gender roles.[30]

For example, when typists were primarily men, it was claimed that typing required physical stamina. But later, when typing became a female occupation, it was said to require a woman's dexterity.[31] Meatpacking and slaughtering establishments in the 1890s had labor forces that were virtually all male and who claimed that women should not be employed in the trimming room and cutting floor because "handling the knife" was not women's

---

28. On long-term trends in occupational segregation using a consistent set of occupations, see Jacobs (1989); for the 1970 to 2010 period, see Blau, Brummund, and Liu (2012). A more relevant index, particularly for the model developed here, would use firm- or city-level data. Blau (1977) analyzes the effects of sex segregation using data on the fraction female by firm for occupation-city cells.

29. According to Garrison (1979), male librarians became administrators during the period of demand growth. On more recent changes in occupational segregation, see Reskin and Roos (1990).

30. Earlier in US history, before the fertile lands of the Midwest were populated, native-born women did some dairying but did not work in the fields. "In [colonial] New England only men . . . were to be seen in the fields," according to Bidwell and Falconer (1925, 116). Recent arrivals from Germany, however, worked alongside their husbands and brothers in the fields. Once again, factor endowments and income levels altered gender roles.

31. See Davies (1982).

work. The use of female strikebreakers in 1904 ultimately led to the hiring of women in sausage making. But even though Slavic women were hired as meat trimmers, women were not given entrée to the cutting floor.[32]

As Caplow (1954) has noted in his insightful work on occupations, "Any job for which only women are employed is likely to be classified as delicate, or even as monotonous."[33] Occupations and industries acquire secondary sex characteristics that serve to reinforce small initial differences in the degree of strength, stamina, or intensity demanded on the job. "The use of tabooed words, the fostering of sports and other interests which women do not share, and participation in activities which women are intended to disapprove . . . all suggest that the adult male group is to a large extent engaged in a reaction *against* feminine influence."[34]

Union rules and firm policy have also been used to restrict the entry of women. Unions have erected barriers to the hiring of women in various crafts. Molders working in foundries in the 1910s were fined for instructing women in their trade.[35] The Cigar-Maker's International Union, organized in 1851, excluded women (and blacks) in its constitution.[36] Rigid, formal barriers have existed in many professions, such as law and medicine.[37] Firms hiring office workers had personnel policies not to hire women in certain occupations but to hire women exclusively in others.[38] Advertisements for jobs listed the gender of the job until sex became a protected group at the federal level through the Civil Rights Act of 1964.[39]

When women manage to slip through the barriers, intimidation is often a last resort. Female firefighters and police officers have successfully sued municipalities for sexual harassment with intent to create a hostile work environment and for tampering with tests to make women, but not men, fail. In *Berkman v. City of New York*,[40] two female firefighters were physi-

---

32. See the account by Abbott and Breckinridge (1911). "There seems to be a strong objection in the community to the employment of women in the trimming-room, on the ground that 'handling the knife' is not women's work. It is difficult to justify this prejudice on any logical ground since it has always been recognized that a woman could suitably handle a knife in her own kitchen" (639). Although women linked, twisted, and tied the sausage after the strike, the packing of sausage in the casing, which used machinery, remained men's work.

33. Caplow (1954, 233).

34. Ibid., 239, italics in original.

35. US Department of Labor, Women's Bureau (1920) reported: "The molders' union did not admit women even during the war. . . . By the rules of this organization members are fined for teaching a woman any part of a trade. . . . A further reason is the fact that core making . . . is regarded as one of the stages in the apprenticeship of a 'molder.' Unless all the stages . . . are open to women the introduction of woman core makers complicates and disrupts trade regulations" (34). See also Kanter (1977) on the training of managers by others within firms.

36. Abbott (1907, 16). The union altered its constitution in 1867 to allow the excluded groups to become members. A decade later, in 1877, women were used as strikebreakers.

37. See Morello (1986) on lawyers and Harris (1978) on professions in general.

38. See Goldin (2006) and the material in section 9.1.3.

39. See Darity and Mason (1998) for examples of advertisements with the specified sex and race and for a discussion of state laws that preceded the Civil Rights Act of 1964 and their lack of enforcement.

40. U.S. District Court, 626 F. Supp. 591, 1985.

cally harassed and the physical test for advancement from the probationary position was altered. Three female firefighters successfully sued the Reedy Creek Improvement District and Walt Disney World for harassment.[41] Male firefighters had displayed lewd pictures in the fire station and engaged in vulgarities with the goal of preventing female trainees from receiving instruction. In *Ramona Arnold v. City of Seminole, Oklahoma*, police officers sexually harassed a female officer with intent to create a "hostile and offensive working environment."[42]

Abbott tells of a woman and her daughters who learned to use the mule in a Waltham textile mill but were forced to leave when the "men made unpleasant remarks."[43] Firm managers and supervisors interviewed at the end of each of the world wars noted that it was virtually impossible to integrate occupations incrementally from 100 percent male.[44]

Even though credentials and tests may initially be barriers to women's entry, a woman who has earned a verifiable and known credential or passed a test of known quality cannot be viewed as a polluter. Thus the growth of credentials can increase integration and reduce "wage discrimination."

9.2.2   Manufacturing Occupations in the Early Twentieth Century

Occupations and industries have been overwhelmingly segregated by sex throughout history, although segregation was more extreme a century ago than it is today, particularly in manufacturing.[45] Integrated occupations in manufacturing around the turn of the twentieth century were found in a handful of industries (e.g., textiles, apparel, tobacco, shoes, printing, and paper). Further, when men and women occupied the same job in the same firm, remuneration was invariably by the piece, not time. Piece-rate work may have enabled firms to pay males and females different amounts despite having the same occupational title and working in the same firm. For example, male piece-rate compositors who worked in integrated firms—those having both male and female compositors—earned on average 36 percent more than did female piece-rate compositors.[46]

Many industries in the early 1900s had no integrated occupations and a large group of them (hiring more than 60 percent of all male operatives) had virtually no female operatives. Industrial segregation by sex in the manufacturing sector measured by an index of dissimilarity was 61 in 1890 and fell to 33 in 1960.[47] Industries were so highly sex segregated in 1890 that more than 60 percent of male operatives could not have shared the same

41. *Orlando Sentinel*, October 29, 1996, p. D1.

42. U.S. District Court, 614 V. Supp. 853, 1985.

43. Abbott (1909, 92).

44. See US Department of Labor (1920). This was particularly true of firms having a large number of men in an occupation.

45. See, for example, the discussion in Goldin (1990, chapter 3).

46. Goldin (1990, table 3.6, 81).

47. The index of dissimilarity is used where the unit of observation is the two-digit SIC industry in 1890 and 1960. See Goldin (1990, table 3.5, 80).

industrial-occupational title with a female. Virtually no female operatives were employed in twenty-three "male intensive" industries (e.g., agricultural implements, iron and steel, lumber) in 1890. Of the 230,000 production workers in foundry and machine shop products in the United States in 1890, just 1,200 were women. Almost 70 percent of all female operatives were in just two industries—textiles and clothing.[48]

Yet "wage discrimination" was rather small among male and female operatives across the manufacturing spectrum around 1900.[49] Attribute differences (e.g., total work experience, years in the occupation, tenure on the job) explain much (65 percent) of the disparity in earnings and another portion is due to differences in the productivity of unskilled men and women paid by the piece (15 percent).[50] Despite the introduction of machinery throughout the manufacturing sector, brute strength was still important and highly rewarded. All of this suggests that the male and female distributions of C were rather far apart in 1890. But these facts cannot explain all industrial and occupational segregation by sex.

Certain occupations and industries were integrated (e.g., in printing and publishing, textiles). Yet other industries were formed entirely around male workers, for whom entry-level occupations were often used as screening and training grounds for higher-level occupations to isolate the higher-level occupations from integration, and to ensure that selection to them was from a pool of male workers, entire industries were segregated.[51] These industries were organized in ways that differed radically from those in the female-intensive and mixed sectors. But it is not clear whether the differences were due to strength and skill requirements, the need for apprenticeships, higher costs of having division of labor, or the absence of piece-rate work.[52]

Because considerable strength was required in manufacturing work in the past, the male and female characteristic distributions may not have over-

48. US Census Office (1895), and also Goldin (1990, table 3.5, 80).

49. On "wage discrimination," see Goldin (1990, chapter 4).

50. The 15 percent figure comes from an analysis of the earnings of men and women in the same occupations (in this instance it was the bundling of kindling wood), paid by the piece in firms that hired both male and female workers. See Goldin (1990, 104).

51. One observer commented on the integration of certain parts of the metal industry: "The displacement of the boy has one serious disadvantage. When boys worked at these tasks it was possible to pick out the clever and ready, who might be expected to become leading men and foremen. The girls do not furnish material for this purpose. . . . This at first unforeseen development will, in the view of many superintendents, check the tendency to replace boys with girls in many of the lighter occupations" (US Senate 1910, vol. XI, 15).

52. Milkman (1987) demonstrates differences in the organization of work between the automobile and electrical industries around 1940. Greenwald (1980) documents hostility toward women workers during World War I. "Ordinarily, welding had been one stage in the apprenticeship of a machinist. During the war the process was separated for the first time from this larger training program. . . . The employment of women as core makers in railroad foundries presented molders with a similar challenge. . . . Since the production of cores was a distinct stage in the training of apprentices, the molders' union strongly objected to the separation of core making from the entire program of training" (117). It is not clear whether these apprenticeship stages were necessary to the entire production process or whether they were maintained to prevent female workers from entering lower-skilled positions.

lapped entirely and the male distribution may have had a longer right-hand tail, whereas the female distribution may have had a longer left-hand tail. In terms of the predictions of the framework regarding where occupational segregation would be found, the evidence corroborates the notion that segregated occupations in manufacturing were found at the tails of the female earnings distribution.

On average, female hourly earnings for occupations that were gender segregated were nearly identical to those that were integrated (weighted by the number of female employees). Among the few integrated occupations were some in printing and publishing, almost unique in early twentieth-century manufacturing in the employment of relatively well-educated production workers.[53] The segregated occupations, however, were found both at the very bottom and at the very top of the female earnings distribution. For example, in clothing and tailoring, women in the female-only trade of buttonhole maker "earn the highest wages among the female hand workers."[54] Most firms, in addition, had female supervisors who were among the highest paid female shop floor workers.

9.2.3   Office Work in the Mid-twentieth Century

With the shift from manufacturing to clerical and office jobs and the substitution of brains for brawn, male and female characteristic distributions began to have greater overlap. In the data set I will soon describe, male clerical workers in 1940 had just 0.4 more years of schooling than female clerical workers (11.5 years for women and 11.9 for men; see table 9.1 columns [5] and [6]). Men in these jobs had more years of college and advanced degrees, but the bulk of office workers at that time had only high school diplomas. Job experience was a bit different by sex. Men worked about 2.6 years more with the current firm (10.2 years for men and 7.6 for women) and 2.4 years more in office work generally (12.8 versus 10.4).

An important implication of the model is that when women first enter the labor force they will be barred from occupations that require skills above the median productive characteristic in the female distribution. Another implication is that firms will find it advantageous to use the talents of these women by creating "all female" occupations around that level of skill. Alternatively or in conjunction, occupations that had previously existed could be transformed into female occupations especially if employment in them was growing rapidly and there had been few men in them to protect the occupation.

To investigate these implications I examine an extensive set of data on clerical and office workers in 1940. The data were gathered from archival records relating to US Department of Labor, Women's Bureau Bulletin no. 188 (1942), which concerned the personnel policies of firms and the characteris-

---

53. See US Department of Labor (1905). Printing and publishing was also unique because its union enabled the integration by sex of occupations in the twentieth century.

54. On women's occupations and earnings in the clothing industry, see US Senate (1910, vol. I, 458).

Table 9.1   Earnings functions for male and female office workers, 1940

Dependent variable	Female (1) Coefficient (s. e.)	Female (2) Coefficient (s. e.)	Male (3) Coefficient (s. e.)	Male (4) Coefficient (s. e.)	Female (5) Means	Male (6) Means
Log of full-time yearly salary					6.95	7.34
Total office experience	0.0320	0.0315	0.0507	0.0483	10.35	12.77
	(0.00220)	(0.00368)	(0.00240)	(0.00608)		
Total office experience squared $\times 10^{-2}$	–0.0588	–0.0577	–0.0804	–0.0766		
	(0.00613)	(0.0097)	(0.00507)	(0.0109)		
Experience with current firm	0.0154	0.0151	0.0131	0.0129	7.58	10.2
	(0.00155)	(0.00199)	(0.00155)	(0.00288)		
Years schooling	0.0393	0.0368	0.0605	0.0551	11.5	11.9
	(0.00364)	(0.00555)	(0.00343)	(0.00632)		
Married	–0.00760	–0.00774	0.140	0.131	0.197	0.484
	(0.0147)	(0.0186)	(0.0169)	(0.0197)		
Sex ratio (fraction female or male) of current occupation		–0.818		–0.588	0.711	0.733
		(0.350)		(0.233)		
Sex ratio squared		0.720		0.659		
		(0.305)		(0.182)		
Constant	6.151	6.339	5.978	6.184		
	(0.0472)	(0.115)	(0.0470)	(0.139)		
Number of observations	1,393	1,393	1,491	1,491		
R^2	0.484	0.504	0.626	0.648		

Source: 1940 Office Worker Survey (see data appendix). Goldin (1990) uses a smaller sample of records; Goldin (2006) uses the expanded sample used here.

Notes: Columns (2) and (4) clustered (by occupation) standard errors are in parentheses. "Total office experience" is the sum of all work experience in offices. "Sex ratio" is the fraction female for column (1) and fraction male for column (2) in each of the seventy-five occupations in the sample. Only observations with complete information on education were used; that is, missing values in any of the entries (e.g., years in high school) are excluded. Earnings use the "usual" salary per pay period and are "annualized" to get the (full-time) annual salary for a forty-hour per week and fifty-two-week per year worker.

tics of office workers in 1940. Two separate sets of related data were collected by the Women's Bureau and later deposited in the US National Archives in Washington, DC: individual worker records and firm-level information.

Individual worker information was collected by the Women's Bureau from personnel records and surveys of individual workers in firms across several major cities (see data appendix). I sampled almost 3,000 records for workers in Philadelphia. These records contain detailed information on the workers' office employment history including information on their first job, current job, marital status, education, and earnings. The number of workers surveyed by the Women's Bureau was so large that about one-fourth of all Philadelphia's office workers were included in the survey.[55]

55. See US Department of Labor, Women's Bureau (1942, no. 188-5, 2). The Women's Bureau noted that only the Philadelphia data had complete education and other personal information.

The Women's Bureau also surveyed firms about their personnel policies concerning office workers. The firm-level records contain information on the numbers of office workers hired and a host of personnel policies including the office occupations that were limited to men or to women by company policy and whether the firm discriminated on the basis of race, ethnicity, marital status, and age (see appendix figure 9A.1). I collected and tabulated all extant information from these surveys for three cities: Philadelphia, Kansas City, and Los Angeles.

Firm responses in these records were remarkably candid and reflected the norms of the day, the absence of regulations concerning protected groups, and, on occasion, the desire of firms to demonstrate generosity by their preferential employment of married men during the Great Depression. Few inhibitions were revealed about discrimination on the basis of race and religion. In Philadelphia, for example, of the ninety-seven firms having ten or more males and ten or more females in clerical positions, thirty firms, or 31 percent, specifically stated that they had a company policy not to hire "Negroes" or "colored."[56] Of the ninety-seven firms, sixty-five had at least one job that was reserved by company policy to men, sixty-nine had at least one job reserved to women, and fifty-nine reserved jobs to both. The data for each of the three cities in the sample are given in table 9.2.

Taking the model's implications to the data is complicated by the fact that, unlike in the model, the characteristic on which productivity is based in the real world is generally not single-dimensional. A weighted average of factors that impact productivity is used to obtain a measure of the level of the characteristic. I use the office worker sample from Philadelphia to estimate a full-time annualized earnings regression for males and females, as given in table 9.1, columns (1) and (3). Log of full-time annual earnings is regressed on a set of productivity enhancing factors: total office experience, its square, tenure with the firm, and years of education; marital status is also included.

Female employees were not necessarily paid their full marginal product due to various factors, including that their occupations were limited to those that did not involve much advancement in the firm. Therefore, I evaluate their aggregate skill level using their observables (e.g., education, experi-

---

Although they collected data from personnel records in other cities, their resources allowed them to do interviews with workers only in Philadelphia, it appears.

56. Many firms did not think they were discriminating when they barred blacks. For example, in answer to the question, "what are the firm's policies with regard to race and color?" the Pennsylvania Railroad stated, "no discrimination as to race; no colored people hired in office." Du Pont's statement "no negroes in clerical jobs" was echoed in many responses. Some firms may have been commenting on the fact that the firm currently employed "no negroes," but many specifically stated the reason why (e.g., Philadelphia Electric stated, "employees refuse to work with colored people in the clerical field") or that they barred a range of workers (e.g., "Jewish girls not for office"). Mr. Simpson, of the Philadelphia Gas Works, gave the fullest statement: "He said they get few Jewish or negro applications for clerical jobs. He doesn't feel that negroes can be placed with the whites on clerical jobs. There are some Jewish clerical workers but a very small percentage of the total. . . . He thought it was better not to have very many." 1940 Office Firm Survey; see data appendix.

Table 9.2   Firms with restricted occupations by race and gender, 1940

City	Firms having ≥ 10 male and ≥ 10 female office workers	Number of firms (%) with race restrictions	Number of firms (%) with any restrictions on occupations by sex		
			Female only	Male only	Both
Philadelphia, PA	97	30 (31)	65 (67)	69 (71)	59 (61)
Kansas City, MO	39	19 (49)	29 (74)	26 (67)	22 (56)
Los Angeles, CA	83	18 (23)	47 (57)	49 (59)	39 (47)

Source: 1940 Office Firm Survey (see data appendix).

Notes: Only firms with ten or more men and ten or more women in office or clerical occupations are shown. Race and gender restrictions were described on a form similar to that in figure 9A.1.

ence) weighted by the coefficients from the male equation. That is, I use table 9.1, column (3) coefficients combined with the female means given in column (5). This method essentially gives the earnings of a female had she been paid like a male. I then add to this value the residual calculated from the female earnings regression in column (1) to account for unobservable traits that made some individuals better suited to certain occupations. The overall mean is, of course, unchanged, but the mean for certain occupations is higher and for others is lower.

Computed in this way the median (full-time, annualized) income for female workers is $1,318 per year (1940 dollars), whereas the raw median for women was $1,020. About 35 percent of male office workers had annualized salaries below $1,318. The median for the male distribution is $1,560. The full-time annualized earnings distribution for all male office workers is given in figure 9.4. The median for females, according to the procedure just outlined, is drawn at $1,318. I now examine which occupations (in firms having ten or more males and ten or more females) were restricted to men only and to women only.[57]

A listing of the clerical occupations in the Philadelphia sample from the Women's Bureau is given in table 9.3. I have matched these occupations to those given in the firm-level surveys and also to those in the office worker sample from which I obtain the annualized earnings. But some of the occupations listed by the firms on the survey were specific to each firm and harder to match.

Firms in Philadelphia (with more than ten male and female office workers)

57. I limit the analysis to firms with ten or more employees by sex to have a sufficient number of employees in each occupation and to have both males and females employed in each firm. Although many of the surveyed firms were small, the vast majority of workers were in firms that met this restriction: 94 percent in Philadelphia, 93 percent in Los Angeles, and 78 percent in Kansas City.

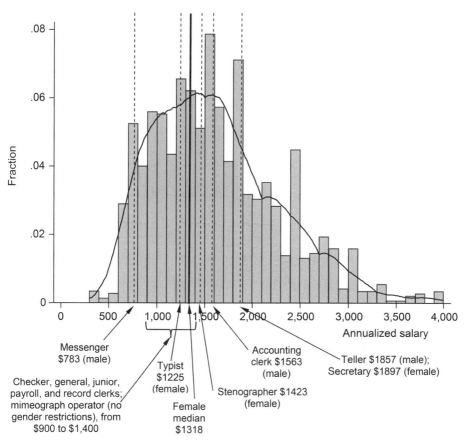

Fig. 9.4   **Earnings distribution for male clerical workers in Philadelphia and mean earnings in certain gender-restricted and unrestricted clerical occupations among Philadelphia firms, 1940**

Sources: 1940 Office Worker Survey and 1940 Office Firm Survey. See data appendix.

Notes: "Annualized earnings" assumes full-time workers (see notes to table 9.1). The male distribution is for annualized earnings in 1940 (histogram with 47 bins of $100 width). The line drawn is the kernel density. For drafting purposes, earnings in the graph are truncated at $4,000, which omits about 3 percent of the sample. The female median is computed by estimating a log earnings regression of the men in the sample who completed elementary school, where the regressors are education in years, office experience, office experience squared, firm experience, and whether currently married (see table 9.1, column [3]). Women's earnings are estimated by giving women the male coefficients. The residual from the equation for women (table 9.1, column [1]) is added to include the unobserved component. There were 1,393 men and 1,491 women in the sample who had completed elementary school. The occupations listed in the diagram above were among the more-common ones given in response to the question, "which jobs are open to men (women) only?" asked on the 1940 Office Firm Survey (see figure 9A.1 for a facsimile of the survey). Each occupation is listed with the group (male, female) to which it was often restricted and the mean annualized earnings for that group. The fraction of all female and male office workers in each of the occupations can be found in table 9.3.

Table 9.3   Clerical occupations and restricted firms: Philadelphia firms, 1940

Clerical occupations	Women's Bureau Bulletin no. 188					Restricted firms	
	(1) No. females	(2) No. males	(3) % of females	(4) % of males	(5) % female	(6) Male occs	(7) Female occs
Stenographic group							
Secretary	1265	58	0.107	0.009	0.956	0	10
Stenography	1721	109	0.145	0.016	0.940	0	20
Typist	1534	183	0.130	0.027	0.893	0	14
Dictating mach. transcriber	195	0	0.016	0.000	1.000	0	5
Correspondent	96	65	0.008	0.010	0.596		
Accounting group							
Accounting clerk	211	312	0.018	0.047	0.403 }	16[a]	0
Audit clerk	48	212	0.004	0.032	0.185 }		
Bookkeeping clerk	239	180	0.020	0.027	0.570	0	5
Bookkeeper, hand	125	176	0.011	0.026	0.415	5	0
Cashier, teller	140	294	0.012	0.044	0.323	6	2[b]
Machine operators							
Address	114	32	0.010	0.005	0.781	0	1
Billing	169	112	0.014	0.017	0.601	0	4
Bookkeeping clerk	430	0	0.036	0.000	1.000	0	6
Calculating	534	114	0.045	0.017	0.824	0	9
Duplicating	60	61	0.005	0.009	0.496		
Key punch	155	27	0.013	0.004	0.852		
Tabulating	57	83	0.005	0.012	0.407		
Other clerks							
Actuarial	54	35	0.005	0.005	0.607		
Bill, statement, and collect.	152	172	0.013	0.026	0.469		
Bond, security, draft	34	181	0.003	0.027	0.158		
Checker	89	71	0.008	0.011	0.556		
Circulation and subscription	153	0	0.013	0.000	1.000		

	(1)	(2)	(3)	(4)	(5)	(6)	(7)
Coin counter	50	36	0.004	0.005	0.581		0
Cost and production	34	317	0.003	0.047	0.097	2	0
Credit	112	64	0.009	0.010	0.636		
Draftsman	0	104	0.000	0.016	0.000	4	0
File	606	170	0.051	0.025	0.781	0	9
Mail	122	74	0.010	0.011	0.622	3	0
Messenger	111	385	0.009	0.058	0.224	14	1
Order and shipping	170	189	0.014	0.028	0.474	2	0
Payroll and timekeeper	174	129	0.015	0.019	0.574		
Rate	0	134	0.000	0.020	0.000		
Receptionist	95	0	0.008	0.000	1.000		
Record	287	174	0.024	0.026	0.623		
Renewal	0	45	0.000	0.007	0.000		
Route	0	62	0.000	0.009	0.000		
Service desk	122	0	0.010	0.000	1.000		
Sorter	108	0	0.009	0.000	1.000		
Statistical	178	226	0.015	0.034	0.441		
Stock	117	324	0.010	0.049	0.265	3	0
Telephone	356	0	0.030	0.000	1.000	0	14
Transit	99	213	0.008	0.032	0.317		
Trouble dispatcher	120	124	0.010	0.019	0.492		
Clerks, n.e.c.:	1309	1246	0.111	0.187	0.512		
TOTAL non-supervisory	11,831	6,675	1.000	1.000	0.639	13	4
Supervisors	379	805	1.000	1.000	0.320		

Sources: Columns (1) to (5) from the US Department of Labor, Women's Bureau (1942, no. 188-5); columns (6) and (7) calculated from the 1940 Office Firm Survey (see data appendix).

Notes: Columns (6) and (7) give the number of firms with ten or more male and female clerical workers that listed the given occupation as one that was restricted to males or to females. There were ninety-seven firms in the data set for Philadelphia that met the size criteria (see text).

[a] The restricted occupation was listed mainly as "accounting."

[b] These were "cashiers" not "tellers."

mentioned twenty-two of the clerical occupations itemized by the Women's Bureau to have been restricted to either males or females (rarely to both).[58] These occupations are noted in table 9.3, columns (6) and (7), which give the number of firms (out of ninety-seven) that mentioned having restrictions. As was noted before, the vast majority of the surveyed firms had some restrictions by sex on occupations. Some firms had just one restricted occupation and some had more than one. Therefore, the number of restricted firms in columns (6) and (7) can sum to more than the ninety-seven firms that had ten or more male and ten or more female clerical employees. Another clear fact is that the occupations that had restrictions were quantitatively important in terms of employment.

Most of the restricted occupations, as I will demonstrate, were those with substantial annual earnings. When a low-paying beginner job (e.g., messenger clerk, office boy) was reserved for males, the restriction was often stated as due to a desire by the firm to use the occupation as a means to select for upper-level positions. In some cases (e.g., stock clerk) the restriction was said to be due to the strength demanded. And in certain other cases (e.g., clerical workers in a steel plant) the position was deemed inappropriate for women who would have to walk through factory areas inhabited only by men.

But in a host of other cases, occupations were listed as being restricted to men with no stated reason. The quantitatively most important of these were in the accounting group. These restricted occupations include accounting clerks, bookkeepers (but not machine bookkeepers), cashiers, tellers, timekeepers, and teller window examiners. About 30 percent of male clerical workers in firms with ten or more male (and female) clerical workers restricted at least one accounting group position to males only. But some firms hired women in these occupations and we know that women were capable of performing these jobs but were barred in some firms. Accounting clerks, for example, were 40 percent female and hand bookkeepers were 42 percent.

Similarly, occupations were often restricted to women only. Among the most prominent were stenographers, typists, various machine operators such as comptometer operators, and secretaries. These, too, were quantitatively important. The three major occupations in the stenographic group that were often reserved for women were almost 40 percent of all employment for women office workers in Philadelphia.

Although I do not know what the earnings were in the precise firms that had occupational restrictions, I do know mean earnings for many of the occupations from the 1940 Office Worker Survey for Philadelphia (see data appendix). As can be seen in figure 9.4, some of the most quantitatively

58. I have listed only occupations that were specifically noted. In some cases the firm representative mentioned "all office jobs" or "all clerks" and in other cases an occupation was mentioned that was highly specific to the firm and probably grouped in table 9.3 in "Clerks, n.e.c."

important positions in the accounting group that were restricted to males had earnings that were higher than the (adjusted) female median.

More surprising is that many positions that were restricted to women also had mean earnings (adjusted female) above the female median. If talented women were barred from a range of positions occupied by men, then firms had an incentive to create positions that used these skills and were restricted to women. The position of accounting clerk was often restricted to males and stenographer to females. Both paid about the same amount and both paid above the female median. Similarly, tellers were a common occupation restricted to males and secretaries were also commonly restricted to females. Once again, they paid about the same amount and considerably above the female median.[59]

What about occupations not listed as restricted? Among the more numerous were certain clerks such as checker, credit, general, junior, payroll, and record clerks; also, correspondents and duplicating machine operators. Female mean earnings for these occupations, calculated in the manner described above, are lower than the median for female office workers; male mean earnings for these occupations are generally lower than the median. Thus there is some evidence that the occupations that were most restricted were those above the female median and the occupations that were least restricted were those below the female median. These occupations were often gender mixed and were not particularly high in the annual earnings distribution.

But I do not want to claim that the model fits the data perfectly. There are several anomalies in taking the data to the model. Typists were generally restricted to females and have earnings just below the female median. Typists for females, just like messenger boys for males, were occasionally used as part of an internal ladder. Telephone operators were almost always restricted to women and their pay was quite low.

To further explore the relationship between earnings and the fraction female in the occupation, I estimate a variant of the (log) full-time annual earnings regression in table 9.1 by adding the sex ratio of the occupation and its square (the sample includes seventy-five separately enumerated occupations). These estimates, and their standard errors clustered at the occupation level, are given in columns (2) and (4).

For women, earnings initially decrease with the sex ratio (females/total employees) of the occupation, hitting a minimum at 57 percent female, and then rise (column [2]). The turning point is almost identical if the controls for

---

59. Kuhn (1993) has developed a different and revealing model to explain the existence of occupations that are reserved for men and women separately. Kuhn's model has specific human capital and a higher mean exit rate for women than men. Employers must bar women from entering occupations that involve extensive training for which the firm will pay. Equivalently, employers have to bar men from entering occupations for which they will receive training but later discover that they would do better to quit and train for a different position.

characteristics (e.g., education, job experience) are excluded and if higher-order terms for fraction female are introduced. Because the average woman was in an occupation that was 71 percent female, female earnings generally increased with the sex ratio of the occupation.[60]

The relationship between the sex ratio (males/total employees) and earnings is similar for the male sample. The turning point occurs at 45 percent male and the average male was in an occupation that was 73 percent male (column [4]). Therefore male earnings, on average, increased with the fraction male in the occupation. Therefore earnings generally increase with gender segregation for women and the same holds for males.

It should also be mentioned that similar relationships are found if education rather than earnings is the dependent variable. The central finding here is that more segregated occupations in office work in 1940 employed women with higher levels of education than average and the same is true for men.[61] Both income and education produce findings that are consistent with the implications of the model that segregation by sex is greater above the median of the characteristic distribution for women.

World War II and the tight labor market of the 1950s were effective in altering gender distinctions in some occupations but far fewer than might have been expected. One of the most radical shifts was in banks. During the war women were employed as bank tellers, practically a male-only clerical occupation in 1926, but after the war men were rarely bank tellers.[62] Interestingly, the relative earnings of bank tellers had declined long before the feminization of the occupation. Thus any real de-skilling of the occupation preceded the entry of women and male bank tellers, it appears, managed to hold on to their occupation long after $\Omega = 1$.

9.2.4   Occupational Segregation Post-1950s

"Wage discrimination" evident in 1940 was strongest for those at the upper end of the education scale and for those with substantial work experience.[63] Occupations reserved for college-educated women were few in number and the list closed to them was extensive. A comprehensive personnel survey

60. This finding might appear to contradict that found in some studies using more recent data, such as Sorensen (1990), although see Filer (1989), who uses 430 occupations and a large group of occupational controls, O'Neill (1983) who estimates a nonlinear relationship, and Macpherson and Hirsch (1995) who use longitudinal data to account for unmeasured individual characteristics and preferences.

61. Among female employees having less than twelve years of schooling, the mean fraction female by occupation was 0.67, whereas the same for female employees having more than eleven years was 0.73.

62. On bank tellers in the mid-twentieth century, see Strober and Arnold (1987) and NICB (1926) for data on the sex composition of tellers and other clerical occupations.

63. Goldin (1986, table 3) reports the coefficients for the male and female earnings equations. "Years of education" has a higher coefficient for females than males, but the college, vocational, and high school dummies are considerably larger for males. Education has a more continuous impact for women, while the effect for men is in steps, possibly allowing them to begin on a different occupational ladder.

taken in the mid-1950s revealed that firms were not accommodating the rapidly increasing group of college-educated women.[64] In terms of figure 9.3, female-only or integrated occupations in the range of *BB'* did not expand and women were crowded into occupations around *B*. It is not surprising, therefore, that when discontent with the labor market was voiced by women in the 1960s the most discontented were the college educated.

Various empirical studies of discrimination in the 1970s and 1980s indicated that the labor market had finally responded and that "wage discrimination" was lower, not higher, among the more highly educated.[65] The decrease in discrimination over the long run may have been due to the emergence of credentialized occupations that could not be polluted by the presence of women. But some of the decline from the 1960s to the 1980s may also have been due to antidiscrimination legislation and to an environment in which discrimination was less tolerated.

There was a time when women with the highest levels of education were barred in subtle and more obvious ways from many high-prestige and high-income occupations and were hired in only a small number of female-dominated occupations, such as teacher, nurse, librarian, and social worker. The clerical data for 1940 demonstrated that higher-educated women in that particular sector were bookkeepers, secretaries, and stenographers, but were rarely found in a host of other occupations in which there were higher-educated men.

But barriers and fetters at the top of the income and education distribution have broken down and most top-earning jobs are far more integrated now.[66] Using the 2009 and 2010 American Community Survey I find that about one-third of all physicians and lawyers (the number one and four occupations by male income) are women and almost half of pharmacists (the number six occupation) are.[67] These fractions would be greater if a younger group were used. The pollution theory would claim that part of the erosion of barriers is due to increased credentialization of women and better information on the abilities of women as a group and of individual women. No stigma is attached to hiring a woman known to be as competent as the existing male employees.

But pollution may still be found in "frog ponds"—workplaces that have highly particular characteristics and skills and in which a group of outside arbiters exists.[68] Frog ponds would include the firehouses and police depart-

---

64. Goldin (1990) discusses Hussey/Palmer personnel surveys taken in 1956–1957 of the major employers in Philadelphia. The fifty interviews reveal that college women, except teachers and nurses, did not have a place in these firms.

65. See Filer (1983) and Blau and Beller (1988).

66. The group of well-integrated occupations still does not include many at the very top including Fortune 500 CEOs, the US Congress, and others at the pinnacle of various professions. See Sandberg and Scovell (2013) for a recent statement about women and leadership with a somewhat different reason for their absence.

67. These rankings use full-time, full-year wage, salary, and business incomes.

68. See Frank (1985) on "frog ponds."

ments mentioned earlier; they would also include trading floors and other parts of the financial sector.[69] But they are, thankfully, rarer now than ever. Pollution may never be eliminated entirely but it has been greatly abated.

9.3 Summary and Implications

I have suggested that discrimination against women is motivated, in part, by the desire of men to protect their occupational status. When work took more brawn than brain, the attribute distributions of men and women were rather far apart. "Men's work" was perceived as better than "women's work" and observing a woman doing a man's job signaled that the man's job had been downgraded, possibly because of a technological shock. In a static context the model predicts ranges of segregation and integration of occupations along the characteristic scale.

As machines substituted for strength, as brain replaced brawn and as educational attainment increased, the distributions of attributes narrowed by sex. The dynamic implications of the framework and the historical evidence are revealing. Important lags existed in the labor market, hampering its ability to devise jobs for new groups of workers. Some lags arose from the institutionalization of occupational barriers, as was the case for firms hiring office workers in the 1930s, and some came from worker expectations about which jobs were appropriate for male and female workers. Older industries remained highly segregated by sex, while newer industries took greater advantage of the newly available female labor supply.

The results of the model depend on the existence of asymmetric information. Women know their own characteristics, as do those who hire them, but others in the community do not. Any mechanism that increases information, such as the credentialization of occupations, will foster integration. Similarly, the visibility of successful women today and in the past may help shatter old stereotypes and increase knowledge about the true distribution of female attributes.

Data Appendix
1940 Office Firm and Office Worker Surveys

Two types of surveys were analyzed in US Department of Labor, Women's Bureau, *Office Work in [Houston, Los Angeles, Kansas City, Richmond, Philadelphia]: 1940*, Bulletins of the Women's Bureau, Nos. 188-1, 188-2,

---

69. On the financial sector, see Smith (2002) on the Salomon Smith Barney $3.2 million arbitration penalty regarding the claim of a sexually hostile work environment in the "boom boom room" case.

188-3, 188-4, 188-5. The originals for both surveys are housed in the US National Archives. These data, in various forms, have been used in Goldin (1990, 1991, 2006).

The surveys were done of firms and of the workers in some of those firms. The firm-level records were filled out by an agent of the firm, often a personnel officer. The individual-level records appear to have been drawn from the personnel records of the firm, although in some cases they appear to have come directly from interviews with the workers.

1940 Office Firm Survey

National Archives, Record Group no. 86, Boxes 496–500. Firms of all sizes were surveyed in the five cities and include those in manufacturing, real estate, retail, banking, insurance, government, telephone, public utilities, railroads, advertising, communications, and professional practices. The surveys covered a large fraction of firms in these cities. For example, fully one-quarter of Philadelphia's office workers were included in the survey (No. 188-5, 2). Records for 539 firms in Kansas City, Los Angeles, and Philadelphia were collected and information was coded on the number of clerical workers by sex employed in 1939, firm policies regarding the employment of women or men in particular occupations, and discrimination with regard to race and ethnicity. See fig. 9A.1 for a facsimile of a 1940 Women's Bureau firm-level survey.

1940 Office Worker Survey

A sample of 1,432 female office workers and 1,564 male office workers was collected for Philadelphia. Information was coded on each regarding age, marital status, education (years and whether individual graduated from each level), total work experience, experience with the current firm, experience in office work, current earnings (measured three ways: earnings last year in 1939, usual salary per pay period, and actual salary for the last pay period), pay period (e.g., weekly, hourly), earnings when the worker began at the firm, whether the worker had ever been furloughed, whether work with the current firm was continuous, current occupation and initial occupation with the firm, among other variables.

Model Appendix

Further Results and Clarifications to the Pollution Theory Model

In the simple form of the model, discrimination and occupational segregation will occur even if the distributions of male and female characteristics are the same. Male employees will treat a female applicant as a polluter in

Department of Labor   Agent _____
Women's Bureau   Date _____
                              OFFICE WORKERS' STUDY 1940

1. Firm name _____ 2. Business_____ 3. Address_____
4. Persons interviewed and positions _____
5. Who are the executives? _____ administrators? _____ professional workers?_____

                                        Men   Women   Total
6. # clerical workers regularly employed 1939 ____   ____   ____
7. # clerical workers employed as extras 1939   ____   ____   ____
8. # new clerical workers taken on in 1939   ____   ____   ____

9. Hours of work: Daily ____ Saturday ____ Total weekly ____ Overtime ____
10. Office organization: list departments _____ types of machines used _____
11. Method of wage payment: monthly, semimonthly, weekly, daily, hourly, piece, bonuses

12. Employment requirements and practices (discuss by job where differences exist)
    a. Hiring: Who hires new employees? _____
        What are beginning rates of pay? _____ system of advancement? _____
    b. Source of applicants _____
    c. Age: Minimum ____ Maximum ____
    d. Marital status:
        Are married women employed? _____
        Are women who marry in service allowed to remain? _____
    e. Sex:
        Which jobs open to men only? _____
        To women only? _____
    f. Educational requirements:
        1. General _____ 2. Special business training _____
    g. Policies with reference to race and color _____

13. General policies:
    Vacations with pay _____ To whom? _____ Length? _____
    Sick leave _____ Dismissal wage and notice_____
    Promotional policy and salary increases _____ Retirement plans _____

Organization: Trade union or other _____

Other welfare activities _____

Fig. 9A.1   Facsimile of 1940 Women's Bureau Office Firm Survey
Note: Questions in bold are those discussed in the text.

occupations above the median and these will remain male-only occupations. The result arises because men enter the occupations in period 1 and women apply to enter only in period 2.

The model can accommodate a symmetric treatment in which both men and women apply for jobs in period 2, although only men enter in period 1. In this case, knowledge of the entire distribution for both men and women is needed. As in the previous setup, no one outside the occupation knows the C level of the prospective entrant although everyone knows the C level of the occupation in period 1. Between period 1 and 2, there is a technology shock Ω that introduces uncertainty regarding an occupation's C level.

The more fully symmetric form of the model treats each new entrant, either male or female, as a potential polluter. Let β = the probability that a male does not pollute an occupation known to have a C level of λ, and α = the probability that a female does not pollute an occupation with a C level of λ. Therefore, using the notation of figure 9.2 where B and E are the upper bounds for the female and male characteristic distributions:

$$\int_{\lambda}^{B} g(C^{F}) dC = \alpha, \text{ and } \int_{\lambda}^{E} h(C^{M}) dC = \beta$$

where, generally, $\beta > \alpha$. Assume that preexisting male workers in the occupation require compensation for hiring a female and that this compensatory payment increases with $[(\beta - \alpha)/\beta]$. That is, the payment increases with the difference in the probabilities that a male and female will not pollute scaled by the probability that one of their own—a male—will. The level of compensation required to hire a female worker will rise with λ, the preexisting C level for male employees.[70]

The results, therefore, conform to those of the asymmetric form of the model, but the compensation demanded will go to zero as the two distributions approach each other and are zero when the distributions are the same. The results will be qualitatively identical to those obtained with the assumption that only women apply for the jobs in period 2. But in this case the range of integrated occupations will widen for any two distributions and will widen progressively as the two distributions approach equality.

The model can be extended to account for different probabilities that a technological shock, $\Omega = 1$, occurred, although there will be little change to the substantive results. Some occupations, firms, and industries can face a higher probability that $\Omega = 1$ and this could enter the likelihood that a female entrant is a polluter.

Similarly, the model can be extended to incorporate the total costs of hiring a woman. In the current model, even one female employee will pollute all male workers in the occupation. The cost of hiring would therefore have to include the total amount of compensation given to preexisting male employees and that would rise with the size of the occupation within a firm. Thus, occupations that are relatively large within firms will be more costly to integrate.[71]

---

70. As in the previous discussion, the amount of compensatory payment will depend on the number of male workers since the hiring of just one woman pollutes the prestige of all men.

71. Other model extensions include: (a) adding a third period to allow men to shift out of occupations experiencing a technology shock; and (b) technology shocks that are positive, as well as negative.

References

Abbott, Edith. 1907. "Employment of Women in Industries: Cigar-Making—Its History and Present Tendencies." *Journal of Political Economy* 15 (January): 1–25.
———. 1909. *Women in Industry: A Study in American Economic History.* New York: D. Appleton and Company.
Abbott, Edith, and S. P. Breckinridge. 1911. "Women in Industry: The Chicago Stockyards." *Journal of Political Economy* 19 (October): 632–54.
Aigner, Dennis J., and Glen G. Cain. 1977. "Statistical Theories of Discrimination in Labor Markets." *Industrial Labor Relations Review* 30 (January): 175–87.
Akerlof, George A., and Rachel E. Kranton. 2000. "Economics and Identity." *Quarterly Journal of Economics* 115 (August): 715–53.
Alesina, Alberto, Paola Giuliano, and Nathan Nunn. 2011. "On the Origins of Gender Roles: Women and the Plough." NBER Working Paper no. 17098, Cambridge, MA.
Altonji, Joseph G., and Rebecca M. Blank. 1999. "Race and Gender in the Labor Market." In *Handbook of Labor Economics*, vol. 3c, edited by Orley C. Ashenfelter and David Card, 3143–259. Amsterdam: North Holland-Elsevier Press.
Arrow, Kenneth. 1973. "The Theory of Discrimination." In *Discrimination in Labor Markets*, edited by Orley Ashenfelter and Albert Rees, 3–33. Princeton, NJ: Princeton University Press.
Beaman, Lori A., Raghabendra Chattopadhyay, Esther Duflo, Rohini Pande, and Petia Topalova. 2009. "Powerful Women: Does Exposure Reduce Bias?" *Quarterly Journal of Economics* 124 (November): 1497–540.
Becker, Gary. 1957. *The Economics of Discrimination.* Chicago: University of Chicago Press.
Bertrand, Marianne. 2011. "New Perspectives on Gender." *Handbook of Labor Economics*, vol. 4B, edited by D. Card and O. Ashenfelter, 1545–92. Amsterdam: Elsevier B.V.
Bertrand, Marianne, Claudia Goldin, and Lawrence F. Katz. 2010. "Dynamics of the Gender Gap among Young Professionals in the Corporate and Financial Sectors." *American Economic Journal: Applied Economics* 2 (July): 228–55.
Bidwell, Percy Wells, and John I. Falconer. 1925. *History of Agriculture in the Northern United States: 1620–1860.* Washington, DC: Carnegie Institution.
Blau, Francine D. 1977. *Equal Pay in the Office.* Lexington, MA: Lexington Books.
Blau, Francine D., and Andrea H. Beller. 1988. "Trends in Earnings Differentials by Sex: 1971–1981." *Industrial and Labor Relations Review* 41 (July): 513–29.
Blau, Francine D., Peter Brummund, and Albert Yung-Hsu Liu. 2012. "Trends in Occupational Sex Segregation by Gender 1970–2009: Adjusting for the Impact of Changes in the Occupational Coding System." NBER Working Paper no. 17993, Cambridge, MA.
Breckinridge, S. P. 1906. "Legislative Control of Women's Work." *Journal of Political Economy* 14 (February): 107–9.
Caplow, Theodore. 1954. *The Sociology of Work.* Minneapolis, MN: University of Minnesota Press.
Coate, Stephen, and Glenn C. Loury. 1993. "Will Affirmative-Action Policies Eliminate Racial Stereotypes?" *American Economic Review* 83 (December): 1220–40.
Darity, William A., and Patrick L. Mason. 1998. "Evidence on Discrimination in Employment: Codes of Color, Codes of Gender." *Journal of Economic Perspectives* 12 (Spring): 63–90.
Davies, Margery W. 1982. *Women's Place is at the Typewriter: Office Work and Office Workers, 1870–1930.* Philadelphia, PA: Temple University Press.

Douglas, Mary. 1966. *Purity and Danger: An Analysis of Concepts of Pollution and Taboo*. London: Routledge and Kegan Paul Ltd.

Filer, Randall K. 1983. "Sexual Differences in Earnings: The Role of Individual Personalities and Tastes." *Journal of Human Resources* 18 (Winter): 82–95.

———. 1989. "Occupational Segregation, Compensating Differentials, and Comparable Worth." In *Pay Equity: Empirical Inquiries*, edited by Robert T. Michael, Heidi Hartmann, and Brigid O'Farrell, 153–70. Washington, DC: National Academy.

Frank, Robert H. 1985. *Choosing the Right Pond: Human Behavior and the Quest for Status*. Oxford: Oxford University Press.

Garrison, Dee. 1979. *Apostles of Culture: The Public Librarian and American Society, 1876–1920*. New York: The Free Press.

Goldin, Claudia. 1986. "Monitoring Costs and Occupational Segregation by Sex: A Historical Analysis." *Journal of Labor Economics* 4 (1): 1–27.

———. 1990. *Understanding the Gender Gap: An Economic History of American Women*. New York: Oxford University Press.

———. 1991. "Marriage Bars: Discrimination against Married Women Workers from the 1920s to the 1950s." In *Favorites of Fortune: Technology, Growth, and Economic Development since the Industrial Revolution*, edited by Henry Rosovsky, David Landes, and Patrice Higonnet, 511–36. Cambridge, MA: Harvard University Press.

———. 2006. "The Rising (and then Declining) Significance of Gender." In *The Declining Significance of Gender?* edited by Fran D. Blau, Mary C. Brinton, and David B. Grusky, 67–101. New York: Russell Sage Foundation.

Goldin, Claudia, and Kenneth Sokoloff. 1982. "Women, Children, and Industrialization in the Early Republic: Evidence from the Manufacturing Censuses." *Journal of Economic History* 42 (December): 741–74.

———. 1984. "The Relative Productivity Hypothesis of Industrialization: The American Case, 1820–1850," *Quarterly Journal of Economics* 99 (August): 461–88.

Greenwald, Maurine Weiner. 1980. *Women, War, and Work: The Impact of World War I on Women Workers in the United States*. Westport, CT: Greenwood Press.

Harris, Barbara J. 1978. *Beyond Her Sphere: Women and the Professions in American History*. Westport, CT: Greenwood Press.

Humphries, Jane. 1987. "'. . . The Most Free From Objection . . .' The Sexual Division of Labor and Women's Work in Nineteenth-Century England." *Journal of Economic History* 47 (December): 929–49.

Jacobs, Jerry. 1989. "Long-Term Trends in Occupational Segregation by Sex." *American Journal of Sociology* 95 (July): 160–73.

Jacobsen, Joyce. 1994. "Trends in Workforce Sex Segregation: 1960 to 1990." *Social Science Quarterly* 75 (March): 204–11.

Kanter, Rosabeth Moss. 1977. *Men and Women of the Corporation*. New York: Basic Books.

Kleiner, Morris M., and Alan B. Krueger. 2013. "Analyzing the Extent and Influence of Occupational Licensing on the Labor Market." *Journal of Labor Economics: The Princeton Data Improvement Initiative* 31 (April): S173–S202.

Kuhn, Peter. 1993. "Demographic Groups and Personnel Policy." *Labour Economics* 1 (June): 49–70.

Lang, Kevin. 1986. "A Language Theory of Discrimination." *Quarterly Journal of Economics* 101 (May): 363–82.

Law, Marc T., and Mindy S. Marks. 2009. "Effects of Occupational Licensing Laws on Minorities: Evidence from the Progressive Era." *Journal of Law and Economics* 52 (May): 351–66.

Lundberg, Shelley J., and Richard Startz. 1983. "Private Discrimination and Social

Intervention in Competitive Labor Markets." *American Economic Review* 73 (June): 340–7.

Macpherson, David A., and Barry T. Hirsch. 1995. "Wages and Gender Composition: Why Do Women's Jobs Pay Less?" *Journal of Labor Economics* 13 (July): 426–71.

Milgrom, Paul, and Sharon Oster. 1987. "Job Discrimination, Market Forces, and the Invisibility Hypothesis." *Quarterly Journal of Economics* 102 (August): 453–76.

Milkman, Ruth. 1987. *Gender at Work: The Dynamics of Job Segregation by Sex during World War II.* Urbana, IL: University of Illinois Press.

Morello, Karen Berger. 1986. *The Invisible Bar: The Woman Lawyer in America, 1638 to the Present.* New York: Random House.

National Industrial Conference Board (NICB). 1926. *Clerical Salaries in the United States, 1926.* New York: National Industrial Conference Board.

O'Neill, June. 1983. *The Determinants and Wage Effects of Occupational Segregation.* Washington, DC: The Urban Institute.

Pan, Jessica. 2011. "Gender Segregation in Occupations: The Role of Tipping and Social Interactions." Working Paper, National University of Singapore. October.

Phelps, Edmund S. 1972. "The Statistical Theory of Racism and Sexism." *American Economic Review* 62 (September): 659–61.

Reskin, Barbara F., and Patricia A. Roos. 1990. *Job Queues, Gender Queues: Explaining Women's Inroads into Male Occupations.* Philadelphia, PA: Temple University Press.

Sandberg, Sheryl, and Nell Scovell. 2013. *Lean In: Women, Work, and the Will to Lead.* New York: Knopf.

Smith, Randall. 2002. "Salomon Is Told to Pay Broker $3.2 Million: Sex-Bias Award Is the Largest to Come from 1997 Settlement after the 'Boom Boom Room' Case." *Wall Street Journal,* December 17. http://academic.udayton.edu/lawrenceulrich /SexualHarassmentSalomonSmithBarney.htm.

Sorensen, Elaine. 1990. "The Crowding Hypothesis and Comparable Worth Issue." *Journal of Human Resources* 25 (Winter): 55–89.

Strober, Myra H., and Carolyn L. Arnold. 1987. "The Dynamics of Occupational Segregation among Bank Tellers." In *Gender in the Workplace,* edited by Clair Brown and Joseph A. Pechman, 107–48. Washington, DC: The Brookings Institution.

US Census Office. 1895. *Report on Manufacturing Industries in the United States, Eleventh Census: 1890. Part I. Totals for States and Industries.* Washington, DC: Government Printing Office.

US Department of Labor. 1905. *Nineteenth Annual Report of the Commissioner of Labor, 1904. Wages and Hours of Labor.* Washington, DC: Government Printing Office.

US Department of Labor, Women's Bureau. 1920. *The New Position of Women in American Industry.* Bulletin of the Women's Bureau, No. 12. Washington, DC: Government Printing Office.

———. 1942. *Office Work in Houston, Los Angeles, Kansas City, Richmond, and Philadelphia.* Bulletin of the Women's Bureau, Nos. 188-1, 2, 3, 4, 5. Washington, DC: Government Printing Office.

US Senate. 1910. *Report on Condition of Woman and Child Wage-Earners in the United States in 19 Volumes.* Washington, DC: Government Printing Office.

Comment   Cecilia Elena Rouse

This chapter is quintessential Goldin. It begins with an important stylized fact, combines that with an interesting cultural or institutional insight, develops an economic model to explain the fact and insight, and then tops it off by testing the model with previously unknown or original data. In this chapter the stylized fact is that men and women work in different occupations; this was particularly true 50 to 100 years ago but continues today, albeit to a lesser extent. Further, women historically have earned less than men when they do work in the (observably) same occupation. There have been many theories advanced to explain these patterns. Among the best known are differences in human capital (both physical and cognitive) (Becker 1957), statistical discrimination (Aigner and Cain 1977; Phelps 1972; and Arrow 1973), and more recently differences in psychological attributes and preferences and social norms (e.g., Bertrand 2011). Perhaps the best-known, and most widely cited, explanation for true discrimination lies in differences in taste for interacting with members of different groups, originally advanced by Gary Becker (1957). However, Goldin's very important insight in this chapter is that while differences in taste, in particular, may explain racial discrimination, many men like women and live along side of them in so many domains. As such, surely differences in "taste"—in its simplest form—cannot lie at the foundation of gender occupational segregation.

And so Goldin sets out to develop what she calls a "pollution theory" of discrimination. The model is not wholly distinct from other models of discrimination but rather pulls them together in a novel way. Basically, the model posits that differences in taste (distaste) for working with women may arise as a desire by men to protect their occupational status. She then adds in some asymmetric information and, in some cases, differences in human capital, to round it out. At the core of the model is a minimum level of a "skill" (which could be any important productivity-related characteristic such as strength, education, or ability) needed to enter a profession. And society confers greater "prestige" on those occupations that require higher levels of the skill. Further suppose that any worker's ability cannot be perfectly observed, but it is generally known/assumed that the mean for women is lower than that for men. If a woman enters a previously all-male profession, that could arise because either she is qualified or because of an unobserved technological change that has lowered the level of skill required to do the

Cecilia Elena Rouse is dean of the Woodrow Wilson School of Public and International Affairs and the Lawrence and Shirley Katzman and Lewis and Anna Ernst Professor in the Economics of Education at Princeton University. She is the founding director of the Princeton University Education Research Section, is a member of the National Academy of Education, and is a research associate of the National Bureau of Economic Research.

For acknowledgments, sources of research support, and disclosure of the author's material financial relationships, if any, please see http://www.nber.org/chapters/c12905.ack.

job. A lower required skill level would decrease the prestige of the job. The problem is that if members of the wider society cannot distinguish these two explanations, the entrance of women will necessarily decrease the prestige of the occupation. Fearing this outcome, men seek to exclude women from high-prestige occupations.

Goldin then examines potentially testable implications of the model. The first is that men in occupations with a required level of the skill above the median of the female distribution will oppose the entry of women to the occupation, and so if firms want to hire talented women they will create female-only occupations (as an example, men are employed as "accounting clerks" and women as "stenographers"). As a result, one should observe these parallel occupations when high levels of skills are necessary and there are women that possess them. The second, related, implication is that occupational segregation will be nonmonotonic with regard to the skill with higher levels of segregation at the tails of the female distribution in the characteristic and integration in the middle. The third is that the development of credentials and other ways of "verifying" an individual's qualification for the occupation should increase gender integration and reduce wage discrimination. And, finally, the model implies technological change that reduces the required level of skill and should lessen occupational segregation as well. Goldin highlights the advent of lighter fire hoses that allow more women to be able to work effectively as firefighters as one example and adding machines (and other "calculators") that do not require one to be able to add large sums of numbers in one's head as another.

The data requirements to properly test these implications, especially the first two, are numerous: detailed information to allow for precise identification of occupations, information on all relevant qualifications for the job, and information on not only individual workers but also others in the same firm (or relevant wage-setting unit). Most readily available data sets do not typically have such information. Nevertheless Goldin, the consummate historian, pieces together data from different sources to kick the tires of the model. For example, she turns to what is known about occupational segregation in manufacturing at the turn of the twentieth century to document the extent of segregation at the time and to provide some insights into the role of skill differences in "strength" versus "academics" as well as the role of credentialing in the evolution of the distribution of women across occupations. The level of detail she presents tells a compelling story about the potential sources of sex discrimination in some sectors and why it may have evolved in the first half of the twentieth century.

She further tests some of the more subtle implications of the model using a remarkable data set that she put together from archival records at the US Department of Labor from 1940. Specifically, she analyses data on approximately 3,000 clerical and office workers in Philadelphia in which she is able to match individuals to firm-level data (which contain information about personnel policies—the respondents were quite candid in their preferences for certain types of workers). Using these data she both documents the rather extensive amount of sex discrimination in 1940 and finds some evidence consistent with the model, such as that highly educated women were employed in more segregated occupations as were men.

Further, while not the focus of the chapter, Goldin indulges the many readers who suspect that discrimination still explains part of the wage gap between men and women today and briefly considers the extent to which the model explains today's labor market as well. To do so she turns to the 2009 and 2010 American Community Survey to document the increased presence of women in some of the top-earning occupations, such as physicians, lawyers, and pharmacists, that may be partly due to increased credentialization of women in these fields as hypothesized by the pollution theory of discrimination. That said, she also acknowledges that there may be some remaining occupations with unusual characteristics and skills in which the pollution theory may still apply such as firehouses, police departments, and trading floors. As such the chapter is quite "satisfying": a thought-provoking model, data from a relevant time period to test it, and some consideration of the extent to which it applies today.

However, intrigued by the contrast of the situation of women in the labor market today with that of seventy years ago, I would like to suggest two broad areas in which I believe further work would provide an interesting addition to the literature and perhaps provide us with a better understanding of labor markets more generally.

First, to what extent can one systematically document continued, and perhaps subtle, segregation in "highly prestigious" occupations for which women are beginning to obtain the requisite skills and are therefore segregated into parallel occupations? For example, according to the 2012 Survey of America's Physicians conducted by the Physicians Foundation, 55 percent of family physicians were female compared to only 25 percent of physicians with a surgical specialty. As another example, according to the 2011 National Survey on Retention and Promotion of Women in Law Firms conducted by the National Association of Women Lawyers, 44 percent of seventh-year associates at law firms were female compared to only 15 percent of equity partners. These differences may be due to other characteristics of the subfields, but they may also be related to perceptions of prestige. That said, to convincingly document a relationship would require detailed data from employers along the lines of those collected by the Department of Labor in 1940 (which could potentially come from administrative data from a firm or a special survey) or an experiment carefully designed to elicit beliefs about the prestige of occupations under different assumptions about the required level of skill, the distribution of that skill among women, and the prevalence of women in those occupations. On a related note, one aspect of the model that would be interesting to develop is to more explicitly incorporate women's preferences into the model. That is, what do women value? It would be nice to expand the model to incorporate such factors as social norms and multiple dimensions of ability/prestige; such factors may also help us to understand continued subtle occupational segregation such as those in medicine and law.

Second, as discussed above, the pollution theory of discrimination implies processes by which occupations can become integrated, namely through changes in technological change and the development of credentials and licenses that document an individual's level of skill in the occupation. Goldin herself writes, "The model is inherently historical: the past affects the present." (2). As such, it would be intriguing to more generally document the relationship between, say, technological change that reduces the importance of physical strength required for a variety of occupations and any changes in the prevalence of women in the occupation over the entire twentieth century and through today. To document such a relationship may not only provide insights into occupational integration, but also into other effects of technological change on occupational distributions more generally. Similarly, over the past fifty years occupational certificates and licenses have grown tremendously. Kleiner and Krueger (2013) estimate that approximately 29 percent of their surveyed workers were required to have a government-issued license in 2008 while less than 5 percent were required to do so in the 1950s. They also show that there is no difference in the licensing rate by gender. To what extent can the growth in occupational certificates and licenses explain the documented decrease in discrimination and increased occupational integration? As policymakers press for more certification to help employers understand the value of different curricular programs, the impact of these "signals" of skill attainment on occupational segregation may prove an additional social benefit.

In short, this chapter by Goldin is thoroughly intriguing. And while the model is stylized, it will undoubtedly spur others to think along these lines, both empirically and theoretically, thereby advancing our understanding of all kinds of group-based differentials in occupation and earnings.

References

Aigner, Dennis J., and Glen G. Cain. 1977. "Statistical Theories of Discrimination in Labor Markets." *Industrial Labor Relations Review* 30 (January): 175–87.

Arrow, Kenneth. 1973. "The Theory of Discrimination." In *Discrimination in Labor Markets*, edited by Orley Ashenfelter and Albert Rees. Princeton, NJ: Princeton University Press.

Becker, Gary. 1957. *The Economics of Discrimination*. Chicago: University of Chicago Press.

Bertrand, Marianne. 2011. "New Perspectives on Gender." In *Handbook of Labor Economics*, vol. 4B, edited by O. Ashenfelter and D. Card, 1545–92. Amsterdam: Elsevier B.V.

Kleiner, Morris, and Alan B. Krueger. 2013. "Analyzing the Extent and Influence of Occupational Licensing on the Labor Market." *Journal of Labor Economics* 31 (2): S173–S202.

National Association of Women Lawyers. 2011. "National Survey on Retention and Promotion of Women in Law Firms." http://ms-jd.org/blog/article/nawls-national -survey-retention-and-promotion-women-law-firms-0.

Phelps, Edmund S. 1972. "The Statistical Theory of Racism and Sexism." *American Economic Review* 62 (September): 659–61.

Physicians Foundation. 2012. "A Survey of America's Physicians: Practice Patterns and Perspectives." http://www.physiciansfoundation.org/healthcare-research /a-survey-of-americas-physicians-practice-patterns-and-perspectives/.

The Supply of Gender Stereotypes and Discriminatory Beliefs

Edward L. Glaeser and Yueran Ma

10.1 Introduction

Why do gender-related beliefs emerge and shift over time? Changes in these beliefs may have played a role in the secular changes in female labor force participation discussed by Goldin (1990) and Olivetti (chapter 5, this volume). According to the General Social Survey, 47 percent of women born before 1946 (and 59 percent of men) agree with the statement "It is much better for everyone involved if the man is the achiever outside the home and the woman takes care of the home and family."[1] Only 29 percent of women born after 1945 share that view. These perceptions not only vary over time, but also across regions. A full 50 percent of female respondents (from all cohorts) agree with that statement in the West South Central Region, while only 26 percent of New Englanders share the view.

We have less survey evidence on discriminatory beliefs about women's ability in the workforce than we do about women's "proper" role in the home. Nonetheless, the evidence that does exist also suggests dramatic transformations about beliefs about women's capacity in the workplace during the late twentieth century. In 1953, Gallup asked "If you were taking a new job and had your choice of a boss, would you prefer to work for a man or for a

Edward L. Glaeser is the Fred and Eleanor Glimp Professor of Economics at Harvard University and a research associate and director of the Working Group on Urban Economics at the National Bureau of Economic Research. Yueran Ma is an undergraduate student of economics at Harvard University.

The authors thank their discussant, Matt Kahn, two referees, and the coeditors for helpful comments. Glaeser thanks the Taubman Center for State and Local Government for financial support. For acknowledgments, sources of research support, and disclosure of the authors' material financial relationships, if any, please see http://www.nber.org/chapters/c12890.ack.

1. To increase the sample size, we combine the waves of 2003, 2004, and 2007 of the General Social Survey to compute these statistics.

woman?" In 1953, 57 percent of women and 79 percent of men expressed a preference for a male boss, as opposed to only 8 percent of women and 2 percent of men who expressed a preference for a female boss. By 1987, the share of female and male respondents expressing a preference for a male boss had dropped to 37 and 29 percent respectively, with men now preferring a female boss (Simon and Landis 1989).

Moreover, an abundance of personal histories, ethnographic work, and field-specific statistical research suggests that men, and often women as well, have often believed that women are less capable in many workplace relevant tasks (e.g., Lerner 1987). The literature on women and perceived math ability is voluminous, and suggests that men and women often believe that women are less able in mathematics (see Gunderson et al. 2012). The women who pioneered their way up corporate ladders have often described a common male presumption that their talents were limited. Major thinkers from Aristotle to Freud have often depicted women as severely lacking in vital decision-making areas.

Section 10.2 further discusses the survey, ethnographic, and literary sources that attest to the existence of patriarchal, discriminatory beliefs against women at various points in history. This section also argues that these gender-related stereotypes cannot be understood as a purely Bayesian response to commonly available facts, but that they are instead a product of persuasion. For example, the surveys discussed above are taken in the same year, by respondents who observe the same labor markets, and yet respondents born before and after 1945 have markedly different opinions about working women, suggesting that an impact of upbringing on beliefs is far stronger that it should be in a perfectly rational world.

Our view complements Goldin (chapter 9, this volume) who argues that discrimination against women in previously male jobs may reflect some aspects of reality. We do not mean to suggest that reality is irrelevant, but rather that there are many cases in which beliefs about women do not correspond to reality. Instead, as in Glaeser (2005), we assume that beliefs reflect persuasion rather than reality, and we focus on the supply of persuasion.

To understand the supply of erroneous beliefs, we must understand the incentives to spread falsehood. After discussing several possible alternative sources in section 10.3, we focus our attention on parents. Parents with a strong preference for own grandchildren will have an interest in persuading daughters to forgo work in the formal labor force (Gunderson et al. 2012). Moreover, parents have far greater resources available with which to influence the beliefs of their children than do coworkers, spouses, or other possible sources of beliefs. Parents have some control over children's time and experiences for many years, during periods where children are less likely to have strong alternative sources of information. This combination of incentives and power leads us to believe that parents are a primary source of gender stereotypes and we model that process in sections 10.4 and 10.5.

Section 10.4 presents our core model on the parental formation of beliefs for female children. Our model follows standard economic assumptions and links the persuasion process to a Bayesian signaling model. Parents can send costly signals, including altering the education of their children or their own workplace behavior, which may shape children's beliefs, either about their own ability or about the ability of women as a whole. While the model uses the word "ability" to describe the source of uncertainty, it could equivalently be interpreted as the psychic returns from working and child rearing, so the model can be interpreted as describing the perpetuation of traditional values.

We focus on differential education choices by gender. If young women believe that parents have access to private information about their children's ability, then choices about educational investment will be seen as a meaningful signal about their own ability. We first focus on women's beliefs about their own ability in section 10.4, but then discuss how the model would shape societal beliefs in section 10.5.

In the model, parents are altruistic toward their children but they have an independent desire to have more grandchildren. This desire creates an incentive for them to try to generate beliefs that lead to more childbearing. If education increases the returns from working in the labor force relative to childbearing, this will generate lower levels of women's education, even if women know their ability levels with certainty. The underprovision of education effect becomes more pronounced if parents, but not their daughters, have private information about the ability of their own daughters or of women generally. Parents of skilled daughters may have an incentive to try to imitate parents of less able children by giving them less education, which may persuade daughters that their own time is best spent in childbearing. If daughters have rational beliefs, this will cause more able women to think that they are merely average, but will not lead to any aggregate misperception about women's ability.

In section 10.5, we turn to three extensions of the model. We first discuss the ways in which parental choices may alter societal beliefs of both men and women. In a rational model that leads to a separating or semipooling equilibrium, mistaken stereotypes get quickly undone. If the outcome in the model is pooling, then these stereotypes persist. The impact of parental persuasion will be particularly strong, and have more extreme consequences, if children are credulous Bayesians who make the understandable error of overestimating their parents' altruism (Glaeser and Sunstein 2009). Trusting their parents too much leads daughters to underestimate their parents' incentive to act strategically. This tendency will heighten the parents' incentive to behave in a strategic manner, by underinvesting in education.

At the end of section 10.5, we discuss the timing of work and child rearing, drawing on Goldin and Katz (2000). In this model, women (of varied educational attainment) choose when to schedule a continuous term of home production for child rearing, either early or late in their life cycle. The critical implication is that parental investment in misinformation makes sense when women have children early but not late. This fact implies that the shifts in the timing of women's childbearing should have had a major effect on the supply of gender stereotypes. Over the long run, technologies such as the Pill, which allows women to control the timing of fertility, may have reduced the incentive to persuade daughters that their time is better spent bearing children.

Section 10.6 concludes and discusses the interplay between sources of incorrect information and real world experience. Working before childbearing means that there is enough information to counteract persuasion. In a similar fashion, gender-related quotas that limit the number of women on the job seem unlikely to persist in the same way as glass ceilings that prevent women from rising above a certain level. Gender-related quotas should be unstable, if they are sustained with incorrect beliefs, because the few women hired for the job end up providing information that counteracts false beliefs. Glass ceilings, by contrast, provide no such evidence, which allow false beliefs to persist and maintain the incentives to perpetuate such beliefs.

10.2   Discrimination and the Social Formation of Beliefs

We have a great deal of information about the relative productivity of men and women in the household, the availability of market-provided household services, and perceived workplace discrimination against women (e.g., Goldin 1990; Blau, Brummund, and Liu 2013). We have less evidence on beliefs about female competence. Perhaps this dearth of information is understandable. In the very recent past in the United States we would hardly expect many respondents to honestly admit to thinking that women are less capable. Nonetheless, the relative absence of polling data about female competence makes it difficult to fully document shifts in beliefs about women and their capacities.

There is, however, a great deal of anecdotal evidence suggesting that women have often faced strong belief-related barriers to employment. Men have often held strong opinions that women were just not up to certain jobs. Often these beliefs have crumbled in the face of reality, but certainly some of these beliefs persist even today.

10.2.1   Attitudes toward Women and Work

In this subsection, we briefly review the polling data that are available about gender stereotypes from the General Social Survey (GSS) and other sources. The General Social Survey and other surveyors have been asking questions about traditional gender roles since the early 1970s. Unfortunately, these gender role–related questions do not map neatly into any particular taste or belief. A patriarchal viewpoint can reflect a higher opinion of female productivity in the household sector or a belief that employers discriminate unfairly against women.

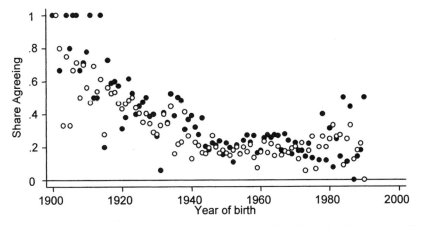

● Men Should Work, Women Not, M   ○ Men Should Work, Women Not, W

Fig. 10.1   Men should work and women should not (multiple years)
Source: General Social Survey.
Note: Response to the question, "It is much better for everyone involved if the man is the achiever outside the home and the woman takes care of the home and family?"

Figure 10.1, for example, shows the average responses to the question, "It is much better for everyone involved if the man is the achiever outside the home and the woman takes care of the home and family?" by birth year for men and women separately. The graph shows a strong downward pattern for both men and women. For cohorts born at the start of the twentieth century, almost all men and women thought that traditional gender roles were best. The share of respondents sharing that view declines to about 30 percent by 1950 and then levels off. There are some odd positive upticks in the responses to the question in the most recent cohorts, but this may reflect measurement error. The basic pattern documents a profound change across cohorts born in the first half of the twentieth century, and this pattern presents itself during every year in which the survey question was asked.[2]

The second figure (figure 10.2) shows a similar response to the GSS question, asking whether mothers' working outside the home is harmful or harmless for young children. Again, cohorts born at the start of the twentieth century almost uniformly believed that children were hurt by women working outside the home. By 1960, almost half of respondents did not state this belief. Even though an overwhelming majority of respondents are comfortable with women working as a general matter, some still say that working while children are young is harmful.

---

2. There is no survey evidence for cohorts born in the nineteenth-century United States. Olivetti (chapter 5, this volume) documents that some, but not all countries, experienced a U-shaped female labor force participation pattern. It would be interesting to know whether attitudes in these countries toward women participating in the workforce roughly track the time series of female labor force participation.

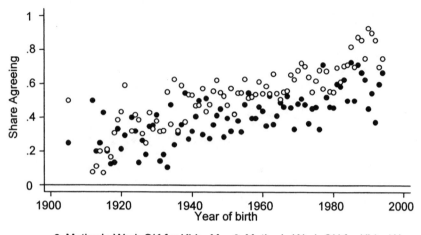

Fig. 10.2   Women working does not harm children (multiple years)
Source: General Social Survey.
Note: Response to the statement, "A preschool child is likely to suffer if his or her mother works."

There are far fewer questions that seem to directly capture assessments of female competence, and most that are relevant concern very particular tasks or occupations. The General Social Survey asks two highly specialized questions for particular years that would seem to relate to female competence.

In 1974 and 1982, the survey asked if men make better political leaders. The cohort pattern, shown in figure 10.3, displays a clear change over time. About 40 percent of people born earlier in the twentieth century think that men make better political leaders. By the latter decades of the century, this belief is down to 20 percent. We cannot generalize from political competence to competence in the workplace, but the effects are still quite striking.

A second question that is potentially related to ability was asked in 1996. Men and women were both asked if women earn less than men because they work less hard. This question about female work effort shows a striking nonlinearity (shown in figure 10.4), where beliefs about greater male effort decline with year of birth during the first half of the twentieth century and then a rise after that date. We have no satisfactory explanation for this pattern, but it does suggest that cohort does have an impact on these beliefs.

10.2.2 The Social Formation of Beliefs

Why do discriminatory beliefs differ radically over groups and across time? The economics of discrimination began when Gary Becker (1957) presented a model based on the preferences of employers, customers, and fellow workers. Becker's approach posits that some members of one group dislike

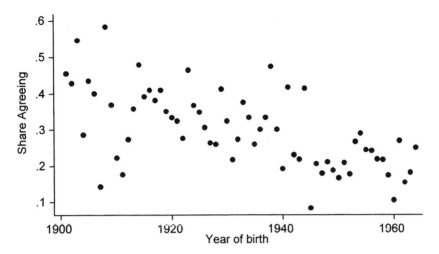

Fig. 10.3 Men are better at politics (multiple years)

Source: General Social Survey.

Note: Response to the question, "Would you say that most men are better suited emotionally for politics than are most women, that men and women are equally suited, or that women are better suited than men in this area?"

Fig. 10.4 Men earn more than women because they work harder (1996)

Source: General Social Survey.

Note: Response to the question, "Men work harder on the job than women do. How important do you think this reason is for explaining why women earn less?"

working with or buying from members of another group. The Becker model describes the reality of the mid-1950s, and provides many keen insights, like the negative impact on profits generated by an employer's discriminatory tastes.[3]

Even if whites had no innate dislike of blacks and men were willing to work with women, members of one group might still benefit if they were able to coordinate to expropriate the rights of another group (Krueger 1963; Thurow 1969), or if there was a society-wide equilibrium that restricts the choices of a disadvantaged group (Akerlof 1976).[4] The South's Jim Crow system was not merely the decentralized preferences or beliefs of ordinary people. It was socially and legally organized, and seems in many contexts to have generated transfers from blacks to whites. Those transfers were perhaps most obvious in the case of segregated schools, which allowed tax dollars to be spent far more heavily on white, rather than black children, especially when blacks were particularly immobile (Margo 1991).

These models certainly fit many aspects of the Jim Crow South, and they may also reflect some forms of gender-based discrimination as well. As Myrdal (1944) discussed in his classic study of American segregation, integration-oriented whites were no more allowed to travel in black railcars than blacks were allowed to travel in white cars. Firms proudly trumpeted their whites only policies, and the system only changed with massive legal intervention from the federal government, which can be seen as breaking the old equilibrium with outside force. Margo (1991) predicts that centralized discriminatory behavior would start to change as blacks could move north and indeed that seems to have happened.

It is less clear that there was an organized conspiracy against women in the mid-twentieth century that was similar to the Jim Crow system in the South, or that the legal pressure exerted by the Equal Pay Act of 1963 or the Civil Rights Act of 1964 had the same cathartic impact for women that it did for African Americans. Moreover, neither centralized discrimination models nor the Becker taste-based discrimination model can explain the changing nature of views toward African Americans and women, because they were not intended to make beliefs or preferences endogenous.[5] In centralized discrimination models, members of the ruling clique rationally respond to

---

3. Lazear's (1999) model of culture and language provides a complementary communication-based explanation for some forms of discrimination in the labor market. Different cultures, or ways of speaking, can make coordination difficult and lead to lower productivity.

4. Akerlof (1976) presents a model where a caste system, such as the Jim Crow South, was an unfortunate but stable equilibrium that reflected a society-wide rule where members of one clique are punished for interacting with members of a second clique.

5. Subsequent work by Becker and Murphy (2000) makes preferences endogenous, and this chapter is strongly indebted to their work. Our decision to focus on belief rather than preference formation reflects our own preference for the greater discipline created by belief-formation models, as in section 10.5, that require at least a partial Bayesian framework. In the case of the model in section 10.4, results would be identical if we allowed preference formation.

incentives, and have neither negative opinions nor disproportionate ill will toward either women or minorities.

Arrow's statistical discrimination model (1973) provides an alternative model that can explain discriminatory hiring practices and beliefs. The model suggests that employers and ordinary people have a low opinion of certain groups and these low opinions lead to discriminatory behavior. Certainly, it appears to be the case that at various times employers have held a low opinion of the competence of both blacks and women. Indeed, Goldin (chapter 9, this volume) is closely related to the statistical discrimination theory suggesting that opposition to women in particular jobs is based on an assessment of female ability generally, which may be lower than the ability level in an occupation at the time.

However, the great challenge of statistical discrimination models is that they typically also assume that people are fairly rational in their belief formation. This implies that attitudes need to be tethered to reality. Yet it is difficult to accept that there was much evidence to suggest that either women or blacks were as inept as many midcentury employers appear to have thought. Previous work (Glaeser 2005) focusing on beliefs about malevolence (rather than competence) emphasized that while southern voters a century ago seem to have been convinced that African Americans were a great threat to their safety, but it was whites, not blacks, who had systematically enslaved, brutalized, sexually assaulted, and even killed members of the other group. It is harder to document the error in beliefs about competence, but it seems quite likely that many people had beliefs about women and minorities that were not based on any real evidence and that bore little resemblance to the truth.

If beliefs about blacks and women systematically differed from reality, it becomes necessary to focus on theories that can generate widespread divergence between the truth and beliefs. There are at least two well-known systematic biases that can potentially generate such beliefs internally, without any external persuasion: the fundamental attribution error and self-serving biases. If the fundamental attribution error leads observers to associate the negative outcomes of others with intrinsic personal characteristics, rather than external constraints, then individuals could readily believe that poor labor market outcomes for either blacks or women represent low levels of innate ability rather than discrimination. Self-serving biases, which lead people to prefer views that make them see themselves in a positive light, could also lead white men to have negative views of blacks and women, because such views prop up white self-esteem.

While these behavioral quirks may have contributed to the negative assessment of blacks and women, there are limits to the power of these theories. For example, women's own belief in gender stereotypes, discussed in the previous subsection, cannot be the result of self-serving biases, since the beliefs do not seem to be self-serving. Moreover, the fundamental attribution error suggests that adverse outcomes for others are attributed to intrinsic factors, but that personal disappointments are blamed on external constraints. Yet women themselves often seem to share patriarchal beliefs.

Here, we focus on the social formation of error, and our critical assumption is that human beings are sensitive to social persuasion. In the discussion and two models that follow, individuals will be reasonably rational, but they will not totally discount falsely generated signals about the characteristics of out-groups.

On one level, the social formation of error runs against a long-standing tendency of economists to assume a high level of rationality and even accuracy in beliefs. Yet if we accept that mid-twentieth-century white males had erroneous opinions of the ability levels of blacks and women, we must consider at least the possibility that some beliefs have little basis in reality. While our approach runs against the economist's predilection for hyperrationality, it fully embraces the role that incentives can play in the generation of all sorts of outcomes, including incorrect beliefs.

Naturally, those incentives must battle against the incentives of listeners to learn the truth. In the political context, those incentives may be quite weak. After all, no individual voter has a strong incentive to ascertain the truth about any particular story, if the truth will only serve to make his or her vote a bit wiser. In the labor force context, those incentives may be quite stronger.

Moreover, we will assume that widely spread falsehoods will not persist if there is obvious evidence to the contrary. In any sensible learning model, this fact will suggest that racial or sex-based quotas are not typically stable, while glass ceilings may be. The existence of a glass ceiling toward women (or perhaps a low dark roof for blacks in the Jim Crow South) ensures that there is no hard evidence on how women or blacks can perform in higher positions. The absence of information allows incorrect beliefs to persist.

10.2.3 Discrimination versus Hatred

These models also help us to distinguish discrimination from hatred. Hatred is modeled as a belief that an out-group is malevolent and prone to engage in harmful behavior if they are empowered. Discrimination is a belief that an out-group is different and perhaps less capable, but not necessarily harmful or malign. Hatred leads to policies such as segregation and genocide, as in-groups attempt to shield themselves from the perceived threat. Discrimination will lead to different hiring practices and perhaps even exclusion from political decision making. Yet policies based on beliefs about lesser ability levels will not attempt to explicitly harm the out-group, because the out-group is not perceived as dangerous. While we might wish to harm people who are perceived to be malevolent before they harm us, we have little incentive to attack people who are perceived as less able.

Historically, African Americans have suffered from both discrimination and hatred. They have been perceived as being less competent, and they have also been perceived as being a threat. These beliefs were able to persist, arguably, because blacks were excluded from positions where they might do (perceived) harm and kept out of jobs where they could have demonstrated ability.

Women have suffered from discrimination but not typically from hatred. The primary experience of extraordinary altruism in the lives of most men is the self-sacrificing behavior of their own mothers, which would make it hard to accept that women are somehow naturally malevolent. Indeed, many of the most profound opponents of women in the workplace or in politics, who certainly subscribe and even promulgate views about female incompetence, have also held up women as the fairer sex that is more generous and good-hearted than men. When Senator Vest of Missouri opposed women's suffrage in 1887 he said, "I believe that [women] are better than men, but I do not believe they are adapted to the political work of this world."[6]

It is historically rare for out-groups to be simultaneously depicted as malign and incompetent. Indeed, such views would be counterproductive if a hate-producer is looking to generate support for policies that are harmful to the out-group. If a group is incompetent, then it is less threatening and that would mean less need to engage in defensive mechanisms. Jews, for example, have historically been depicted as both malign and powerful, which together justified the use of extreme anti-Semitic policies. The Soviet Union was depicted as an evil empire, which called for massive US military spending at the time. If the Soviet Union was merely an evil bumbling bureaucracy (arguably an accurate description during the Reagan era) then there would have been far less need for military spending.

In the case of patriarchic beliefs, it is possible to conceptually distinguish beliefs about ability and societal norms. A woman, for example, might stay in the home because she believes that her workplace productivity is relatively low in comparison to her productivity in the household. Alternatively, she may believe that staying home is just the "right" thing to do. But while these two notions may differ in some deep sense as a practical matter, they are indistinguishable. There is a conceptual distinction between believing that women are less able in the workplace or more able in the household sector, and surely both beliefs have existed, but when it comes to time allocation decisions the beliefs are interchangeable.

10.3   The Entrepreneurs of Error: Sources of Sexism

If common beliefs are socially formed, then they are unlikely to be produced by accidents. Instead, interested individuals must have incentives to spread falsehood. In this section, we discuss various potential sources

---

6. *The History of Women Suffrage,* vol. 4, ed. Susan B. Anthony and Ida Husted Harper (Indianapolis, IN: Hollenbeck Press).

of misinformation about female ability levels and explain our decision to focus on one particular source, parents. We focus on cases where spreading misinformation is intentional and instrumental. There have certainly been countless instances where politicians, for example, have uttered gender stereotypes, but most of the time, this seems more likely to reflect preexisting norms rather than any conscious political strategy. We therefore look for a setting where someone with the power to persuade also has the motive to depict women as either less capable or more suited for work outside the labor market.

10.3.1 Political Entrepreneurs

In Glaeser (2005), political entrepreneurs spread hatred against an out-group because hatred complemented the policies proposed by those politicians. The model suggests that a steady supply of erroneous beliefs requires low costs of widespread persuasion, persistent policy differences between parties that disproportionately impacted an out-group, political weakness of the out-group, and the relative segregation of that out-group to reduce alternative sources of information.

These conditions are far less likely to hold for women than for blacks or Jews, and they certainly do not hold in the more distant past, when we believe gender-related beliefs were already strong. Cheap political persuasion, outside of cities, requires both the printing press and voter literacy. For this reason, politically induced hatred of groups, as opposed to religiously induced hatred, appears to have been a largely nineteenth-century innovation.

Two prominent gender-related issues emerged in US politics during the nineteenth century: female suffrage and temperance (eventually, prohibition). Prominent leaders in female suffrage, like Elizabeth Cady Stanton, also led temperance organizations and prominent temperance leaders, like Frances Willard, were also suffragists. Prohibition was partially justified as a policy that would protect wives and children from abusive, drunken husbands, and suffrage was justified as the means of passing prohibition. The rise of gender-related issues made it possible at least that the opponents of these issues would have turned to sexism, just as the opponents of policies that granted modest aid to blacks or Jews turned to racism and anti-Semitism. Beliefs about female competence would be particularly relevant to the issue of female suffrage, and arguments about female incapacity were routinely made by the opponents of suffrage.

Yet even in these cases the political language was limited, perhaps because the parties never split decisively on suffrage and politicians had far less chance of changing male beliefs about women than they did of conjuring the fear of a race riot. The early connection between these issues and abolitionism (Fogel 2000) may have made them a more natural fit for the Republican Party, and Republicans were stronger supporters of the bills that eventually led to the Nineteenth Amendment, but neither issue became a major party plank until 1916, when both platforms supported extending voting rights to women.[7] Neither party endorsed prohibition before the passage of the Eighteenth Amendment. By 1916 a large number of states already allowed female suffrage, especially in presidential elections, making it politically unwise to insult a large voting bloc.

Moreover, since the Nineteenth Amendment was passed, women have gone from being politically absent to the second largest and now the largest voting bloc. While there has been plenty of vilification on both sides of the debate on abortion rights, the suggestion that abortion limitations are justified by broad limits on female decision-making ability has been fairly rare (suggestions that teenage girls are incapable of making wise decisions are more common), presumably because telling a majority of voters that they are stupid (or evil) would seem to be immense electoral folly.[8]

Opponents of the Equal Rights Amendment (ERA) were more likely to have voiced their opposition to unnecessary federal regulation rather than to say that discrimination was broadly justified on ability-related grounds. The Republican Platform of 1980 affirmed "our Party's historic commitment to equal rights and equality for women," and supported "equal opportunities for women," but also claimed that "states have a constitutional right to accept or reject a constitutional amendment without federal interference or pressure," and that federal "pressure against states which refused to ratify ERA" must cease. Phyllis Schlafly was the most prominent political entrepreneur opposed to the amendment, and she based her opposition both on a defense of traditional family structure and by claiming that the amendment would strip women of traditional privileges, such as avoiding the draft. While there have been instances where politicians do seem to have actively promoted gender stereotypes, particularly around the issue of female suffrage, this seems to have been a relatively minor phenomenon, at least relative to the spread of stereotypes by other actors.

10.3.2 Market Entrepreneurs

A belief that women are less capable in the marketplace has one obvious beneficiary: competing male coworkers, as suggested by Goldin (chapter 9, this volume). This would suggest that men should have the incentive to spread the idea that women are less competent. Within a corporate hierarchy, presumably the sensible strategy would be to emphasize the limits of

---

7. In 1916, the Republican Platform "favors the extension of the suffrage to women, but recognizes the right of each state to settle this question for itself," while the Democrats "recommend the extension of the franchise to the women of the country by the States upon the same terms as to men." The Republicans are endorsing suffrage, but not an amendment to force it on unwilling states, while it is unclear if the Democrats are supporting such an amendment or not. In 1872, the Republican Platform provided the amorphous words "The Republican party is mindful of its obligations to the loyal women of America for their noble devotion to the cause of freedom " and "the honest demand of any class of citizens for additional rights should be treated with respectful consideration."

8. Democrats do, of course, assert that Republicans are waging a "war on women," a charge that Republicans hotly deny.

a particular woman. In other settings, where no single female competitor exists, then it may make more sense to disparage women more broadly.

Spreading false beliefs will be more common when women really are a potential threat, and this means that we can make sense of the rise of female discrimination in certain jobs that is discussed by Goldin (2000). During the early twentieth century, the threat of a female competitor was small and this meant that men spent little effort on persuading prospective bosses not to hire women. During the mid-twentieth century, the threat became more obvious and men began to persuade more assiduously. At the end of the twentieth century, there were enough positive examples of women working that misinformation had much less effect.

Several factors would be necessary for this persuasion to represent a dominant force. First, people making hiring decisions would need to be susceptible to persuasion from the subordinates who will compete with the new employee. This is not inconceivable—deans, for example, are quite reliant on faculty members when hiring—and junior faculty members are often allowed to weigh in on junior faculty hires. This process does suggest that persuasion would be occupation specific. It may be possible to persuade a superior that one's particular task (mathematics, construction work) requires male attributes, but it is unlikely to be as easy or as sensible to try to persuade the superior that women are less capable at all workplace tasks. However, if women are accepted as being less able in enough occupations, presumably the natural inference is that there is something more general at play.

Second, the persuaders would need to solve the free rider problem. No single worker has much of an incentive to persuade. The propagation of these beliefs would therefore be more likely in small firm settings, or in cases where other organizations exist to collectively represent the interests of male workers. For example, in 1941, the United Auto Workers (UAW) filed a strike against the Kelsey-Hayes wheel plant, demanding "the removal of girl employees from machine work" (Milkman 1982). But while the UAW might demand segregation-by-job in particular plants, and would regularly fight for equal pay provisions that reduced the possibility of men losing jobs to lower-cost female employees, the union was far more interested in representing female employees than disparaging them.

Third, if beliefs have some connection to evidence and Bayesian reasoning, then discriminatory beliefs in the workforce can only persist when there is no evidence to the contrary, which is true even if beliefs come from other sources. Hard discriminatory barriers, justified by these beliefs, may be able to persist, while quotas, based on incorrect beliefs, seem unlikely to be stable. Many have argued that women working at typically male jobs during World War II helped dispel the idea that they were incapable of doing these typically male activities. The relative durability of glass ceilings may be connected with the formation of beliefs, because they ensure that there is no direct evidence on upper-level administrators in one particular company, and advocates of discrimination can more plausibly argue that upper-level jobs are more heterogeneous across firms than lower-level jobs. That heterogeneity makes it easier to deny the relevance of female achievements in other firms.

Individual workers might disparage women, and unions might occasionally strike against female employment, but overall discriminatory beliefs spread by coworkers do not appear to have been a major force, presumably because of the relatively weak incentives and limited ability for workers to spread discriminatory beliefs to employers. Industrialists have every incentive to see through male claims about female incompetence and look for low-cost labor, as Lowell did when he started his textile mills almost two centuries ago. While coworkers may have served as an occasional source of discriminatory beliefs, they are unlikely to be a significant force, especially in more traditional societies.

The alternative market entrepreneur who has an incentive to promulgate gender stereotypes is the consumer goods company. Friedan (1963) is the primary proponent of this point of view. For the Friedan argument to be persuasive the industry must be oligopolistic, consumer goods must strongly complement not substitute for women's time at home, and the costs of persuasion must be low. It is possible that these conditions existed when Friedan wrote *The Feminine Mystique* in 1963, although they seem unlikely to hold today. Many important home products—the dishwasher, premade meals—substitute rather than complement time spent in the home, suggesting that their sellers should have been advocates of women working, not the opposite. There is little doubt that magazines and advertisements provided many examples of the joys of homemaking, but the instrumental aim of those examples seems far more likely to generate positive associations for using a particular product. Even a washing machine company has the incentive to show a happy woman at home with her washing machine, not because the company wants to her to stay at home, but rather because it wants her to think about how wonderful having a washing machine can be.

10.3.3   Family Entrepreneurs

The long history of patriarchal attitudes, before mass media, before widespread democracy, before even the possibility of significant female integration into the workforce, suggests that these attitudes ultimately have a deeper source. Perhaps the deepest source of all is the family or clan itself and ancient institutions such as the church, that are often allied with adults in the family. If patriarchic views are common, if not ubiquitous, then it seems reasonable to believe that they are delivered for deep reasons and there is no deeper motivation than the perpetuation of the gene pool.

A particularly natural reason for supplying patriarchic beliefs is that these beliefs increase childbearing. Fertility is typically seen as a complement toward being in the home and substitute with being away from home.

Children typically need child care and that is typically most cheaply provided at home. Multiple pregnancies are often more difficult for working mothers to fit into their schedules. Given that fathers always bear far less of the costs of pregnancies and often far less of the cost of child rearing, empowering men within the household may also lead to higher levels of fertility, especially in cultures that lack inexpensive, reliable birth control.

For basic biological reasons, grandparents will often want more children than their own children will independently desire, because the grandparents receive a direct benefit from grandchildren, over and above the indirect impact that grandchildren have through their children's own welfare. If children have maximized their own welfare with respect to their own progeny, the envelope theorem implies that grandparents will desire a higher number of grandchildren. There are multiple means of prodding children to be fertile, including bribes and verbal haranguing, but investing in beliefs may be a reasonable tool.

Parents have both a strong motive and abundant means of influencing children's beliefs, such as exposing children to gender stereotypes in childhood literature. Weitzman et al. (1972) examines children's storybooks in the United States, and finds pervasive differences in the ways that genders are depicted, with boys being adventurous and girls being pretty and passive. Bereaud (1975) examines French children's books and similarly finds that they portray girls as "timid, passive and dependent" and women "in the traditional housewife role or in low-paid, unskilled occupations." Children's books are bought by parents, so it is reasonable to believe that parents want such images broadcast to their own children.

In the pluralistic United States today, parents can also choose other influences, such as religion. If parents want to encourage childbearing, then they can take their children to religious institutions that encourage childbearing. Some of the most extreme examples of pro-natalist religious entities are the Mormon church and various ultraorthodox groups. These institutions and the traditional Catholic church also encouraged large families and traditional female lifestyles. Religious support for childbearing may reflect both a desire to cater to parents who want grandchildren, but also a desire to fill the pews in decades to come. Religious groups that did not support childbearing, such as the Shakers, tend to disappear over time.

As we will model, parents can also engage in more costly signals to children about their abilities. A mother may herself adopt a traditional lifestyle to convince her daughters to do the same and her sons to marry someone who acts similarly. Providing little education for daughters is another means of suggesting that her possibilities in the workplaces are limited, and that she should focus more on producing grandchildren. We will formally model undereducation of women.

We will focus on the signaling choices of individuals, which will inevitably lead to some heterogeneity in the population. That heterogeneity may be smoothed out by institutions, such as churches, which will lead to a more ubiquitous set of attitudes. A state may also embrace traditional lifestyle choices for pro-natalist reasons, which may in turn be motivated by the desire for a large army. Hitler's Germany, for example, pushed a strong ideology of motherhood and traditional female roles (Rossy 2011).

Empirically, demographers have documented that parental preferences do affect children's preferences and decisions on marriage and childbearing. Axinn, Clarkberg, and Thornton (1994) show that mothers' preference for the size of their children's families is significantly positively correlated with the children's family-size preferences when the children are young adults. Barber (2000) shows that both sons and daughters whose mothers prefer early marriage, large families, and low minimum education for their children end up entering parenthood earlier. This effect is significant controlling for family income, parental education, the mother's work choice, and other family background variables. Such evidence corroborates our idea that parental influence is possibly quite powerful.

10.4   Gender Stereotypes, Education, and Daughters

The critical assumption in our model is that the parents care about the welfare of their children *and* their grandchildren. Parents would like to prod their children to have more children themselves, thereby increasing their total number of descendants. Evolutionary theory would seem to suggest such preferences, as would ordinary observation. In particular, popular culture is replete with examples of parents wanting their children to get married and have at least one child of their own.

This assumption about parental preferences then influences parental investments in their children, especially when those preferences shape the beliefs of those children. Parents have many tools for influencing beliefs about female competence in the workforce, including telling stories, attending religious services, maternal behavior, and so forth. We will focus on the provision of education for daughters. Female education is a particularly important signal that parents can send daughters about their productivity outside the home.

We will focus on beliefs about female competence, but this is only one possible interpretation of the model. The "competence" parameter can also be interpreted as the psychic benefit of working. An alternative interpretation, therefore, is that parents attempt to persuade their daughters that there are lower returns from working in the formal sector than from bearing children. In a sense, the model can be interpreted as suggesting that to increase the size of the third-generation parents are trying to persuade their daughters of the virtues of "traditional values."[9]

9. This interpretation relates to Boustan and Collins (chapter 6, this volume) that documents that nonworking mothers are more likely to have nonworking daughters. If nonworking mothers have stronger preferences for both their own children and for grandchildren, then they will indeed be willing to invest more in changing the preferences of their progeny.

Table 10.1   **Assumptions and implications**

Assumption	Implication if eliminated
1: Grandparents desire more grandchildren than the middle generation.	The model's results disappear and grandparents no longer try to persuade their daughters. This is the critical assumption.
2: Ability increases the returns from market work more than childbearing.	If ability complements childbearing more than work, then assumption 1 implies that parents would want daughters to think that they are more, not less, able.
3: Cash expenditures cannot eliminate the time costs of childbearing.	Women who are more productive in the workforce might have more children rather than less, this would similarly eliminate the incentive to perpetuate stereotypes.
4: Binary ability level	Multiple-ability types would complicate the model, but not eliminate the basic result that parents want to shade daughters' assessment of their workplace productivity downward.
5: Children infer the off-the-equilibrium-path assumptions come from parents that would benefit from such a deviation given a narrower range of response (the D1 assumption).	There are multiple equilibria that include the one on which we choose to focus.

Our model assumes three generations (grandparents, parents, and children). The grandparents act first in period 1. They select the investment in human capital for a specific child in the second generation. We assume that we are looking at the decision of grandparents after their own fertility decisions have been made. In period 2, the parents' generation then decides on the number of children that they have and the human capital of those children. The children make no choices in the model and are assumed to be homogeneous. Table 10.1 discusses the core assumptions of the model and the implication of eliminating those assumptions.

10.4.1   The Period 2 Decisions by the Second Generation

In period 2, daughters in the second generation (parents) choose fertility levels, N, human capital levels for their boy children (H_{CM}), and human capital levels for their girl children (H_{CF}) to maximize:

$$(1) \qquad \text{Consumption} + \alpha \big(V(N) + .5Ng_M(H_{CM}) + .5Ng_F(H_{CF}) \big),$$

where $V(.)$, $\phi(.)$ $g_M(.)$ and $g_F(.)$ are all increasing, concave functions. We assume that one half of all children are male and that the benefits of skill may be different between boys and girls.

Consumption is assumed to equal $\delta W(H_F)A_F(1 - T_{HF}) + Y_0 - .5NH_{CM} - .5NH_{CF}$, where $\delta W(H_F)A_F(1 - T_{HF})$ reflects the wife's earnings, which equals

$\delta W(H_F)A_F$ (the wife's wage rate) times $1 - T_{HF}$ (the time spent working), and Y_0 reflects any other income, including husbands' earnings. Household time is proportional to the number of children, so $T_{HF} = N t_c$. The wage equals a discrimination level, denoted δ, times a wage function that is increasing in the women's human capital ($W(H_F)$) times an ability level A_F. We further assume that $W(.)$ is increasing, concave, and that $\lim_{x \to 0} W(x) = \infty$. We first assume that women make fertility decisions before observing their workplace productivity, and make work-timing decisions based on an estimate: $\hat{A}_F$. We relax that assumption in section 10.5.

The first-order conditions that determine human capital level investments are $\alpha g_M'(H_{CM}) = \alpha g_F'(H_{CF}) = 1$. We let G_T denote $.5(g_M(H_{CM}) + g_F(H_{CF}))$, and H_T denote $.5H_{CM} + .5H_{CF}$ evaluated at the welfare-maximizing levels of human capital investment. We assume that $G_T \geq H_T$.

Three assumptions together ensure that the investment in children's human capital is independent of the number of children: quasi-linear preferences, the benefits from investing in children scales up linearly with the number of children, and the costs of human capital investment similarly scale up linearly with the number of children. Quality and quantity of children are not completely independent, however, as the net benefit from investing in quality will impact the incentive to have more children.

The optimal fertility choice is characterized by the first-order condition $\delta W(H_F)\hat{A}_F t_c = \alpha(V'(N) + G_T) - H_T$. Differentiating this equation implies that the number of children is increasing with α and decreasing with δ, H_F, t_c and $\hat{A}_F$. Other than α, all of these parameters effectively increase the opportunity cost of having more children.

We use this equation to implicitly define a function $N(W(H_F)\hat{A}_F)$, which represents the number of children that a women will have depending on her level of human capital and beliefs about her workplace ability. The other elements that determine utility have been suppressed because they are fixed. Holding $\hat{A}_F$ and other parameters constant, the derivative of N with respect to H_F is $[\delta W'(H_F)\hat{A}_F t_c]/\alpha V''(N) < 0$. The second derivative of N with respect to H_F is negative as long as $V'''(N)$ is not too negative, as it would not be if $V(.)$ has a standard form such as vN^σ, with $\sigma < 1$.

The total welfare of a female child equals $Y_0 + \delta W(H_F)A_F(1 - N t_c) + \alpha(V(N) + NG_T) - NH_T$, where N will be optimally chosen in response to the other parameters. This welfare level and the choice function N are then ingredients into the decision making of the first generation.

10.4.2   The Period 1 Decision by the Grandparents' Generation

We now turn to the grandparents' generation, and focus on their choice of investment in human capital for a single, female child in the second generation. The grandparents choose only the level of human capital, which carries a cost H_F, just like the human capital by the next generation. The grandparents' welfare will equal α_1 times the daughters' direct welfare,

$Y_0 + \delta W(H_F)A_F(1 - N\underline{t}_c) + \alpha(V(N) + NG_T) - NH_T$, plus the utility that grandparents get directly from the third generation, which equals α_2 (a second altruism parameter) times $V(N) + NG_T$, which is also the welfare that the second generation receives from the third generation.

Throughout the model, we will assume that the first generation accurately assesses the ability of their children in the second generation. This assumption can be relaxed, as long as the grandparents retain some private information. For example, the grandparents could have some private information about the state of the labor market or a private, imperfect signal about the daughters' ability level. As long as the grandparents have some private information then a signaling game will still occur, but if the grandparents were known to know nothing more than the second generation, then they would have no ability in a rational model to influence the beliefs of their children.

Assuming that individuals in the first generation accurately assess the daughter's ability level A_F, their welfare (that is related to a specific child) equals:

(2) $\alpha_1[Y_0 + \delta W(H_F)A_F(1 - N\underline{t}_c) + \alpha(V(N) + NG_T) - NH_T]$

$$+\alpha_2(V(N) + NG_T) - H_F,$$

where H_F refers to the investment of human capital in the second generation. The parameter α_1 reflects the direct impact of the second generation's welfare on the welfare of the first generation. The parameter α_2 reflects the impact of the third generation's welfare on the welfare of the first generation. If the second generation chooses their fertility level to maximize their own welfare, then the derivative of grandparents' welfare with respect to N, the number of grandchildren equals $\alpha_2(V'(N) + G_T)$, which is strictly positive. Given these preferences, grandparents will always want their children to have more progeny than they will naturally choose on their own.

Standard evolutionary preferences suggest that animals act as if they care about reproducing their gene pool, not just for a single generation but for generations to come. One approach that grandparents might have is to provide cash assistance that is tied to the number of children produced. Many grandparents do explicitly subsidize grandchildren, if they have the resources, by providing funds for education or even buying a house in a neighborhood with a good school district.

Grandparents may also want parents to spend a bit more investing in their children's human capital, and this might reverse the results of the model. We have structured preferences and production functions so that there is no tradeoff between quantity and quality, and where the daughters' human capital does not increase the human capital of the next generation. If daughters' human capital did contribute directly to the human capital of their own children, then grandparents would have a stronger incentive to invest in their daughters. This effect would tend to mute the implications of the model.

We have chosen a stark and simple case to highlight how a desire for own grandchildren may lead to lower human capital investment in girls, and the generation of beliefs about female inability in the workplace, but we are well aware that reasonable perturbations of the model could generate alternative predictions. For example, grandparents could conceivably care so much about grandchildren's quality that they might actually not want higher fertility levels. We have also assumed that maternal human capital only impacts childbearing by increasing opportunity costs. If maternal skills help generate human capital in the next generation, then this would create a grandchild—related incentive for investment in daughters, as described above.

We first focus on investments in a daughter's human capital, assuming that A_F is known at every point. We then turn to the possible scenario in which the parents, but not the daughter, have received a private signal about the daughter's ability, in which case investing in education can serve as a costly signal to the daughter of her skills. Finally, we address sexist indoctrination of sons.

When the future mother's ability level is known to all, then the first-order condition for the grandparents is:

$$(3) \qquad \alpha_1 \delta W'(H_F) A_F (1 - N \underline{t}_c) + \alpha_2 (V'(N) + G_T) \frac{\delta W'(H_F) \underline{t}_c}{\alpha V''(N)} = 1.$$

We assume that second-order conditions (see Glaeser and Ma 2013) hold for this to be a maximum.

Given our assumption on the second-order condition, Proposition 1 follows:[10]

PROPOSITION 1: *Parents will invest a positive amount in daughters' education if* $-[(N_0 V''(N_0))/(V'(N_0) + G_T)] > (\alpha_2/\alpha\alpha_1)(N_0 \underline{t}_c/(1 - N_0 \underline{t}_c))$ *where* N_0 *represents the number of children chosen by a daughter with no education. If this condition holds, and parents do invest in a positive amount of education, then the level of education is declining with* α_2 *and increasing with* α_1. *The level of education will increase with* δ *and* A_F *if and only if* $[(-\alpha V''(N))/(\delta A_F \underline{t}_c)^2 W'(H_F) W(H_F)] > \{(\alpha_2/\alpha) - \alpha_1 - [\alpha_2 V''(N)(V'(N) + G_T)/\alpha(V''(N)^2)]\}$.

Proposition 1 implies that parents will always invest a positive amount in their daughter's education if α_2 is sufficiently small, and that the amount of education that their daughter receives is decreasing as α_2 rises. The incentive to underinvest in daughters is directly a function of the altruism toward grandchildren, but of course, this would diminish if daughters' human capital were an input into the human capital of the next generation. By contrast, as the grandparents care more about their daughters relative to their grandchildren, investment in the daughters' education will rise.

The parameters δ and A_F are complements to daughters' education, and they will typically cause the investment in the daughters' education to rise,

10. Proofs may be found in the working paper version of this chapter (Glaeser and Ma 2013).

as long as α_2 is relatively small, so the dominant effect of these parameters is to increase the payoff to daughters' education. A somewhat less intuitive possibility is that if α_1 is sufficiently low, higher values of δ and A_F, which increase the returns to work, may actually reduce the tendency to invest in daughters' education. If α_1 is low enough, then the grandparent only cares about investing in human capital because it impacts the supply of eventual grandchildren. As higher values of δ and A_F reduces the number of grandchildren directly, this may sufficiently increase the grandparents' demand for more grandchildren that they may offset these higher labor market returns with less investment in human capital.

A crucial assumption of the model is that the second generation's human capital does not influence the "quality" of the third generation. To briefly illustrate how drastically results can change when this assumption is relaxed, assume that $G_T = G_0 + g(H_F - H_F^0)$, where G_0, g and H_F^0 are constants. The parental first-order condition is now $\alpha_1(\delta W'(H_F)A_F(1 - N\underline{t}_c) + \alpha gN)$ $+ \alpha_2\{(V'(N) + G_T)[(\delta W'(H_F)A_F\underline{t}_c) / \alpha V''(N)] + gN\} = 1$. The first generation will still have an incentive to underinvest in daughters' education to increase fertility, but the comparative static on α_2 is reversed if $(-V'(N) + G_T)[(\delta W'(H_F)A_F\underline{t}_c) / \alpha V''(N)] < gN$, so the grandparents who care about their grandchildren invest more—not less—in their daughters. We will drop this assumption now, but return to it in our later section on credulous Bayesians.

In sum, in the model with perfect information there is an incentive to underinvest in daughters (in order to induce them to have more children), but there is no attempt to shape the beliefs of daughters about themselves or about women in general. We now turn to the situation in which the parent has some private information. When modeling the investment in daughters, we assume that this information is about the young woman herself. When discussing investment in sons, we will assume that this information is about women more generally.

10.4.3   Belief Formation

We now turn to the core of the model—the formation of daughters' beliefs. The first-generation parents know their daughters' ability, but daughters themselves only infer their talents from parental investment in their human capital. In equilibrium, a daughter whose parents invest heavily, both personally and through external investments, will typically infer that she has abundant raw skill, since we assume that such skill is a complement with investment in the model. If parents ignore a daughter's education, then she will naturally infer that she has little innate talent. At this point, we focus on the formation of beliefs by a single individual, but in the next section, we discuss the implication of this for beliefs by sons and by society as a whole.

The timing of the model, preferences, and production functions are just as before, but we now assume that A_F can take on two values 1 and $1 - a$, and daughters are more able with probability p. Parents learn their daughter's skill, make an investment, and then the daughter infers her skill from their investment levels and then makes her own fertility choice. We define the investment level chosen under perfect information as H_F^{Skill} for skilled daughters and $H_F^{Unskill}$ for unskilled daughters.[11] These are benchmark quantities that would be chosen if the daughters knew their ability level. We also define $H_{Skill}^{Unskill}$ as the level of human capital that would be chosen by parents of unskilled daughters if their daughters believe erroneously that they are skilled. We let π denote daughter's assessment that she is high skilled, based on the human capital level that she has received, and $N(H_F, \pi)$ denote her fertility level, which is decreasing in both H_F and π. First-generation welfare can then be denoted $U_i(H_F, N(H_F, \pi))$ for $i = u$ and s, depending on whether the daughter is skilled or unskilled.

We have assumed that there are only two groups in the population and that the parents of the more skilled wish their daughters thought that they were less skilled. This feels particularly harsh, but that harshness can be reduced if we instead assumed that there were a variety of subgroups in the population and daughters knew their subgroup. Then the assumed desire to push the daughter's assessment of her ability downward only means that parents wish that the daughter thinks she is less able relative to her subgroup, not relative to the entire population. In this setup, the parents of a talented daughter would be happy to have her realize that she is more able than most women or prevalent gender stereotypes, but would still want her to shade her self-confidence downward slightly. As discussed above, the ability parameter can also be interpreted as reflecting the value of working inside or outside the home, and can therefore be seen as capturing values rather than innate ability.

Locally, the welfare of the grandparents is decreasing with π—the daughter's belief in her own competence—but we go further and assume that this derivative holds globally as well, so that parents would always prefer their daughters to think that they have a lower probability of being able. This assumption implies that skilled parents would like to imitate unskilled parents. If that assumption does not hold, then there will be little incentive to manipulate beliefs. This assumption follows automatically if a is sufficiently small, so that the fertility choices by less skilled children are only slightly greater than the fertility choices of more skilled children.

We further assume a minimum level of investment that parents are legally required to make, which is denoted $\underline{H}_F$, and that this is less than $H_F^{Unskill}$. Thus in a world with perfect information, this lower bound will not bind.

In a Bayesian-separating equilibrium where skilled and unskilled daugh-

11. The values of N_{Skill} and H_F^{Skill} satisfy $\delta W(H_F^{Skill}) \underline{t}_c + H_T = \alpha(V'(N_{Skill}) + G_T)$, and $1 = W'(H_F^{Skill}) \delta \{\alpha_1 (1 - N_{Skill} \underline{t}_c) + [\alpha_2 (V'(N_{Skill}) + G_T) t_c] / \alpha V''(N_{Skill})\}$, and other values are defined similarly.

ters receive different levels of education, then daughters learn their "type." If both types of parents choose a level of investment in equilibrium, then daughters will believe that they are skilled with some probability weakly between zero and one. We will use an equilibrium refinement to suggest which equilibrium seems most likely to exist.

What are possible outcomes if the parents of skilled and unskilled daughters choose different levels of education? In these outcomes, the parents of skilled daughters must choose H_F^{Skill}, since that maximizes $U_S(H_F, N(H_F,1))$. Any other investment level will not change daughters' self-assessments, and will only reduce parental welfare. Moreover, any alternative candidate-separating equilibrium investment level will generate a deviation to this point, since the parents of the skilled cannot change the daughters' beliefs in an adverse way—as long as there is separating—and they can better match between their daughters' skill and her human capital level.

Since the welfare of the parents of skilled, in any separating equilibrium, is determined by $U_S(H_F^{Skill}, N(H_F^{Skill},1))$, it is helpful to determine the range of values of investment for the parents of the less skilled, which would induce the parents of the more skilled to imitate them:

Lemma 1: There exists one value of H, denoted $\widehat{H}$, at which $U_S(H_F^{Skill}, N(H_F^{Skill},1)) = U_S(\widehat{H}, N(\widehat{H},0))$, and for all values of H between $\widehat{H}$ and H_F^{Skill}, $U_S(H_F^{Skill}, N(H_F^{Skill},1)) < U_S(H,N(H,0))$, but if $H < \widehat{H}$, $U_S(H_F^{Skill}, N(H_F^{Skill},1)) > U_S(\widehat{H}, N(\widehat{H},0))$. If $H > \widehat{H}$, then $U_U(H,N(H,1)) < U_U(\widehat{H}, N(\widehat{H},0))$. At $H = \widehat{H}$, holding beliefs constant, the welfare of parents of skilled daughters is strictly increasing in H, and $\widehat{H}$ is rising with δ and α_1 and falling with α_2.

Lemma 1 helps determine the structure of a separating equilibrium. The value of H, denoted $\widehat{H}$, is the highest investment of human capital by parents of the less skilled that will not induce the parents of the more skilled to attempt to imitate them. If the less skilled invest more than $\widehat{H}$, then the parents of the more skilled will choose to imitate them, for $U_S(H_F^{Unskill}, N(H_F^{Unskill},1)) < U_S(H,N(H,0))$, but if the parents of the less skilled invest less than that amount then the more skilled will not benefit by imitating them. If the parents of the less skilled are investing $\widehat{H}$, then they will not benefit by mimicking the parents of the more skilled.

In a separating equilibrium the unskilled parents, however, may well end up choosing an investment level other than $H_F^{Unskill}$. While that skill level is perfectly matched to their daughters' ability and their preferences, it may not be an equilibrium since if $H_F^{Unskill} > \widehat{H}$, it may lead the parents of the skilled to want to imitate them. Moreover an alternative investment level will not necessarily generate a deviation, since a deviation toward an alternative investment level may cause beliefs to change in a way that hurts the welfare of the parents of the less skilled.

A pooling equilibrium is also possible, but generically, it will not be possible for the two types to pool at more than one human capital level. In an equilibrium where parents of the same type choose two different levels of human capital, these parents must be indifferent between the two levels of investment. The beliefs that make one type of parent indifferent between two levels of investment will not make the other type of parent indifferent between two types of investment. Formally if $U_S(H_F^1, N(H_F^1, \pi_1)) = U_S(H_F^2, N(H_F^2, \pi_2))$, where H_F^1 and H_F^2 represent the two different investment levels and π_1 and π_2 represent the beliefs at the two investment levels, then generically $U_U(H_F^1, N(H_F^1, \pi_1)) \neq U_U(H_F^2, N(H_F^2, \pi_2))$.

If we place no further restrictions on off-the-equilibrium-path beliefs, then multiple equilibrium are possible. For example, it is possible for there to be a continuum of pure separating equilibrium, where parents of skilled daughters choose H_F^{Skill} and parents of unskilled daughters choose any value of H below $\widehat{H}$, as long as the parents of unskilled daughters prefer that value of H and being known to have an unskilled daughter to choosing $H_{Skill}^{Unskill}$, which is the best that they can do if their daughters believe that they are skilled. It is also possible for the unskilled parents to choose two levels of H that yield equal utility levels, as long as one is above $H_F^{Unskill}$ and one is below H_F^{Skill} and both yield equal utility. It is also possible for there to be a pooling equilibrium, where both parents of skilled and unskilled daughters choose a common level of H, as long as the payoff for the parents of skilled daughters is better off than if they choose H_F^{Skill} and the parents of unskilled daughters are better off than if they chose $H_{Skill}^{Unskill}$. Semipooling equilibria are also possible, where some fraction of both groups mix and choose a common equilibrium, as well also choosing some separate investment level.

However, many of these seem like unlikely outcomes since if $H_F^{Unskill} < \widehat{H}$, daughters who observed a deviation to $H_F^{Unskill}$, which would yield higher welfare for the parents, would surely still infer that they were less able, since choosing $H_F^{Unskill}$ would produce less welfare for parents of the more skilled than they are already receiving in equilibrium. Separating equilibrium, therefore, seem most likely to yield exactly two investment levels, one for each skill level.

To formalize this intuition and generate a unique equilibrium when $\widehat{H} > H_F^{Unskill}$, it is sufficient to assume a perfect Bayesian equilibrium where daughters believe that if one type of parents would never deviate to a human capital level H, given any rational fertility response, then the deviation must come from the other group. This assumption leads to Proposition 2a:

PROPOSITION 2A: *If $\widehat{H} > H_F^{Unskill}$, then there is no pooling equilibrium, skilled parents choose to invest H_F^{Skill} and unskilled parents choose $H_F^{Unskill}$.*

This proposition suggests that there is one most likely outcome if $H_F^{Unskill}$ is sufficiently low. Since the parents of the skilled would not choose $H_F^{Unskill}$ even if their daughters would change their beliefs, then daughters reasonably believe that such an investment level cannot come from parents of the more skilled. Since they believe that an investment level of $H_F^{Unskill}$ must come from the parents of the unskilled, then parents of the unskilled will choose that investment level and a unique equilibrium results.

Proposition 2a describes the equilibrium for a range of parameter values, when the parents of the skilled have little incentive to imitate the parents of the weak. In this case, the outcomes with imperfect information are identical to the outcomes with perfect information. There is some incentive to reduce the education of daughters of both skill levels, but little actual deceit or misinformation.

But what about situations in which $\widehat{H} < H_F^{Unskill}$, and the parents of skilled daughters would like to pretend to be parents of unskilled daughters? In these cases, there is the potential for misinformation, and no possibility that parents will behave exactly as they did in the full information case.

All sorts of possible outcomes seem to coexist. For example, skilled and unskilled might pool at some relatively high level of schooling. This equilibrium would be maintained if daughters interpreted any deviation as coming from parents of the more skilled. Alternatively, the less skilled might choose some extremely low level of schooling (less than $\widehat{H}$) and this would be maintained if daughters believed that any deviation came again from parents of the more skilled.

To select a single-equilibrium prediction for a wider range of parameter values, we now assume a variant of the D1 refinement (Cho and Kreps 1987): if an off-the-equilibrium-path investment level is more attractive for one type of parent, given any set of beliefs by children, then children assume that this type of parent has generated this deviation with probability one. In this model, the children's response to the parents' human capital investment is their fertility level. If $N_s^*(H)$ and $N_U^*(H)$ makes the parents of skilled and unskilled children respectively indifferent between their equilibrium payoff and any deviation H, then if $N_s^*(H) > N_U^*(H)$ the deviation seems more likely to have come from a parent of a skilled child. If $N_s^*(H) < N_U^*(H)$ then the deviation seems more likely to have come from a parent of an unskilled child. The D1 refinement requires children to think that the deviation comes, with probability one, from the parent of an unskilled child if and only if $N_s^*(H) < N_U^*(H)$. This is a strong assumption that produces a single equilibrium for all parameter values:

PROPOSITION 2B: *If $H_F^{Unskill} > \widehat{H} > \underline{H}_F$, then skilled parents choose H_F^{Skill} and unskilled parents choose $\widehat{H}$. If $\widehat{H} < \underline{H}_F$, then all unskilled and some skilled parents choose $\underline{H}_F$. In that case, the number of parents of skilled daughters choosing $\underline{H}_F$ will decrease with α_1 and increase with α_2.*

The equilibrium then follows the value of $\widehat{H}$, which as discussed in Lemma 1, is a function of the labor market discrimination against women. When the value of δ is very low and women have weak opportunities in the labor market, then $\widehat{H} < \underline{H}_F$. In this case, it is impossible for parents of the unskilled to choose a level of education that separates themselves completely from the parents of the skilled. In this case, the parents of the skilled and unskilled both choose the minimum level of girls' education, and skilled and unskilled daughters alike are both less educated than they would be under complete information. This may represent the setting in highly traditional societies where parents radically underinvest in their daughters.

Ultimately, there can be a complete pooling equilibrium where all parents end up providing girls with only the legal minimum of education. Any deviation upward will be seen as an indication that the girl is skilled, and will generate lower fertility levels. This force essentially traps society in a world where women are less educated and unable to distinguish among the more or less skilled.

For higher levels of δ, where labor market discrimination is less severe, the desire to distort views influences the education choices of the parents of the less skilled, but not the parents of the more skilled. The parents of the less skilled provide less education for their daughters in order to distinguish themselves from the parents of the more skilled. Their daughters end up having more children both because their opportunity cost of time is less and also because they know that they are less able in the workforce.

When δ is high, and there is little labor market discrimination, then $\widehat{H} > H_F^{Unskill}$, and a separating equilibrium will exist with no distortion of parental incentives as discussed in Proposition 2b. The parents of the less skilled educate less—the parents of the more skilled educate more.

Parental altruism works throughout this model. As parents care about their daughters more, relative to their grandchildren, pooling is less likely and skilled daughters receive more education. But if parents are particularly focused on their long-run genetic legacy, then daughters pay the cost in lower educational outcomes.

The model has several implications. When labor market discrimination is strong, then parents of skilled and unskilled daughters alike choose to provide them with minimal education. The skilled daughters may particularly suffer, because their parents are trying to ensure that they do not realize their skills.

As women are less discriminated against, this leads to more investment in the skilled daughters, and there can be a discrete jump in educational investment for this group. Previously, some members of the skilled group will be treated like less skilled children, and a lucky few will receive more schooling. Afterward, all members of the skilled group will get more schooling. We think of this as capturing the gradual rise in women's college education in the United States during the early twentieth century.

Eventually, signaling concerns lose power in a pure separating equilibrium, and the skills essentially serve to maximize grandparents' welfare. Of course, all daughters will still be undereducated, because parents are trying to engender more fertility, but they will at least become informed about their talents. The underinvestment in female education may vanish altogether, if parents lose control over the educational investment of their daughters, if female education does little to reduce fertility, or if daughters' education leads to more investment in the quality of grandchildren, which grandparents value.

This model suggests that the population would have only two levels of education for women, but that would not be the case if there were visible differences in parameters across the population. In that case, different parameters will lead to different equilibria, although for any given set of observable parameters, parents will still use education to influence their daughters' beliefs.

If taken literally, then in the parameter space when pooling occurs, skilled daughters do not know that they are skilled, but at least they, and everyone else, correctly infers the share of women in the population who are skilled. Yet children may be unable to actually know the true share of skilled daughters, since they do not observe any daughters being well educated. Since there is little hard evidence on skills, parents may be able to persuade sons and daughters alike that skilled daughters are rare even if they are common. Such stories would not be falsified by anything in the children's experience.

Once separation occurred, then such stories would fall apart. We believe that this signaling model therefore may be connected to broader societal beliefs, even though the model itself contains no improper updating. In a regime in which women are not differentiated by skill, it would seem possible for parents and their allies to argue that the share of skilled women is low, which would encourage both sons and daughters to produce more grandchildren.[12]

10.5   Extensions: Systemic Beliefs, Credulous Bayesians, and Work Timing

The previous section described our core model, in which parents deceive daughters about their ability level by underinvesting in education. In that setting, we assumed that daughters knew the population's propensity to be unskilled, although not whether they are skilled themselves. As such, there will be some daughters who underestimate their own skills in the pooling

12. The core assumption of our model is that parents want more grandchildren than their sons and daughters naturally will give to them. The same parental preferences should also generate incentives to engage in other forms of belief investment, most notably inculcating opposition to homosexual lifestyles. If homosexuality leads to less own grandchildren, then parents who value own grandchildren will invest in their children's beliefs to that end. They will attempt to convince them that homosexuality will lead to unhappiness and perhaps worse. In this setting as well, religious organizations may offer parents a means of perpetuating beliefs that serve their biological interests. If the church supports traditional lifestyles and opposes homosexuality, then parents may have an incentive to take their children to church despite their own private religious beliefs.

equilibrium, but no society-wide tendency to diminish women. We now drop the assumption that children know the society-level distribution of skills, and assume that parents but not children have this knowledge.

10.5.1   Society-Wide Discrimination

The previous discussion focused on the formation of beliefs of daughters about their own ability, but we now perturb the model to focus on systemic beliefs about women's ability. In this case, we assume that children are unsure about "p"—the probability that women have less ability and specifically that they initially assume that p is uniformly distributed between p and 1. Parents are assumed to have no more knowledge of p than children, and children do not observe the society-wide level of skills among daughters until after they make fertility choices. To simplify matters, we assume that the actual value of p is arbitrarily close to one, so that there are only an arbitrarily small number of parents with less able girls. The actual ability of the daughters will only be revealed after they make their fertility and work choices.

If children correctly understand their parents' preferences, then the model is essentially unchanged. There are ranges of values at which there is separating, semipooling, and pooling. We are in a situation quite similar to the one discussed above. Assuming our version of D1, Proposition 3 follows:

PROPOSITION 3: *If the second generation initially does not know the share of daughters who are capable, they will learn that share if they observe the education decisions of the first generation when α_2/α_1 is sufficiently low, so that there is either a separating or semipooling equilibrium, but not if there is a pooling equilibrium.*

The intuition of this proposition is that observing the ex post distribution of skills can typically enable observers to deduce the true distribution of skills in the female population, unless there is full pooling. If there is a separating equilibrium, then there will obviously be complete revelation. If there is semipooling, then the proportion of parents of skilled daughters who undereducate them can be inferred from the parameter values. The actual share of undereducated women then would allow observers to infer the actual distribution of skills.

Only in the case of full pooling, where there is literally no information about the underlying distribution of skills does ignorance persist. In that case, a belief that women are less able can persist, because parental knowledge never gets transformed into action.

There are reasons, however, that we might doubt this version of the world. This suggests a very stark difference between female and male education. It suggests that as discrimination decreases, there should be sharp societal jumps in beliefs as soon as some women receive more education and this education is observed. The proposition does require widespread information and a fair amount of rationality, neither of which may exist in reality; that said, it does suggest that discriminatory beliefs can disappear in a generation, even if parents persist in undereducating their daughters.

10.5.2   Credulous Bayesians

An alternative approach, which is somewhat less attractive given strict assumptions about hyperrationality but which perhaps lies closer to the truth, is that children misperceive parental preferences, and believe that $\alpha_2 = 0$. As such, they believe that parents make decisions only to improve their children's welfare, and not to manipulate their children's beliefs. This is a version of Glaeser and Sunstein's (2009) "Credulous Bayesianism" where agents use Bayes's rule to make inferences but they underestimate the incentives of people around them to persuade. Given the pervasive altruism that exists in parent-child relationships, it would be particularly natural for children to think that parents are particularly benign.

If α_2 is thought to be zero exactly, then children will look at parents' investment in daughters and believe that these investments maximize: $\alpha_1(Y_0 + \delta W(H_F)\hat{A}_F(1 - N\underline{t}_c) + \alpha(V(N) + NG_T) - NH_T) - H_F$, and hence $\hat{A}_F(H_F) = 1 / \{\alpha_1\delta W'(H_F)[1 - N(W(H_F)\hat{A}_F(H_F)]\underline{t}_c\}$ and $\hat{A}_F{}'(H_F)$ is positive as long as children believe that their parents' maximization problem is concave. Proposition 4 follows:

PROPOSITION 4: *If children believe that $\alpha_2 = 0$, then parents will choose to invest in daughters' education so that both sons and daughters believe that women are less talented than men. Higher values of α_2 will cause human capital investment to fall, the belief in women's ability to decline, and fertility to rise.*

Since children may believe that parents lack ulterior motives, underinvestment in daughters is interpreted as meaning that daughters are expected to be less able. This belief will occur in both daughters and sons, and it will become more extreme if parents have stronger preferences toward grandchildren.

In a more complicated version of the model considered in the working paper version of this chapter (Glaeser and Ma 2013), with both sons and daughters, we found that the underinvestment in daughters becomes more extreme when there are more boys in the household and less extreme when there are more girls. The logic of this effect is not that boys take up girls' resources (there are no income effects in this model), but rather that boys present an added target for indoctrination. While the logic of this argument appears clear, it runs counter to the finding of Butcher and Case (1994) that women with only female siblings receive less, not more, education. Of course, these findings could reflect forces outside of the model, such as spillovers from boys to girls during the mid-twentieth century.

To illustrate the importance of our assumption that daughters' human capital does not influence the "quality of her own children," we return to the assumption that $G_T = G_0 + g(H_F - H_F^0)$. In this case, parents who care about the next generation would have competing incentives. They would want to invest more in their daughters so that their grandchildren end up being more skilled, and invest less in their daughters so that their grandchildren are more abundant. If the two forces are perfectly balanced, then the credulous Bayesians will actually be right.

This possible extension offers one suggestion about why gender-based discrimination may have faded. If daughters receive more investment because the returns to human capital in the next generation increase, then they and the men around them will infer that they have a higher ability level themselves, assuming that they incorrectly underestimate the altruism toward the next generation. If this hypothesis is correct, then the rise in returns to skill might have the added impact of reducing gender stereotypes.

10.5.3 Timing of Work and Persuasion

The models of persuasion that we have discussed ultimately assume that women are choosing their fertility levels with little direct knowledge of their workplace ability, but that would seem to depend on the timing of work and childbearing. If the mother works initially, she will surely have a better assessment of her talents from that direct source than from anything she may have inferred from either refrigerator advertisements or even her parents' investment in her human capital. That knowledge will then essentially eliminate the incentive to persuade initially.

For simplicity, we continue to assume that each child requires a fixed-time investment of $\underline{t}_c$, although we ignore investment in children's human capital. We assume that mothers maximize the expected value of $y_0 + \int_{t=0}^{1} y(t)dt + \alpha V(N)$, where $y(t)$ is the earnings at each t, so there are no discounting issues. Women end up being paid their expected or realized productivity level multiplied by $\delta W(H_F)$.

We only consider two options in childbearing. First, the mother has children immediately, basing her fertility decision on her expected workplace earnings. Second, the mother delays childbearing to the point where she has learned her actually productivity in the workplace and then decides on fertility knowing her actual ability level. We ignore more complicated strategies, and assume that the primary costs of delay are health or time related, so that the expected time cost of N children, when childbearing begins at time t_0, will be $g(t_0)N\underline{t}_c$ where $g(0) = 1$ and $g'(t_0) > 0$. These assumptions capture both the added difficulty of having children when older and that the ability to produce children has historically been impossible for women beyond some age. We ignore other benefits of later childbearing (more experience in life) and other costs (more human capital may depreciate during the childbearing period).

Moreover, we continue to assume A_F equals either 1 or 1-a; hence the probability that ability equals 1 is given by $1 - (1 - \hat{A}_F) / \alpha$, where $\hat{A}_F$ is the women's expected ability level. The expected payoff from having children immediately will be $y_0 + \delta W(H_F)\hat{A}_F(1 - N\underline{t}_c) + \alpha V(N)$, meaning that as before N satisfies $\delta W(H_F)\hat{A}_F \underline{t}_c = \alpha V'(N)$. With delay, the woman learns her true ability level and eventually chooses fertility to maximize $g_\psi \delta W(H_F)A_F \underline{t}_c = \alpha V'(N)$, where we let g_ψ denote the health cost of delaying fertility until the point of knowledge. This leads to Proposition 5.

PROPOSITION 5: *There exists a value of g_ψ at which women are indifferent between postponing work or postponing childbearing, and for higher values of g_ψ women will postpone childbearing and for lower values of g_ψ, women will postpone work. If women postpone childbearing, then changes in the initial beliefs about workplace will have no impact on their fertility decision.*

Proposition 5 suggests that medical advances that permit delayed child-bearing may have far-reaching impacts on social beliefs. If women are making fertility decisions early in life, then those decisions will be based not on their actual workplace productivity, but rather on the information that they have gleaned about the relative pleasure of working and childbearing. That position of ignorance creates a possible role for persuasion for grandparents interested in encouraging fertility, or anyone else interested in persuading men and women.

But if women obtain substantial work experience before having children, then the impact of any such persuasion is highly muted. The knowledge gained in the labor force will surely swamp the knowledge inferred from parental education decisions or the persuasion of consumer goods companies. As such, the delay in childbearing can powerfully change the incentives for persuasion. This effect connects the time series of female labor force participation with the time series of opinions about female competence at work. As Goldin (2006) describes, women were initially prone to work after marriage and then the pattern switched and more women worked earlier. That switch should, if the model's assumptions are correct, act to reduce the incentive to invest in gender-related beliefs and stereotypes. If women are waiting to learn their type before having children, then they are likely to be less responsive to parental misinformation about their ability level or likelihood of enjoying work.

10.5.4   Explaining the History

The model suggests that parents have an incentive to persuade their daughters that the returns to the workplace are lower, in order to increase the number of grandchildren that they in turn produce. This is, without doubt, a partial story. As in Goldin (chapter 9, this volume), there is also workplace discrimination that occurs when male incumbents suggest that women are bad at particular jobs. But discrimination in the family seems likely to be more powerful, and could potentially shape women's beliefs about their deepest abilities, not just their talents at a particular task.

Can the model help us explain the decline in gender-related stereotypes that seems to have occurred over the course of the twentieth century? We have discussed two potential causes for changing beliefs. One possibility is that rising returns to skill also increases the returns for investing in daughters, even if those daughters never work, because their skills will translate into more capable grandchildren. This is a possibility, but it does have some trouble with the timing of the changes. We typically think of rising returns to skill as a post-1975 phenomenon, and clearly gender stereotypes changed significantly before that date. The women's movement preceded rather than followed that great widening of wages in the US economy.

The alternative hypothesis is that the timing of women's work and childbearing changed, which ensured that stereotypes were less important, because women could base their decisions on harder facts, and consequently the incentive to inculcate such stereotypes also declined. Indeed, in almost any sensible model of error, delaying childbearing would have decreased incorrect beliefs about workplace productivity and decreased the incentives to generate those incorrect beliefs. This suggests that the power of the Pill may have been both to increase women's options and help change wider beliefs about women.

10.6 Conclusion

This chapter has discussed different sources of gender stereotypes. In our model, parental persuasion is seen as the likely force driving the perpetuation of gender-related beliefs.

We recognize that this model will run counter to the experience of many daughters, who experienced parents who pushed them to succeed, and gave them nothing but positive affirmation of their own talents. While such occurrences do run counter to the literal structure of the model, we do not believe that they are incompatible with a somewhat richer view of the world.

In many cases, parents may have been more interested in grandchildren quality than in grandchildren quantity. If daughters' human capital, and even workplace success, ended up leading toward more investment in grandchildren, then grandparents would indeed have an incentive to push their daughters toward education and success in the workforce.

Moreover, we have treated parents as the only source of information available to children. Consider a world in which there are a variety of social institutions that broadcast messages about women's ability in work. We may even assume that these institutions exist to cater to parents who want allies in prodding children toward childbearing. Churches, for example, often seem to have served that role.

If parents believe that their daughters or sons are already exposed to information depicting women as less competent, and they also believe that their daughters will invest too little in themselves if they adopt those social beliefs (even given the parents' pro-grandchildren preferences), then the parents may work against those social beliefs. For example, assume that the prevalent social belief is that women have ability level $\underline{A}$ and that parents know that their own daughter has ability level $\overline{A}$. Those parents may not want the daughter to behave as if she knew her full ability level, but they may still want to think that she as an ability level higher than $\underline{A}$. They will then tell their daughter to disregard the negative stereotype, even if they would prefer it if she thought her own ability was slightly less than $\overline{A}$.

Gender-related beliefs do seem to have had an impact on labor markets and family choices. Those beliefs do not seem to have always been based on reality. We have adopted an economic approach to error that emphasizes the incentives to mislead. We hope that future work develops further models along this line, and does more to subject our model and related theoretical work to serious empirical tests.

References

Akerlof, George. 1976. "The Economics of Caste and of the Rat Race and Other Woeful Tales." *Quarterly Journal of Economics* 90 (4): 599–617.

Arrow, Kenneth J. 1973. "The Theory of Discrimination." In *Discrimination in Labor Markets*, edited by Orley Ashenfelter and Albert Rees, 3–33. Princeton, NJ: Princeton University Press.

Axinn, William G., Marin Clarkberg, and Arland Thornton. 1994. "Family Influences on Family Size Preferences." *Demography* 31 (1): 65–79.

Barber, Nigel. 2000. *Why Parents Matter: Parental Investment and Child Outcomes.* Westport, CT: Bergin & Garvey.

Becker, Gary. 1957. *The Economics of Discrimination.* Chicago: University of Chicago Press.

Becker, Gary S., and Kevin M. Murphy. 2000. *Social Economics: Market Behavior in a Social Environment.* Cambridge, MA: Harvard University Press.

Bereaud, Susan R. 1975. "Sex Role Images in French Children's Books." *Journal of Marriage and the Family* 37:194–207.

Blau, Francine, Peter Brummund, and Albert Yung-Hsu Liu. 2013. "Trends in Occupational Segregation by Gender 1970–2009: Adjusting for the Impact of Changes in the Occupational Coding System." *Demography* 50 (2): 471–92.

Butcher, Kristin F., and Anne Case. 1994. "The Effect of Sibling Sex Composition on Women's Education and Earnings." *Quarterly Journal of Economics* 109 (3): 531–63.

Cho, In-Koo, and David M. Kreps. 1987. "Signaling Games and Stable Equilibria." *Quarterly Journal of Economics* 102 (2): 179–221.

Fogel, Robert William. 2000. *The Fourth Great Awakening and the Future of Egalitarianism.* Chicago: University of Chicago Press.

Friedan, Betty. 1963. *The Feminine Mystique.* New York: W.W. Norton.

Glaeser, Edward L. 2005. "The Political Economy of Hatred." *Quarterly Journal of Economics* 120v(1): 45–86.

Glaeser, Edward L., and Yueran Ma. 2013. "The Supply of Gender Stereotypes and Discriminatory Beliefs." NBER Working Paper no. 19109. Cambridge, MA.

Glaeser, Edward L., and Cass Sunstein. 2009. "Extremism and Social Learning." *Journal of Legal Analysis* 1 (1): 263–324.

Goldin, Claudia. 1990. *Understanding the Gender Gap: An Economic History of American Women.* Oxford: Oxford University Press.

———. 2000. "Labor Markets in the Twentieth Century." In *Cambridge Economic History of the United States, Vol. III, The Twentieth Century*, edited by Stanley J. Engerman and Robert E. Gallman, 549–625. New York: Cambridge University Press.

———. 2006. "The Quiet Revolution That Transformed Women's Employment, Education, and Family." *American Economic Review* 96:1–21.

Goldin, Claudia, and Lawrence F. Katz. 2000. "Career and Marriage in the Age of the Pill." *American Economic Review* 90 (2): 461–5.

Gunderson, Elizabeth, Gerardo Ramirez, Susan Levine, and Sian Beilock. 2012. "The Role of Parents and Teachers in the Development of Gender-Related Math Attitudes." *Sex Roles* 66 (3/4): 153.

Krueger, Anne O. 1963. "The Economics of Discrimination." *Journal of Political Economy* 71 (5): 481–6.

Lazear, Edward P. 1999. "Culture and Language." *Journal of Political Economy* 107 (6): 95–126.

Lerner, Gerda. 1987. *The Creation of Patriarchy.* Oxford: Oxford University Press.

Margo, Robert A. 1991. "Segregated Schools and the Mobility Hypothesis: A Model of Local Government Discrimination." *Quarterly Journal of Economics* 106 (1): 61–73.

Milkman, Ruth. 1982. "Redefining 'Women's Work': The Sexual Division of Labor in the Auto Industry during World War II." *Feminist Studies* 8 (2) 336–72.

Myrdal, Gunnar. 1944. *An American Dilemma: The Negro Problem and Modern Democracy.* New York: Harper & Brothers.

Rossy, Katherine M. 2011. "Politicizing Pronatalism: Exploring the Nazi Ideology of Women through the Lens of Visual Propaganda, 1933–1939." *Graduate History Review* 3 (1). http://journals.uvic.ca/index.php/ghr/article/view/6478.

Simon, Rita J., and Jean M. Landis. 1989. "A Report: Women's and Men's Attitudes about a Woman's Place and Role." *Public Opinion Quarterly* 53 (2): 265–76.

Thurow, Lester C. 1969. *Poverty and Discrimination.* Washington, DC: Brookings Institution.

Weitzman, L. J., D. Eiffel, E. Hokada, and C. Ross. 1972. "Sex-Role Socialization in Picture Books for Preschool Children." *American Journal of Sociology* 77:1125–50.

11

Claudia Goldin

Stanley L. Engerman

I have known Claudia Goldin for over forty years—about two-thirds of her life and over 50 percent of mine. We met when she started working on the economics of slavery with Robert Fogel at the University of Chicago. From that initial meeting followed more or less continuous contacts at various meetings of the Cliometric Society, the Economic History Association, and the American Economic Association, the latter two groups of which she subsequently became president. There was also the Development of the American Economy Program (DAE) of the National Bureau of Economic Research and its two annual meetings. At first, with Robert Fogel as DAE director, Claudia and I were members of the DAE advisory committee, along with Lance Davis, Robert Gallman, and Clayne Pope. In return for service we were rewarded with a lavish dinner after each meeting. When Bob Fogel stepped down as DAE director and Claudia took his place, Lance commented that this would be the end of the advisory committee and its lavish meals, and so it was. Let me add, however, as I will return to, that Claudia has done such a great job organizing and running the DAE program that clearly the advisory committee and the meals were expendable, and the NBER's money was put to much better use.

Although counting years is customary in personal relations, I realized that I could also have divided this period into the eras of three wonderful dogs. First, the long-lived Kelso (no doubt named after the famous racehorse—the fourth best thoroughbred of the twentieth century according to

Stanley L. Engerman is the John Munro Professor of Economics and professor of history at the University of Rochester and a research associate of the National Bureau of Economic Research.

Blood-Horse magazine). After that I may have missed one or two dogs before Prairie and the current Pika.

Claudia's educational background is quite interesting in that she was clearly part of the expansion of female education that she and Larry Katz subsequently wrote so much about:

- As a high school student, she was one of the few females attending the prestigious Bronx High School of Science—limited for its first years to males only. Its graduates have won eight Nobel Prizes, mostly in physics (none, so far, in economics). This is no doubt the greatest number of any high school in the United States and possibly the world. Bronx Science later began to admit more women among those who passed their stringent entrance exam, but the gender ratio remained unbalanced. When in high school Claudia was interested in the sciences, which she later found made a useful contribution to her work as an economist.
- Claudia then moved on to Cornell, where she graduated with a major in economics. This shift was influenced by Alfred Kahn, a distinguished scholar of industrial organization, considered by many to be the father of airline deregulation. At this time, the share of women among Cornell undergraduates was only about one-quarter (statistic courtesy of George Boyer and Ronald Ehrenberg). Finally, Claudia went to the University of Chicago, receiving a PhD in 1972. From my observation the gender ratio at the time was quite different from more recent cohorts.

Since receiving her doctoral degree, Claudia has written in excess of one hundred articles, some coauthored, many singly done, and three important books. She also edited four conference volumes on a wide range of topics. Such impressive output and great breadth of subjects make it difficult to describe, let alone examine, all or many in this brief space. We are all quite familiar with her work on gender and educational issues—in particular, *Understanding the Gender Gap: An Economic History of American Women* (Goldin 1990) and *The Race between Education and Technology* (Goldin and Katz 2008). Both are path-breaking works, as close to definitive as possible in these most contentious areas. Rather than focus on these, however, I want to return to some of Claudia's earlier important work on other topics—work that has demonstrated commendable staying power among historians, economists, and economic historians. This description should be especially useful to those who know her career based on her entry on Wikipedia, which has article summaries only after 1990.

Her first book, *Urban Slavery in the American South, 1820–1860: A Quantitative History* was an important contribution (Goldin 1975). Superficially, the book seems to start from a small issue, but one that has considerably broader implications. Previously, it was argued by historians of the American South that the decline in the share of slaves in southern cities (relative to the countryside) meant that slavery was proven to be inefficient and doomed to collapse fairly soon. By extensive primary archival research, collecting data on slave prices and occupations, and with a clever application of supply and demand, she showed that the relative decline of slavery in the cities was not due to economic inefficiency but rather the opposite—demand was booming in the rural (cotton) sector. This argument has won the day among historians and the book may still be found on many reading lists in history and economic history, achieving a consensus, unlike other research on slavery at the time.

In the late 1970s and into the 1980s Claudia coauthored several excellent articles that have remained important to economics and economic history, all based on clever theoretical models, along with primary and secondary quantitative analyses. One, with Frank Lewis (Goldin and Lewis 1980), is a reexamination of the particular pattern of US economic growth after independence, which tested a frequent hypothesis of the time, the impact of exports on economic growth. Another, also with Frank Lewis, estimated the economic costs of the Civil War and the nature of the postwar recovery, showing that the costs were extremely high in both human and physical capital—much greater, for example, than the market value of slaves in 1860 (Goldin and Lewis 1975).

Two classic articles with the late Kenneth Sokoloff (Goldin and Sokoloff 1982, 1984) raised many issues for the study of antebellum economic growth and the effects of age-sex composition in the labor force, such as the size of industrial firms and the role of patterns of crop production in leading to economic differences in agriculture between the North and South. These articles opened up new bodies of research among economic historians, as well as development economists, and remain frequently cited.

In closing I will point to other types of significant contributions that Claudia has made to numerous students and colleagues with her very generous and helpful comments, suggestions, and encouragement. She has been a mentor to a large number of students. Some of her benefits to others came when she was editor of the *Journal of Economic History*, others from her teaching and advising, and still others with letters and discussions with colleagues and other economists.

Thus she has had a great impact on scholarship in economics and economic history going beyond her publications. In addition, as director of the DAE, her main focus has been to provide an entry for younger scholars into the profession along with opportunities to interact with senior members, and more generally, to demonstrate the central importance of economic history to economics as a scholarly discipline.

In all regards, Claudia Goldin has been a model of the scholarly life, worthy of emulation by all.

References

Goldin, Claudia. 1975. *Urban Slavery in the American South, 1820–1860: A Quantitative History*. Chicago: University of Chicago Press.

———. 1990. *Understanding the Gender Gap: An Economic History of American Women*. New York: Oxford University Press.

Goldin, Claudia, and Lawrence F. Katz. 2008. *The Race between Education and Technology*. Cambridge, MA: Harvard University Press.

Goldin, Claudia, and Frank Lewis. 1975. "The Economic Cost of the American Civil War: Estimates and Implications." *Journal of Economic History* 35:299–326.

———. 1980. "The Role of Exports in American Economic Growth during the Napoleonic Wars, 1793–1807." *Explorations in Economic History* 17:6–25.

Goldin, Claudia, and Kenneth Sokoloff. 1982. "Women, Children, and Industrialization during the Early Republic: Evidence from the Manufacturing Censuses." *Journal of Economic History* 42:741–74.

———. 1984. "The Relative Productivity Hypothesis of Industrialization: The American Case, 1820–1850." *Quarterly Journal of Economics* 99:461–88.

Contributors

Martha J. Bailey
Department of Economics
University of Michigan
611 Tappan Street
Ann Arbor, MI 48109

Francine D. Blau
Department of Economics
Cornell University
268 Ives Hall
Ithaca, NY 14853-3901

Hoyt Bleakley
Booth School of Business
University of Chicago
5807 South Woodlawn Avenue
Chicago, IL 60637

Leah Platt Boustan
Department of Economics
8283 Bunche Hall
University of California, Los Angeles
Los Angeles, CA 90095-1477

William J. Collins
Department of Economics
Vanderbilt University
VU Station B #351819
2301 Vanderbilt Place
Nashville, TN 37235-1819

Dora Costa
Department of Economics
Bunche Hall 9272
University of California, Los Angeles
Box 951477
Los Angeles, CA 90095-1477

Stanley L. Engerman
Department of Economics
University of Rochester
Rochester, NY 14627-0156

Joseph Ferrie
Department of Economics
Northwestern University
Evanston, IL 60208-2600

Carola Frydman
Department of Economics
Boston University
270 Bay State Road
Boston, MA 02215

Edward L. Glaeser
Department of Economics
315A Littauer Center
Harvard University
Cambridge, MA 02138

Claudia Goldin
Department of Economics
Harvard University
Cambridge, MA 02138

Nora Gordon
McCourt School of Public Policy
Georgetown University
37th and O Streets, NW
Washington, DC 20057

Melanie Guldi
Department of Economics
University of Central Florida
4000 Central Florida Blvd.
Orlando, FL 32816

Brad J. Hershbein
W. E. Upjohn Institute for
    Employment Research
300 S. Westnedge Ave.
Kalamazoo, MI 49007

Lawrence F. Katz
Department of Economics
Harvard University
Cambridge, MA 02138

Ilyana Kuziemko
Graduate School of Business
Columbia University
Uris Hall
3022 Broadway
New York, NY 10027

Adriana Lleras-Muney
Department of Economics
9373 Bunche Hall
University of California, Los Angeles
Los Angeles, CA 90095

Shelly Lundberg
Department of Economics
University of California, Santa
    Barbara
Santa Barbara, CA 93106

Yueran Ma
Harvard University
Cambridge, MA 02138

Robert A. Margo
Department of Economics
Boston University
270 Bay State Road
Boston, MA 02215

Claudia Olivetti
Department of Economics
Boston University
270 Bay State Road
Boston, MA 02215

Robert A. Pollak
Washington University in St. Louis
Arts and Sciences and the Olin
    Business School
Campus Box 1133
1 Brookings Drive
St. Louis, MO 63130

Sarah J. Reber
Department of Public Policy
University of California, Los Angeles
3250 Public Policy Building
Los Angeles, CA 90095

Cecilia Elena Rouse
Woodrow Wilson School of Public and
    International Affairs
Princeton University
Princeton, NJ 08544-1013

Author Index

Subject Index

Education policies, US: changes in federal polices, 70–73; changes in local policies and practices, 74–76; changes in state policies, 73–74; recent changes in, 68–76. *See also* High school dropout; High school graduation rates; Teacher labor market

Electricity revolution, 15–16, 24

Elementary and Secondary Education Act (ESEA), 70–73

Establishment size: female/child labor and, 31–32; manufacturing and, 19

Family entrepreneurs, 369–71

"Family macro" subfield in economics, 277–78

Female labor: demand for, industrialization and, in nineteenth century, 165–66; establishment size and, 31–32; regressions of, 29–30t, 29–31; role of, in early industrialization, 28; steam power and, 31

Female labor force participation, 2–3, 161–64; American experience versus other developed countries, 167–71; black versus white differences in, 205–6; decline in, in early US industrialization, 166; and economic development, 174–76; and economic development, 1950–2005, 176–82; evidence on intergenerational transmission, 221–32; female slaves and, 206, 206n1; long-run trends in, 171–73, 172f; personal characteristics and racial differences in, 1870–2010, 213–21; trends in, by race, 207–13

Female occupational distribution, racial differences in, 210–13

Fertility: changing relationship between mothers' education and, 296–302; integrating neoclassical model with supply side for, 278–81; timing of work and persuasion and, 385–86

Fertility declines, US: conclusions for post-1960 period, 302–8; exceptionalism of post-1960 period, 281–90; literature on causes of, 273–76; models of, in economics and demography, 277–78; neoclassical theory of, 277–78. *See also* "Second Demographic Transition" (SDT)

Fertility rates: across educational groups, 249; similarities in early and later twentieth-century period, 281–84

Fertility transitions, twentieth-century US, 276–77

Frog ponds, 341–42

Fundamental attribution error, 363

Gender, structural transformation and, 182–88; in developed countries, 183f, 184–88, 187t

Gender equality, economic development and, 164–65

Gender-related beliefs: attitudes toward women and work, 358–60; discrimination and social formation of, 358–65; emergence and changes in, 355–58; social formation of, 360–64; systematic biases an, 363

Goldin-Katz framework, 21, 22–23

Hatred, discrimination versus, 364–65

Health: commonly used contemporary samples, 134; comparisons with US slaves and developing countries, 148–53; data, 129–34; educational attainment and, 121–24; height as measure of, 122–24; theoretical framework for, 124–29; Union Army soldiers data, 129–33; World War II enlisted men data, 133–34. *See also* Height

Height: effects of, on education, 138–42; as measure of health, 122–24; trends in, 134–37; wealth and, 142–48. *See also* Health

High school dropout: literature on, 64–66; regional variations in, 63f, 65–66

High school graduation rates, 59–64, 62f; income inequality and, 59–60, 77–84; literature on factors influencing, 66–68; relevance of, 60–61; by US regions, 62–63, 63f. *See also* Education policies, US

High school movement, 19, 61–62

Hollowing out, 35–38; defined, 16–17; of occupational skill distribution, in twentieth century, 47

Human capital, Becker's model of, 60

Immigrant assimilation, 97–99; children and their parents, 99–100, 110–16; data, 100–106; discussion of results,